ANOTHER MOTHER TONGUE

GAY WORDS, GAY WORLDS

JUDY GRAHN

UPDATED AND EXPANDED EDITION

BEACON PRESS · BOSTON

Beacon Press
25 Beacon Street
Boston, Massachusetts 02108

Beacon Press books
are published under the auspices of
the Unitarian Universalist Association of Congregations.

95 94 93 92 91   8 7 6 5 4 3 2

Library of Congress Cataloging-in-Publication Data
Grahn, Judy, 1940–
Another mother tongue : gay words, gay worlds / Judy Grahn.
p.   cm.
Includes bibliographical references and index
ISBN 0-8070-7911-1
1. Homosexuality — Terminology. 2. Homosexuality — Miscellanea.
3. Lesbianism — Miscellanea. 4. Lesbians — United States—
Miscellanea. 5. Life style — United States — Miscellanea.
I. Title.
HQ76.25.U5G73   1990
306.76'6 — dc20   90-52597

To Yvonne Mary Robinson
Lover, guide, and friend

To Robert E. McDaniel
Mentor and friend, who predicted in 1967
that I would do this work

To Paula Gunn Allen
Who gave me a place to stand
on "the other side"
so I could have the mirror image
necessary for true vision

Contents

Author's Note

In the five years after *Another Mother Tongue* was first published, I received a multitude of testimony confirming its ideas. In addition to enthusiastic response from the Gay/Lesbian Press, Gay American Indian founder Randy Burns and Mattachine Society Founder Harry Hay each came to book signings urging people to buy the book, the American Library Association awarded it, a mural in Oakland displays me reading from it, and I hear that Black film director Marlon Riggs displayed that scene in his movie *Tongues Untied*. Queen Boudica has joined the Gay Freedom Day parades. And most moving to me, a New Zealand Maori warrior dike, after reading the book, fell weeping into my arms because at last she could recognize her life story.

This expanded version has given me a chance to add more words and phrases on Gayness from the Spanish language, in which the vocabulary of Gay culture is endlessly rich. By splitting the last chapter I have added half a chapter each to chapters 10 and 11, so the book is increased by 8 or 9 percent, with material describing the birth of Lesbian feminism and the special role of working-class women and women of color in that drama. I also get to tell additional stories of Gay/Lesbian presence in history, notably in the earliest signed poetry of ancient Sumer, at the founding of what we call Western civilization.

Oakland, CA

Preface

In 1961, when I was twenty-one, I went to a library in Washington, D.C., to read about homosexuals and Lesbians, to investigate, explore, compare opinions, learn who I might be, what others thought of me, who my peers were and had been. The books on such a subject, I was told by indignant, terrified librarians unable to say aloud the word *homosexual*, were locked away. They showed me a wire cage where the "special" books were kept in a jail for books. Only professors, doctors, psychiatrists, and lawyers for the criminally insane could see them, check them out, hold them in their hands. The books I wanted to check out were by "experts" on the subject of homosexuality as it was understood at the time. The severe reaction of the women librarians, who by all rights should have been my allies, plus the censorship of the official, professional written material of which my own person was the subject, constituted some of the serious jolts I experienced in my early twenties concerning the position of Gay people in American society.

These jolts, which included being given a less-than-honorable discharge from the armed services with its attendant demoralizing treatment, having my parents and friends notified of my "crime" of Lesbianism, being denied jobs and housing, being beaten in public for looking like a dike—these taught me everything I would ever need to know about the nature of the oppression of Gay people. And made me angry and determined enough to use my life to reverse a perilous situation.

In 1963 I picketed the White House with the Gay rights group Mattachine Society, one of a little band of fifteen Gay people, three of us women. In 1964 I published an article in *Sexology Magazine* under a pseudonym, stating that most Lesbians were "not sick" but were normal, ordinary people. Since my letters and notes had been seized and used against my friends in the service, I was afraid even in civilian life of having my writing notes grabbed; I burned some cards I had been keeping about Lesbian couples in Washington, D.C. Then in 1965 I wrote an angry satire,

"The Psychoanalysis of Edward the Dyke," storing it away because of the impossibility of getting it published. I did publish a few short poems, also under a pseudonym, in the Lesbian magazine *The Ladder*.

In 1970, tired of waiting for a publisher radical enough to handle my material, I printed poems myself on a mimeograph machine, which grew into a complete, productive press. As the wave of Gay Liberation, Lesbian, and feminist groups became the huge groundswell of organized transition that characterized the seventies (on the heels of the civil rights and Black power movements and the peace and hippie movements of the sixties), I became a poet and a voice of Lesbian/feminism and "the common woman," among other things. In 1974, after writing "A Woman Is Talking to Death," I began to work on long prose pieces. I decided to investigate women's history and Gay history.

In finding and recording some of the Gay cultural histories, I have drawn upon my own life history as a Lesbian and as a Gay activist during the last third of the twentieth century in America. I have recalled my utter isolation at sixteen, when I looked up *Lesbian* in the dictionary, having no one to ask about such things, terrified, elated, painfully self-aware, grateful it was there at all. Feeling the full weight of the social silence surrounding it, me, my unfolding life. I have gone over and over in my mind the careful teaching my first lover Von gave me, as she recited in strictest secrecy the litany of words and phrases related to the forbidden subject of our way of being: *Gay, faggot, tribadism, round, straight, in drag, coming out,* and a mysterious word she had no definition for: *catafoil.* In addition, I have remembered words and phrases used about Gay people by heterosexual culture. The list I made to research consisted originally of twelve words: *dyke, queer, butch, femme, Gay, camp, fairy, faggot, purple, pansy, bulldike, Lesbian.* I have used both *dyke* and its alternate spelling *dike,* because I love both words; they are still in an oral tradition, not yet standardized into one spelling. *Catafoil,* I now believe, came from a Gay book Von read while standing in a drugstore — a habit she had, especially with Gay books since it was socially embarrassing if not dangerous to buy them. This book was *Quatrefoil,* a Gay novel by James Barr first published in 1950.[1]

My methods for gathering information can be called eclectic. I used dictionaries and history, anthropology and sociology, poetry and the occult. I used a lot of common sense and an uncommon amount of perseverance. I spent more than one evening in complete frustration sitting banging a dictionary against my knees screaming, "I know you're in there!" after months of chasing the word *bulldike*. I read and read, filled boxes with notebooks of notes, thought and thought, wept, cried out to the phantoms of history, muttered to myself. I am a poet and a Gay cultural theorist, not an etymologist. Word derivations find their way into dictionaries after etymologists have gathered information based on the contexts in which the words may have been used. There has been no acceptance and exploration of the Gay context that would allow our subterranean slang words to enter the world of dictionaries. It is as a Gay person, using Gay cultural contexts and meanings, that I have explored words such as *faggot, fairy, bulldike,* and so on. These words have a far different meaning for Gay people than they have for straight people in general, including etymologists. This is because heterosexual people have a different mindset from Gay people just as Anglos, for example, have a different mindset from Navajos. Even when Anglos study Navajo culture, therefore, they do not ascribe the same meaning a Navajo does to what they see. Nor does the Navajo tell everything to the Anglo, as some things in Indian culture are kept secret for protection. Gay culture too keeps secrets for its own protection.

Gradually I formulated theories that Gay culture is ancient and has been suppressed into an underground state of being, that everything has meaning, that slang is not necessarily a transitory language form, that old traditions transform, they do not really perish. If Sappho's fragments were preserved, why not other elements also? Once I had gathered a few clues, people began to bring me information, from other countries, from specialized fields of study, from their lives as bar dikes and faggots; and I was beginning to know what questions to ask. Years passed. I began to see that my own life fit into a pattern of Gay culture too, and I undertook to use stories from my own experience as examples of a dike's life. And now that I knew what kinds of questions to ask I did some interviews of other Gay people or people with expertise that was pertinent to my subject. The worlds that began unfolding were exciting beyond my imagining, as my little list of taboo words turned out to be keys to knowledge.

The Culture Is Everything

What gives any group of people distinction and dignity is its culture. This includes a remembrance of the past and a setting of itself in a world context whereby the group can see *who it is* relative to everyone else.

I have always been bothered by the definition of homosexuality as a *behavior*. Scratching is a behavior. Homosexuality is a way of being, one that can completely influence a person's life and shape its meaning and direction.

In *Another Mother Tongue: Gay Words and Gay Worlds* I am suggesting parameters and characteristics of homosexual culture as I have experienced it and as others have spoken or written about it. In doing this I have often used stereotypes, even derogatory ones, very deliberately, as points of entry into the history, for *something* about stereotypes is usually true and therefore open to study.

The Gay culture I have set about to describe is old, extremely old, and it is continuous. The continuity is a result of characteristics that members teach each other so that the characteristics repeat era after era. I have found that Gay culture has its traditionalists, its core group, that it is worldwide, and that it has tribal and spiritual roots. Gay culture is sometimes underground, sometimes aboveground, and often both.

Another Mother Tongue: Gay Words and Gay Worlds traces Gay cultural attributes, words, and phrases—both those used *within* the Gay underground and those used by outsiders about it. Chapter One deals with the antiquity of lavender as the Gay color, taking us back in time to tribal traditions. Having described some tribal holdovers in our modern industrial culture in Chapter Two, "The Original Underground," Chapter Three establishes the high public positions frequently held by Gay people in American Indian tribes in the recent past, while Chapter Five, "We Go Around the World," extends these positions to references from cultures around the globe. Chapter Four, "Fairies and Fairy Queens," applies the same Gay attributes to the tribal vestiges underlying European societies, an important connection since the slang phrases of the Gay underground in America virtually all stem from European languages, particularly English of course. I next examine the French terms *butch* and *femme* as well as the English *bulldike*, with an eye toward establishing modern Gay offices that have some similarity to their counterparts in the more openly Gay-tolerant European pagan cultures of centuries ago. Chapters Seven, "Riding with the Amazons," and Eight, "Flaming, Flaming Faggot Kings," also examine offices (very unofficial) that Gay people hold in society. The last two chapters concern more generalized functions of Gay culture in our society, such as the importance of women bonding and the effect Gay leadership has had on our society. The last chapter considers whether there is a special Gay philosophical attitude that can help us in today's crisis-oriented mass universe.

My own life story weaves in and out of the other Gay stories, and the book is addressed to my first lover Von, whose memory kept me company throughout.

To this work I bring my understanding that "women's history" parallels, crisscrosses, and influences Gay cultural history. I also have come to understand while working on the book that "women's history" and "tribal history" have certain things in common.

Some of the names of modern Gay people in the book have been changed or the surname has been omitted for protection, the persons preferring anonymity to the threat of losing a job or family love. Yet the number of people who are able to live as openly Gay is astounding compared to the case in former decades and speaks of a growing place Gay people occupy in the arena of public life. I hope this book clarifies and intensifies that influence.

¹ James Barr, *Quatrefoil* (Boston: Alyson Publications, 1982).

Acknowledgments

Any book is more than the work of the author; it is also a composite of the work, experience, and generosity of many minds. I would like to credit, with all my thanks and gratitude, some of those who contributed to this book:

Karen Sjöholm first, my friend and research assistant who throughout did an uncannily accurate job of understanding what I needed and in culling it with great patience and enthusiasm from the library and from people she knew, without once pulling me off course or down dead-end streets. Who waited years while I painstakingly pieced it together, buying me books, coming around with new ideas exactly when I needed to hear them, remaining steadfast in her optimism and goodwill; I can simply never thank her enough.

Paula Gunn Allen, teacher supreme, whose ideas fill out the other half of my own, who generously gave of her mind, her library resources and her patient, critical eye to guide me into a perspective that jumped the book onto a more intelligent plane of vision than I was able to do alone. She gave me a place to stand based in the tribal traditions of this continent, which then served as a standard and a mirror for viewing the Anglo-European tribal traditions that have survived intact in modern Gay culture. In addition, she conceived the cover design.

For library assistance, for doing an early presentation with me, and especially for giving me feedback in the foundation efforts and Boudica chapter I want to thank Wendy Cadden; also for years of giving me love and of patiently listening to my doubts and complaints. For generous use of her work and for her continual encouragement, I want to thank my friend Linda Marie. And Audre Lorde for writing The Black Unicorn and for giving her loving assistance with Chapter Three. I want also to thank Luisah Teish, Tede Matthews, and Ginny Berson for their generous interviews; then Laura Tow, Ann Shellabarger, and most especially the National Endowment for the Arts for financial assistance helpful to this book. Special thanks to Marie Cantlon, my editor at Beacon Press, for her thoughtful assistance with the final writing and organizing of the book, to managing editor Jeff Smith, and to the production staff for a beautiful design job. I want to thank Gloria Greenfield and especially Pat McGloin of Persephone Press for editorial assistance; Louise Merrill for lending me some of her books for ten years; and Paul Mariah for letting me walk away with his copy of *Geography and Plays* when copies were in short supply; Vivian Cadden for a gift of old family encyclopedias; Kate Winter for the loan of her *Oxford English Dictionaries*; Coletta Reid and Casey Czarnik for belief in what I was about to do; Kirsten Grimsted, Peggy Kimball, Arlene Raven, and other women of the *Chrysalis Magazine* staff for having the foresight to publish my first completed chapter, "The Queen of Bulldikery," even though some people thought it was the strangest article they had ever seen. Thanks to the Lesbian and Gay History Archives for sponsoring a presentation of the early material; Ollie of Ollie's bar in Oakland for sponsoring a series of presentations of unfinished chapters; Sherry Thomas and Carol Seajay of Old Wives Tales bookstore in San Francisco for sponsoring a series of presentations of unfinished chapters; Laura Tow for organizing a reading of preliminary material. Eloise Klein Healy and other women in Los Angeles for sponsoring and organizing readings of unfinished chapters. For feeding me vital bits of information, I want to thank Robert Gluck, Lee Francis, Aleida Rodriguez, Tonia, Kate Clinton, Ursula Steinegger Pat Parker, Eric Thomas, Nellie Wong, Johnnie Louie, Julia Stanley Penelope, Emily Warn, Michael Taylor, Avotjca, Carol Robertson, Ginny Berson, Michelle Cliff, Blanche Wiesen Cook, Clare Coss, a sailor who wrote me a letter, numerous others whose names escape or are unknown to me. Thanks to Gloria Anzaldua and to Randy for reading me his Rufus poem.

For their work I want to thank Elizabeth Gould Davis, Robert Duncan, Edward Field, Gertrude Stein, Arthur Evans, Margaret Murray, Jonathon Katz, Walter Williams, Maurice Kenny, Carl Morse, Willyce Kim, Eloise Klein Healy, Ann Allen Shockley, Adrienne Rich, Mary Daly, Lillian Faderman Charlotte Bunch, Rita Mae Brown, Pat Parker, Olga Broumas, Evelyn Blackwood, and dozens of others whose work sustained and furthered me.

I certainly want to thank Dr. Nathan Hare, my teacher at Howard University in Washington, D.C., who one day in 1964 displayed to his primarily Black, middle-class, and highly conservative sociology students a copy of the (at that time) completely

underground Lesbian magazine *The Ladder.* "You should all read
this," he said, "to help you understand the problems and social
position of another minority in America." Sitting in the back of
the room a stranger on two counts, being white and Gay, I remember trembling and trying to keep from bursting into tears, for this
was the first openly positive response to Gay culture I had ever
heard from a straight person, and I was singularly impressed. I
want to thank him for teaching me the sociological tool of partici-
patory observation through which I was better able to view my
own life and the lives of my friends as examples of social behavior.

Last I want to thank those who went before me, Dell Martin,
Phyllis Lyon, Barbara Gittings, Barbara Grier, Frank Kameney,
Henry Hay, other founders and prime movers of DOB, Mattachine,
One, *The Ladder,* bar owners who fought for civil and social rights
of gathering and touching, and my own fellow organizers during
the West Coast New Lesbian Feminist Movement wave beginning
in 1969 and flooding into the seventies: Wendy Cadden, Linda
Wilson (who now has a different name), Alice Molloy, Carol Wil-
son, Natalie Lando, Naomi Groeschel, Pat Jackson, Pat Parker,
Louise Merrill, Brenda Crider, Anne Leonard, Pat Norman, Red
Arobateau, Marnie Hall, and the others who should just put their
names right here. Bless us all.

Grateful acknowledgement is made to the following for permission to reprint: From "Lament for a maidenhead," from *Sappho: A New Translation*, translated by Mary Barnard, reprinted by permission of The University of California Press, copyright © 1958, by the University of California Press; the lines from "The Spoon Ring" from *This Light Will Shine*, by Paul Mariah (ManRoot 1978), by permission of the author; the lines from "Some Like Indians Endure" from *Skins and Bones*, unpublished manuscript by Paula Gunn Allen, by permission of the author; quotation from "Beloved Women: Lesbians in American Indian Cultures" by Paula Gunn Allen, from *Conditions 7*, reprinted by permission of the author; "Beloved Women" by Paula Gunn Allen, from *Conditions 7*, by permission of the author; the lines from "WINKTE" from *Only as Far as Brooklyn* by Maurice Kenny (Good Gay Poets, 1979), by permission of the author; "To Demeter" from *The Homeric Hymns*, translated by Apostolos N. Athanassakis (Johns Hopkins University Press, 1976), by permission of the publisher; the lines from "The Curse of the Future Fairy" by Carl Morse, first printed in FAG RAG #40 (Boston, 1983) copyright © 1983 Carl Morse, by permission of the author; "Woman on Fire" from *The Night Sun* by Aaron Shurin (Gay Sunshine Press, San Francisco, 1976), by permission of the author; the lines from "I Spent the Day with You" from *A Packet Beating Like a Heart* by Eloise Klein Healy (Birds of a Feather, 1981), by permission of the author; the lines from "Timepiece" and lines from "125th Street and Abomey" and "The Women of Dan" are reprinted from *The Black Unicorn, Poems by Audre Lorde*, by permission of W.W. Norton and Company, Inc. Copyright © 1978 Audre Lorde; excerpt from "Antonia" and "The Rhani of Jhansi" from unpublished manuscripts by Linda Marie, by permission of the author; "My Lady Ain't No Lady" and "From Deep Within" from *Movement in Black* by Pat Parker, copyright © 1978 by Pat Parker, reprinted by permission of the author and the publisher, The Crossing Press; excerpt from interview with Evelyn Torton Beck from *Lilith: The Jewish Women's Magazine*, reprinted by permission of Evelyn Torton Beck; lines from "Athens" from the "Voyage to Lesbos" sequence, by Jacqueline Lapidus, from *Conditions 7*, reprinted by permission of the author; lines from "Four Songs the Night Nurse Sang" from *Roots and Branches* by Robert Duncan (Charles Scribner & Sons, 1964), by permission of the author; quotation from *Elements of a Coffee Service* by Robert Glück (Four Seasons Foundation, 1982), by permission of the author; "(THE FLOATING POEM, UNNUMBERED)" in "Twenty-One Love Poems" from *The Dream of a Common Language, Poems 1974–1977* by Adrienne Rich, is reprinted by permission of the author and the publisher, W.W. Norton & Company, Inc. Copyright © 1978 by W.W. Norton & Company, Inc.; the lines from "with the clear/plastic speculum" by Olga Broumas, from *Lesbian Poetry*, edited by Elly Bulkin and Joan Larkin (Persephone Press, 1981), reprinted by permission of the author. An earlier version of chapter 6 originally appeared in *13th Moon*, volume 8, 1 and 2.

ANOTHER MOTHER TONGUE

CHAPTER ONE

Sashay Down the Lavender Trail

A purple robe he wore, o'erwrought with gold
With the device of a great snake, whose breath
Was a fiery flame: which when I did behold
I fell a-weeping and I cried, "Sweet youth,
Tell me why, sad and sighing, thou dost rove
These pleasant realms? I pray thee speak me sooth
What is thy name?" He said, "My name is Love."
Then straight the first did turn himself to me
And cried, "He lieth, for his name is Shame,
But I am Love, and I was wont to be
Alone in this fair garden, till he came
Unasked by night; I am true Love, I fill
The hearts of boy and girl with mutual flame."
Then sighing said the other, "Have thy will,
I am the Love that dare not speak its name."

From "Two Loves,"
Lord Alfred Douglas[1]

"OUR COLOR is purple, or lavender," my first lover affirmed, intensely whispering to my avid and puzzled young ears the forbidden litany of who we were or might be. "No one knows why this is, it just is," handsome Vonnie said, her lips against me like the vibrant breasts of birds, her voice timbered as an alto song, her words like half-remembered ballad or blues lyrics that sounded stranger than ancient English describing fragments of a story neither of us could recognize. She taught me the words of Gay life; she could not tell me what they meant. She wore a ring on her little finger as a badge of her Gayness, and the first thing she bought for me as a love and Gay-entry token was a slender silver and turquoise ring for the little finger of my left hand.[2] She could not tell me what this had to do with our love for each other and our decision to attempt the difficult task of living together as lovers instead of taking the socially ordained path of marrying men, a continual pressure we were subjected to by every person we knew. Except other Lesbians.

Well, Vonnie, teaching-lover, here I am now so many years and such a distance later trying to fill out a picture from the shadow you passed on to me, an opera from the little whistled melody you first gave me with such curiosity and eagerness.

Eighteen and nineteen years old in the year 1959, we were equally baffled and in wonder at ourselves, as secret lovers, Lesbians, spinsters, something called "Gay." Why the word *Gay?* Why purple? And why so hated? So denied? So dangerous? When our love was like a flower?

A Little Local Color in a Grey Landscape

Watching the two of us becoming lovers, a frightened heterosexual friend accused us bitterly, "It's all them damn books you guys read that's ruining you." But though we both read voraciously, we disappointingly could not find books with which to "ruin" ourselves. The words associated with being Gay, (including *Gay*) were not written down so that we could find and decipher them. Words describing us as lovers and as people with unique characteristics were oral history we heard in a line passed on from our first lover's first lover's first lover. Some of the words were so secret they seemed never to be used by the not-Gay, and we did not speak these words in their presence (*closet* or *straight*, for instance).

3

As my first lover, the woman who "brought me out," Vonnie taught me a potently alive underground vocabulary. We were not living in a center of urban sophistication where she might have been expected to learn it, but in a sparsely populated, rural portion of the world, in an economically poor and spiritually depressed late 1950s New Mexico desert town near the hellish border of West Texas. There, it seemed to me, virtually everything was prohibited except low-level wage slavery and mandatory, joyless marriage. "How do you drive through West Texas?" we joked. "As fast as you can." We didn't even try to make the joke entertaining.

At eighteen I had "eloped" to be with my exciting raven-haired Yvonne, having fallen in love with her in three days and gone to stay illicitly and ecstatically on the small campus where she was patiently putting herself through college to become what she most admired: a teacher, one of the dedicated kind. The town was arid and alkaline and grey, tightlipped and guilt-ridden, the (mostly) white Protestant town people appearing to view all life forces as a hellfire to be stamped out whenever possible. To my hot-for-life sensibilities, they seemed to value only what beat them down and made them old before their time. Pleasure was forbidden, intellectual ideas were suspect (as was music), and outsiders were seen as subversive. Anything that made the juices flow was "off-color." Any color at all seemed to be "off-color" in that grey, grey world. Life was seen as something to suffer. All dancing was prohibited, even when the high school students modestly requested special permission from the town council to hold a senior prom.

The college cafeteria stuffed the milk and bread with great gobs of gummy white saltpeter in a vain and hideous attempt to suppress the sexual feelings of the students. Alcohol was prohibited, the entire county being dry. Sex of any kind was never mentioned out loud. Men had little money and women none. People worked desolately and women married without love; everyone looked out for their own and no one else, bitterly stressing a "survival of the fittest" doctrine. The citizens believed they were being punished for something. And so they were; they punished each other for the slightest infraction of "God-given" regulations.

Though the campus was a little more lenient than the town, Vonnie and I had no difficulty being bohemians in such a place. I was considered an outright juvenile delinquent merely for being an eighteen-year-old female on the loose, unattached to husband or father or institution.

Even in that wasteland of human relationships and social rigidity, where we had to be so utterly secretive about so much and where Yvonne's territory consisted of half of a closet and the top bunk in an open dormitory room shared with three innocently heterosexual roommates, even in that walk-on-eggs place we knew at least five other "out" Lesbians. We had a secret Gay culture. We knew about the color purple.

We had our fun and flirtations and arguments. We had our philosophical discussions and our parties and jokes and special signals and Lesbian clowning. We had heated love affairs, where we locked burning eyes and made love all over the floor because the bed seemed suddenly too far to go, and we had our serious long-term relationships. We admired each other's (forbidden to women) minds. We had found the local bootlegger, a Spanish-speaking gypsylike woman who was probably Gay herself, with wonderful humor, a big family, a mouthful of gleaming gold teeth.

We had our cigar-smoking sessions using Monopoly money and our horsey, beer-drinking Saturday nights ending with someone taking care of someone else who was sick on liquor. We played competitive sports. We admired each other's (forbidden to women) muscles. We had our cultural in-group expressions and gestures.

"Never go straight, always go forward," we joked inevitably when anyone was giving directions in a car full of Lesbians or Gay men. We had our little finger jokes. On Halloween we brazenly wore mustaches all over campus and fell down laughing at each other's funny faces. We shared danger — both physical and social — together. We stood watch for each other as lovers do in jail. We admired each other's (forbidden to women) courage. We knew about cunnilingus, though only the boldest among us practiced it. We knew about the Mound of Venus. We knew about tribadism and about butch and femme. We admired each other's (forbidden to women) sexual appetites. We knew that Gay was our generic name, that people who were not Gay were "straight" and that many of them called us "queer" with unfathomable hatred and fear, that Sappho had written love poems to women in 600 B.C., that Oscar Wilde, a faggot, had gone to jail for his Gayness, that little finger rings were a secret means of Gay identification though heaven would not help you if you were wrong.

We knew that purple was our special color, though we did not know what this meant. We did not wear purple or collect purple objects or dye our curtains purple. We did not use lavender soap or sew with mauve material or have magenta bedspreads or

5

carry bunches of violets; we had no purple flags. We simply repeated what our lovers had told us their lovers had told them: purple or lavender is the Gay color.

Eleven years and many travels later, in February 1969, in California at the first West Coast meeting in the new wave of Gay Liberation that was to sweep across the country throughout the seventies on the heels of the Feminist movement, which was on the heels of the Black movement, and on the eve of marching off with six other women to form a Lesbian/feminist separatist configuration, I presented a paper calling for all Gay people to organize, as other groups had organized. In honor of our subterranean culture, I called the paper "The Purple Fist." When radical Lesbian/feminists made themselves visible as a group in New York City in the early seventies, they called themselves "The Lavender Menace." Lesbian poet Fran Winant called her publishing enterprise "Violet Press." Soon a songwriter/singer, Alix Dobkin, produced an album, "Lavender Jane Loves Women." In Baltimore, Lesbian-owned Diana Press published an anthology, "Lavender Herring." Purple book jackets appeared on books and dictionaries produced by Gay poets and writers of both sexes, and purple T-shirts announced Gay slogans of affirmation from diverse groups of people from all over the country. As though some mysterious hand had planted bulbs all over the land, we lavender folk sprang up, spontaneously flowering in the color we had learned as an identifying mark of our culture when it was subterranean and secret.[3]

The Color of Transition

The connections between purple and ancient Gay stories and traditions indicate that it has considerably more significance than simply a mixture of "female red" and "male blue" colors. Nor is it just a remembrance handed down loyally like school colors; it has meanings from the tribal civilizations that preceded and underlie our modern world and has a place in the shamanic sciences and arts that prevailed in the long, woman-centered ages of human history before this primarily patriarchal era.

Purple represents, brings about, and is present during radical transformation from one state of being to another. Purple appears at twilight and at predawn. It stands at the gate between the land of the material flesh in one world and the land of the spirit or soul in another and is present in the envelope of energy that surrounds the body, usually called the "aura." It is especially prominent in the aura during the transformational events of birth and death; at such times it serves as a protection and a medium or transformative vehicle. During Lent the Catholic Church covers statues of the saints with purple cloth, saying that Jesus is hidden at this time until his resurrection. Perhaps this is a holdover from pagan tradition when the dying god might have been described as "in the underworld."

Many people can see the body's aura. A thirty-two-year-old woman described to me in detail her ability to do this for the year following a stroke that partially paralyzed one side of her body and temporarily altered her perceptions. During that period of heightened sight, she saw energy pour from her friends' hands and arms when they gestured; she watched an auditorium fill with the brilliant amber aura of an enthusiastic rock concert audience. And she spent time in her hospital bed studying the vivid purple aura of her roommate, who lay dying of cancer, having decided to die in peace without the use of chemotherapy.

I asked a traditional witch to tell me the qualities of purple. She was a member through her Irish family, of a coven in the "Craft," as the underground remnants of the Old Religion are called by practitioners. "In the Craft," she replied in a big voice, fixing sharp blue Irish eyes upon me, "purple has always meant power, spiritual power. It's connected to birth and death and all kinds of transformations, and to the number seven. And it's also a color associated with the moon. But more than anything, it means power."

The claim Gay culture has to the color purple is not a recent innovation. In truth, it is of remotest antiquity, with connections reaching back as far as human memory can recall, into times before recorded history, even into the shamanic times of so-called Stone Age people with their occult interpretations of the color spectrum. And even if no other Gay trait had lasted through the ages of history to identify Gayness, purple alone would be a clear statement of the great antiquity of Gay culture.

I have spent years searching out the stories, listening and learning. I will be the teacher now, my beautiful-spirit Yvonne, first love. I will try to answer some of the questions that made our life together seem so mysterious. I will use the clues you gave me as

7

you tried to teach and protect me. I will start by telling you some old, old stories about the color purple and what it says about some other qualities of being Gay, and you may be very surprised.

Say It With Flowers

"Pansy" is a derogatory name applied to men who are a bit swishy, especially by straight men who want to believe that they themselves are stiff and upright. In Shakespeare's play about mixed identities, *A Midsummer Night's Dream*, the Fairy-King Oberon sends the Fairy, Puck, on a special mission to gather a magic purple flower that changes a person's sexual inclinations: "The juice of it on sleeping eyelids laid, / Will make or man or woman madly dote / Upon the next live creature that it sees." [4] The flower Puck gathered was the pansy. Violets, which are related to pansies (both are in the viola family) were worn by both men and women in sixteenth-century England to indicate that they did not intend to marry. Pansy is also one of the names suggested for the purple flower that sprang from the blood of a male lover whom one of the Gayest of the Greek gods, Apollo, accidently struck dead. [5] "Love lies bleeding" is another name for the pansy and also for the purple-and-crimson-flowered amaranth, sacred to Artemis at her Ephesian shrine. According to Mrs. Grieve in her *Modern Herbal*, the name *amaranth* came from the Greek *unwithering* and signified immortality. Mrs. Grieve lists menstrual disorders among the plant's medicinal uses. [6]

The Greeks, who took homosexual love for granted, told a story about still another purple flower and a young man who fell in love with the reflection of a handsome young man. Narcissus scorned the love of maidens, and this especially affected one whose name was Echo. She was so hurt by his indifference that she hid in the woods and mountains, wasting away until she had no more flesh; nothing remained of her except her voice. Anyone can hear her still, especially in the remote areas of the earth, where she hides. One day another maiden, who knew Echo's sad end, was sympathetic to her, and had also tried in vain to attract the attention of Narcissus, prayed to an avenging goddess to make the indifferent man feel what it was like to love without having the feeling returned. In response to her prayer, the avenging goddess cast a spell upon a shining clear fountain, as mythographer Bulfinch describes, "with water like silver, to which the shepherds never drove their flocks, nor the mountain goats resorted, nor any of the beasts of the forest; neither was it defaced with fallen leaves or branches; but the grass grew fresh around it, and the rocks sheltered it from the sun." Here, Narcissus one day wandered and stooped to drink and for the first time saw his own face. He thought the young man he saw was a water-spirit and fell instantly in love with him.

Overcome with longing for the bright eyes, glowing cheeks, parted lips, and spirit of liveliness and health, he could not stop gazing at the image. His lips touched the lips of the spirit for a kiss, but the image immediately broke apart. He tried every way to embrace the beautiful man, and every time he touched the surface of the water the spirit left. He wept over his loss, and his tears chased the face further from him. Finally he, like Echo, pined away and died. When the maidens came to bury him he had altogether gone. In his place grew a flower with a purple center, surrounded by white leaves, which bears and preserves the memory of Narcissus.[7] We get the word *narcissist* from this story. The flower described is not the narcissus we know today, which belongs to the lily family. Mrs. Grieve quotes Pliny saying that our narcissus was named for *narce*, narcotic sleep, and not "the fabulous boy." [8]

The purple flower called "narcissus" figured prominently in another Greek story, this one a religious rite with many Lesbian undertones — the story of Demeter and her daughter Persephone. A long poem, "The Hymn to Demeter," [9] written down about 1500 B.C. tells how the Maid Persephone was gathering flowers with twenty-three other girls when she reached for one spectacular narcissus, a special flower grown particularly for her by her great-grandmother, the earth goddess Gaia. Gaia's shrine was guarded by a great python of renewal and transformation. As Persephone touched the brilliant purple flower the earth suddenly opened up beneath her and Persephone was swept into the spirit-world. Perhaps she fell into a shamanic type of trance induced by the narcotic bulbs of the flower. As a result of her subterranean journey, Persephone became a Queen of the Underworld, mistress of the spirits along with the crone goddess Hekate, who also became her lifelong companion.

Apollo's Love Lies Bleeding

The hyacinth is another flower named, like narcissus, for the love between two men, and in the stories about them, both are purple.[10] The Sun god of Greece, Apollo, was once in love or, as Bulfinch puts it, "passionately fond" of a youth named Hyacinthus. The upstart Sun god, who overthrew the powerful matriarch, the earth goddess Gaia at her ancient snakey shrine, followed Hyacinthus everywhere he went. Apollo carried the nets when the two of them went fishing, led the dogs for the hunt, trailed after the young man in excursions into the mountains, and even neglected his own lyre and arrows, so foolishly head over heels was he in love with Hyacinthus. One day they played a game of discusthrowing, Apollo tossing the discus very high and far. Hyacinthus, overexcited with the sport, ran forward to grab it when the discus unexpectedly bounced on the ground, hitting him in the forehead. The horrified Apollo lifted him up and tried to stanch the blood from the wound, but no pressure could help it. Bulfinch describes Hyacinthus' dying: "As, when one has broken the stem of a lily in the garden it hangs its head and turns its flowers to the earth, so the head of the dying boy, as if too heavy for his neck, fell over on his shoulder." [11]

The stricken lover Apollo vowed to commemorate his lost love in song and story; moreover, he turned the dead youth into a flower. Where his blood had stained the earth, a purple flower grew up, and on the petals the god inscribed his woe with his arrow in marks that spelled "Ah! Ah!" [12]

This is certainly a lovely and poetic story. A different sort of poet has left us references to purple, to certain flowers, and to the love of women for women. These remain in the lines of the original Lesbian poet, Sappho.

Coming from Well-Built Lesbos

About one hundred poems, many of them in fragments of only a few words, remain to us of the work of Sappho, the beloved, "little and dark," as she was described. In these precious remnants she made seven references to the color purple, five to violets or "violet-colored," and two to purple hyacinths. Love, she said, wore a purple mantle.[13] Her mother had worn a purple headband in her dark hair when she was young, considering it high style. Describing something beautiful but overlooked, Sappho wrote, "Like a hyacinth in / the mountains, trampled / by the shepherds until / only a purple stain / remains on the ground." [14]

Sappho's contemporary Alkaios, a male poet, described her as "violet-haired," and Sappho's poetry mentions, among other flowers and herbs, the violet tiaras she and her lovers made for one another as part of the love of life they shared.

Purple also appears in the oldest known poem that explicitly records the use of the word *Lesbian* as a reference to a woman who loves other women and not just to a native of the island of Lesbos. Living a generation after Sappho, Anacreon described an attractive Lesbian he wanted for himself:

> Golden-haired love strikes me again
> with a purple ball, and calls on me to play
> with a motley-sandled girl. But she,
> for she comes from well-built Lesbos,
> finds fault with my hair, for it is white,
> and gapes after another girl.[15]

The Great Greek Transition

The emergence of Greek civilization after the fall of Troy in 1200 B.C. marked a great change from the old gynarchical states that had earlier culminated in the predominance of Black Egyptian science and architecture. The matrifocal worlds of Egypt, Mesopotamia, and Old Europe gave way to the rising military patriarchal states of the northern Mediterranean with their new artistic emphasis on the individual and male body, the individual and male mind, the individual and male god/rulership. During all these centuries of painful transition and transference of control, emphasis, and ritual from primarily female to primarily male hands, Gay culture played and continues to play an enormous part in the change. Gay culture acts as a buffer and a medium between clashing worlds and helps effect the transitions of power and knowledge from one sex to the other. In the ancient Greek cities, who better to interpret the "mysteries" of female-based religious rite and science than Gay men, who gained access by masquerading as women in the temples and the sacred rites? Who better to explain to ignorant grooms in the rising new system of heterosexual marriage how to make love to women and how to respect brides than a Lesbian poet/songwriter? Sappho, mistress of a school for training young women, filled her work with advice on how to approach and treat women, as well as the gods.

Purple became a national color before there were nations. Numerous ancient cities, such as Sidon and Tyre, became famous for the quality and beauty of the purple dyes developed by their

11

craftworkers and the purple cloth of their weavers. A name for one Greek purple dye, *Paideros*, also meant "boy-lover." When the prominence of the Greeks gave way to newer and ever more military/masculine-based states, in both Rome and medieval Europe high-grade purple cloth remained associated with power. I believe the original spiritual power of tribal sorcerer/shaman/priests was later vested in kings and high clergy, royalty and court leaders. Purple graced court scenes that included the traditional wisewomen and wisemen, the Gay jesters, astrologers, diviners, soothsayers, advisers, acrobats, archbishops and abbesses, troubadors and bards. The medieval courts were guarded and further graced by knights, the templars, who were accused of sodomy and tortured and destroyed as an order, perhaps because they drew their customs in large measure from the old gynarchies and goddess/religious states and most of all from ancient Gay pagan traditions with a tribal, "prehistoric" base. As the overt remnants of the older woman-directed ways such as the Old Religion of Europe were increasingly suppressed, overthrown, and driven underground by wave after wave of patriarchal domination, masculine religion, and militarism, Gay culture was also forced underground. The half-secret acknowledgment of lavender as the sacred color associated with Gayness was submerged into veiled mythological stories or the simple memory of purple as the "Gay color" passed on through secret Gay culture networks of lovers and friends.

The sources of this underground have apparently been numerous, stemming from all parts of Europe and found in any stratum of contemporary society, whether upper-class Gay people or lower-class, urban or rural, religious or pagan or atheist, professional or blue collar, secretary or street person, bohemian artist or business executive. In all its strata the Gay underground knows that its traditional color is purple.

The Special Little Finger Ring

Many of the Black peoples of the South and North American continents brought their African religions, arts, and sciences with them, sustaining them as best they could in secret, in a covert or barely veiled underground in spite of monumental attempts by the white slave owners to utterly suppress the powerful cultures. The Yoruba religion of West Africa survived in the southern United States, the West Indies, and South America, where it is known as *Macumba*. It is a pantheistic religion (having many gods and spirits, rather than one primary one). For protection, its practitioners often cover it with a thin veneer of Catholicism. This living religion, which is currently attracting American white people as well as people of color, includes a powerful trilogy of goddesses. The oldest is Lemanja, the Great Ocean; the youngest sister is Oshun, whose provinces are clear rivers and streams and whose attributes are beauty and grace. The middle of the three is a warrior and storm goddess who appears (through the offices of mediums at spiritual meetings) wearing men's clothing and carrying weapons. Her name is Oya, and her special color is purple.[16]

Purple plays a major role in a story from North American Indian tradition. The story, gathered at the turn of the century from the Caddo Indian tribe in what is now Texas, tells of a Gay shaman, a pacifist with great powers whose people were moving toward a more patriarchal/military conception of masculinity. The shaman still had the bewitching powers of a sorcerer, and his life was protected from attack by the presence of a purple spot located on his left little finger.

According to George Dorsey in *Traditions of the Caddo*, there once was a Caddo man who always went about dressed as a woman and doing the work of women, never that of men. The other men made fun of him but he did not care. Then a war broke out between the Caddo and another tribe, with all the men joining the fray except this man, who remained with the women. After the war party of men had left, one man, too elderly to join them, came to the cross-dressed fellow and threatened to kill him if he would not go to war with the others, saying it was a disgrace to have such a man in the tribe. But he refused,

> saying the Great Father did not send him to earth to fight and did not want him to. The old man paid no attention to his excuse, and told him if he did not go to fight he would have the warriors kill him when they returned from battle with the enemy. The man said that they could not kill him, that he would always come to life, and would bewitch people and cause them to fight and kill one another. The old man did not believe him, and when the war party came home he told the men that they would have to kill the man because he was a coward, and they could not let a coward live in the tribe.
>
> They beat him until they thought he was dead, and were just ready to bury him when he jumped up alive. Again they beat him until he fell, then they cut off his head. He jumped up headless and ran about, frightening all of the people. They

13

were just about to give up killing him when someone noticed a small purple spot on the little finger of his left hand. They cut that out; then he lay down and died. Soon after many people began to fight and quarrel, and even killed their own brothers and sisters and fathers and mothers. The other people tried to stop the fighting, but could not, because the people were betwitched and could not help themselves.

After that the old man remembered what the cross-dressing pacifist had warned, and he told the rest of the people, and they regretted killing him.[17]

The fact that the protective magic dot of purple was on the shaman's little finger makes this a very Gay story indeed. Wearing a little finger ring, especially on the left hand, is a common way of indicating Gayness to other members of the secret or semisecret Gay underground in America. When a tennis star in modern America decided to indicate her Lesbianism openly, she not only had her lover sit boldly in the box reserved for players' spouses, she also used a close-up publicity photograph that included her hand held beside her face. Posted on her little finger was a little ring signaling to other Gay people her solidarity and identification with them.

The Caddo Indian story reveals the antiquity of the special nature of little fingers in the Gay domain, illustrating that the little finger was not always used as a secret identifying signal but rather is an indication of special powers, a badge of office. It becomes a secret signal only when Gay culture is suppressed by patriarchal cultural bias.

The Little Finger of Hermes Is Very Long

Well, Von, I still remember the magical thrill I felt watching your beautiful, strong square hands and your heavy silver ring, as you talked excitedly with them in the air, making gestures like drawings of your ideas. The ring you gave me for my own little finger was more than a love band, though it certainly was that. It was also a mark of something else we had in common, our belonging to a secret, different world and way of life than other people, not superior, not cultish, just: itself.

Paul Mariah, a Gay poet who served a prison term in Illinois solely on charges of homosexuality, says that the spoon ring was

14

invented by prisoners to give to each other when they made a love
bond.

> The secret vows
> Of prisoners
> Exchange rings,
> Silver contraband
>
> (Whenever a spoon
> Is stolen from chow
> Line, frisks happen,
> Search for lost silver
>
> Either a shiv appears
> In some hidden corner
> Or a lover announces
> His bond, shows his hand.)
>
> A spoon, a wedding ring
> Crest of prison despair
> That knows the ritual song
> "To spoon the empty air." [18]

Why is the little finger the finger of Gay designation? [19] Clues
about this lie in the occult, divinatory arts. The occult tradition
says that each finger is named for a particular god. Each god has
particular attributes, and so does each finger. Venus, for instance,
with her love interests rules the third finger, the traditional position on the left hand for the bond-ring of heterosexual marriage.

The little finger is named for Mercury, whose dominions are
change, communication, science, spiritual power, and wit. These
qualities are attributed to the little finger by the art of palmistry.
The winged Roman god Mercury was called Hermes in Greece.
Hermes had a number of offices, including herald and messenger
of the gods, giver of increase to herds, and guardian of boundaries
and of roads and their commerce. He was god of science and invention, of eloquence, of cunning, trickery, and theft, of luck and
treasure trove, and the conductor of the dead spirits to the underworld of Hades. His graphic symbol is a woman's symbol, taken
from the Ankh, the life symbol of Egypt, with two horns added
to the top. According to Neoplatonic philosophy, Hermes' function in Egypt, where he was identified with the god Thoth, was

"scribe of the gods." His works embodied mystical, theosophical, astrological, and alchemical doctrines.[20] Hermes was the messenger who wrote down the basic laws of occult practice, and in the West the occult tradition is called the Hermetic tradition.[21]

The god with the same characteristics as Greek Hermes was called Wuotan or Wodin in northern Europe. Wednesday is named after him — Wodin's Day — just as Thursday is named for the storm god Thor — Thor's Day.[22] The character of Wuotan is mercury and quicksilver, changeability and transformation; and his color is purple. Sexual rites that included homosexuality were part of his worship. In the Middle Ages, Christian authorities seeking to suppress the Old Religion of Europe specifically condemned weekly festivals honoring both Thor on Thursday and Wuotan on Wednesday. The texts of confessions extracted from people who honored the old pagan deities repeatedly described sexual rites on these weekly festival occasions (as well as other holidays). The sexual rites included numerous references to "men lying with men and women lying with women." [23]

Opals and Amethysts

The occult sciences gave the color purple the same attributes as palmistry does: spiritual knowledge and transformation.[24] The little finger is also designated as having these attributes, and wearing a ring on it helps bring the attributes to the forefront, according to occult stone specialists.[25]

At least two gemstones have ancient Gay traditions of their own. The opal, or moonstone, a milky, translucent stone shot through with blue and purple (and more colors if it is Mexican), gets its name from the Latin *opalus*. The Greeks called the opal *paideros*, a name they also gave to a purple vegetable dye. *Paideros* was also the name of a thorn plant with a head shaped like a penis. The writer Pliny says that *paideros* comes from *pais, paidos,* "boy, son" and *erotis,* "beloved," and that it is related to the Greek *paiderastes,* "boy-lover, pederast." He says the opal earned its name because of its exceptional beauty.[26]

The purple amethyst is used by occultists as a crystal of divination. Known as a stone of the spirit, of change and transformation it is traditionally selected as the material for the crystal ball. Modern scientists also say that the amethyst has peculiar properties for effecting some molecular changes in other forms of matter, and it is used in certain types of delicate tissue surgery.

The origin of the stone's name is told in a basic Lesbian warrior rescue story involving the goddess Diana. The Roman god of wine and good times, Bacchus, was also given to another of alcohol's characteristics: rash decisions made in a fit of rage. One day in a bad temper he decreed that the next person to cross his path would be devoured alive by wild tigers. Meanwhile, one of Diana's many worshipers, who were almost always women, was on her way to the shrine to pay her respects to the goddess of hunting and childbirth. She was a lovely, clear, and rather colorless maiden named Amethyst. Seeing her cross the drunken wine god's path, and knowing what he had vowed to do, Diana intervened before the tigers could begin their merciless attack. Using her store of transformational tricks, Diana turned the young Amethyst into a pillar of colorless quartz. When Bacchus sobered up, he regretted his harsh, vindictive edict and the permanent mineral state into which the once-living woman had been frozen. Using his own magic, he spilled wine over the pale Amethyst-stone, giving it a lovely, rich lavender hue and endowing it with the power to prevent drunkenness.[27]

Worlds of Change

So, Von, you can see that purple is of the spirit and denotes a change from one world or life position to another. In recent times, the election of Ronald Reagan in 1980 marked the greatest single change in the American economic and political viewpoint since the time of the Great Depression, the New Deal, and Franklin Delano Roosevelt fifty years earlier. And the fashion industry responded in kind, reflecting 1981 as a year of change by coming out with racks of clothes for men and women that featured every shade and hue of purple.

I know, Von, my dear "Bab," as we used to call each other privately, that you would be astonished and pleased to see how many lavender stories are connected to Gay themes. And I know I have barely scratched the surface. Think what it means, already: that we are not just an arbitrary group, like "all the people who like chocolate mocha ice cream." We have a history, or more appropriately several histories, that give our way of life meaning beyond its simple mechanics. Being Gay is not just falling in love with or having sexual relations with members of the same sex. What Gay people as a group have in common is not simply same-gender bonding and sexual proclivities coupled with shared op-

17

pression from anti-Gay forces in the larger society. Being a Lesbian is more than a "political choice" made by consciously feminist women of the seventies who were bonding with women while at the same time vaulting over or combating the sexism they perceived in the institution of heterosexual marriage.

Gay people have a history because Gay culture has histories that give us a continuity with the past and that give us connections with Gay people in other cultures and countries, places, and times. We're the inheritors of a distinct cultural background with very long roots, long buried to be sure. I want to dig out some more of the clues, especially from the words you vested with me as my first lover, Von, in the act of bringing me out and attempting to protect and prepare me for life in an underground culture. Where do the other attributes we once pondered together come from: the prohibition of wearing green on Thursday, for instance? That one really baffled you. And faggots and fairies, bulldykes, butches, and femmes? The sexual term neither of us shy butterflies could bear to use, "eating you out"? Why those particular words for such exact social characteristics in a well-defined cultural underground that used the same terms from one end of the country to the other, as we found once we had left our backland of New Mexico? Why those particular terms, where do they come from, why are they passed along the grapevine?

In proceeding with my task of researching Gay underground slang words, phrases, and characteristics, is there, I wondered, such a thing as a coherent Gay culture? Could it be that Gay people play certain roles in society that are a necessary and natural part of socialized life and, if so, is this true in any part of the world? I wondered why such a deep, suppressive silence surrounded the subject of Gayness when Yvonne and I were coming of age in the early sixties. We heard rumors of Gay geese, in a natural animal world otherwise universally described as living in heterosexual family groups. We heard rumors of Gay men in Russia. (We heard they were getting severe jail sentences, so it wasn't joyful news.) We heard of Lesbian and Gay men imprisoned in Cuba. But even if they were imprisoned, at least they *existed*, and that was important information in our isolated and frightening circumstances. Tiny taps heard on the wall of our own mental and emotional prison.

All the authorities of the 1950s — religious, psychiatric and political, literary and familial — appeared to agree: Man and woman are "born" to cleave one unto the other and any other ar-

18

rangement, particularly same-gender attachment, is unnatural, a sin, a crime, a sickness, a decadence, a fault, a shame, a waste, and a deliberate attempt to "hurt" the friend or family member to whom we tried to explain our everyday lives. Perhaps, our families suggested, we were simply rebellious and busy doing "the opposite" of what we had been taught was "the right way" to be.

I thought that if Gayness has cultural characteristics, then it exists as a separate entity, complete in itself, and not as a reaction to a heterosexual social model, not as a reaction to any social model, including sexism, patriarchy, the way men or women are treated by each other, the fact that families stay together or split up, that sexuality is open or closed, that the economy is flourishing or depressed. If Gayness has a culture of its own, it exists in the midst of but is not caused by any of those conditions.

CHAPTER TWO

The Original Underground

Great Woman down there
Will she, i wonder, feel a desire to move?
Great Woman down there
Will she, i wonder, feel a desire to move?
Come out, you down there
Those who live above you
Call you
To see you, savage and snappish!
Come out, you down there.

Eskimo shaman song to summon Sedna[1]

Von, my dear first lover, I don't believe you consciously thought that you were bringing me out to be a part of an underground culture. You just did what your lovers had taught you to do. There seemed to be so few of us out there in rural areas during the late 1950s. I don't think we could have imagined an extensive network of underground people; I'm not sure we even knew about Gay bars then. Because so many people around us appeared to be "straight," which was defined as normal, the norm, we thought of ourselves as aberrant from the main culture rather than people entrusted with a distinct cultural tradition of our own. The deep silence surrounding homosexuality and Lesbianism, of course, is why we thought this way.

I Am the Skeleton in My Family Closet

ONE GAY PATTERN common to all modern or "emerging" nations is the closeting of Gays into an underground society. Apparently this shift from visibility to invisibility happens in the often centuries-long changeover from tribe to village to modern industrial state. The compulsory hiddenness of Gay life is evident to Western Gay people. "Being in the closet," that is, hidden, and "coming out of the closet," that is, being revealed, are expressions that have recently escaped from Gay slang into American pop culture as a result of the impact that Gay writing, Gay mass demonstrations, and other Gay organizing endeavors have had on mass consciousness during the 1970s. At present the term "closet" implies a scandalous personal secret, or skeleton, in the family closet. In the case of a Gay person, it refers more precisely to *being* the skeleton in the family's closet.[2] That skeleton is the reality of Gayness itself. The sometimes violent and always frightening suppression of Gay culture often forces Gay people to live in the closet, in a secret world. And this suppression prevails throughout the modern industrial world.

Living in the closet does not eliminate Gay sex or lifelong Gay relationships, but it does hide Gay culture from view, channeling it into a closely guarded and psychologically dangerous, though vital and lively, undergound. Social suppression of Gay culture is reflected in such statements as "No one cares what you do in private, just don't flaunt it," that is, don't express it, make it public. But without flaunting there is no culture; there is only the imitation of heterosexual culture and the illusion that only one culture exists. Closets exist to maintain this illusion.

23

The current antihomosexual campaign in America expresses very well a determination to maintain the illusion of universal heterosexuality: "We love homosexuals as persons. What we resist is the attempt to incorporate their chosen lifestyle under the heading of a minority group." This statement is from a newspaper article quoting men who advocate that homosexuals be executed for "sins" because, according to Scripture, homosexuality is against the law. "We want to minister to homosexuals and win them to Christ," one man says.[3] What is threatened is Gay *culture*, especially as it has become organized, open, and accessible to its members, operating as a community like any other.

Adrienne Rich has written of the compulsory orientation of women toward heterosexuality.[4] Within the Gay population itself is another, related phenomenon: the compulsory *illusion* of heterosexuality. In fact, in our society even animals are depicted, displayed, and imagined in heterosexual couplings, although in the wild state they live entirely differently, often with the sexes separated.

Many Gay people marry a person of the opposite sex to produce a front for both of them. When society insists that everyone pretend to be heterosexual and punishes anyone who does not give that appearance, Gay people live solidly in the closet, in a secret underworld known only to themselves. They display one image to the world, a truer one to each other. And straight people live in a world of self-blinding false assumption. When this happens the straight people may find their Gay friends and family members — unrecognized by them — to be a little peculiar and socially clumsy. Gay people are likely to find their straight friends and family stupid and cruel. Both sides are participating in the illusion.

Gay Is a Grand Old Dame

Of course sometimes high humor is involved in maintaining all this secrecy; Gay people of all social strata develop intricate codes and language inflections that operate within ordinary-sounding language patterns to convey information that members of the Gay culture can understand. The idea is that hidden things may be least noticed when contained in what is most obvious.

Gertrude Stein perfected this style in an apparently innocuous story published in 1922. Consequently, I first heard the word *Gay* used with reference to homosexual love in a high school literature class, although I didn't know that members of the homosexual underground culture called themselves Gay, and neither did my teacher. The teacher read to us in class Stein's inexpressibly clever and completely overt Lesbian story of two women learning to be lovers, "Miss Furr and Miss Skeene." First the two live together in the city, learning "ways of being gay," and ending each day in "a gay way," until Miss Furr finds that "She was gay enough, she was always gay exactly the same way, she was always learning little things to use in being gay . . . she would always be gay in the same way, when Georgine Skeene was there not so long each day as when Georgine Skeene was away." And so they broke up, without any long-term unhappiness. The story is guileless and utterly typical of the behavior of Lesbians. It is my favorite coming-out story. And Stein slid it perfectly through the censorship of the era, so that everyone could read it, but some could decode it and learn more about themselves than others could.[5]

Maintaining Secrecy

The secrecy some Gay couples maintain about their relationship to each other can reach great extremes. I have known women lovers together for fifteen years who pretend to live separately, going one night to the house of one and the next night to the house of the other, each time carrying the gear, suitcases, changes of clothing they will need for the next day, for the sake of fooling a few family members and straight friends. Other Lesbian couples go to even greater lengths to ensure secrecy. One couple has lived together for nine years and also works together in the same office, where they are so fearful of being discovered as lovers and lifetime mates that they pretend not to know each other at all.

When I was working in a laboratory as a medical technician, I had a clear lesson in the secrecy of the closet. Six of us were standing around getting ready to take off our white coats and go home for the day, when one woman told an ugly anti-Gay joke. She was a young aide in training to do minor tests, nowhere near as skilled as the rest of us, and she recently had been married; no one expected her to stay long at her job. The point of her joke was See-how-stupid-and-wrong-faggots-are. It made me sick inside to hear it, but following the rule of appearing heterosexual or else, from years of habit and the desire to stay employed and reasonably accepted among my co-workers, I obediently pretended to laugh.

25

As I did so my eyes met the sparkling blue eyes of our boss, a man who had worked his way up to become the chief laboratory technician of the hospital. In his fifties, he had never married and was continually teased as "most eligible bachelor." His eyes flashed into mine now as, mouths guffawing, we acknowledged with a special look that straight people simply had to be indulged, that that was part of The Life. My eyes flicked from him to his lover Robert, a technician like myself and a friend of mine. Large, broad-shouldered, and with his short hair plastered to his skull, Robert looked as if the word *straight* was invented just to describe him. He and I were teased in the laboratory for going out together, which we occasionally did as a front. But I knew Robert and our boss had been lovers for several years and owned a business together outside the laboratory, operating it on weekends; I had been there to have dinner with them.

From Robert's distorted, pretending-to-laugh face, my gaze passed to another technician, Rita. She was beautiful, graceful, smart, and gutsy. She had recently led all of us in a strike for better wages. The highly skilled Rita was head of the bacteriology department and a specialist in her work. I had a terrific crush on her at the time, and now to my disgust here she was pretending to howl at the rude joke, and so was her lover Alberta who stood next to her with her coat on, ready to go home. The two Lesbians worked together in the laboratory, owned a house and a couple of horses, having lived together for at least ten years. I closed my mouth and stopped laughing. I was too astonished at what my eyes had registered: Of six people standing in the laboratory laughing at a vicious anti-Gay joke, five were Gay — everyone except the woman who had told the joke. The walls of the closet are guarded by the dogs of terror, and the inside of the closet is a house of mirrors.

Being in the Closet

The modern closet, or secret world, of the typical Gay person is partially defined by the fears we share of dreadful repercussions inflicted on us by the straight world simply for Gayness itself. Threat of harm more than genuine experience of harm defines the modern American closet. Fear of being fired and losing all economic security is another high closet wall. Fear of being ostracized by family, friends, and neighbors is another. Gay people can usually expect as much punishment and oppression from members of their own families, including their grown children, as from strangers, and for the sole reason of their identification as Gay.

The Nazi terrorism during the thirties and World War II has altered permanently people's ideas of the ability of "civilization" to care for its citizens. Among the populations condemned to torture, grotesque physical debasement, and death were Europe's Gay people. As for the Jews, the fact of genocide was even more bitter after the experience of an openly tolerant pre-Nazi Germany. Jewish intellectuals said the Jews had never been closer to total acceptance in Christian society. Berlin before Hitler published Gay books and supported a lively Gay culture that was active in the arts and the universities.[6]

I don't remember the exact moment that I understood that Nazi Germany had destroyed hundreds of thousands of homosexuals solely on the basis of their Gayness. But I know that the fact will haunt me all my life, for I can never trust my citizenship, never take for granted that my neighbors will not stand idly by while I am killed for my way of life. The Holocaust will be with us forever; in any event, centuries of anti-Gay oppression in Western society has produced our response of secrecy.

The Gay closet has many points of discomfort. One is the sheer shame that life must be so secret, that one's citizenship is always dependent on how camouflaged as a heterosexual one appears. The necessary double life means that the Gay person can never simply stand flat-footed on the earth; there are aways two people operating in one body, and one of them is a liar. This creates problems of distrust and disorientation. Fear is always present and affects every part of Gay life.

And the fear causes many Gay people to feel that no matter how you love your family and friends, you can never feel they completely love you, for being in the closet means they do not even know you, they know a projected false image of you. And if they did know you, would they hate you? Push you out of the family? Act superior and condescending? Lock you in a torturous mental hospital? Cut off your funds? Sock you and hit you? You can never trust them, for whether they choose it or not, they are allied with the Nazis as long as a Gay family member has to lead a secret life on account of fear.

Moreover, the fact that Gay people are closeted prohibits expression of liberal views on the part of straight people who would be open and tolerant, even joyful of the free expression of Gay culture if anyone would just provide an honest context. Of course

27

people are already openly tolerant, even grateful for the richness and use of Gay culture. But when a Gay person is in the closet, there is no way to know who are the friends and who are the enemies. There can be no friends in an atmosphere of suspicion and terror.

Most ironically, the closet cuts off members of the Gay community from each other. Some Gay people are so avid to be seen as straight that they go out of their way to persecute open homosexuals as a way of diverting attention from themselves. There is no safety in this behavior.

An Underground Bar

In the closeted world of the late 1950s, when you brought me out, Von, we worried a great deal that you might lose your teaching credentials if we were seen as Lesbian. We made up stories for people about phony boyfriends and husbands. We told some people we were sisters-in-law. And we were frightened all the time. Yet still we found our world exciting and wouldn't have stopped being Gay for anything. We loved being able to love each other and to explore areas of human behavior that didn't seem to be open to other young women we knew. We were part of a secret network of Lesbians who knew each other, who were busy learning the stances and attitudes of Gayness, and who met for parties or to play cards. There was yet another part of the Gay underground culture that I would get to know in the next couple of years: the Gay bar. This was to be the only public expression of Gay culture that I would find in a closeted world.

During the late fifties and early sixties, my Von, when virtually everyone was in the closet, including you as you finished college after tearfully sending me on my way out into the world to become a "real writer," the only place I found to locate a gathering of Gay people was a downtown big-city bar. I was living alone then, working first as a sandwich girl, then as a medical secretary, waiting for you to come live with me again. Which you eventually did. During that time of being apart from you I was SO lonely. I made the mistake of enlisting in the armed service only to get myself kicked out for being Gay. I was at the bottom of the world, twenty-one, entirely on my own, cut off from everyone I had known in the past, including most of my family, trying to get started with an education and a career, trying to locate myself in the mysterious, biting world called "Gay." It was very different *from your warm arms, your concern that I be protected and taught, led into the world of Lesbianism gently, "brought out" by your strong sense of responsibility. The world I now entered without your company was not like that. This was urban, cold, sophisticated, tough, indifferent, and even outright cruel. No arms caught you when you fell, nor wiped the blood from your cheek when you were wounded. And we, in that little urban underground of Gay people, we were all wounded.*

I can see now it was a necessary part of my initiation; going to my first Gay bar certainly felt as terrifying, mystifying, and life-altering as any ritual procedure could have felt.

The bar was on a sleazy street of pawnshops, clubs featuring women dancers pushing watered-down drinks on a quota system between dances, tattoo parlors, rundown hotels, and hamburger counters staying open till just past bar-closing time to serve coffee and sobering-up food to customers too drunk to walk to a bus stop. A nearby bus stand for service personnel dropped off loads of sailors and soldiers with weekend passes and just enough money to get drunk and do a little carousing. MPs patrolled the block as often as did the city police.

The street had a permanently dislocated look, unwashed and untended, a look of transience and worn-out baggage. Our fresh young faces, not yet wary, cynical, or bitter, were a startling contrast to the environment. Dim, multicolored neon lights added to the dinginess and aura of danger. Brassy whores in tight, bright miniskirts were trailed down the street by knots of self-conscious sailors and singular, decrepit winos.

Nothing distinguished the Rendezvous Bar from any of the others except that its reputation among queers was that it was "ours." Why we should have wanted it is anybody's guess. Perhaps we took what dregs were available. All the world at that time was divided very severely into male and female, with no one crossing the line easily; there was no androgyny. Women did not wear pants on the street; men did not make graceful gestures, let alone carry purses or wear makeup. In those days homosexuality was so closely guarded and so heavily punished that it might as well have been illegal just to gather in a bar together. Only heavy payoffs, I have heard, kept any of the bars open for business to a Gay clientele. Quite a contrast to the snazzy, clean, well-lit, beautiful, and often Gay-owned bars of today. (*My Von, you are missing out on seeing them too; you have such bad timing.*) But the sleazy Ren-

29

dezvous was where we bottom-of-the-world overt Gay people could go and be "ourselves."

I went there one night with another Lesbian I had met in the service; I remember the fear I felt on the bus ride downtown. The bus passed through a dark tunnel and the driver had a black curtain wrapped around his seat. I felt I was on a journey to hell and had to laugh at my young self for undertaking such a perilous journey. There would be no turning back for me once I had entered such a place; I knew very distinctly that I had "crossed over."

From the minute I entered the doors of the Rendezvous, past the Gay bouncer (who looked exactly like Li'l Abner in the comics), and gaped in thrilled shock at the self-assured, proud Lesbians in pants and the men in makeup and sculptured, displayed, eerily beautiful faces, I saw myself as part of a group that included some very peculiar characters and characteristics. I ceased then to be a nice white Protestant girl with a tomboy nature who had once had a secret and very loving Lesbian relationship with another nice girl who was attending college to become a teacher. That definition no longer applied, as I stepped into my first Gay bar to become a full-fledged dike, a more-than-a-Lesbian.

Imitating the women I found at the Rendezvous, I dressed for the dike part each evening before riding the bus to my new world. I combed my hair back from my face, having cut it as short as I could and still hold my job. Using men's hairdressing I slicked it into a duck tail; with peroxide I streaked a blond swath into the front and arranged a curl to fall down the center of my forehead. Next came boys' trousers and either a black turtleneck sweater or a boys' white shirt with a T-shirt underneath. Black clothing was the color of choice. Cigarettes tucked in the front pocket, boys' black loafers, and a comb completed the outfit. No makeup of any kind, certainly no purse. A jacket, if it were pouring rain or freezing cold. The boys' heavy black loafers that I had invaded a men's shoe store to buy were a special point of pride; they had taken real courage to get.

No one in the bar used a last name in front of the others, and I suspect that all first names were assumed: We had names we took for ourselves as dikes or fairies in that particular setting, just as we had a special slang language. I took the name Sonny.[7]

For all our boyish clothes and mannerisms (known as being "butch") we women did not pass as men or boys. We dikes did not want to be taken for men and were insulted and ashamed (I certainly was, anyhow) when someone said we were "trying to be men" or when a clerk called me "Sir." In fact, on those rare occasions when a woman came in who was passing in society as a man, word about this went around the tables and we studied her secretly and gossiped about her. For our point was not to be men; our point was to be butch and get away with it. We always kept something back: a high-pitched voice, a slant of the head, or a limpness of hand gestures, something that was clearly labeled female. I believe our statement was "Here is another way of being a woman," not "Here is a woman trying to be taken for a man."

The fairies also held something back that prevented them from passing over into the female gender; no matter how many sequins or feathers she wore, a drag queen was a Gay queen, not a man-passing-as-a-woman. Proper bar etiquette required that the drag queens be called "she." They referred to each other as "sister" (by which they meant friends with whom one did not have sex).[8] "Mary" was another term for male homosexuals, and so was "Nellie" (used as an adjective). We dikes were sometimes spoken of as "he," but this was relatively rare compared to the use of female pronouns to indicate the queens.

A hawk-eyed, bent-over old crone with a heavy European accent and not a trace of warmth or goodwill owned the bar, cheating us nightly on the beer and refusing to supply toilet paper or other niceties. She glared at all of us equally with apparent rank contempt when we stood at the bar to order our beers. Her standard method of letting us know it was closing time was to shine a blazing searchlight into our beer-sodden faces until we got the message, stumbling out into the starkly unwelcoming streets.

The bar had considerable dangers. Sailors lurked in the alleys outside, waiting to prove their "manhood" on our bodies; more than once they beat someone I knew — dike or faggot — on her or his way home. A brick crashed through the front window one night, scattering glass splinters over the dance floor where, fortunately, none of us were clenched together swaying to early sixties "Moon River" melodies, thrilled to death (in my case at least) to be holding a member of the same sex in her arms, to be two women publicly dancing.

One night a furious femme wearing a tight dress and carrying a purse attacked one of the dikes at another table — a woman dressed like myself in sedate dark colors and men's clothing, slicked-back hair. The femme stormed up behind the dike, who was probably her girlfriend, beating her on the head with the sharp peg of her high-heeled shoe. It was my first understanding that women fight each other.

Another night two policemen came up to the table where I sat with my friend from the service. They shined a flashlight into our eyes and commanded us to stand up or else be arrested. Then they demanded that we say our real names, first and last, several times, as loud as we could. Sweat poured down my ribs as I obeyed. After they left, my friend and I sat with our heads lowered, too ashamed of our weakness to look around or even to look each other in the face. We had no internal defense from the self-loathing our helplessness inspired and no analysis that would help us perceive oppression as oppression and not as a personal taint of character. Only the queens with their raucous sly tongues helped us get over these kinds of incidents. They called the policemen "Alice Blue Gowns," insulting them behind their backs. "Alice Blue Gown tried to sit on *my* nightstick but I said No! You dirty boy! I know you're menthtrating!" one plump faggot in a cashmere sweater would begin and soon we would be laughing and feeling strong again.

The dikes had a special way of talking, with a minimum of inflection, a flat matter-of-fact, everything-is-under-control effect. It was considered more dikish to be planted solidly in one place than to flit, to use tightly controlled gestures rather than anything grandiose.

The dikes and femmes of the bar provided a kind of low-key, solid background of being; the queens (often with a sailor or two in tow) took the foreground, talking in loud voices, using flamboyant costumes and body language to create a starry effect. Sometimes they came in full drag, with wigs and makeup, and at other times just with a big fluffy sweater for a costume but always with the particular broad gestures, lilting voice, and special queen talk. Or shrieking. The special language of a queen, or even an ordinary garden-variety faggot, is so distinct I find I can distinguish it even in a crowd of men in a restaurant or on the street, far from any Gay scene. It's a full or modified lisp coupled with dramatic inflection and, as used in full-drag queen style, it accompanies a running monologue of commentary, jokes, puns and "Gay talk," most of it sexual but with a great deal of social and political content. Bruce Rodgers's dictionary of Gay slang, *Gay Talk* (originally called *The Queen's Vernacular*), has more than 12,000 entries. This slang talk is used most particularly by Gay men, especially the fairy queens, and less so by the bar dikes.[9]

I noticed some differences between my experience as a single woman in that Gay bar and my experiences in other kinds of bars, where, of course, I did not dress in an extreme dyke fashion. In the Gay bar I could sit and drink and not be surrounded by men demanding my attention. I could ask someone to dance. I could lead when we danced, or I could find someone who liked to lead and let her do it. I could dance with either men or women. I could sing along with the lyrics and not be embarrassed to be using the "wrong" gender. I could sit with a serious face and not have smiles and pleasantries demanded of me. I noticed also great differences in Gay coupling; for the most part, lovers who were going together for any length of time were of similar size; one did not tower over the other. In the playing they did together in company, there was not the same stress on conquering-male, conquered-female that I saw in straight bars, where the pairing was different, with different purposes and a different social structure to support it.

Well, Von, those are my memories of my first Gay bar experience; my entry into that world was shocking and endlessly fascinating. I often thought I was losing my mind. Sometimes on the street I would feel that the whole world was reversed, and I would be unable to tell the men from the women, since I could see that each had qualities of the other. I tried to believe that they really knew this too and were only play-acting their roles, so rigidly defined and so in opposition to each other. But of course at that time they didn't see any such thing, and this only increased my sense of craziness. I was going through a serious transformation, one not defined by American society, except as an "aberration." Without realizing it, I was doing something remarkably similar to the initiation rites of my dikish forerunners.

Earth with Its Wide Roads Gaped

The prototype of transformation ritual for Western civilization, if not for others, is the Demeter/Kore story, the tale of the maid Persephone's journey to the underworld and her mother Demeter's retaliation. These rites were practiced for a thousand years in the part of Greece called Eleusis, long before and as late as two hundred years following the time of Sappho. The "Hymn to Demeter," a Greek text dated speculatively at around 1500 B.C., tells in beautiful language the story of the anguish and rage of the Earth

Mother, Demeter, over the abduction of her daughter Persephone by Hades, the lord of the Underworld. One bright day, out in the meadow with twenty-three maiden companions, the young woman Persephone ("She Who Gathers Everything") was collecting roses and crocuses and violets, irises too, and hyacinths, without danger, until she reached for a fatal purple flower, the narcissus. The "Hymn to Demeter" describes the special narcissus, which Gaia

> . . . made blossom there . . .
> for a girl with a flower's beauty.
> A lure it was, wondrous and radiant, and a marvel to be seen . . .
> A hundred stems of sweet-smelling blossoms
> grew from its roots. The wide sky above
> and the whole earth and the briny swell of the sea laughed.
> She was dazzled and reached out with both hands at once
> to take the pretty bauble; Earth with its wide roads gaped.[10]

Superficially, the story is of the abduction of a girl, "She Who Gathers Everything," by a patriarchal figure, the lord of the Underworld. Through a trick she is forced to return to the lower domain for six months out of the year. The story is agricultural and menstrual, of the land lying fallow in the months of winter and of being reborn when two women are reunited. It tells of the power of Demeter to withhold the fruits of the earth during the barren, bitter time of her grieving search for Persephone. Some researchers believe that the innermost secret rites of the Demeter/ Persephone mysteries were Lesbian, or, to use a more specific description, tribadic. Others have suggested that people had hallucinatory experiences during the rites from eating ergot, an LSD-type drug-mold that grows on rye. Perhaps what the ergot induced in a mass audience the priestesses produced by rubbing each other into a trance state, using sex to arouse the aura that surrounds the clitoris, the *aura clitoridis*.[11]

Several elements of the story as it was acted out in the Greek rites are Lesbian. The only person who aided Demeter when her daughter was kidnapped by Hades was Hekate, who came out of her cave when she heard Demeter crying, and the two women together searched for the lost girl. Hekate and Demeter searched with torches by night for Persephone, whose title was the Kore, meaning the Maid, the unmarried one, the Dyke.

Once Demeter knew her daughter was in the underworld, she rendered the earth barren in her anger and then went traveling on some adventures of her own. While she was in her deep mourning and depression, a female jokester appeared to her and made her laugh. This jokester was Baubo, who caused Demeter to laugh by telling her obscene sexual jokes and lifting up her skirt so Demeter could see her genitals.[12] Images of the female pudenda abounded in the ancient religious ritual world, in Egypt — where they were called *Baubo* — in European pagan temples, and even in early Christian churches.

When Persephone was finally found, Hekate embraced her several times and then became her minister and companion for the remainder of their lives, that is, eternally.[13] As a result of their relationship, Hekate became goddess of the Underworld along with Persephone, the two of them ruling jointly along with Hades. A child of Gaia and Uranus, Hekate was goddess of the crossroads; she was worshiped well into late-medieval European times as the three-part goddess of the witches, whose celebrated rites were despised by the Inquisition authorities as orgiastic and Lesbian in their essence. Dogs were sacred to Hekate, as were honey and black female lambs.

When Persephone was reunited with her mother and with her new companion Hekate, she could no longer spend all her time on the earth but was required to become goddess of the Underworld of spirits after she ate a sacred food, six seeds of the pomegranate, the food of departed spirits. The ruby seeds of the Pom Grannie — as one warmly flirtatious, gorgeous Black dyke called the fruit I was munching on as she leaned in the window of my car talking to me at a gas station in San Diego — the Pom Grannie means far more than "fertility"; it also means the blood and sex powers special to women. The bowl-shaped red "Chinese apple" has tightly grouped seeds in clusters, clear, red, living fruit crystals. More profoundly, they mean female power, menstrual and clitoral, from the intense red of their coloring and the oblong bud shape of each luscious seed. They *feel* like a clitoris, especially to the tongue. To Lesbians the Pom Grannie is the "rubyfruit," the delicate, sexual, acid-sweet crystal-psychic universe of women at the essence of existence, of women who "eat each other out" from one living world of perception into another.[14]

Modern Lesbians are women who initiate each other into a way of life that even in the present industrial/electronic state requires some of the same sensibilities and social functions that were required of our shaman/priest ancestors, whose path we follow whether we consciously know it or not.

And this is what I am trying to tell you, Von, that nothing ever really changes. That you brought me out and then sent me even further into the underground Gay world, coming back later to put back the broken pieces just the way you were supposed to, just as if you'd been trained for it. I should say, though, that you and I were far too inhibited to use the expression "eat each other out." It would take the freewheeling, loudmouthed sixties to free up my tongue.

Brownies and Girl Scouts

The formal institutions for shamanic apprenticeship have been suppressed or have faded from historic memory in our Western, American culture, so rational-minded is it. Faint vestiges of initiation with its spirits and terrifying journeys to underworld realms are mostly relegated to horror comics, the carnival fun house, and sci-fi movies. But I remember one such vestigial initiation that happened to me as it happens to many little girls and boys.

The year the members of my small Girl Scout troop were thirteen, I arrived late to a Scout meeting one afternoon. Four of my Scout friends met me at the door in a state of excitement more than usually intense, even for that charged period of our opening adolescent lives. Our Scout leader, they said, had left unexpectedly for the afternoon, and in her absence they had decided, instead of a regular meeting, to hold something more interesting: an initiation. And I was to be the initiate, the others having already gone through it. To my horror and fascination, they put a blindfold on me and led me through a dank basement labyrinth of sudden weird sounds, bizarre objects pressed into my reluctant hands, and strange feelings like webs whisked across my face.

"Know what this is?" they screamed, thrusting my disgusted fingers into applesauce or liver or folding my clammy palm around a peeled grape. "These are eyeballs!" they shrieked, rolling the grapes on my outstretched fingers. "This is brains! Stomach! These are leg bones!" My hair stood on end and my knees bobbed while I stiffened into my dikely habit of revealing no fear toward anything girls were expected to fear.

"Oh, this is not scary," I scoffed, upping their ante, making them try harder. They led me on through a labyrinth of sudden wind, the breath of ghosts, the shrill voices of ghosts, the brushing bloody bodies of ghosts. Then at some grisly point the deathly humor and grotesqueness overflowed in us, and we collapsed hysterically laughing, and it ended. I was unblinded; they showed me what the mysteries, the sticky "innards" were made of. I acted distantly interested and matter-of-fact. Yet I had been truly horrified, the hair had bristled on my neck. I carry forever the sensation of peeled grapes as part of my understanding of the vulnerability of eyeballs. They had taken me on a small but true girls' puberty journey into the land of blood and guts and dead people. And I had not shrieked nor fainted nor run away. I was, in a thin, paltry imitation of women's lives in bygone days, initiated and prepared in small measure for the blood and gore of womanhood.

Eyeballs of the Other World

A genuine initiation accompanies the training of shamans, both Gay and straight, in the tribal world. They prepare to enter domains other people never go near, to be able to take the bodies and personae of plants and animals, to walk under the ocean or behind the moon, to fly thoughts and pictures thousands of miles, to imprint drawings on cliffs hundreds of feet above the head of the tallest person among them. They must enter many worlds. As we shall see in later chapters, for the Gay shamans, the *angakok* and *Winkte*, the *Sahacat* and *koskalaka*, uniting with spirit doubles is part of their selected task in life. As Elie Reclus described the initiate Gay male of the Far North, "the soul of the *angakok* flies upon the wings of the wind, and quitting the body at will, sails swift and light through the universe. It is permitted to probe all hidden things, to seek knowledge of all mysteries, in order that they may be revealed to those who have remained mortal with spirit unrefined." [15] After his initiation and training, the *angakok* has become a medium, able to visit the spirit world and bring back its knowledge to share with his own people. Indeed, he is not only able to visit the other world, he is able to unite himself with it.

Underworlds of all kinds have long been a part of Gay life. Coming out from one world into another is a Gay cultural attribute, and fear probably always accompanies it. In tribal shamanic life, the fear is brought about by wolves' teeth, by exposure to the elements and storms; in modern life it is brought about in an environment consisting almost entirely of other people, and they too have teeth, teeth of harsh judgment and storms of fury and brutality.

Coming out from one world into another is reflected in the Spanish word for Gay men, *Mariposa,* the butterfly, and in the

37

German expression for Gay, *Vom Anderen Uffer*, "from the other side" of the river or the world. The ordeal of the *angakok* or any other shaman/priest, the long years of preparation, of fasting and learning, of discipline and controlled study are what give her or him the extraordinary skills and sensibilities not only of healing and predicting and knowing, but of being able to visit the spirit world, to revive the dead, to locate the departed spirit and bring it back reunited with its earthly body.

Sickness, purging, catharsis, isolation, and meditation; certain kinds of chanting, dancing, and intense sexual sensation; celibacy and fasting; comas, exposure to extreme temperatures, lengths of time spent in the wilderness; the experience of high fevers; the use of hallucinogenic drugs and ordeals of prolonged pain — these are all methods by which shaman/witches/wisemen of every description have traditionally arrived at their visions and at their special abilities to heal, predict, know, create, and transform.

Dike Is Some Kind of Shamantic Title

Understanding tribal initiation procedures and how widespread they are has been of special interest to me personally because of certain extreme events in my own life. Had I been born into a tribal society as were my European genetic ancestors, I believe I would have been the European equivalent of a shaman: a hag, a wisewoman, a sorcerer, a dervish, a runic bard, a warrior/priest, a wiccan-woman. Born into an American white Protestant family in a modern industrial democratic state I became, instead, a very purposeful Lesbian poet. It has become clear to me that I am some kind of modern ceremonial dike. I think there are in our country hundreds of thousands of such people, as well hundreds of thousands of ceremonial faggots, and many varied avenues to these traditional Gay offices.

My own experience was that of being raised in a poor and very isolated family under stressful conditions. I felt myself apart from others and categorically different. Illness after illness beset me as a child, with high fevers, deliriums, close brushes with death, or light bouts of frightening diseases such as rabies, polio, the dread tuberculosis that had killed my grandfather as a young man. These near-misses plus a terrifying year in high school of aphasia kept me — to say nothing of my startled parents — in a state of high drama throughout my childhood.

Yet I was a tomboy; I never once thought of myself as sickly, just as I wouldn't have thought of our family as poor if others hadn't pointed it out and humiliated us. I took a dyke's-eye view of myself as tough and hardy, smart, muscular, and athletic. I was also talkative, cheerful, and witty. I began writing articles at six, performing dramatics at nine, writing poetry at ten or eleven. By then you could add sulky and moody to my list of character traits. Neighbors and teachers alike said I was born to be a poet. I had an intense sense of destiny and a strong philosophical bent. I hated being a child, and I strained to grow up as fast as possible. By the age of twelve I had a stack of rejection slips from magazines to which my mother and I had sent my poems, typed on a borrowed typewriter and with the pen name Amelia Silver, which I thought sounded appropriately like Emily Dickinson. I saved my meager allowance to buy Modern Library editions of Shakespeare and technical manuals on how to write poetry.

Spending most of my time alone, I talked to trees, the irrigation canal, the hateful desert wind (at which I would curse and scream), animals, the moon, the air. I learned not to tell other people that the elements all talked back to me, too. I was not actually talking to my "self"; answers came telling me what to do and reassuring me that my course was true and that I should continue. I worked hard to develop my poetry.

But after I left home at seventeen, my life as a young Lesbian and as a single woman trying to get along in the world were so difficult I virtually stopped writing. After getting in so much trouble as a dike and living for a while in the heavily demoralized urban Gay ghetto of the times, I concentrated on becoming a good girl, an obedient worker, a socially acceptable person. I visited a psychiatrist, worked as a medical secretary, took some night classes, and was very much off course. My life seemed fixed, and I did not know how to change it or how I could ever take charge of it.

Then as we were moving to a Maryland suburb outside Washington, D.C., I contracted a rare infection — cat-scratch fever — which was misdiagnosed and mistreated by a series of doctors. After six weeks of fever and slurred speech, one night I fell over on the couch, unconscious and in convulsions. I was living at the time with Yvonne, in our second attempt to stay together as a couple. We had a roommate, a woman who had previously been my lover for a couple of years while I was separated from Yvonne when she was beginning her career as a teacher. Terrified for my life, the two women rushed me by ambulance to the nearest hospital, Yvonne with her fingers pressed on my tongue to keep me from choking. Her nails were black for weeks from the bruises my grinding teeth gave her, as wracking convulsions contorted my whole body. At two o'clock in the morning they were told that I was not going to live through the night, that the convulsions were too severe, and that I had brain fever — encephalitis — of unknown origin.

Before dawn and my certain death, an ambitious young doctor who happened to be studying rare diseases was passing through the hospital and was called in on my case, and he made an accurate diagnosis. He sent to a nearby military hospital that happened to stock the necessary rare serum antidote.

My lovers were told then that even if I lived I would likely be a "vegetable" (a carrot?). And when finally I opened my eyes three days later, I recognized no one, at first not even my parents: two strangers standing at the foot of my strange, strange bed. I was a transformed person. My vocabulary was gone — good-bye to all those medical transcription terms. Even simple nouns like *jug* eluded my new tongue, although friends reported that at times I would burst out with pages of Shakespeare or Samuel Coleridge, memorized years before. I was emotionally volatile, breaking into tears when someone told a joke and laughing hysterically when someone told a serious story. I remember throwing shoes at the TV in uncontrolled rage. What fun *that* was. Friends became condescendingly uneasy over my mental state. They mourned that I would never be "right."

But oh I woke from my deadly coma in such a happy state, high as a kite, singing a little children's song from Archibald MacLeish's play *J.B.* concerning the aftermath of a nuclear war. Even though I could not speak properly, I could sing. And because I had crossed into or close to the domain of death and then returned, I became freed from the restraints of my former workaday world, freed to proceed with the values, ideas, pursuits that mattered most to the expression of the artistic sensibilities I had developed and worked so hard at as a child. I sang the happy little child's song for a year while I gradually realigned my senses and my speech. By the time I turned twenty-six I was well again.

During the healing period I consorted with other magical characters. For a solid month, my head, in which my brain had swelled and rubbed against the inside of my skull, ached with such pain I could barely crack one eye to see what I was eating. The pain became an entity of its own, and I took to talking to it.

Lying on a couch in one of the rooms we had rented near Rock Creek Park, to my delight I was visited by creatures from the Maryland woods. Lively jay birds hopped through the room to get the cheese crackers I scattered blindly on the floor for them. A large raccoon moved into the attic above my head. Mistakenly named Roger, she came in at first for water, which she got by cleverly turning on (and never turning back off) the faucet in the kitchen sink. Later she would take dried cat food from a box and eggs and butterscotch candies from my hand. She would take the time to feel the palm of my hand with the soft pads of her own little hand. She unwrapped the yellow candies from their cellophane wrappers, chewing them vigorously and without humor. She always tried to take the egg home. Clutching it in one hand she waddled up the steep roof to the attic. Several times the egg got away from her and rolled down to splat on the little porch outside my room while she watched sadly. Many times she succeeded and I could hear the twitters of pleasure from the attic. Roger had three babies up there, and with their bright eyes, round middles, and stubby ringtails I had never seen such dear things.

The night she brought her children out for their first midnight stroll, I was well enough to get up when I heard their unusually frantic squealing. Ordinarily they all twittered, like birds speaking in long, rapid sentences. Creeping along the dark floor until I could see onto the porch, I had a fine moonlit night to watch Roger get her two-month-old children from the roof to the porch. Child number one was hanging backward from the three-story eave, twittering and shrieking hysterically. Three feet below on the porch rail Roger stood urging and urging the baby to let go its grip; then minutes later it did, free-falling into her outspread arms as she broke the impact. The two went rolling onto the porch in a round bundle. After reassurance of success, she began nagging and urging the second one down. It too hung squealing from the roof and had to decide to trust her open arms. When she had persuaded them all to come down, she led them onto a long, tremulously thin tree branch and took her family for their first trek into the woods. I watched the great long limb swaying in the moonlight as the parade of raccoons marched along it. I had not been so glad to be alive in years. And I knew what they meant: Just let go, trust your own powers and the power of those around you.

41

Don't hang forever on the eave of the roof overlooking the great creative forest, trying to control something. Let go, trust the twitter all around you.

Mice, squirrels, and small birds also came into the house during those weeks, in addition to the big jays and the several cats who lived there. They all told me: Live, act, be yourself.

Surrounded by creatures who have always given me such fine company and advice, I began to write as soon as I could function at all, determined that never again would I let anything deter me from my course or purpose in life. If being a poet meant flinging myself over the parapet of safety and learning to fly, then I would do it. And so again, as had happened when I was a child, I had access to the spirit world, to shadows, to animal understanding, to guides and voices, visions, odd ways of thinking, all the altered states of consciousness necessary for the core of artistic creation. From then on my course was fixed: My work centered on forging a new definition of Gay people in my writing and in my public performances.

And though of necessity I am using my own life as an example, it is not to single myself out as a special case. I have heard other Gay people, as well as artists, describe similar experiences. Recently one lifelong dike, Michaele Uccella, told me, "I was diagnosed with cancer. I went into the hospital and let them administer chemotherapy. When I got out I moved into the barn for a couple of months. I listened to the birds and animals show me what to do to heal myself."

To celebrate my rapid recovery, Yvonne painted three life-size Katchina figures in brilliant colors on one wall, and in the bedroom she printed one of my poems in thick lettering. Soon afterward, we moved back to New Mexico, for we were homesick.

Visions

My psychic powers had been buried under my fear that I needed to be a good, white, agreeable working girl in order to survive on my own and not go down the drain of life. My intuitive and spirit-centered knowledge was locked in a closet of its own lest it contradict the straight, academic, Freudian, super-materialist Western medical techniques I had absorbed in school and in my job as a medical secretary and laboratory technician. No poetry entered into me during those years. But now through the intense "initiation" experience of my coma, I was learning how to pass between two worlds: the world of the Gay underground and the world of the straight, socially sanctioned aboveground.

A few months after my hospitalization, shortly after returning to the desert of New Mexico, I had an intense vision. Three of us had driven to an old Spanish church eighty miles southeast of Albuquerque, at Quarai. Roofless, the steep rock walls of the edifice, built by the forced labor of the newly conquered Indians centuries before, still stood. The bare stones, shaped by hand into bricks and carefully stacked, rose into the brilliant blue autumn sky. Here the Spanish fathers demanded of the men, "Build us a church," and the Indian women fell on the ground laughing, for construction and architecture had always been the domain of women. Now we could see where owls had left feathers and piles of vomited mouse bones in the shadows of the terrible holy place. Nearby kivas lurked in the earth like great vine-filled pots. We were too afraid of guardian rattlesnakes to explore them.

In this place of beauty and aesthetic creativity, fraught with destiny and anger and terror, I went walking in the arroyo that runs near the old colonial ruin. My two companions walked in the opposite direction. They were my lover Yvonne, whom I was about to leave for the second time in eight years, and a new friend we had made recently, Wendy Cadden.

As I squatted down to finger some potsherds among the pebbles suddenly I saw an Indian woman sitting on the bank behind me. In her fifties, she was dressed entirely in black and was looking directly at me. She was very dark-skinned and with a narrow rather than a broad face. Her attitude was one of silent watching and of waiting. Looking at her I was filled with a great sense of self-respect and of being on course. "Just proceed," she seemed to be conveying. "What you will do matters. All you need is to do it." Ever after, whenever I feel despair and futility beyond my capacity, I remember her, how she looked on the arroyo bank silhouetted against the stark sky, and I am renewed. Of course, no embodied person was on the bank; the watcher was a spirit woman. She conveyed as strong a message to me as if I'd known her all my life.

When I had completely recovered from the encephalitis, late in 1966, I walked into a bar in Albuquerque and announced that I was a poet; I walked up to a woman on campus who I thought was a dike (she was) and announced that I was a Lesbian. I proceeded on a course of openly Lesbian writing. When I could not get my work published because of its controversial nature, I founded a press, producing not only my own radical work but that of other women as well. Along with Wendy Cadden, who became my lover for fourteen years, I learned all the skills necessary to run a complete print shop and to promote the work of Lesbian writers nationwide. In the formal manner of a public performer of Lesbian poetry, poetry addressed to the society as a whole but written from the base of a Lesbian life perspective, even without an established "tribal" context to help me, I established my public dyke office in contemporary America.

Shamanism Is a Romantic Idea Until You Really Do It

Shamanism is a popular subject, especially in the western United States. Tribal people of America still retain the ritual and initiation teachings to produce genuine shamans. It is easy, especially for white people, to imitate and romanticize this by borrowing heavily from what they have read about other cultures while totally ignoring the ritual history of their own Euro-American culture. In our society, as in any, the "shamanic" office is a charged, potent, awe-inspiring and even fear-inspiring person who takes true risks by crossing over into other worlds. A drag queen of the 1960s screaming through downtown Manhattan and risking being blown away by a shotgun full of anti-faggot rage was performing a loaded, shamanic act. He was leading men into the dangerous world of women; he was crossing the abyss between the sexes.

In many parts of the society during any given era, this abyss is wide, deep, and heavily guarded by members of both sexes. Yet thousands of examples of such crossing over and risk taking led, for instance, to the entry of millions of American women into occupations formerly designated male-only and to the participation of many men in nurturing aspects of parenting, formerly considered feminine. Modern Gay people stand on extreme thresholds. We are likely to be the first women in "men's" sports and other endeavors developed by men in recent centuries. And we are equally likely to be the first men in "women's" domains.

The modern closet masks our path-breaking habits. Billie Jean King catapulted women's tennis into a highly paid, well-attended spectator sport during the early 1970s, and during this period she wore her hair short and used butchy mannerisms. Heterosexual society supported her in her efforts to professionalize and popularize women's tennis, short hair and all. She has said publicly that she had a woman lover in 1976. During this period she was, in my opinion, functioning publicly as a ceremonial dike, making the crossover between two worlds that would open the way for highly paid professional tennis to be seen as a woman's game. Ten years later, when the task of path breaking was done, tennis fans and reporters no longer wanted to see a dike image for women players. Then Billie Jean King's marriage to a man became of primary importance to the public eye. In 1982 she denied being a Lesbian any longer and, according to the *New York Times*, said that her lesbian affair had been a "mistake," for which she accepted full "responsibility." In her case, as in so many others, Gay culture helped her forge a new path for women into an area formerly denied them. But when the path was made, the Gay culture was denied and pushed back into the closet.[16]

In ancient times the first men let into women's sacred rites were men in drag. These men led the way, they risked the abyss. At first they were ripped apart by angry women — and no doubt by angry men as well. But what they learned from the rites they taught other men, paving the way for men to learn what women had developed: Agriculture science, astrology, midwifery, all the skills and human attributes and bodies of ancient knowledge that had developed in women's hands passed into the masculine sphere through the medium of cross-dressing and the ability of a small number of men — Gay men — to identify with the opposite sex and to act it out.

The old wisewomen's skills passed over so thoroughly that men have now reached a stage whereby they have developed their own independent versions of science and astrology and weather control and have excluded women from their institutions for several centuries. Now the passing must reverse heavily in the other direction. With Lesbians or, more specifically, women heavily influenced by contact with Lesbian culture often leading the way, we will for the next few centuries absorb the sciences that men have been harboring in their exclusive ranks. Meantime men, led by Gay men, will continue taking over the last vestiges of childbirth and child care, attempting to duplicate the womb under laboratory conditions. As we always have, Gay people will make many of the paths, will lead the way over from the world of one sex to the world of the other. Lesbians will do a great deal to open the space programs to women, to develop computer technology for the use of civilians, to open up the "hard" sciences of physics and mathematics that have been prohibited to women for centuries. As a result, the sciences themselves will become much more integrated with each other. Eco-astro-physic-psycho-dramas of a much more balanced future will unfold if society allows this exchange to happen. And perhaps the more quickly the balance unfolds, the less likely we will be to be caught in a nuclear conflagration, since one usual consequence of war is accelerated technological development.

The Dike in the Matter

A dike learns much of her social function from other dykes, even those so firmly in the closet as to never have heard the word *dike*. It is true that a certain amount of cross-gender imitation goes into the formation of a modern dyke or faggot, as of old. A girl watches the gait and mannerisms of her brothers and her father, her uncles and the neighbor men. She identifies with them. She learns to handle the tools, weapons, particular ambitions, and stances known in her society as "men's." And when she grows up, lo she becomes a dyke. But then something else happens, something more complex. She enters the Gay underground. She meets other Lesbians in a Gay network that is everywhere, however covert and subtle. Whether she ever has the chance to enter a Gay bar or not, she imitates dykes, not men. She may identify with traditionally dyke figures: Diana the Huntress, Beebo Brinker, Gertrude Stein, Bessie Smith, Natalie Barney, Queen Christina, Joan of Arc, Amy Lowell, Oya, St. Barbara, modern athletes, and other leaders. She may understand that men sometimes imitate dykes, or she may believe that dykeness is imitation of men and is therefore anti-woman and to be suppressed. She may hang keys from her belt to signify, "I hold the keys." She may cut her hair very short, shorter by far than any men are wearing it, because short hair is a dykish thing. She may dress exactly like her own brother and then pitch her voice unexpectedly high, so that everyone who meets her is thrown a little off-balance in their perceptions of accepted truths about the nature of the world. She may grow her hair long and wear one earring only, or three in one ear and two in the other, or mismatched socks or other signs of asymmetry that say, "I cross over. I belong to more than one world." She may dress exactly like her brother and then be highly indignant and chagrined if she is mistaken for a boy or a man, called "Sir" by a clerk or waiter. Because the social message she bears and is delivering is not "I am a man" but rather "Here is another way to be a woman."

A dyke, especially if she is young and rebellious, may notice that most progressive women in her society clip their hair, wear plain faces and "man"-tailored clothes, and do work traditionally assigned to men. And so she may redesign herself with lavish, even garish hair and brilliant makeup to make the statement "Here's still *another* way of being a woman." And that's a dykish thing to do, a balancing thing.

That's literally what *dike* means — balance, the path. The name of the goddess Dike of Greece, who was old Gaia's granddaughter, meant "the way, the path." And her social function was natural balance, the keeping of the balance of forces. With her two sisters Eunomia ("Order") and Eirene ("Peace"), she was present at the birth of Hermes. The three sisters were known as the Hours and were worshiped in conjunction with Demeter as a foursome, mostly by women. Dike was a storm goddess. In times when men were challenging the old woman-oriented traditions, Dike was a warrior/avenger against those who broke the old traditions. She is called "Natural Justice," and her close companion (lover) is Aletheia, "Truth." Dike is depicted riding in a cart holding scales of justice and a measuring rod. At her feet is a wheel of time, and she is called "she from whom none may run away." [17]

> I am the sky his Lord and I am the earth her Lady
> — Inscription of the Sumerian Goddess Inana

Great bodies of knowledge and skill, understanding and perspective have had to pass over the millennia from the hands of one sex into the hands of the other. Otherwise women and men would live in universes as totally different from each other as those of antelope and grains of sand. In some societies, in fact, men and women have gone so far as to speak entirely separate languages. What the Gay historical functions reveal, among other principles, is that within any society men and women develop differently and have, each, a subculture of their own that is overbalanced in the importance it places on particular jobs, attitudes, amount of aggressiveness, roles it plays, amounts of expressed physicality and tenderness, and that has different understandings of children, of the universe, of the sciences or different access to parts of the economy, the healing arts, transportation services, and so on. One of the major homosexual/shamanic functions in any society is to *cross over* between these two essentially different worlds and reveal them to each other. In this way the knowledge special to women becomes known and comprehensible to men, and vice versa. Access to worlds inaccessible to most people has always been a Gay cultural function; we have always had underworlds of every description.

A society, or an institution within a large complex society, whose members want the sexes to be kept polarized and unable to identify with each other, to share jobs, knowledge, economic and political power, child care or other functions equally, will be suppressive of Gay culture so there can be no crossing over and therefore no exchange of important cross-gender information. A rising patriarchy acts in this manner, especially a newly industrializing state that is busy passing productive control into the hands of men. The result is the suppression of Gay culture into its modern form of the closet.

I am happy to report to you, my dear Von, in case you had gotten worried, that the suppression is never permanent. I know you would be happy with the definition of dike that I have formulated; the title certainly fit you.

CHAPTER THREE

Gay Is *Very* American

dykes remind me of indians
like indians dykes
are supposed to die out
or forget
or drink all the time
or shatter
go away
to nowhere
to remember what will happen
if they dont

they dont
anyway
even though it
happens
and they remember
they dont

because the moon remembers
because so does the sun
because so do the stars
remember
and the persistent stubborn
grass
of the earth

From "Some Like Indians Endure,"
Paula Gunn Allen (Laguna/Sioux)[1]

THE GROUPS often considered "polar opposites" in our culture — men and women, Gays and straights, Blacks and whites — serve as mirrors for each other, giving each of us vital information concerning our roles in society. Without mirrors, how well would any of us know ourselves? For the purpose of perceiving contemporary Gay culture and its possible functions, I was fortunate to be given an invaluable mirror: the experience and history of Gay people among American Indian tribes indigenous to North America.

Indian tribal culture is known above all for its emphasis on balance and harmony. No one element, force, or impulse dominates the others — not men over women, not people over nature, not god over people, not economic necessity over spiritual or aesthetic necessity, not life over death, material over etheric, or youth over old age. And there is much to indicate that the spiritual heart of the ancient Indian Way was Gay leadership including both sexes.

Growing up as we did in the great American desert of the West and in the state of New Mexico where ancient Indian pueblos, Spanish land-grant towns, and Anglo merchant towns stand next to each other everywhere, my first lover Von and I shared some understandings that few Americans have outside that area. We understood that real cowboys and real Indians have many of the same characteristics and are often one and the same person. That Spain, not England, was the first colonizer of the "New World." That Indians go to school, drive cars, watch TV, and live in the modern world while they also keep their thousands-of-years-old traditions.

As native southwesterners Vonnie and I retained a deep suspicion of tourists, of easterners, and of the military bases that occupy so much of the territory. In particular, and in spite of our identification of ourselves as intellectuals with sophisticated and objective minds, we shared a suspicion (and something also of envy) for the anthropologists who filled southwestern museums with tools, arts, dishes, and other common leavings of Indian people that they called "artifacts." We often went looking for similar objects ourselves in the arroyos and deserted Indian towns of handmade stones and mortar. It seemed romantic to walk through the past in the old ruins, as romantic to us as Greek or Cretan temple ruins or old European cathedrals.

But the museums and the anthropologists acted, we thought, as though the Indian people themselves had disappeared alto-

51

gether from the area, were relegated to some distant realm spoken of as "the past, the stone age." Indians, the authorities implied with words, postcards of feathered warriors, and labels, did not live in the modern world; they "belonged" to the past. Yet we could see Indians walking around town on any Saturday night, as contemporary and modern as we. They wore khaki-colored clothes just as my own father did.

We went to school with Indian children, we bought their parents' wares. As a child, I watched a black-clad Indian woman come once a week to our neighbor's apartment, where she worked as a maid. When we went to Gay bars in Albuquerque or Santa Fe, the man sitting at the bar on the next stool was as likely to be an Indian as an Anglo, and when I took a summer creative writing class the one writer whose work I remembered after fifteen years is a Pueblo Indian man, Simon Ortiz.

Years and much distance and life experience after my southwestern childhood, I would confront for myself what it means to be studied and collected by anthropologists and I would feel repeatedly, as a closet Lesbian, something of what a "vanishing American" feels: that everyone around you has "vanished" you whether you like it or not.

Although we grew up side by side with Indian children, there were huge gaps in the information we non-Indian children were given about our neighbors. And peculiarly, though we could "see" the real persons of real Indians, the images we were given in school, on postcards in the tourist shops, and in the movies caused us to gradually superimpose a made-up Indian image over the person we knew or thought of when we said or heard the word *Indian*. In such ways do people "vanish," do cultures go underground.

What Was Unknown

The idea that Indian people have and always have had Gay customs never occurred to me, nor did I know anything about the roles played by American Indian women and men within the tribes until I lived with a Laguna Indian writer and teacher, Paula Gunn Allen. The images I was taught in school about American Indians led me to believe that they were utterly straight. I was taught that the men were savage warriors, violent and "manly" in a rigid, militaristic way. Hollywood helped with this stereotype image by casting white men in the leading "Indian" roles and by creating an image of "Indian" based on an interpretation of the Plains Indians, buffalo hunters who were economically dependent on horses and young men. The Hollywood version was quite a contrast to most Indian tribes, particularly those living around me, who were gatherers, gardeners, and farmers and much more dependent on women and the gentleness of men than the Plains tribes to the east. Indian men created by Hollywood image-makers were either "braves" (like baseball players?) or stern, grim-faced, "noble" chiefs without a sense of humor or an erotic impulse. Hollywood's Indian women were passive (as well as impassive) squaws, obedient to their husbands to the point of walking behind the men like servants, doing menial work, and suffering nameless humiliations.

The supposedly liberated white settlers were portrayed as representing freedom and independence from the Indian world of female drudgery and male barbarism. The word *squaw* was used with contempt by white boys, and we girls assumed that Indians similarly held women in contempt. Thus were we taught, in school, we white people who though we take and teach so many history classes, know so little of what lies under our feet and holds us up, of what lives side by side with us, of what the sources of our own ways of life are.

I did not know, for instance, until Paula Gunn Allen explained it to me, that the white settlers, my ancestors among them, escaping the brutality of feudal and industrial slavery, oppression, and war in Europe, were actually helpless in the wilderness of a strange continent and completely dependent for two centuries on the goodwill and educational assistance of the various Indian peoples, who ensured their survival. Modern Americans seldom recognize that most of the food we eat and the medicines we take were developed through the agricultural sciences of Indian women centuries before the time of Columbus.

Nor have we been taught that Indian women had genuine political and economic power in their tribes or that Indian culture teaches gentleness toward nature and often calls its male chiefs by names whose origins mean "mother" or "motherly." Perhaps most important, we have never learned to give proper credit for the ideas and forms of freedom and democratic government learned by the white European forefathers from the Iroquois and other Indian peoples who had created and used them for centuries. The Iroquois, a matriarchal people, had in their councils women warriors who acted as "peace chiefs" to prevent wars from

53

starting or from escalating. We did not know that the marriage customs of Indian tribes from one end of the American continent to the other do not treat women and children as property. And we were not taught that Indian tribes openly included Gay people and that these Gay people held positions of power and office, some of which *required* Gayness, cross-dressing, and homosexual love bonds and sex. This we certainly were not taught. And that women sometimes married women and men sometimes married men — this we never, never were taught.

How different, my beloved Von, our lives together would have been if we had known that we were not strangers in the world, having to invent and discover our purposes entirely on our own and from what we could learn from each other, pull out of each other in bewilderment and strife.

"Strange Country, This"

"Strange country, this," a white man wrote of the Crow Indians in 1850, "where males assume the dress and perform the duties of females, while women turn men and mate with their own sex." [2] Not only the Crow, but most and in all likelihood every Indian tribe on the American continent, exhibited this same "strangeness." Sue-Ellen Jacobs studied written records from the last few centuries for references to Gay people in American Indian tribes. Her figures reveal how prevalent Gay traditions have been for the people who occupied this continent when the European colonial population arrived. Out of ninety-nine tribes with recorded material, there were references to Gay culture in eighty-eight, with twenty including specific references to Lesbianism. The latter references are more remarkable considering how little information has been recorded about anything concerning women, let alone information about one of our deepest secrets. Eleven tribes denied any homosexuality to the anthropologists and other writers. All the denials of Gay presence came from East Coast tribes located in the areas of heaviest and longest contact with those segments of white Christian culture that severely punish people who admit to Gayness. The eighty-eight tribes that reported Gay culture include many familiar Indian names: Apache, Navajo, Winnebago, Cheyenne, Pima, Crow, Shoshoni, Paiute, Osage, Acoma, Zuni, Sioux, Pawnee, Choctaw, Creek, Seminole, Illinois, Mojave, Oglala, Shasta, Aleut, Fox, Iowa, Kansas, Yuma, Aztec, and Maya. Less familiar are the names of the Tlingit, Naskapi, Ponca, Menomini, Maricopa, Klamath, Quinault, Yuki, Chilula, and Kamia, to name a handful.[3]

Jacobs lists the exact offices held by Gay persons in twenty-one tribes, presenting a cross section of the functions, especially those of cross-dressing people who take on the work, dress, and social position of the opposite sex while establishing sexual and even marital bonds with their own sex. These are people who in English are called *bulldikes* and *drag queens*. Among the Crow, for instance, who once had many such people, cross-dressing homosexual men are responsible for cutting down the tree that is used for the Sun dance ceremony. In twelve of the twenty-one tribes Jacobs cites with regard to Gay functions, Gay transvestites were the medicine people or shamans of the tribe. In four — the Crow, Cheyenne, Dakota, and Illinois — they were essential for high spiritual ceremonies, in three they served a special function at funerals, in one — the Winnebago — they acted as oracle, and in one last tribe their role is reported as "good-for-nothing."[4] I rather favor that last one, having felt just that way on numerous occasions myself in relation to my society.

In *Gay American History*, Jonathon Katz has collected accounts mentioning the names Indians have used to designate their Gay tribal members. Each tribe had or continues to have special names for Gay men and Lesbians, especially when referring to cross-dressing and special tribal offices rather than to casual homosexual relations, although these may also be present. The Pomo use *Das*, the Kalekau, *Das* and *Murfidai* (for hermaphrodite); the Mojave say *Alyha* and *Hwame* (Lesbian) while the Navajo call their Gay priesthood *Nadle*; the Winnebago say *Siange* ("sigh-an-gee"). The Oglala call Gay magic men *Winkte*, the Omaha and Ponca both say *Mingu-ga*, the Zuni of the Southwest say *Ko'thlama*, the Yurok's word is *Wergern*, and the Acoma Pueblo people say *Mujerado*, a term believed to come from the Spanish *Mujerhado*, "man-witch-woman"; the Chippewa use *A-go-kwa*, the Lakota *Adi-wa-lona* and *Koskalaka*; the Inuits say *Choupan*, the Konyagas of Alaska say *Achnutschik*. The Kamchadale of the Bering Strait call their Gay magicians *Koe'kcuc*; the Kodiaks call theirs *Ke'yev*. The Absaroke Indians of Montana use *Bo-te*, meaning "not-man, not-woman." Gay queens among the Indians of the Santa Barbara region were called "Jewel," and so the Spanish recorded it as *Joya*. The transvestites of both sexes of the Klamath people are called *Twlinna ek*, when Lesbians live together it is known as *Sawa linaa.* Yuma Indians call Lesbians *Kwe rhame,* and Gay men *Elxa;* female transvestites are *War'hameh* for the Cocopa people and *Warharmi* for the Kamia of California.[5]

What's in a Name

The European soldiers, trappers, explorers, and settlers were contemptuous of Gay traditions in their own cultures, and several centuries of persecution under the Inquisition had taught them to deny all Gayness. The heaviest persecutions in Europe happened concurrently with the heaviest periods of colonization of the Indians in North America, according to Paula Gunn Allen. Small wonder, perhaps, that Gay people were often the first Indians killed and that even when tribes were tolerated by the white people, their Gay people were mocked and persecuted to the point of changing their behavior for the sake of the safety of their people. Balboa, for instance, set wild dogs on the Gay medicine men of California tribes, killing them, the "Jewels" of their own people.[6]

The white people coined a term for the Gay Indians they saw, the cross-dressers who lived among members of the opposite sex. They called them "Berdache," sometimes translated "Bowdash" or "Bundosh." *Berdache* is a French word meaning "slave boy," probably stemming from the period when patriarchal Moroccan customs were brought to southern Europe by invading Muslims.[7]

That the Indians themselves had extremely high opinions of their Gay population is best illustrated by the offices Gay people held within tribal life and by the openness with which they lived, even marrying members of their own sex in some tribes. A Kutenai woman of Montana, for instance, who dressed as a man and was accompanied in her travels by another woman, described by the white writer as her "wife," held the occupations of courier, guide, prophet, warrior, and peace mediator.[8] In white men's terms this would be equivalent to a high position in the State Department.

Matilda Coxe Stevenson, an anthropologist, wrote about Gay men in the Zuni tribe of the late nineteenth century, speaking of two cross-dressed men in particular as "being the finest potters and weavers in the tribe. One was the most intelligent person in the pueblo, especially versed in their ancient lore. He was conspicuous in ceremonials, always taking the part of the captive Kor'kokshi in the dramatization of the Ka'nakwe."[9] Stevenson

56

also wrote a remarkable account of the death of her close friend, We'wha, a Zuni man who "passed" all his life as a woman and was prominent in the tribe. "Owing to her bright mind and excellent memory," Stevenson wrote, "she was called on . . . when a long prayer had to be repeated or a grace was to be offered over a feast. In fact she was the chief personage on many occasions. On account of her physical strength all the household work requiring great exertion was left for her, and while she most willingly took the harder work from the others of the family, she would not permit idleness; all had to labor or receive an upbraiding from We'wha, and nothing was more dreaded than a scolding from her." [10] She once spent six months in Washington, D.C., visiting President Grover Cleveland and other politicians.

Overall, the collected accounts indicate the high status accorded Gay male transvestites who, usually at adolescence, took on the dress, language, gestures, and occupations of the women of the tribe. In part this high status can be attributed to the high status occupied by Indian women in most tribes. For instance, the pottery making and weaving for which the Zuni Gay man was noted were occupations constituting a major source of income for the Zuni people, and both are women's work. Land was and is usually held in trust by the women of a tribe, who also own the houses, hogans, teepees, yurts, and pueblos.

Paula Gunn Allen helps explain the woman-based philosophy prevalent in Indian tribalism, especially in Allen's own southwestern pueblos. You cannot understand Indians' ways of thinking, she says, without understanding that they stem from a spirit-based, rather than a family-based, system. "Among American Indians," she writes, "Spirit-related persons are perceived as more closely linked than blood-related persons. Understanding this primary difference between American Indian values and modern Euro-American Judeo-Christian values is critical to understanding Indian familial structures and the context in which Lesbians functioned. For American Indian people, the primary value was relationship to the Spirit world. All else was determined by the essential nature of this understanding. Spirits, gods and goddesses, metaphysical/occult forces, and the right means of relating to them, determined the tribes' every institution, every custom, every endeavor and pastime. This was not peculiar to inhabitants of the Western Hemisphere, incidentally; it was at one time the primary value of all tribal people on earth." [11]

In the Indian belief system, human beings live in a universe that is, as Allen says, "alive, intelligent, and aware," and the spirits have as much to say about it as humans do. A number of spirit people belong to one's family, and one or more of them act as a person's personal spirit guide. Put very simply, when these spirits tell a person (often in adolescence), through dreams, visions, or public rites, to put on the clothing, language, habits, and occupation of the opposite sex, the person does so. Not to follow the guidance given would mean a serious breach of the cultural value and a danger to one's self.

Modern patriarchal society has usually defined "natural" to mean rigid adherence to sexually dictated roles delineated by a body of authorities over what constitutes the masculine and what constitutes the feminine sphere of society. The Indian idea of what is natural to a person means what the person's visions and spirits tell her or him to do with life. Some tribes have described the quality of Gayness as something a being is born with; others say it comes with a vision or is given to a person by a spirit. Others have special "tests" to find the boys who seek girls' tools and the girls who seek boys' tools. In the past, according to Jacobs, California tribes frequently used the method of seating a boy on the ground: "On one side of him are placed the tools or weapons representing manhood, on the other side some implements of woman's work. The grass is set afire around the boy. As he flees from the burning grass, he will grab something from one side or the other. His selection will be the factor determining his future." [12] In other tribes, such as the Aleut and Tabatulabal, parents might deliberately raise a boy to be a girl if he is particularly handsome.[13] Or a shaman may choose the change for a boy or a girl.

Records indicate that having a Gay nature and undertaking cross-dressing created a pool of initiates from which certain priesthoods of shamans drew their apprentices. Edward Carpenter reports that Gay people abound among the tribes of the Bering Strait — the Kamchadales, the Chukchi, the Aleuts, the Inuits, and the Kodiak Islanders — flourishing under the direction and leadership of the shamans. A Chukchi lad of sixteen who puts on women's clothing, takes up women's work, and moves a husband into his yurt is encouraged by the shamans, who take it to be an injunction of their own particular, and Gay, deity. Such youths, called "choupans," often went on to become priests, although not all of them met the requirements of character, temperament, and calling.[14]

Entrance into the spirit world of shamanism is difficult and requires tremendous effort, as writer Elie Reclus described: "Disciplined by abstinence and prolonged vigils, by hardship and constrain he must learn to endure pain stoically and to subdue his bodily desires, to make the body obey unmurmuringly the commands of the spirit. Others may be chatterers; he will be silent as becomes the prophet and the soothsayer. So the young novice becomes a solitary figure in the northern landscape, wandering through long winter nights across great plains with the white moon over him and the wind for his companion. Absorbing the chill moonlight he feels himself in the presence of his greatest god: Sidne, the Eskimo mother goddess." Like Demeter, Sidne visits the underworld, and so will he. Reclus continued: "He sees stars unknown to the profane; he asks the secrets of destiny from Sirius, Algol and Altair; he passes through a series of initiations, knowing well that his spirit will not be loosed from the burden of dense matter and crass ignorance, until the moon has looked him in the face, and darted a certain ray into his eyes. At last his own Genius, evoked from the bottomless depths of existence, appears to him, having scaled the immensity of the heavens, and climbed across the abysses of the ocean. White, wan and solemn, the phantom will say to him: 'Behold me, what dost thou desire?' Uniting himself with the Double from beyond the grave, the soul of the [apprentice] flies upon the wings of the wind, and quitting the body at will, sails swift and light through the universe. It is permitted to probe all hidden things, to seek the knowledge of all mysteries, in order that they may be revealed to those who have remained mortal with spirit unrefined." [15]

Girls of this region also undertook the Gay crossover. Carpenter says that among the Eskimo people and other populations, especially in the Yukon, girls sometimes declined marriage and childbearing. "Changing their sex, so to speak," he writes, "they live as boys, adopting masculine manners and customs, they hunt the stag, and in the chase shrink from no danger; in fishing from no fatigue." [16] They are dykes, in other words, not alienated modern dykes, but dykes with a well-defined and respected social function.

In "Transformations: Shamanism and Homosexuality," Mike Wilken points out that the Mojave Indians have, or once had, a special song cycle for the initiation of a sacred Gay person, whose role was "highly elaborate and well integrated into Mojave cosmology." [17] An early recorder, George Devereux, said cross-dressers were exceptionally powerful shamans, especially the *Huame*, the

59

women. Gay Mojave shamans sometimes specialized in curing venereal diseases and were considered lucky in love. They took marriage partners of their own sex.[18]

Formerly, the leadership among Navajos was reported by Navajo informants to be the Gay shaman/priesthood, the *Nadle*. Each family tried to have at least one person within the *Nadle*, as such a sacred Gay person brought wealth and success to the whole family. As a group the *Nadle* were put in charge of the clan's wealth. Sources quoted as late as the 1930s said that the *Nadle* were sacred and holy and that without them the Navajo would perish as a people. One speaker compared their leadership to that of President Roosevelt. The word *Nadle*, like Gay, encompasses both women and men.[19]

Manly Hearted Women

Paula Gunn Allen says that among the Sioux were women known as "manly-hearted women."[20] They functioned as warriors and at least sometimes married other women. Allen says, "Among the Cherokee there were women known as Beloved Women who were warriors, leaders, and influential council members. But among the Cherokee, all women had real influence in tribal matters until reorganization was necessitated by American removal attempts."[21]

BELOVED WOMEN

It is not known if those
who warred and hunted on the plains
chanted and hexed in the hills
divined and healed in the mountains
gazed and walked beneath the seas
were Lesbians
It is never known
if any woman was a Lesbian
so who can say that
she who shivering drank
warm blood beneath wind-blown moons
slept tight to a beloved of shininghair
curled as a smile within crescent arms
followed her track deep into secret woods
dreamed other dreams
and who would record these things
perhaps all women are
Lesbian though many try

to turn knotted sinew and stubby cheek
into that ancient almostremembered scene
perhaps all know the first
beloved so well
they can shape the power
to reclaim her

The portents in the skies —
the moons forever growing and falling
away, the suns concentric orbits
daily crossing themselves like a nun —
who's to say that these are signs
of what has always been?
And perhaps the portents are better
left written only in the stars,
etched on cave-walls, rosewindows,
the perfect naves of brooding
cathedrals. Perhaps
all they signify is best left
unsaid.

Nobody knows whether those women
were Lesbians. Nobody
can say what such an event
might mean.[22]

Actually, Allen herself has plenty to say about what such an event might mean. Indian women spent most of their time with each other, and men with men, as is common among all tribal peoples. Sexual attitudes were very free, and Allen feels it is likely that Lesbianism was an "integral part of Indian life." Simple sexual bonding with accompanying warmth and friendship is only one aspect of being Gay, however, though it may be the most prevalent as well as the easiest to hide. What of the cross-dressing person, the Lesbian warrior or chief, the shaman who seeks and finds visions? "It might be," Allen says, that

some Indian women could be seen as "dykes," while some
could be seen as "Lesbians," if you think of "dyke" as one who
bonds with women in order to further some Spirit and supernatural directive, and "Lesbian" as a woman who is emotionally and physically intimate with other women. (The two
groups would not have been mutually exclusive.)
    The "dyke" (we might also call her a "ceremonial Les-
bian") was likely to have been a medicine woman in a special
sense. She probably was a participant in the Spirit (intelligence,

force-field) of an Entity or Deity who was particularly close to earth during the Goddess period though that Deity is still present in the lives of some American Indian women who practice Her ceremonies and participate actively and knowingly in Her reality. Signs of this Deity remain scattered all over the continent: Snake Mound in Ohio is probably one such holdover. La Virgin de Guadalupe is another. There are all sorts of petroglyphs, edifices, and stories concerning some aspects of Her, and Her signs are preserved in much of the lore and literature in many tribes.[23]

In Allen's own Laguna tribe, the chief deities are female, and tribal relations were built around *soroates*, or sisterhoods. The Keres creator goddess, Thought Woman, created her two sisters by the power of Creative Thought, and together the three "gave rise to all creations."[24]

Given that in white Euro-American terminology a dyke is a woman who cross-dresses at least to some extent and is often found doing work, sports, games, and other activities that have formerly been the exclusive preserve of men, "manly hearted woman" is an Indian title that could translate "dyke."

A detailed account of such a "ceremonial Lesbian," a Kutenai Indian in Montana in the early 1800s, appears in Katz's *Gay American History*. A member of a Plains tribe that valued hunting above everything else, she achieved a lively reputation as a courier, guide, prophet, warrior, peace mediator, healer, as well as hunter. She changed her married name, Madame Boisverd, to one of her own language and choosing, *Kauxuma Nupika*, "gone to the spirits," after returning to her tribe after a year's absence. She said that while living among the whites she had magically changed her sex. Thereafter she wore only men's clothing, gambled, warred, and "took wives" just as the men did, traveling with them over the countryside. Just how "wifely" some of her lovers were, however, is indicated in this record, kept by frontiersman Alexander Ross: "In the account of our voyage I have been silent as to the two strangers who cast up at Astoria, and accompanied us from thence; but have noticed already, that instead of being man and wife, as they at first gave us to understand, they were in fact both women — and bold adventurous amazons they were."[25]

"Gone to the spirits," who also called herself Sitting-in-the-water-Grizzly, having lived a shaman's life, was given a shaman/warrior's death; that is, she was nearly impossible to kill. Set upon in a Blackfoot ambush, she did not falter until a number of shots had entered her body, and when several warriors slashed her with knives on the chest and abdomen the cuts were said to have healed themselves. Finally one of the warriors opened her chest and cut off the lower portion of her heart. Only then did she die. The Indian informant who passed on the story, ended it by saying, "No wild animals or birds disturbed her body, which is said to have gradually decayed." [26]

This woman is an example of a Gay female shaman, a "ceremonial dyke," to borrow a phrase from Allen's analysis, which holds that the initiate is "required to follow the lead of Spirits and to carry out the task they assign her." Such stories, Allen says, are frequent in the literature and lore of American Indians, pointing to a crisis in the life of the initiate that results in her "death" or deathlike trance, and then

> her visit to the Spirit realms from which she finally returns, transformed and powerful. After such events, she no longer belongs to her tribe or family, but the Spirit teacher who instructed her.
>
> The Lakota have a word for some of these women, *koskalaka*, which is translated as "young man," and "woman who doesn't want to marry." I would guess that its proper translation is "lesbian" or, colloquially, "dyke." These women are said to be the daughters (that is, the followers/practitioners) of *wila numpa* or Doublewoman. (Pronounced Weeya-Noompa). Doublewoman is a Spirit/Divinity who links two women together making them one in Her power. They do a dance in which a rope is twined between them and coiled to form a "rope baby." The exact purpose or result of this dance is not mentioned, but its significance is clear. In a culture that values children and women because they bear them, two women who don't want to marry (a man) become united by the power of *wila numpa* and their union is validated by the creation of a rope baby. That is, the rope baby signifies the potency of their union in terms that are comprehensible to their society, which therefore legitimizes it.[27]

That the ceremonial or shamanic Lesbian of tribal times often perceives virginity as a necessary part of her office is evident in this description of a female warrior in Carolyn Neithammer's book *Daughters of Earth*: "Among the Kaska, in Canada, lesbianism was not only accepted but actually initiated and encouraged at times. If a family found itself with too many daughters, one of the girls was selected to be a son and was raised like a boy. When the child was five, her parents tied the dried ovaries of a bear to her inner belt. She wore them for the rest of her life as an amulet to prevent conception. Dressed in male clothing and performing the male role, these persons became outstanding hunters. Their sexual experiences were with other women, and orgasm was achieved by clitoral friction while one woman lay on top of another. If a male ever made advances to such a man-woman, he risked having his bow and arrows broken by the object of his attentions, for any sexual contact with a man was believed to ruin a lesbian's luck with game." [28]

A similar understanding that sexual relations with the opposite sex will ruin a shaman's power is expressed by Maria Sabina, a poet-shaman of contemporary times who practices healing, divining, and envisioning among her people, the Mazatec Indians of Mexico. Sacred hallucinogenic mushrooms help her with her craft. She describes herself in her chants as a spirit woman who can speak with the dead "because I can go in and out of the realm of death." [29] She has been married more than once, and during those periods she does not eat the mushrooms or practice shamanism because, as she says, "the woman who takes mushrooms should not have relations with men." [30] "When one goes to bed with a man their cleanliness is spoiled. If a man takes them [the mushrooms] two or three days after he uses a woman, his testicles rot. If a woman does the same, she goes crazy." [31]

Womanly Hearted Men

The Oglala Sioux call their Gay male prophets *winktes*. A Sioux medicine man, John Lame Deer, once took it upon himself to interview one of the *winkte* as part of his book *Lame Deer, Seeker of Visions*. No one, he says, had bothered to interview a *winkte* before. He explained their origin: "We think that if a woman has two little ones growing inside her, if she is going to have twins, sometimes instead of giving birth to two babies they have formed up in her womb into just one, into a half man-half woman kind of being. We call such a person a *winkte*. He could be a hermaphrodite with male and female parts. In the old days a *winkte* dressed like a woman, cooked and did beadwork. He behaved like a squaw and did not go to war. To us a man is what nature, or his dreams, make him. We accept him for what he wants to be. Still, fathers did not like to see their boys hanging around a *winkte*'s place and told them to stay away." [32]

Lame Deer went to a bar where a *winkte* was sitting and bought him a bottle of wine in exchange for some information about himself.

> I told him he could have all he wanted if he told me the truth about *winktes*. He told me that if nature puts a burden on a man by making him different, it also gives him a power. He told me that a *winkte* has a gift of prophecy and that he himself could predict the weather. In our tribe we go to a *winkte* to give a newborn child a secret name. Most often this is done for boys, but sometimes he could give such a name to a girl. Ida, for instance, got one. A name given by a *winkte* is supposed to bring its bearer luck and long life. In the old days it was worth a fine horse — at the least. The *winkte* told me that these names are very sexy, even funny, very outspoken names. You don't let a stranger know them; he would kid you about it. Having a *winkte* name could make a man famous. Sitting Bull, Black Elk, even Crazy Horse had secret *winkte* names which only a few people know. The *winkte* in the bar does a little prophesying. He told a woman she would live to be eighty years old, and she gave him a fine pair of moccasins for that. He also does certain cures and uses herbs known to *winktes*. Well, this man-woman told me that in the old days the *winktes* used to call each other sisters and had a special hill where they were buried. I asked him when he died, when he went south, what he would be in the spirit land, a man or a woman. He told me he would be both.[33]

In his poem "WINKTE," Maurice Kenny, Mohawk, describes the peaceful as well as the peacemaking powers of the Gay shaman in former times:

> The Crow and Ponca offered deerskin
> When the decision to avoid the warpath was made,
> And we were accepted into the fur robes
> Of a young warrior, and lay by his flesh
> And knew his mouth and warm groin;
> Or we married (a second wife) to the chief,
> And if we fulfilled our duties, he smiled
> And gave us his grandchildren to care for.
>
> ... We were special to the Sioux, Cheyenne, Ponca
> And the Crow who valued our worth and did not spit
> Names at our lifted skirts nor kicked our nakedness.
> We had power with the people! [34]

Ceremonial rites marked the status of certain Gay people in the tribes. The ceremonial Lesbians of the Mojave, the *huame*, have a special song cycle for their initiation. In the eighteenth century the Sioux, Sacs, and Fox Indians of the Plains gave once or more a year a special feast for the I-coo-coo-a, "who is a man dressed in women's clothes, as he has been all his life." [35]

Among the Pueblo peoples of the Southwest, as among other tribal folk, gods and spirits appear on earth and participate in tribal life. Ceremonial functions include humans dressed "as the gods," acting out some of their functions, which include dispensing justice, distributing goods to make sure no one goes without, blessing new houses, and ensuring an atmosphere in which the people flourish. Clowns and trickster figures abound in this pantheon of lively spirits. The Keres call this group of gods "Koshari." They are highly sexual, "in polymorphous array," as writer Hamilton Tyler puts it. Like other trickster gods in other cultures, they advocate homosexual as well as heterosexual relations. Hermes of Greece was such a god, with a clown aspect. One group of clown gods of the Zuni are the "Koyemshis"; they are said to have once been supernatural, and their name is believed to have been derived from words meaning "god husband." [36] The sacred clowns go to great extremes in their behavior, acting out impulses other people hold in restraint or wouldn't dream of doing; they roll on the ground, say forbidden words, display their penises or artificial phalluses, eat dirt, excrement, and rotten things, and undergo pain with no apparent ill effects, for they are in a special god-state. They are sacred in the tribal sense of sacredness, which is a different sensibility from that used by the mass, organized, and patriarchal religions. Remnants of the clown aspects of Old European tribal religions remained for centuries in the "Fool's Popes" ceremonies and the masquerades of New Year's. [37]

Myths with Gay Plots

Among people with a thriving Gay culture and with ceremonial positions held by Gay members, there must be an ample number of Gay gods as well. Jonathon Katz cites an origin story with a Gay god, taken from a study of a California tribe and published in 1931. The Kamia, who lived east of San Diego, had formerly camped on the Salton Sea, then scattered from it. "The dispersal of the people from their camping place at Salton Sea was due to fear created by the appearance from the north of a female transvestite (Warharmi) and two male twins called Madkwahomai. These were the introducers of Kamia culture ... the transvestite and the twins ... were the bearers of the seeds of cultivated plants." [38] According to Paula Gunn Allen, this may be a description of Spider Grandmother, also known as "Thought Woman," creatrix supreme of southwestern farming tribes, and her twin grandsons.

Another origin story, recorded by Allen's great-uncle John Gunn, concerns a battle apparently between Gay and non-Gay factions. Gunn's version is called "The Battle of the Sto-ro-ka and the Ka-tsi-na." The Sto-ro-ka are described as a race of Ko-qui-ma, or hermaphrodites. They occupied the country in the vicinity of the lake known to the Ke-res as the Arrosauk and now called Mormon Lake, south of Flagstaff, Arizona.

According to Gunn, the Sto-ro-ka hermaphrodites won a battle against the Ka-tsi-na faction north of Zuni Salt Lake. He credits their victory with assistance they received from a storm: "The Sto-ro-ka went into the battle with bow strings made from the fibers of the soap weed, while those of the Ka-tsi-na were of deer and antelope sinews. While the battle was in progress, a terrific storm of rain and hail came down upon the warriors. The bow strings of the Ka-tsi-na were wet by the rain and soon became limp and useless; while those of the Sto-ro-ka, being made of vegetable fibre, were only rendered more tense and consequently more efficient, by the wetting." [39]

Sue-Ellen Jacobs recounts a mythic story with a Gay theme. She says the Southern Okanagon of Washington State credit the great Indian trickster god Coyote with predicting the future occurrence of Gay cross-dressing "when he left the Cougar's house disguised as a woman. Tlingit mythology says they exist because a 'half-man, half-woman' was reincarnated in a certain child because the woman of this child married the sun and had such a person as her 8th child." [40]

One Navajo creation story tells how in the East lived the Turquoise Hermaphrodite, a man in woman's clothing. Near him grew the Male reed. In the West lived the White Shell Girl, also a hermaphrodite, and near her the big Female reed grew. When Turquoise Boy visited First Woman she told her husband First Man that the Hermaphrodite "was of her flesh and not of his," meaning that First Woman and the Turquoise Hermaphrodite represented the female principle. Turquoise Boy, or *Ashon nutli'*, was called *Nadle*, meaning "that which changes," because he was the first man to change into a woman. His big Male Reed was planted in the Third World. It grew so large that people crawled up into it to escape flood waters. When they had climbed far enough they entered the Fourth World. In this world White Shell Girl's big Female Reed was planted, and it became the roof of the Fourth World.[41]

White Culture Suppressed Indian Gay Traditions

The influence of anti-Gay elements in white culture has altered the social position of Gay Indians within their tribes in the centuries of white colonization. This has correlated with a similar loss of power within the tribes of Indian women. Numerous writers have commented on the change in attitude toward Gay medicine people. In 1940 A. L. Kroeber wrote, "While the institution was in full bloom, the Caucasian attitude was one of repugnance and condemnation. This attitude quickly became communicated to the Indians, and made subsequent personality inquiry difficult, the later berdaches (Gay people) leading repressed or disguised lives." [42] Arthur Evans went so far as to suggest that the repulsion for Gay behavior felt by the whites caused them to use harsh and genocidal methods against the tribes, annihilating many of them.[43] Most contemporary scholars believe the purpose of such brutal attacks was to acquire the land and resources of the Indians, and of course this did happen. But that is only the physical side of the story. I believe that the suppression of the often woman-centered and pagan tribal life was a powerful underlying motive.

By 1889 shame already was attached to the Gay role among the Winnebago people, who had formerly considered Gays highly honored and respected persons. But the tribe "had become ashamed of the custom because the white people thought it was amusing or evil." [44] Another writer noted that a Chippewa Gay man was "scorned, insulted and greatly belittled by the American travelers who met him." White writers referred to sodomy as a "beastly and loathsome sin." Navajo men seldom dress as women now because they fear the ridicule of white people. Those who persist are considered queer and are referred to jokingly by white and Indian society alike, and children are discouraged in cross-sex affiliations.[45] As Allen has pointed out to me, much of the anti-Gay sentiment among modern American Indians can be attributed to their attempts to secure a "safer" position among the dominant whites as well as to their contact with Euro-American anti-Gay forces in school, religious training, the army, and other institutions.

Along with the increasing repression of Gay culture among modern Indian tribes trying to survive in a sea of Euro-American pressures, American Indian women have suffered and continue to suffer abuse and loss of their traditional powers. Gay culture goes hand in hand with a strong woman-based society, and such a society was at the very heart of the Indian culture that has been most under attack by white philosophy and practice. I believe that Gay people from tribes, villages, groups, and clans all over the earth are presently experiencing, or historically have already experienced, the transitions of suppression and loss of publicly acknowledged "office" that have been happening for three centuries among American Indian Gay priests and medicine/shaman people.

Gay Indian Love in Modern Life

Three distinct patterns of Gay life appear from the stories that have managed to survive and the studies that have been done, daringly, on Gay American Indians. One pattern is simple sexual bonding, friendship, or companionship. The model for male friendship among Indians was very likely that of two Gay companions, especially among the warriors. Katz documents an example recorded by H. Clay Trumbull: "An officer of the United States army, who has given much study to the customs of the North American Indians, tells of the warm friendship sometimes existing between men of the same tribe, or even between two men of hostile tribes, under the name of 'brothers by adoption.' Speaking of the Arapahoe warriors in this connection, he says: 'They really seem to "fall in love" with men; and I have known this affectionate interest to live for years, surviving lapse of time and separation.' " [47]

Katz also reports that some Indian women had simple sexual Lesbian relationships and that conditions of sexual tolerance and high status of women in the culture must have encouraged the development of such friendships. Exactly how prevalent this was, as Allen's poem "Beloved Women" says, cannot be known for certain.

A second Gay pattern of Indian tribal society is that of the cross-dresser, or "Gay dresser." These are the men and women who take cross-sex roles, or special "Gay" roles, such as the carriers of the dead reported among the Miami Indians, male nonwarriors who were not only litter bearers but nurses who took on dangerously infectious cases others would not touch. The Miami "hermaphrodites" were described by whites as "effeminate," that is, huskier and larger than other men. (This surely can only mean that the women of the tribe were larger and stronger than the men.)

The hermaphrodites were special men trusted to do women's work, as well as "Gay" work, such as special nursing and care of the dead warriors.[48] Reports in Katz indicate that cross-dressed tribal homosexuals do the work of the opposite sex and also sometimes have their own special categories of work that others do not do. Titles given to such work are often complimentary — "best runner," "best potter in the tribe" — and often the cross-dressed homosexual man was considered a prize "wife" by the men and women alike. Although like everyone else cross-dressed Gays took some teasing, they were in general admired. They can be roughly compared to fairies and dykes in white culture for the functions and offices they fulfilled in traditional tribal life, although their white counterparts must act out their functions without social sanction and in a fractured social context.

A third Gay pattern is that of the ceremonial Gay person, who underwent formal initiation and had priestly, shamanic, or "sorcerer" powers. Public rites accompanied the taking of the office by the shaman, who was considered "gone to the spirits," "Manitou," sacred. The shaman had special, publicly acknowledged powers. These powers, along with other qualities such as sensitivity, endurance, and "calling," made the person eligible for ceremonial priesthood because of her or his Gayness. Such people operated under the protective spirit of certain gods and served highly sacred ceremonial functions, using magical powers requiring special training and special skills. Their stories, with Gay themes, were present in tribal myth and history, taught as a matter of course to every person in the tribe.

There is no correlative to such positions in modern white culture, although there are intriguing parallels between shamanistic performers and the actors, jugglers, clowns, ventriloquists, and other performers of Western "show business." [49]

Of all the elements in Western society, perhaps performing artists come closest to the ceremonial Gay people in traditional Indian society. Superstars are not exactly worshiped in Western society, but they are accorded extremely enthusiastic attention, high status, pay, and sometimes genuine power. Their heavily stressful lifestyle is accompanied by visionary eccentricity and often overlaps into a deviant, often mind-bending drug subculture. Actors take on a masked persona with makeup, feathers, and furs. They take part in frequent cross-dressed performances, and they have a mediumship quality of malleability, as though they are "taken over" by the spirit they are acting out, who in Western terminology is a "character."

Still, a performer's qualities are a thin imitation, a tiny shadow of the kind of social and personal powers held by Gay people whose whole being was focused on directing spirit power for their tribe's well-being and on maintaining a balanced relationship with the rest of nature and with other tribes. According to one account, the Gay shamans, the *Bote* (described as similar to drag queens) of the Plains Indians knew each other and formed special groups of their own across tribal lines, even among enemy tribes.[50]

Two of the three patterns of Gay Indian customs have their counterparts in modern white society. The first pattern, that of sexual bonding or friendship, can be seen in Lesbians and Gay men and their relationships. The cross-dressing pattern has its counterpart in dykes, fairies, and faggots with their cross-dressed or special mannerisms, social jobs, offices, and functions. There are no direct correlatives for the ceremonial Gay functions in patriarchal, mass society.

Indian Values

We had no idea of the Gay customs barely suppressed or still functioning in the Indian cultures around us, Von, as we grew up each in her isolated small Anglo town. By the time we were eighteen, we were cut off from our own Euro-American people by their hostility toward the very essence of our lives, our Gayness. We felt their grim silence on the subject to the marrow of our bones. We felt and acted rejected, alienated, and thoroughly "queer."

I know that if we could have known anything about the Navajo Nadle, of the Bo-te of the Crow, of the Hwame women of the Pima, so much of our alienation and terror would have left us. We could have understood our own behavior, or specialness, as a gift as well as a burden and as an asset to our society as well as its apparent nemesis. We could have played the American game of cowboys and Indians with a brand-new twist. We might have recognized more personal reasons for the deep attraction we both felt for the ancient Indian cultures everywhere present in the Southwest. You and I often went out into the deserts and mesas to walk arroyos near abandoned stone villages, peering into vine-filled underground kivas amber with October light, turning over in the fine-ground sand potsherds left from hundreds of years ago. We did not particularly collect anything. We just went there to feel the oldness of the places, to think about what might have been. We felt at home there, as "at home" as we felt anywhere. We took comfort in this feeling.

The Western stigmatic view has historically defined Gay men as less than men and Lesbians as not really women, as less than fully female. And what contortions people, both straight and Gay, have often gone through to "prove" that they are all man, or all woman. The traditional Indian view of the Gay person differs most distinctly from the Western version in that it sees Gay people as having more of themselves than others do, not less, as being in effect double persons and as such connected to doubling and to the ability to couple, to join, with forces outside the usual ken of the human mind. As John Lame Deer explained, the *winkte* begins as two babies joined as one being in the womb. And he said that adult, magical *winkte* men could endow others with another side to themselves, a secret name. Reclus described the apprentice *angakok* shaman's capacity for uniting, after much seeking, with his own spirit double from the world beyond material flesh, under the guidance of the Mother Goddess Sidne. Paula Gunn Allen described the ceremony of the old Lakota tribe whereby two ceremonial Lesbians, *koskalaka*, are bonded together in a public ceremony in the spirit of the god Doublewoman, *wila numpa*.

The tribal attitude said, and continues to say, that Gay people are especially empowered because we are able to identify with both sexes and can see into more than one world at once, having the capacity to see from more than one point of view at a time. And that is also an Indian way of seeing.[51]

CHAPTER FOUR

Fairies and Fairy Queens

The unborn fairies are angry,
and the interplanetary anthill future is saying
step up the search for lifedust in new galaxies,
for the ground is no longer here, the air not here,
not here the sweethearts of the satellites.
And the 19th century is dead,
and the 20th century is dead,
and the 21st century is dead,
and the 22nd century is full of fairies!

From "The Curse of the Future Fairy,"
Carl Morse[1]

*We never thought of ourselves as "Fairies," Vonnie, nor did
we dream there had ever been such people as that, tribal Fairy
people with Gay customs. Recently I have been looking at pictures
of you, my Von, and remembering how your ears stuck out. You
wore your hair in such a way as to accentuate this feature and
never to hide it. I believe you were as proud of your stuck-out ears
as you were of your distinguished-looking salt-and-pepper hair. I
am remembering how bright your eyes and smile were, what a
lively, animated person you were. And how very short you kept
your hair; how often you wore Levis and a turquoise inlaid cowboy
belt even though it singled you out from other women so distinctly, and in such a butchy manner. You did this even while you
scaled the professional ladder in your occupation. You could have
been a conventionally handsome woman; instead, you chose to
be handsome and at the same time clearly a dike, clearly a jester
who kept conventional social situations slightly off-balance.*

*I am remembering how animatedly you handled your
physical being. You talked with your hands and arms and with
the rich up and down of your voice. I remember the gurgle of your
laugh, as though a brook tumbled out of your mouth. I really
took you for granted; I suppose we all do that with our first love.
I idolized and adored you, and then I just took your special qualities for granted. After all, you were "mine" during those first
years. Since then I've not met anyone with the lively spirit you
had, especially when you talked about ideas. You loved ideas the
way people love flowers or babies or new electronic devices. You
loved to talk for hours about the nature of ideas the way some people talk about cars or politics or their careers. You believed that
teachers could teach students in public schools pure ideas and that
the students would love it. You were a very intellectual Fairy,
Von, and I think too far ahead of your time, weren't you? The
pictures of you remind me of your great spirit, and how very
funny you were in your way of talking, never cutting or cruel,
never biting as I sometimes am. I don't remember a deliberately
cruel or vindictive thing from you; you appeared baffled by those
qualities in others. I remember you being witty and fun-loving
the way we imagine a Fairy person ought to be.*

BUT THIS is all a made-up idea of what a "Fairy" might be.
Usually the word isn't used about Lesbians, although sometimes
it means Gay people in general. Nor is there any reason for women
not to adopt the term for themselves once we know its meaning

75

for Gay people. I have heard it most often as a derogatory term, indicating a certain kind of Gay man, meaning what *pansy* means: effeminate, not rigidly masculine in manner. A circular path led me to the clues about why such a word is used about Gay people, beginning with another idea entirely: the color green.

Never Wear Green on Thursday

A people's culture does not exist as one big puddle into which everything flows indiscriminately. Like vast oceans, cultures have their own geography, currents and tides, pools and backwaters. The separate streams of a culture flow together in multiple currents of classes, age groups, regions, and ethnic backgrounds, each adding a very specific variety to the whole swirl of life.

Children recite and teach each other games and songs that may be hundreds, perhaps thousands, of years old. The cadences and stanzas were also chanted by children in sixteenth-century London or Moscow, in medieval France or Tunis, in ancient Jerusalem or Goa. What may be true, or "known," when a person is one age may never be known again in the same lifetime. Many children's games and sayings belong only to them, as part of a children's subculture; adults do not play the games and may no longer be aware of their content. London's bridge has been falling down for many generations of American children who live far from London and far from any understanding of the event. In 1975, Black children on my block in Oakland sang a modern version: "London's britches falling down," and so the song spins on, still alive and meaningful.

My primarily English-descended high school class had subcultures in every group — among the army brats, for instance, or the mysterious secrets of the country club set. Some of the Hispanic boys and a few of the more daring girls were *pachucos*, marked by a particular cross tattooed or drawn in blue ink into the hollow between the thumb and forefinger. All this was intriguing, the more so because the details were not accessible to me.

What was of most immediate, excruciating interest were the increasing references, among the Anglo students at least, to "queers" and "fairies" that began to surface in the ninth grade and gradually intensified as we were pressured into pairing off for the purpose of marriage. Ninth graders repeated the words with a contempt not related to whether anyone really understood the definition. The animosity was apparently what mattered. In sophomore and junior years, when most of us were sixteen and seventeen, a new element was added to the generalized baiting of queers. It became suddenly a known "fact" that anyone who wore the color green on a Thursday was automatically a queer or a fairy. This puzzling, illogical formula was repeated dozens of times throughout the school year.

Those of us who had secretly realized our own queerdom, and had come out to ourselves, nearly dropped dead every time we heard the dire slogan. For in those years, 1956 and 1957, to be openly identified as queer or fairy would have meant complete social shutdown, ostracism, persecution, expulsion from school with subsequent treatment as a criminal or mentally ill person — a pit of horror with no bottom. Fairies were definitely underground, no matter what they were believed to wear.

During those years I had banded with some other "strange ones." Although we had no names for ourselves and no genuine awareness of what made us similar, we were basically quite queer, together with one "fag hag," as I would much later learn to tag her. We operated unconsciously, the six of us. For instance, we celebrated Halloween together, going to the huge annual bonfire and then winding through town in the yearly "snake dance," with long lines of teenagers holding hands to make a chain, or snake, for the exciting, twisting rush up streets and sidewalks, around poles and hydrants. We ended one Halloween by going to the art teacher's house and trick-or-treating, to her great displeasure. Years later I learned she was a Lesbian, barely closeted. How she must have feared seeing us on her doorstep, the limp-wristed, sexual, clownish boys and the athletic, intellectual, clownish girls. All of us Gay as geese, inexpressibly.

Needless to say, those of us who secretly knew our queer state never, under any circumstance, wore green on Thursday. I refused to wear green at all, even long into adulthood and far away from that little town. The curious formula about being a queer if you wore green on Thursday seemed to be part of the subculture of the sixteen- and seventeen-year-olds of my hometown exclusively, for I did not hear the expression used after high school or in any other place. Not that I was listening for it. Only when I undertook to research Gay cultural history did I remember the peculiar custom. Since the Anglos in my high school were heavily North European, especially from the British Isles, I began searching for material on the Fairies from those parts.

Margaret Murray was an anthropologist who, though an expert in Egyptology, decided it would be more appropriate to study her own white European culture. She spent much effort uncovering the old pagan religious structure underlying European folk culture and several hundred years of various degrees of assimilation of Christianity. According to her, the Fairies were genuine flesh-and-blood folk, real historical people, the indigenous tribal folk populating the British Isles and parts of Europe when the fair, blue- or grey-eyed Celtic tribes arrived in the centuries preceding Caesar's conquest of them in 58 B.C., much as Indians populated the North and South American continents. Small of stature and dark-skinned, the Fairies were also called "Brownies" and one of their queens was named *Brunissen*, "brown." They were not portrayed as tiny or as other than human until the time of Shakespeare. Practicing magicians, diviners, and healers, knowing much about herbs and plants, they were extremely skilled in crafts and music and were often consulted by the women and men of the general population even when it became dangerous to do so because of late-medieval persecution of Fairy influences.[2]

The Queen of the Fairies was the genuine ruler, the king having secondary place; according to Murray, "marriage-laws were non-existent . . . and the fairy-queen in particular was never bound to one husband only." [3] Either Fairies did not recognize individual paternity or, as one report has it, "just occasionally a fairy child was born, and then there was great rejoicing — every little fairy man, however old and wizened, was proud to be thought its father. 'For you must remember that they are not of our religion, but star-worshippers. They don't always live together like Christians and turtle-doves; considering their long existence such constancy would be tiresome to them.' " [4] In other words the Fairies did not pair off into male/female couples, nor did they put sexual restrictions on women. It seems likely that whenever this is true of a people, homosexual bonds have been acceptable, if not recognized as an important part of tribal life, with such lack of restriction reported for other areas of sexual behavior.

Green was the primary color worn by the Fairies, who were famous for the beauty of their tailoring and their spun cloth. They used yellow, blue, black, and red dyes and sparkling white linen cloth, but above all they wore green. They had green hoods, caps, tunics, gowns, and capes. "Greensleeves" is a haunting medieval song said to refer to the Queen of Fairy; and one of the four great pagan festival days, May 1, is attended by the "green man" and a special processional dance, "Green Garters." Murray says, "Green was the favourite colour, the reason, probably being that the fairies were originally hunters, and green made them less visible to their quarry. Later, when they themselves were hunted, green was the best colour in which to move unobserved in a forest or to lie hidden on a moor." [5]

The Fairies had two sacred dances, the processional and the round dance. Both resemble the snake dance of my high school days. Murray describes them as

> the Furry dance of England and the Farandole of France. In both these dances the performers hold hands to form a chain, and wind in and out of every room in every house of the village; where the leader goes the others must go, what the leader does the others must do. The dancers of the Farandole must be unmarried; and as the dance is often performed at night they either carry lanterns or "wear a round of waxen tapers on the head" like the fairies . . . The processional dance could be in itself a complete act of worship, but it was most frequently used to bring worshippers to the holy places where the round dance or "Ring" was to be performed.
>
> The ring dance was specially connected to the Fairies, who were reported to move in a ring holding hands. It is the earliest known dance, for there is a representation of one at Cogul in northeastern Spain (Catalonia), which dates to the Late Paleolithic or Capsian period. The dancers are all women, and their peaked hoods, long breasts, and elf-locks should be noted and compared with the pictures and descriptions of elves and fairies. They are apparently dancing round a small male figure who stands in the middle.[6]

This figure was the impersonation of the god, a person dressed in skins.

The witch covens, twelve wisewomen or -men plus one person who on occasion dressed as the god, were a continuation of the Old Religion practiced by the Neolithic Fairy, or tribal people, and the medieval witches and other heretics celebrated the same yearly quartet of sacred days as the Celtic Druids had and as the Stone Age pagans had before them. The Sabbats were held quarterly, on the Second of February (Candlemas Day), the Eve of May, the first of August (Lammas), and the Even of November (All Hallow E'en). Great fires were lit on those four great holidays, the chief of them being Halloween, originally called Winter Even, New Year's Eve, for the Fairies ended their year on October 31.

Witches and Fairies

During the official suppression of witchcraft, that is, of the ancient, tribal, and often female-controlled arts of healing, herbology, astrology, divination, spirit communication, and the ritual use of sexual energy, charges brought against the witches included consorting with the Fairy people as well as using homosexual sex and illicit heterosexual sex in the rituals. Medieval people known to visit the vanishing habitats of the Fairies and to associate with any of them were suspected of witchcraft. In her trial, Joan of Arc was repeatedly questioned about the Fairy tree she visited as a child, because an admission of knowledge of the Fairy arts would have automatically branded her a heretic.[7]

From A.D. 1100, the records contain repeated reports concerning the homosexual customs of the witches, such as the custom following or during a ceremony or Sabbat of the men laying with the men and the women with the women. However, homosexuality was seldom a formal charge leveled against the witches. Since women far outnumbered men in the covens, Lesbian rites must have predominated in the covens' "orgies," as the Christian authorities called the ritual or collective use of sexual energy.[8] In addition to Gay coupling, the witches were known for having sex with the god-impersonation and also for having heterosexual intercourse from behind, a position frowned on by Church doctrine, which advocated that the only acceptable sexual position was with the woman lying on her back with the man on top.

Ceremonial cross-dressing was another magical feature of the Old Religion, so much so that medieval Church laws were enacted prohibiting men from dressing as women (or in skins, as the animal-god) during the New Year's festivals, which were characterized by costume dressing as spirits.[9]

The most important and frequently mentioned day, to the Fairies and the witches alike, was Thursday. Jeffrey Burton Russell notes, "The witches of Dauphine constituted a sect, and they assembled at sabbats, usually on Thursdays... At the sabbat, the witches danced, held sexual orgies, and frequently had intercourse with demons."[10] Even some of the four yearly pagan holidays were held especially on Thursdays. Weekly Thursday festivals sacred to the rain god Thor had to be strictly prohibited by Church authorities opposed to the Old Religion, because the festivals were so popular and drew attention away from Christian festivals. Under torture, one witch confessed that her coven practiced different sexual rites on different days of the week, and Thursday was the day for homosexuality. Thursday was the day women all over Europe rode out at night to worship under the leadership of the greatest "god of the witches," the Maid Diana, Queen of the Underworld of Spirits as well as supreme huntress and midwife on earth. As late as the sixteenth century, in Italy, "her followers went out in procession Thursday nights to a meeting where they feasted and danced in her honor to insure the fertility of their fields. They also put out food and drink for wandering night spirits and could depart their bodies to journey in their souls," according to Russell.[11]

So I could begin to understand the story underlying my high school taboo about wearing the color green on Thursday: The green-wearing Fairy people and the Celtic wisewomen and wizards had used Lesbian and Gay sex rites in ceremonies held especially on Thursdays and had been heavily punished, murdered, publicly terrorized for it — ancestors of my high school contemporaries, ancestors of mine had been those witches and witnesses to their fall from power. So the strange little warning phrase of never wearing green on a Thursday lest you be taken for one of them creates a bond with them over the centuries.

I asked about five hundred people whether they knew of the taboo about wearing green on Thursday. About half of them remembered the prohibition from their own high school years. A few people reported variations. In one Kansas town, wearing green and pink together, especially on Thursday, branded a person a queer. Sixty miles away, the colors were green and yellow. From one Boston school a woman told me the formula was the wearing of orange and yellow together on a Thursday. In a small town in Idaho the color was yellow, the students were of Welsh descent, the school mascot was a dragon, and they practiced the annual snake dance. In Midland, Texas, knots in tennis-shoe laces gave a person away as being queer, with no reference to a day of the week. In another school, leaving the tag in the collar of a new shirt is the giveaway for boys, and this tag, used for hanging up the shirt, is called a "fruit loop." No doubt there are plenty of variations on these particular themes throughout the country, but the most common by far is green on Thursday.

The children's subculture in my high school was remembering some crucial information concerning Fairies and queers, witch hunts of the thirteenth and fourteenth centuries, and Thursday sexual rites of many centuries past. In effect the students were warning each other away from behavior that had once been, and could be again, subject to hideous punishment, torture, seizure of property, and death by public execution. Gay behavior today is still at times punished by humiliation, ostracism, economic deprivation, beatings, murder, family hatred — a long legacy of the products of the Inquisition and other rigid social orders. The high school warnings reinforced at the precisely appropriate time the pressure the students felt to act in a rigidly heterosexual manner in order to take an approved place in the social order.

The Gay Holiday

Halloween, All-Spirits' Eve, is one of four holy days celebrated apparently from Paleolithic times by the tribal Fairy people and by the Celts who succeeded them and absorbed much of their culture. The Celtic Halloween was originally called Samhain (pronounced "Sah-wan"), meaning "Summerset," and was the most important of their holidays. It is the time when the New Year begins, and therefore the time when two different worlds come together. "The Celtic year does not fit together very neatly at the ends," a Celtic specialist, Daniel Melia, explains,[12] and a person can slip at that dangerous time from one world to another. The other world is the one where the spirits live, not thought of as either a heaven or a hell, just another kind of world. Its exact location for the Celts was underground, especially in the vicinity of large burial mounds left by Stone Age Fairy people. Spirits wandered out of their usual world on Halloween and walked among mortals doing extraordinary (trick-or-treat) things. They could be placated by a jack-o'-lantern imitation of themselves and by gifts. Just as the spirits slip into the mortal world on the ill-fitting evening, so a mortal might easily be "swallowed" into the spirit world if precaution is not taken. So impersonating a spirit is the only safe way to travel outdoors on Halloween. And who could best imitate spirits than the Gay people whose traditional priestly shamanic role required just such intercourse with the spirit world?

Jewish culture, too, has retained a cross-dressing holiday from prepatriarchal times, known as Purim. Novelist E. M. Broner describes how "all the stars converge at Purim time, the season for the breaking of laws: the law against drunkenness, transvestism, and the law against teaming together unlike animals."[13] On this special day Broner's women characters divine the future with the Ouija board. "At this time men can have the curliest of wigs, smear their mouths with lipstick, stuff their chest with stockings and rags, borrow earrings for unpierced ears, shadow their eyes. At this time girls tuck hair into caps, mustache the hairless skin above the lips, charcoal in sideburns, speak gruffly." [14]

The qualities of impersonation and the dangerous business of crossing over from one world to another help explain why Halloween is the most significant Gay holiday. Elaborate drag balls often accompanied by costume parades and attendance by stars and political figures, large parties, processions, limousines, and mass public turnouts in Gay ghetto areas on Halloween mark it as the Night of Nights for the Gay community.

Butterflies of Halloween

On Halloween 1980, my lover and long-time partner Wendy Cadden and I deck ourselves out, she as a determined pirate, I as a rakish, caped dandy in purple and blue, my gold tooth gleaming specially for the occasion, my breasts daringly (for me) displayed. We decide to go to San Francisco to look at the Fairies and Queens. As we drive through the city on Halloween just at dusk, we know we are close to the Gay section when we see an immensely tall, well-built blond man eating a hamburger on display in full view through the front plate-glass window of a busy restaurant. He is completely decorated from head to foot as a silver butterfly, large filament wings flowing out behind him three or four feet and impressive lovely antennae curling from his head. Not a soul is near him, and he looks as though he has just arrived from another world, a world where gigantic butterflies sit in display windows eating hamburgers as a matter of course.

A few minutes later, as we are walking farther down the same street, we pass two men completely encased in black leather, at first giving the impression of invulnerability that leather imparts to its wearers. However, everything else about them is out of kilter: They are too skinny, and walking too close to each other; their center of balance isn't really in their shoulders, it's in their hips and hands, and they are talking a mile a minute to each other in gabby voices. The impact is uncanny. These are leather queens.

Behind them, equally skinny and babbling just as rapidly, float two barefoot swishy men dressed only in moth-eaten, saggy long johns, as tender looking and as vulnerable as adult humans can look on a city street.

83

We see several Gay male couples outfitted as "man and wife," wearing slightly exaggerated clothing and postures, with the grim, black-suited "man" dragging by one arm the babyish, passively protesting, pink-fluffed "wife" across the crowded street, as genuinely heterosexual couples stop short, look embarrased, or glower threateningly at this open and totally conscious satire of their own prescribed roles.

Wendy and I lounge aggressively on a street corner. I am having a great time making faces at the tourists, flirting with the dykes who go by, winking at the fairies who notice us appreciatively, being rude and belligerent to the people who have come without costumes to gape at the freaks. We watch the continuous parade flitting by. The queens are out in full regalia. We see pink-skinned queens dressed as whores with immense blond wigs and sequined, stuffed pink bras and dark Southeast Asian queens bearing on their graceful heads three-foot-tall clusters of cream-colored feathers, their sleek gowns held off the cement by a small active retinue of their own brothers and sisters. We see slender, nearly nude queens of all colors in brilliant full body paint, their cubist designs as striking as those used in any modern painting or any tribal ceremony. We see queens in ultratight skirts slit up the thigh revealing shapely, cared-for, self-conscious legs or lumpy, furred, self-consciously satirical legs. And though there are plenty of interesting characters, of devils and spirits, of Pan figures and Puck figures, satyrs, nurses, accident and nuclear holocaust victims, mock soldiers and mock police, mock babies and cowboys, the primary theme is enacted by the queens, queens, queens.

LADY * QUEEN * DOLL * WOMAN

Using these words
not to belittle women
not to mock them.
Not to speak about women at all;

to speak of ourselves.
Unnamed regions —
        rose-pink and rust-fire —
beyond the stern
 and arrogant borders of manhood.

A shortage of terms, perhaps.
language caught

in the vice of opposites, of only
two, so that what is not
man in us
we call *woman*.

From "Woman on Fire," Aaron Shurin[15]

The Core Group Carries the Culture

Most members of any distinct group fit in most of the time with the society at large. Most American Jews cannot be distinguished from most American Christians by appearance, clothing, or the earlocks worn only by the very orthodox; most Scottish-descended men wear modern clothing, not kilts; most American Indians do not paint their bodies or wear headdress; most Gypsies do not swath their heads or use crystal balls. Yet some do. Sheltered within each community, at its heart, are the core members who do keep the older ways, even when these ways are disparaged and discouraged as stereotypes that prevent the group from assimilating. These are its historians and "true" practitioners, its fundamentalists, traditionalists, and old-timers, the orthodox who retain the dances, chants, laws, festivals, customs, clothing, sciences, meanings. They retain the culture in a continuous line from one century to another, one government to another, one economic state to another, one land to another, even one language to another.

Among Gay people, this core or heart group is made up of the blatantly Gay, the drag queens and bulldykes who congregate, whether separately or together (and they do both), in certain urban and rural areas. They are drawn from every immigrant group entering America from every continent, and from the immense Black population (whose Gay people sometimes congregate in bars that cater primarily to them), and from those original Indian tribal people who have managed to survive massacre and cultural erosion by the whites. And from every group, as far as I can tell, are drawn the special categories or, informally, the "offices," of butch women and fairy queen men. They may be called "bullbitches," if the culture they come out of is rural American Black or "Mahu" if it is Hawaiian or Polynesian, but the idea is the same. The blatantly and most nearly ceremonial Gays constitute and maintain an extreme, a center, of the oldest as well as the most recent Gay traditions. They attempt to act out positions of social influence and meaning *as open homosexuals*. All other Gay people in the current culture line themselves up and measure

85

their own behavior in relation to this core or heart group on a continuum stretching into its extreme opposite, which is assimilation or the imitation of heterosexual stereotypes for the purpose of camouflage, that is, closetry, being "in the closet."

Even though at any given time the number of permanent, lifelong members of this central core may be small, multitudes of other people, straight as well as Gay, pass through their influence for periods of time — weeks or months or years — trying out the roles and stances, values and valences, the aura of danger or magic and the topsy-turvy thought patterns, learning enough for their own purposes before moving on to establish their own identities in more hidden and apparently safer positions within the society at large. There they pass the values into the major cultural streams.

In the heart group of traditionalists lie the clues to the ancient Gay traditions, which are contained in the names, words, puns, and special phrases; in the gestures, intonations, lisping, swaggering body language; in the feathery costumes, rings, tattoos, leather jackets of Gay transvestism; in the derogatory names *faggot, queen, dyke, queer, fairy, bulldagger.* In these fragments rest the remnants of ancient Gay tribal traditions: the social functions, offices and domains, the stories of origin and magical powers, of rebellions and sorcery, of witches, wizards, gods, spirits and shamanism, warriors and wars.

A Modern Drag Queen

I remember the drag queens, both Black and white, whose apartments I visited as a young dyke in Washington, D.C., watching them stand on chairs to have their gowns or dresses (culled from secondhand stores) fitted by each other, hearing their incessant witty verbiage, gossipy, outlandish, repetitive, poetic, and philosophical in the most elemental sense. Sensual, barbed, informative, revolting, political — Fairy speech is a living art. They called each other the names of particular movie stars — Miss Garbo, Miss Horne, Miss Taylor, Miss Davis, or sometimes just: Miss Thing. Adhesive stars from the dime store pasted on their cheeks, they swung their hips and their purses, calling each other "she," making splashy entrances and exits, louder than anyone and funnier, more daring, taking up a lot of space and always with a smart remark, a critique, a commentary cutting through hypocrisy, conformity, or rigid manners, revealing the bones of the matter. The

86

drag queen is like the king's jester without the king, some theatrical combination of the Fool, the Hanged Man, and the Empress all rolled into one and without a true territory. Without an intact ceremony. Queens can be found holding court wherever court may be, like nomadic urban gypsies.

Queens are oracular as a rule, loquacious, helpful people as a rule, though also with a reputation for sharp-tongued, shrewish self-defense. Their usual character of speech is a spewing of a running stream of advice, predictions, protection, commentary, gossip, "truth-saying."

The modern Queen of Fairy is a male in flaming female attire, airy gestures, swiveling hips, and a distinct lisp. The queen, especially the older queen, is frequently a social focal point among Gay men, an organizer and a doer, a person to go to for advice and aid, the one who knows about people and events.

Though still a young man, Tede Matthews is an example of a modern queen who devotes much of his time to organizing. In the aftermath of the Gay Movement of the 1970s, his organizing is as consciously political as it is social. I interviewed him at his storefront studio in San Francisco where he was living with his lover and two Lesbian roommates.[16]

Interview with Tede Matthews
About Fairy Queens

TEDE: There is this baby picture of me; my sister had this big floppy hat, and I was just learning to walk and I grabbed the hat from the porch and went running across the yard. My parents took pictures. There I was posing like this when I was two years old or something. (Imitates a girl imitating a movie star.) It was just a natural thing to do. Before I knew such a thing as a queen existed I was into it, into being a woman-identified faggot instead of male-identified. I was always in rebellion against the polarized roles of masculine and feminine. I was more interested in the arts, sensitivity, and cooking, and I took this identity on myself, so I became less of a man. I did drag as a kid by myself and with little girls. I would rub colored chalk on my eyes and cheeks in front of the teacher and wear lipstick at three or four and stuff.

I mostly hung out with my mother, I didn't hang out with kids my own age, especially boys my own age, and I hardly ever took gym. When I was in high school my mother took me out of gym, because in the ninth grade the star team tried to rape me for refusing to give one of them head. She went to the principal.

I remember the first time I learned about drag, the first time I went to a Gay bar. I went in, and there was this drag queen there who I thought was a woman, this tall, Black drag queen named Bee who I later became friends with. And Bee was a radical queen and came up to me and said, "Hey, are you a straight man?" And I went, "Oh, no!" So it was a queen who actually got me to come out and say, to a stranger, that I was Gay. It had a real phenomenal effect on me; I just couldn't take my eyes off this ravishing creature. I never felt an attraction to a woman like that, and yet at first I couldn't really define this person. For all visual effects, he looked like a she — but it finally dawned on me.

I remember also around that time I saw the film *Trash* by Andy Warhol, and Holly Woodlawn was in it, who is this drag queen actress. The first time I saw her, I thought Holly Woodlawn was a woman, because of the way the film is shot. The second time I saw it I was consciously in drag as a woman, and I sat and cried through the whole film, and in fact I had three boys thrown out of the movie house for laughing at her. I went to the manager and said, "These men in there are harassing me; a woman can't even go to the movies alone anymore, you're not safe." And so he tossed them out, on my behalf.

JUDY: You don't think of queens as passive, obviously.

TEDE: No. To be anything close to a woman — I mean, it takes guts to be a woman under patriarchy. I mean, Dolly Parton is like an image of a super-femme, but she has this certain brassiness, she just has to have total guts to survive around men and to have her image be so female. She's the kind of person that a drag queen would emulate, because she is using that female, or femme facade, which is like Marlene Dietrich or Mae West or Dolly Parton or any of those gutsy women over the years who drag queens have chosen to emulate, especially the ones who do female impersonation. There's the other edge to them besides the femme facade that is totally gutsy and a real survivor of the world and I think that's why you don't see many Tuesday Weld drag queens.[17]

JUDY: Who are the other women that drag queens emulate? I know Judy Garland is a big one, and I know she has also appeared in drag with a top hat and a tuxedo — so has Lily Tomlin.

TEDE: Just like Marlene Dietrich has too, and flirted with women in movies. Greta Garbo, Kate Hepburn, Tallulah [Bankhead] — a lot of these movie stars have been reputed to be Lesbians, you know, there are rumors and beliefs, just about all the ones that I've named. These things aren't really intentionally thought out by the queens, who to identify with.

There's no place in this society to fit in if you're a queen. Even in the Gay male community you get ostracized, or you're brought out when it's time to be entertained; or once a year you have a night on Halloween. A lot of the Gay men treat you like a servant; and when you walk into a bar, they'll pinch you or grab you. A lot of the queens, a lot of the guys who do drag for special occasions, put on big false tits, and just act, they act like whores, pretty much — that's their definition of what a liberated woman is.

JUDY: So you think of drag as this satirical parody, that you play with, except it's living theater because it's dangerous and it really has its genuine reactions from other people.

TEDE: Yes. Drag balls give a chance to flaunt, to throw back all the insults and humiliation that are in the sexism in the society. You know, being oppressed heavily as a drag queen (who I think of as probably a real butch woman) breeds insanity and insecurity and then finally breeds conformity as far as drag queens who get into wanting to have husbands, play these mimicky roles and stuff which are the things that women really hate. A lot of feminists really hate when they see men doing this because they see this as men perpetuating male oppression against women, which it does in a way because it keeps those roles alive and keeps a good audience for those roles, especially in the Gay male community.

JUDY: Who are the drag queens you admire, or what do you admire when you do drag?

TEDE: I saw *Rosie the Riveter* the other day, the movie [about women in the work force in World War II], and I realized that those were a lot of my role models, 'cause I do my mother when I'm in drag. There's this one poem I have, "I knew / I wasn't a star / I knew I was real." I do drag as a housewife. And my mother just spent hours talking about her past, so there was this whole mythology in my mind about her life during the thirties and forties, when she was working at a gas station with my father, during the war when she had padded shoulders and pants on and doing these aggressive things that a woman was not supposed to do. I guess that excited and titillated me, the thought of a person doing what they're not supposed to do.

JUDY: What's the difference between a queen and a flaming faggot?

TEDE: *Queen* is a word used to describe a Gay man who is into

89

really anything, like Leather Queen is a man who goes in drag wearing leather, and there are some other sort of racist things — or a Movie Queen likes to go to movies and a Kitchen Queen likes to cook. *Queen* has a much broader meaning; a flaming faggot is just an outrageous, obviously Gay man. It doesn't mean the same as a *drag queen*. He might go around in bright shirts and big flamboyant jewelry and bleach his hair.

JUDY: What would a Leather Queen wear? Pants?

TEDE: Oh yeah, leather pants like the Folsom Street queens [Folsom Street being called the Leather Belt], it's really masculine-looking but then a lot of them talk in high voices like a total drag queen. That's another outrageous, flamboyant homosexual attire that a straight person will look at and think, well, hey, that person's Gay. Being a Leather Queen is being a parody of a parody.

JUDY: Wearing leather while using a high voice is another way of making fun of or refusing to play the accepted masculine role, in the same way as a Gay man I knew of, whose first action in joining Gay Liberation was to go to a wedding in his family, a formal wedding, in a bright red dress and a beard.

TEDE: A dress *and* a beard? Well, if you did that, there's no way that people could come up to you and politely say, well, you Gay people are *nice*, you know, you look just like any normal other person. For me, being Gay isn't trying to be as nice as straight people in the sense of bourgeois politeness. I mean, we're very nice but . . . we're not nice.

I don't think it's so much that we are born this way as I think it's like racial memory, in the sense of what is in our blood or in our spirit. It's not, really, I think, biological. I believe in reincarnation and that there are other lives that we've led. I remember when I was little I was told that I walked like a girl, by my brother, who was my main male oppressor in life; so I remember trying to understand how a man walked. But then when I got dressed up in drag I would just totally accentuate the way I was walking. I remember asking my mother, but she said, Don't worry about it, you'll walk the way *you* walk. So I mean, I'm really lucky that I had her.

JUDY: Thank you, Tede, for granting me this interview.

TEDE: Thank you, Judy, for writing this book.

In many ways Tede's story parallels the stories of traditional Gay figures selected for Gay offices within tribal cultures. The Mahu of Polynesia often chooses to wear girls' clothing at an early age and is even gently teased into doing it by adults in his family. The *Choupan* initiate, the *Achnutschik* youth, the Sioux *Winkte*, the Navajo *Nadle* are often selected or self-selected by their childhood behavior for the special offices they will hold within their societies. And, once selected, no doubt the apprentice is initiated and brought all the way into his special office by other members of the Gay priesthood — in Tede's case informally and unceremoniously by Bee, the Black queen who challenged him to reveal himself and then became his friend to introduce him to Gay culture.

Come Out, Ye Lesbian Queens

Male impersonations of the Queen of Fairy are an obvious, vigorous, and nearly formalized part of Gay life. But where, I wondered, were the Lesbian Queens of Fairy? Lesbians are called *dyke*, not *queen*. Everywhere I went within the Gay underground culture I found that the men had queens to look to and admire or despise; many of the men *are* queens of one description or another — bold, vehement, very much present, colorful, influential even when they were being most derided. I often wondered where the Lesbian queens might be; why do we not call each other "queen"? Of course, Sweden had a Lesbian queen, Queen Christina in the 1600s, who, raised as a boy by her father, abdicated rather than marry a man and who apparently loved a certain countess, her lady-in-waiting. And of course, the Amazons had many queens, and Lesbians are closely connected to the female warrior tradition and often identify with it.

But where are the traditional Lesbian Queens of Fairy? What connection do we have with the European tribal folk? Perhaps the answer is obvious, right in front of us. When Wendy and I had finished watching the butterflies flitting in the Polk Street Gay ghetto on Halloween, we crossed the Bay Bridge into Oakland and dropped in to a large women's bar to see what the dykes were wearing on a Gay holiday. Many pirates, like Wendy, were in evidence in red and black trappings with one gold earring and an old-fashioned knife or sword at the belt. One neighbor of ours had dressed as an old woman; she spent the evening showing photographs of her nude lovers and friends, having fun acting out everyone's stereotype of a modern witch figure, the "dirty old lady." Two lovers of Asian-American descent, both Lesbian writ-

91

ers, one Korean (Willyce Kim) and one Chinese (Kitty Tsui), danced by sporting identical black mustaches. A magnificent bee costume in black and yellow stands out in my mind, and a great deal of leather, some leather pants but most especially leather jackets and belts, a kind of lightweight biker drag. Many women sported tattoos, either permanent or inked on for the Halloween occasion. Remembering that the tribal Pict people tattooed, I came home and hunted through my witch history books for signs of tattooing. It was all there.

"The Devil Leaveth Markes"

The first Lesbian I met with a picture inked into her skin was a handsome blond woman who appropriately enough had been in the navy. She was a small-boned, delicately made person with very short hair and a taut, dykely body of the slender Nordic variety. To my delight, she had a large, garish, three-colored tattoo on her left shoulder blade. The design was of a seahorse, a curvy, friendly looking character with wonderful detail. I met the wearer in a Gay bar sometime in 1961 and invited her to my room where we had a pretty good time in bed and then she overstayed her welcome for a few days until I imagined she would never leave, and I rudely threw all her stuff into the hallway to get her to go away.

Later I met many more Lesbians with tattoos and often wistfully pictured getting one myself. These tattoos included pictures, geometrical designs, names, and once even numbers—in the unusual and militant example of two Jewish Lesbians who recalled the Holocaust by tattooing numbers on their wrists, as was done to the victims in the camps, including relatives of these women. Most Lesbians who get tattooed do it as a form of self-assertion, of pride, and as the expression of a daring personal aesthetic. There is a dashing romantic piratelike quality of traveling to other worlds, dangerous worlds, as Eloise Klein Healy describes in her poem "I Spent the Day with You":

> I spent the day with you like a drunken sailor
> wanting you tattooed inside my life
> drawn dark blue
> as the memory of dangerous foreign cities
> and intricate

as unimaginable promises
shore lights make from the deep . . .

I shook to tell what shudder filled me
high to low as I went willingly
to the ends of my map for you,
diving headfirst through every wave
like the figure of a wooden woman
spearing through the seas,
vibrating with equal force
to a sense of passage and a sense of arrival.

I glittered like an earring made of gold,
like a tale you alone would tell,
throbbing with oriental opulence,
where beaches curled around the turquoise coves
and every spice I saw you
I could smell.

So chose to keep the needle working
deep and deep,
such colors blooming through my skin:
a heart your name unfurls,
the red swell that aches,
this strange design
I bared my body to you for[18]

Modern-day Lesbians may get themselves tattooed as a sign of daring, self-assertion, and dykeliness. Ancient Lesbians and other witches were marked in a more formal manner and for more sacred reasons. Many pagan people have used tattooing, on the American continents and in Africa and Europe, and all across the Northern Arctic territory. The designs tell the bearer's position in the tribe or village. The best-known tattooists were a people also known for fierce female warriors: the matrilineal Picts of the northern British Isles, so called because of the blue pictures they decorated their bodies with, from head to foot.

Pagan customs, including the Gay offices, passing underground during the Roman military and later Christian occupations, apparently kept such of the old traditions as they could get away with, even in an altered form. An authority in 1645 stated of the witches that "the Devil leaveth markes upon their bodies, sometimes like a Blew-spot, or a Red-spot like a flea-biting." [19] The god of the witches, known as "the Devil" to the Christian authorities, tattooed the initiated witches with a little mark, the witches' mark. In *The God of the Witches*, Margaret Murray described the witches' tattoo: "The evidence shows that the mark was caused by pricking or cutting the skin until blood came; the operator then passed his hand over the wound, there was considerable amount of pain which lasted some days or even longer; when the wound healed the resultant red or blue mark was indelible." [20]

No special place on the body was singled out for marking, though in some regions the left side and the left shoulder were repeatedly mentioned. Witches reported being marked with blue on their fingers, shinbone, hip, between the shoulders, and other places. The pain from the ritual tattoo might last as long as three months, and a sensation of heat penetrated the flesh when the marking was done. [21]

Lower-class white people brought the habit of tattooing from the British Isles and spread it especially through port cities, so famous for bordellos, prostitutes of both sexes, exotic food, sailors and pirates, Gayness, and tattoo parlors. Lesbian writer Sharon Isabell tells a story about going with a woman friend to the tattoo parlor to cheer themselves up with some body decoration after a doctor has reported that the friend is dying of cancer. [22] Many tribal people would find nothing strange in that, as they believe that the markings help the gods to claim their own children, to recognize them after death as one of their own, and to welcome the spirit into the other dominion.

Earrings are another tribal method of marking, and a Gay cultural characteristic; they are worn differently by Gays than by straight women. The Gay method, by both men and women, is to wear them out of balance, that is, one in one ear only, or two in one ear, three in the other; or ten in one ear, four in the other, or some other mismatch. One night, riding through the Southwest with a Gay Indian man, I was attracted to an entire row of tiny stones ringing the outside wall of his ear. "How did you come to get those?" I asked, expecting to hear a Gay story. His Gay name is Princess of the Plains, a double pun, on Indian Princess as well as Gay Queen. (Indians, of course, never had princesses or queens; kingship is a European and African tradition.) Instead of telling a tale of the Gay underground, he told me an Indian one. "At an Indian conference in the early sixties," he said, "a couple of Sioux matrons decided it was time I had my ear pierced. So they put me in a chair, held me down and did it. After that I've added another for each of my special occasions."

Impersonating a God-On-Earth Is Just Another Form of Drag

Although one of my slang dictionaries suggests that the term *drag* refers to skirts dragging on the ground as was the fashion among European women in the seventeenth through nineteenth centuries, I feel that the meaning of that most venerable term *drag queen* is a much older and more profound one.

Drag as a Gay term means cross-dressing, whether by a man or a woman, and in tribal/pagan realms cross-dressing often meant entering a magical state involving taking on the persona or spirit of a god-being for public ceremonial purposes.

Expressions for being in drag were recorded in the English slang of 1850; "on the drag" or "flashing the drag" meant "men dressed in women's clothing for immoral purposes." "Drag" also was slang for coach or cart.[23] It seems that the Fool's King New Year celebrations included a procession in which the god-king (a goat, stag, or bull) and the female god were hauled through the village in carts. In even older traditions the gods were pulled in carts during processions. I once saw the picture of a sculpture of Dike, a rain-maiden goddess of Greece, being pulled in a cart. According to *Witchcraft in the Middle Ages*, "The chief pagan festival that continued to exercise the attention of the authorities was the beast masquerade at New Year's, with its accompanying belief in shapeshifting. Condemnations of this festival became . . . standardized . . . The most common accusation is that people went about on New Year's dressed as stags or calves, though an interesting variant is 'in a cart.' Other kinds of disguises are suggested by a Spanish penitential that condemns wearing skins or disguising oneself as a woman. The *indiculus superstitionum* mentions a rite whose particulars include dressing as women or in torn clothes or skins to represent animals."[24]

If cross-dressing sacred men stood in a cart during certain festivals throughout the Middle Ages, they would be said to be "queens in drag," that is, taking the person of the (female) god or ruling queen mother while being pulled in a procession in a ceremonial cart. If cross-dressing women took the (male) god's part or that of the god-king Puck (who was usually a stag or goat), they too would have gone through the village in procession and "in drag" as butches (in male clothing) on certain holiday occasions. Moreover, in the sacred disguise as stags, calves, or goats, members of both sexes would have worn animal skins, or "leather." In its most historic sense, being "in drag" is a reference to cross-dressing during New Year's processions when the Fool's King, a female queen god, or the goat-king Puck was pulled in a cart.

Leather queens, drag queen balls (which feature startling arrivals by limousine), and dykes in leather pants and jackets are beginning to sound like something we might expect from a group of people with traditions in a tribal and medieval/pagan past.

One dilemma of the modern Gay drag queen is that he is impersonating a female god and female characteristics that people around him may despise, and he may be seen only as a mocker of women, sometimes most of all by his Lesbian sisters. Perhaps our history of connection to the Old Religion has been even more deeply suppressed than has his.

The Dildo and the Devil

Lesbianism is closely related to the witch tradition; the phrase *women with women* repeatedly surfaced in the Inquisition's reports on the sexual activities of the witches. And since most witches were women (some authorities believe the ratio of women to men burned was as much as ten thousand to one), references to sexual orgies simply mean that the witches were often Lesbians being public with each other and using sex for bonding with each other and for worship, and perhaps for magical purpose. The coven leaders were the High Priestess, the Maid, and the person impersonating the goat-god.

The other god worshiped by the witches was a female and had a variety of names, depending on the region. Diana was one prominent name. The Teutonic tradition called the leader of the Sabbat, or "wild rout," Berhta, Herla, Herechin (hence Herlequin, Harlequin, Hellequin, Hillikin). Arthur Evans in *Witchcraft and the Gay Counterculture* gives the Horned God, Cernunnos, credit for *harlequin*, saying it meant "the horned king." [25] In central Germany the goddess' names were Holt, Holle, Hulda, Faste, Selga, Selda, Venus (from classical sources); in France, Abundia and Satia; in Italy, Befania, Epiphania, Bezezia. *Witchcraft in the Middle Ages* reports, "Almost always it was a female spirit, rather than a male, and it was most commonly named Perchta or Hulda. The usual translation of this deity's name by Latin writers was *Diana*." [26] Occasionally the thundergods, Odin or Wuotan, were named.

The dildo, or artificial penis made of any material from

polished wood or plastic to inflatable rubber, has persistently been associated with Lesbianism by straight society — in jokes and remarks — in spite of the fact that few Lesbians have seen one, let alone used or owned one. When women en masse in the seventies regained access to their own sexuality, the phrase of the day was the "rediscovery of the *clitoris*," not the vagina, and the mechanical devices employed to help "preorgasmic" women learn to experience their sexual feelings were electric vibrators designed mostly to stimulate the clitoris rather than electric dildos imitative of the penis. Modern Lesbians are usually sensitive to any intimations that they want penises or that their lovemaking needs anything phallic. The last thing I would expect a Lesbian contingent in the annual Gay Day parade to be carrying would be a dildo.[27]

Evidently the witches did not think the same way about it. Sexual ritual was (and is) a major part of most pagan religions on all the continents. Perhaps Lesbians are associated so often in stories and jokes with the dildo for historical reasons. Goddess worshipers and tribal pagans who include sexual rites as part of their religion use dildos in their ceremonies, carry them in processions (while making lewd jokes), wear them as part of the costumes of the god-on-earth — any of the gods and spirits, Katchinas, loas, and orishas who manifest themselves through mediums, visions, dreams, and reality during ceremonies or Sabbats or weekly meetings.

In ancient Egypt it was common for statues to be made so that the phallus was of a different material from the figure and could be removed and carried in a procession.[28] A straw phallus is worn by the priestess as she acts out the part of the Yoruba trickster god Eshu. The maidens who celebrated the Baccant festival in Greece carried penis-shaped wands, the *thyrsus*; the stolid matrons of Rome carried dildos in the festival of their Great Goddess Bona Dea; American Indians carried dildos for certain festivals and also practiced much ritual sex; female-only sex rites that include dildos have been recorded in tribes and societies from around the world.

The god of the European witches used a dildo in the sex rites carried out by the witches in their Sabbats. This is clear from the descriptions some of the women gave to the Inquisitors. The god's penis was cold, they said, and "no man's memberis ar so long and bigg as they ar."[29] Sexual intercourse with him caused pain, and he "was colder than man, and heavier." Isobel Gowdie

97

testified that he had "a huge nature, verie cold, as yce." [30] From all parts of Europe the devil's "nature," by which was meant his penis, was reported as physically cold, hard, heavier and larger than any human's and painful during intercourse. Pregnancy did not come of it; only when the woman gave special consent did she get pregnant from ritual intercourse. Murray describes his body: "The coldness of the devil's entire person, which is vouched for by several witches, suggests that the ritual disguise was not merely a mask over the face, but included a covering, possibly of leather or some other hard and cold substance, over the whole body and even the hands." Other descriptions, of the devil's coldness, hardness of his flesh, blackness and hairiness, suggest that animal hides were used as a covering for the impersonation.

According to Murray, women sometimes took the male god's part. In the testimony of the witches, "he" is often described as a small man, dressed in black, with a "hollow, shrill voyce" as heard by Thomazine Ratcliffe, a Suffolk witch; another said he was "A Pretty handsom Young Man," another that his voice was high and ghostie. Two witches named Anne in 1653 saw two Spirits in the likeness of boys.[31] A small person with a high voice, masked and wearing black leather, using a dildo for sexual rites in a circle of women infamous for homosexuality certainly sounds like a bulldike to me — or a leather queen.

Certainly men impersonated the European god of the witches; they impersonated him as a Black man, as a man dressed in black, as a goat, horse, cat, bull, deer, dog, or other animal. Women also impersonated him at times, even for the sexual rites, since the devil's organ did not have to be real; in fact, there is no reason for it to have been real unless the witch who took it within herself specified that she wished to bear a child by the god.[32] Modern dildo jokes to the contrary, the dildo itself was not invented by women to give them sexual pleasure in the absence of a male lover. The dildo developed as a ceremonial instrument, an attribute of the Old Religion, representing male sexual and reproductive power as it was used by women in their most sacred and usually woman-only rites of the wild, of animal keeping and of agriculture.

The brown-skinned tribal Fairy people who lived in Europe and mixed their culture with the Celts contributed quite a few qualities to modern Gay culture. Knowing about them makes me one hundred percent more willing to call myself a Fairy, makes me less ashamed of jokes that link Lesbians with dildos, even more admiring of Lesbians with colorful dragons on their thighs and shoulders, more loving of lisping drag queens calling each other Mary. Merry Sunshine, Mary.

Clearly there is more tribal connection in being a Fairy than having pointed ears and an elfish humor, my Von. We were more Fairy than we realized, just by being regular dykes. We were Fairy Queens, I suppose.

CHAPTER FIVE

We Go Around the World

In other destinies of choice
you could have come redheaded
with a star between your thighs
and morning like tender mushrooms
rising up around your toes
curling like a Shantung woman's toes
pausing to be loved
in the rice fields at noon
or as sharpened young eyeteeth
guarded in elegant blackness
erotic and hidden as yam shoots
in the parted mouth of dawn
balancing your craft as we went
upstream for water
Elegba's clay pot whistling upon your head.

From "Timepiece," Audre Lorde[1]

AROUND THE YEAR 1978, a well-known feminist organizer of the decade walked into a meeting of her ten-woman staff. "Do you know why we all get along so well?" she crowed. "Because we don't have any goddamned Lesbians on our staff, that's why." She said this, and the four known-only-to-each-other Lesbians on her staff cringed and failed to reveal themselves for the one-thousandth time, believing she would fire them, even though they were forty percent of her work force, and then there would sure enough be no Lesbians on her staff, at least for a while. And she could continue fooling herself.

Heterosexual and homosexual people alike who enforce or submit to the suppression and continual disappearance from sight of Gay communities or openly Gay influence live in a big false bubble of their own invention. "There are no homosexuals in China," official policy says; "no homosexual customs in Africa," some anthropologists insist; "no lesbians in *my* barracks," the (Lesbian) officer testifies to the Office of Special Investigation. And there are no Lesbians in the American family, as one Lesbian's father declared when he caught her back up in the hills with a notorious Lesbian at the age of fifteen: "I know you're not a Lesbian, and if I ever find out that you *are* a Lesbian, I'm going to kill you."

Remember how, as young lovers, Von, we believed the threats against Gay people that we heard on every side; how it deepened into terror, anger, and some unwanted suspicion that we must be dreadful people — no matter how our logic and sensibilities told us otherwise?

Because of this deep-rooted insistence that there simply *are* no queers, ever, anywhere, at all, my life has been a series of surprise realizations. That people are Gay all the world over, for instance. That almost all of the white and profoundly respectable spinster schoolteachers who eased my mother's sometimes battered life and strengthened my sense of destiny and hope when I was a child, and who I hoped were queer, *were* queer. And that the athletes, singers, actors, writers, poets, thinkers I'd ever suspected might be Gay, were and are Gay.

Now, my Von, after twenty years of unraveling a skein of heterosexual wool-over-the-eyes that said, "Nobody is queer, and if they are, they're terrible people and should be destroyed," I have

103

devised new formulas for understanding what is, what really is,
that will reveal more than we ever dreamed, more than simply:
Did those people have sex with each other? Did they fear their
family's rejection, as we did? Were they anything like us?

I now believe there must be more Gay people in places like
China than anywhere, or the state would not need so vehemently
to deny that they exist at all. I now believe that the death penalty
for homosexual love on the lawbooks of Spain and Austria speaks
eloquently for the strength of the Gay cultures that have been so
forcibly suppressed in those regions. I now believe that no culture
on earth can exist without Gay people, whether we are acknowledged and rewarded for our contributions to the fabric of society
or not, whether we are titled, honored, cherished, named, followed, and protected or whether we are disgraced, impoverished,
murdered, negated, sacrificed, and utterly lied about: Gay people
remain central to the functioning of society. In their behavior societies acknowledge this by treating us as gods or devils, intriguing
heroes or subterranean, taboo people. "We Are Everywhere" became an organizing slogan and parade banner for Gay marches
during the seventies, but "we are everywhere" seems to be more
true than any of us dreamed.

Not only are there words that point to the worldwide presence of individual women and men who engage in same-sex love,
more significantly there is a worldwide pattern, both in historical
and in modern times, of institutional Gay power, of special Gay
functions within the context of societies. These include gay spiritual magic, Gay shamanism, women warrior/sorcerers, healers, and
diviners, and even pagan religious homosexualism with gods and
spirits worshiped with homosexual sex in order to direct a particular kind of energy toward a particular social end.

The information about worldwide Gay cultural customs and
traits often has been suppressed by anti-Gay forces, or it has been
incorrectly reported, especially on the subject of women. In addition, Gay information has been hidden from Western eyes because many societies incorporate homosexuality and Lesbianism
in ways that are not understood by us. Our own cultural bias
keeps us from seeing.

I spent many years in ignorance of most other Gay people; at
times I knew only of the American, urban, highly visible, blatant
Gay underground world: a tiny though vital group. I could not
believe the (largely socialist) attitude that Gayness is a decadent

by-product of industrialized capitalism any more than I could accept the equally negative judgments, no different in their effects, of Gayness as a sin or a "mental illness" or "criminal behavior."

The day I saw a poster declaring the existence of an organization of Gay American Indians, I put my face into my hands and sobbed with relief. A huge burden, the burden of isolation and of being defined only by one's enemies, left me on that enlightening day. I understood then that being Gay is a universal quality, like cooking, like decorating the body, like singing, like predicting the weather. Moreover, after learning about the social positions and special offices fulfilled by Indians whose tribes once picked them for the tasks of naming, healing, prediction, leadership, and teaching precisely because they displayed characteristics we call gay, I knew that Gayness goes far beyond simple sexual/emotional activity. What Americans call Gayness not only has distinct cultural characteristics, its participants have long held positions of social power in history and ritual among people all over the globe. The problem is not how to find them so much as it is first how to *see* them, the trees in all those forests, for suppression has caused them to deliberately hide from our view and cultural bias has caused our view to be blind to what is before us. I would like to suggest a few clues about learning to look.

Only Two of Many Words

Gay and *Lesbian* are only two of many words humans use for formalized, socially recognized homosexual bonding. Both belong to Western culture and stem from the oldest Greek civilizations, one from the island Lesbos that was made famous and infamous by the woman-loving poet/priestess Sappho. The other name, *Gay*, comes from the grand old Earth Goddess of Greece, the lady whose temple was guarded with a python and who reigned long before the patriarchal invasions overthrew and replaced her: the great Gaia. Western homosexual people truly deserve to consider themselves the children of Gaia, having kept her name alive for thirty or forty centuries after her fall from grace, mostly by word of mouth.

But *Gay* and *Lesbian* are only two names. The world over, there are thousands more, most of them kept secret by or from the people who write things down in European languages and who so often seek the destruction of what is Gay in any culture, according to their own prohibitions toward it. But some of the words and names for Gay have escaped into written records, words of description and also of special Gay office, such as *Winkte, Choupan, Das, Sahacat, Wick, Mariposa, Koe'kcuc, Achnutschik, Omasenge, Nadle, Links, Finnochio, Fricatrice, Koskalaka*. And what are the relationships of function, the affinities of spirit, the similarities of office and social function among them all, and their relationships to the loaded Gay English slang terms such as *Bulldyke* and *Drag Queen* and *Flaming Faggot* and to the words in other languages and cultures for Gay women and Gay men?

I have answered these questions for myself, but not before I had tried to sort out some of the information about Gay people in cultures other than my own so I would have a way to see, and to begin to define what I was seeing, of my own Gay cultural experiences. Here are a few of the things Gays and Lesbians are called in other languages.

Stirring the Bean Curd

In Spanish, a word that most closely translates as "dyke" is *marimacha*, "strong female." *Mari* is a reference to Mary, the Mother. Many Gay slang words in Spanish are a comparison with her: *marimacha* is "strong Mary," while *maricona* is "weak Mary" and means "faggot," effeminate male, as does *maricoa*. Gay men are also called *mariachi*, referring to the festival musicians who dress in old-fashioned, decorative, tight-fitting clothing and are much like the troubadors of Europe. Another word similar to *faggot* is *mariposa*, the Spanish for Gay male, meaning literally "butterfly." In many cultures the butterfly signifies the soul or spirit of a person. Another slang word for queer in Spanish is *joto* for men, *jota* for women; the conventional meaning is of an old-time courtly dance. There is also *invertido/invertida*, meaning "inside out," *volteado/volteada*, "knocked over." A term strongly suggestive of the Indian tribal Heyoka trickster clown who was said to "go backwards" is *marcha atras*, "marching backwards," Gay.[2] These Spanish Gay slang terms are used in Mexico and southern South America, at least.

Lesbian nomenclature includes references to traditional female dominion in the world's kitchens: A Dutch word for Lesbian is *lollepot*, a particular kind of pot. *Lollepotten* are Lesbians. A term translating as a "pot off balance" designates a Lesbian who is currently looking for a lover.[3]

Although in Mexico the Spanish *tortillera* refers to someone who makes tortillas, in Cuba *tortillera* suggests tribadism, in the sense of two tortillas (women's bodies) rubbing together.[4] Lesbianism in Tahiti is referred to a *vahine pa'i'a*, meaning woman-rubbing-genitals-without-penetration.[5] And a Chinese word for Lesbian, referring to the Lesbian act of frigging, fucking with the fingers, translates as "stirring the bean curd." [6]

In England, a Lesbian may be called a "wick," and a Barbadian/American friend told me the same word is *wicker* in Barbados.[7] In France, *la tapette*, "wallpaper," suggests what *Nellie* does in English. Italian *finnochio*, the vegetable fennel, means something similar to fairy or faggot.[8]

German straight people have an expression, *Vom Anderen Uffer*, "from the other side" of the water, of the other shore, the opposite side of the river. They use it to mean "someone who doesn't belong" and also for Gay. *Warm Bruder* is another derogatory German name for a Gay person, meaning "warm brother," someone who wants to be close and tender with a member of the same sex. *Warmen Schwester* imparts the same meaning for Lesbian. *Links* is another German word for Gay, indicating "left," on the left side, that is, the moon or female side. German Gay people themselves use the word *Schwul* to mean Gay; a related word, *Schwnel*, means the warm, calm weather before a storm breaks out.[9]

Those are a scattering of examples in this brief travelog. But let me get more specific and see if it is possible to determine some patterns in what the words for Gay in various parts of the world might mean, especially with regard to the idea that Gayness involves three levels: same-gender relationship, socially acknowledged function, and mythic/ceremonial dimension. The following is a story about a friend of mine who went traveling in southern India and got involved in a Gay relationship despite a world of language, class, and cultural differences. I think of this story as simply about a relationship. It does not reveal any possible role of Lesbians within Indian society.

Sister, Sister

Delicate shell-bead necklaces in warm subtle tones of brown, orange, and cream cascade from my neck as I write. They are a gift from my friend, Linda Marie, who brought them from the south coast of India, where the shells were gathered from a sparkling beach that slopes into the intense blue water of the Indian

Ocean. They are then strung into slender necklaces by the women and children of the village Kanya Kumari. As Linda explained to me, these Tamil-speaking dark-skinned Hindu people are descendants of the original women-centered tribes who, centuries ago, were pushed to the south of India by the invading patriarchal Aryans who began to dominate the north. Still matrilineal, the women, as so many others around the world, have been reduced to selling necklaces to tourists for a living.

They worship the goddess Kumari, a Spinster God who never took a lover and never married. The great temple of Kumari overlooks the blue sea at the very south tip of India. Huge wooden doors two stories high once opened to allow the goddess, as she sits in her large statue form, to look out over the sea. Long beams of light were said to reflect over the water, gleams of the torchlights held by her worshippers and reflected from the diamonds set into her nose. But once years ago, a Portuguese colonial ship caught in a storm had mistaken her diamond light for a lighthouse signal and crashed on the rocks. Since then, the great doors of Kumari's temple are closed to the sea, though her temple services go on as before.

The local people live in thatched houses of their own making. Rape is unknown in this region, and the men are very shy around the women. The title of respect is "Mother." Linda Marie, an American woman married to an Indian man from a more northern province, had traveled to the south coast villages in 1966 and made a special friend named Antonia. Now in 1978 she returned to find her again. This time she sought an added dimension to their friendship, for in the meantime in America she had divorced her husband and had come out as a Lesbian. What follows is her account of the second visit; she has used an autobiographical character name, Cassie, as the short, red-haired, white American traveler.

TWO-SARIS-TOGETHER

The next morning Cassie brought saris for Antonia and her daughter and sisters. Then she took Antonia to her hotelroom and asked her to stay until Cassie went back to the USA. Cassie asked the question by pointing to the floor, then to the two beds, then to herself and the other woman. Antonia agreed, and they put the mattresses on the floor next to one another. Then so many hours were spent talking, talking, each in her own language and the language of women, tossing their heads and waving their hands . . .

They bathed in the bathroom. Antonia filled a bucket with water, pouring a dipper of cool water over Cassie, then over herself. Antonia was upset because Cassie had pubic hair, and she ran her hand straight across Cassie's pubic bone and said in English, "Blade." When they dressed she said it again, "Blade." She dressed quickly and left through the wooden back door, and disappeared into the night. Cassie thought she said she was coming back but wasn't sure. She could hear the people in the hotel kitchen banging pots and talking loudly and rapidly. A young couple across the hall were arguing and a baby was crying somewhere. "She was disgusted because I have pubic hair," Cassie thought.

"Madam, Madam!" Antonia was calling Cassie from the window. She had brought a blade, and it was the first thing she showed Cassie when she walked in. They both giggled and Cassie undressed again. She stood with her legs apart and Antonia squatted between them. It felt as though Antonia was splitting each pubic hair into four parts. Cassie could hear the blade scratching the hair, scraping the skin. She was very nervous and thought terrible things. (What if this woman hates Americans or thinks women should have clitorectomies?) Antonia patted her thigh a few times to make her relax.

Cassie learned from Antonia that her mother had died when she was small but before dying she had a hex sign tattooed on Antonia's arm. Antonia taught Cassie what the word was in her language, Tamil, for two-turbans-together; then another word for two-saris-together. But as for a-sari-and-a-turban-together, even when Cassie repeated the word in a near-whisper, Antonia would bite her lip and blush. Since she didn't seem to mind Cassie saying the words for two saris or two turbans out loud, Cassie surmised that a-sari-and-a-turban together was a dirty word in Tamil . . .

Antonia was humming, holding up her hands with her eyes closed and weaving back and forth. She knew the word "Love." She pronounced it "Luva." She understood love to mean our secret, the one we keep from the world. What would happen if the world knew an Untouchable from India and an Outcast from America shared a secret? Would it start world wars? Would the United Nations forbid women from traveling alone? If these two were caught, would they be cast to the sea and fed to the sharks? Or worse yet, would they be treated as lepers, would dogs bark and children laugh and point as they passed by? Cassie wondered. The best that could happen if everyone knew this secret would be that women from all over the world would mingle shamelessly and the men would become silent before their power.

Antonia gave Cassie some sticky stuff to chew. She opened Cassie's mouth and pushed it against the soft part of her jaw. Then she told her to hold it there for some time. After a while Antonia pointed her finger to her head, rolled her eyes and raised her eyebrows up and down. Then she pointed to Cassie. Cassie's head was floating. They were on a magic carpet floating between the floor and the ceiling. A tidal wave could have dragged them to sea and it would not have affected these two friends. Antonia was laughing. Her teeth were perfect except for the red stains from the betel nut. Although she was full in build there was not an ounce of flabby tissue on her. She was the color of warm chocolate milk and she tasted as sweet as coconut. Her body was smooth as satin and olive oil as they began to make love.

During the night Antonia wrapped her arms around Cassie's head and whispered, "Sister! Sister!" in her ear like a friendly snake. She had chosen Cassie as her sister. They were twins sharing the same womb and their life experiences only began then.[10]

Antonia, member of the Untouchable caste, long-haired, full-bodied, and clad in a sari, being a sister among her village sisters, married and mother of two children, and citizen of a country whose Lesbians say they are allowed no open expression,[11] is unlikely to be easily singled out for recognition as a Lesbian by a Western observer or anthropologist; indeed, she would not be recognized as such by the majority of Western Lesbians. Perhaps this is because she is not a "Lesbian," and certainly not a dike, not a wick or a fricatrice or a marimacha or a "manly-hearted-woman." In her own terms, she is a *two-saris-together*, and when she speaks to her lover she calls her a family name, "Sister, Sister." I find a number of things significant in this account. The mention of tattooing, for instance, is intriguing because it appears so often in accounts of tribal homosexuality and is also a trait of the Gay underground in the industrial state. "Butch" Lesbians in particular are drawn to it.

I am interested that Linda Marie describes a woman-centered culture with a goddess religion; Antonia's people are one of the last matriarchal cultures on earth, and they are excruciatingly poor and pushed to the bottom of the caste system, as "untouchable." Antonia's easy use of the terms "two-saris-together" and "two-turbans-together" implies that homosexual relations are taken as everyday occurrences and a major basis of social relationships, whereas heterosexual coupling is charged with embarrassment. Her affectionate term "Sister" to describe her lover is reminiscent

110

of Paula Gunn Allen's idea that sisterhood, the soroate, lies at the matrix of woman-centered society.

The next story indicates to me a possible "office" (unofficial to be sure) held by Lesbian spinsters, especially those described in certain parts of Chinese society.

Spinsters Spinnin' All Around

Not all Lesbians are spinsters, and certainly not all spinsters are Lesbians, but many are, and, like Gays, spinsters are weighted characters on both the positive and the negative ends of the contemporary human value scale. Thus, a European folk belief held that a pregnant woman should beware in particular the glance of a spinster, lest her baby be cursed with the evil eye of envy. On the other hand, Welsh mothers considered the child especially blessed with good fortune and promise if a spinster walked in and out of the room during childbirth.

The spinster was the subject of both scorn and admiration when I was growing into my station in life as a dyke and a young Old Maid. My mother (and, grudgingly, my father) admired my independent, tough-minded spinster teachers; and I had so many of them that *spinster* and *teacher* seemed almost the same word. Yet the children's card game my mother played with me, Old Maid, spelled out a different message: The player left holding the card with the ugly Spinster's picture on it loses the game. The Old Maid was portrayed with buck teeth and a lumpy nose, freckles and a high-necked, prudish dress. Later, we hard-headed New Mexico dykes gathered in Vonnie's dormitory room smoking cigars and turning the game around. We huddled over the cards playing the same child's game but loudly reversing the rules: whoever managed to hold on to the fated card until the end won and got to be an Old Maid. We tried to blunt the pain of her obvious ugliness and undesirability with jokes. When I called Vonnie a Spinster Teacher I felt great admiration. Even then we understood the hidden, ancient connection between spinsters and dykes, although we couldn't have known how hidden or how worldwide that connection is or how women's history in the patriarchy has used the one to hide and ostracize the other.

Unmarried women have had a special and specially charged position in American/European-based history. Poet and artist Carol Lee Sanchez reports that in the Spanish communities of her northern New Mexico homeland unmarried women sometimes live together and are referred to as "Las Tias," or, in even closer social relationship, as "comadres," literally "co-mothers." However, open Lesbianism and any hint of sexual relation between spinsters is heavily censured in the overwhelming religious atmosphere, as occurs in tight-knit communities everywhere.[12]

In the New England family, historically secretive about sexual matters, spinsters were family nursemaids and special caretakers, often severely exploited (as were married women) yet often also the only women in the family with their own private rooms. They became teachers, setting a particular tone, morality, value system, and style for teaching. The spinster teacher became a familiar American figure in the landscape of the industrial Northeast, the expanding West, the Great Plains, and the New South.[13]

In the industrial areas, spinsterhood has taken on its full, original meaning of "female spinner," because most female mill workers in the clothing industry, performing tasks of spinning, weaving, dyeing, and sewing, have historically been, though certainly not exclusively, unmarried women. The industrial alternative to marriage for women has been work in a spinning or similar mill to earn money. The cash has helped women to be more independent within the marriage system, but it has also meant that women could delay marriage, sometimes forever.

Spinsterhood As a Lesbian Domain

To the extent that spinsterhood is a Lesbian domain (whether Lesbian sex is acted out or not), it is a Lesbian economic domain that also has cultural and historical elements. Spinsters and weavers led strikes in Europe, America, and China; and I have witnessed strikes in my own work life in other industries such as hospitals and restaurants that were led by closeted Lesbians and Gay men. Spinster teachers have long been the backbone of the American educational system through the twelfth grade, and so many of them are aware of being Gay that Gay teachers were one of the first occupational groups to openly organize for Gay rights and declare themselves in public demonstrations as Gay people struggling for a redefined position in the modern state.

"Spinster" is the Lesbian connection to the old, magical, female-formed domain of the Heavenly Weaver Creation Goddesses, from the ages when baby blankets were woven with astrological symbols and charms that foreordained and predicted the pattern of each person's tribal or village life and identity. Production of thread and cloth remained in women's hands through the office of spinsters — single women, women unattached to men.

If the physical production of cloth was part of the female domain, the public display of finished goods has been a province of Gay men, as the stereotype of Gay men as fashion designers testifies. In ancient England, the Gay Fairy people and Elves were tribal folk noted for their skill at weaving and clothing design. From Fairies/Elves, men's skill with fine clothing continued from the Norman homosexual/foppish courts into Elizabethan times. When only men were allowed to act onstage, women's costumes and mannerisms were of prime importance to the cross-dressed actors. And the theater boxes and pits were filled with fairies, queens, fops, and dandies of every description. The connection between Gay men and that ancient time still continues with the large number of Gay men visible in certain aspects of the clothing industry, particularly in female fashions and trend setting. Stereotypically, fairies (modern "effeminate" Gay men) are expected to have special skill with cloth, especially skill in displaying it on the body, and also with color coordination and related decorating skills.

Lesbian spinsterhood is a Gay office that has passed through the transition of women's central and controlling position in societies to the patriarchal systems of today's world. Because the office allows women to avoid marriage and establish or maintain an independent economic base, it has been of primary importance to the survival of women's freedom, hope, and ability to express ourselves outside of family life. In times of severe restrictions on women's mobility and rights, spinsterhood has sometimes been the only independent female institution.

So for Yvonne and myself, young unmarried maids who wanted to be a teacher and a poet, respectively, *spinster* was a part of our self-definition. We could sense that the tradition went back, say, to Sappho, who was a spinster teacher and poet. But we did not know that throughout the Northern Hemisphere the spinning industry was recorded in myth and story as ever a province of single women and magic men: fairies and elves. We couldn't know that in China, for instance, spinsters, Lesbians, and weaving are sometimes bound into one story.

Lesbian Spinsters in China

In China, centuries ago, the Empress Liu Tsu, Lady of the Yellow Empress Si-Ling, first discovered and developed the difficult art of extracting silk from the pupa of the silkworm mother. She taught the skill to the ladies-in-waiting of her court, and silk weaving became a Chinese spinster's art.

According to Kay (not her real name), who is an American-Chinese dyke raised in China, the Chinese silkworm industry is where the "bad girls" go to work — girls who are aggressive, disobedient, loose with boys, or, most especially, Lesbian. "Be good or you'll be sent to work in the silk factory" is a parental threat used on girl children. Kay herself was brought up to be a boy by her parents and is now an American dyke. A photograph of the children in her family shows a line of beautiful young women in dresses; in the center sits a handsome young man in a suit, sleek hair pressed close to his head, walking stick in hand. This was Kay as her family knew her in China. Having conceived only girl children, her father picked Kay, the oldest, to become the "son" for social reasons, so that the other girls could function in the world outside the family and not be confined at home. Dressed in boy's clothing, Kay escorted her younger sisters when they went out walking on the streets or to social events. She lives now in California with another handsome Chinese-American Lesbian.

As Kay said, Chinese spinsters of the silkworm industry have a notorious reputation. Agnes Smedley, an American observer who wrote about China in the 1930s,[14] described her guide's opinions of the thousands of women spinners in the silk-producing regions. Hostility and contempt rang in his voice as he told her how the spinners in the silk-filament factories were infamous throughout China as Lesbians. They refused to marry, he told her, and if their families insisted on it, the rebellious women would use a portion of their wages to bribe their husbands to take concubines. If this extraordinary "nonmarriage bribe" still didn't free them, the most they would do to comply with their marital obligations was to produce one son, then go back to work at the factory and refuse to live with their husbands. Sometimes two or three spinsters were known to have committed suicide in a group protest when their families insisted on marriage.

In 1930, according to Smedley's account, the Chinese government issued a decree forbidding women to bribe themselves out of marriage. The spinners ignored the decree. And when Communist cells and trade unions were prohibited in the spinning factories, the spinsters formed "Sister Societies" and struck for higher wages.

Smedley's antagonistic escort complained bitterly of the status of the silk workers. They earned too much, he felt. Though they supported parents, grandparents, younger sisters, and brothers, they "squandered" their money, he said. He had "never gone to a picture theater without seeing groups of them sitting together, holding hands."

Smedley reported that only in the silk-working provinces were the births of baby girls accorded celebration. Like their sister spinsters in the New England mills of the nineteenth century, "Consciousness of their worth was reflected in their dignified and independent bearing." [15] Agnes Smedley felt she had never seen such handsome women, and she described how they dressed in black jackets and trousers and wooden sandals. They wore their shiny black hair in a thick, long braid to their waists, with a wide band of brilliant red yarn braided into it. Visiting some of them at home, she learned more about them from sign language, drawings, and songs. Her anti-Lesbian interpreter had deserted her by then, disgusted that she wanted to talk to Lesbians. The spinners told her they had once worked fourteen-hour days and had struck the factory to get a ten-hour workday plus a raise in wages. They were being paid just enough money to tip them into the status of industrial wage-earner in rural China and to buy their independence from the marriage system. To demonstrate how they accomplished their independence from men, they linked hands to form a circle, including the American reporter in it, and, accompanied by a brother or uncle on the flute, they sang songs and ballads about their high spirit and love and solidarity as well as about their ancient village traditions.

Smedley's account, though invaluable and extraordinary, is nevertheless that of a wide-eyed liberal attempting to show how these responsible, handsome, brave, and progressive women were not *really* Lesbians but instead were simply an example of the "goodness and unity" of the common people. In this unrealistic, puritanical, and condescending view, Smedley showed herself to be almost as anti-Lesbian in her own way as was her contemptuous and envious Chinese escort.

Her attitude reminds me, Von, of your roommates in college. They were well-meaning, kind individuals who liked and respected both of us. When they heard rumors that we were Lesbians, they vehemently denied that we could possibly be any such thing. And so they helped us to "pass" and also to be denied for who we were.

115

Even Without Sex
She Could Be Gay

The group of six or seven spinster teachers who lived next door to my parents at various times as I was growing up were of a class, generation, and social standing that allowed no sexual love or romantic expression to develop among them. They could be single, but in no way could they be publicly Lesbian. Their particular closets were celibate, at least by the time I knew them, when they were in their early fifties. They lived in individual apartments near, but never with, each other.

Yet they operated as Gay spinsters anyway, using and passing on to me the same values they would have had if they had been openly Lesbian, the same values that openly, highly visible, political Lesbians of the seventies developed and projected: independence, courage, physical adeptness, concern for women trapped in other kinds of lives, pacifism, and consciously modeled morality. These closeted, celibate spinsters solved many of their personal needs for companionship by living in adjoining apartments, staying utterly loyal and supportive of each other in their lives, in old age, and in their times of dying. I never heard any of them speak a single bad word toward another. Although they always wore dresses, they always also had shorter hair and more aggressive demeanors than other women. Without creating neighborhood antagonism or openly confronting men, they provided a safety net of protection and understanding for some of the more isolated wives who also lived in the apartments. On occasion they allowed a frightened wife and child to stay over when a husband had gone over the edge of violence; they watched out carefully and consistently for any mistreatment of children, of young women, of the elderly, of plants and animals in their little dominion, and they delivered quick critical judgments on these subjects. They protected the apartment complex, even catching a prowler or two, like the true warrior/teacher women they were.

Although this group of spinsters regrettably (and it made them sad) could not be sexual, romantic, or in any way openly Lesbian, they were nevertheless, and in their proper way, acting out a traditional Gay women's office with nearly all its functions intact. And they had such a tremendous influence on me from the age of ten to eighteen that I might have been their child-apprentice, well prepared by their attention and their rigorous, relentless discipline to leave my hard environment for an even

116

harder one, to seek my own vision and my own place and office in a spinster world. In some other culture they could well have been a group of Machi shamans, or Huame of the Mojave, or Koskalaka of Lakota or Gwyddonot warrior/shamans of the Celts, or Sahacat of North Africa, or Sapphic priest/teachers. They even kept, in the arid desert town where we lived, a carefully tended bed of flowers; and wouldn't you know it — the flowers were pansies.

Nevertheless those women missed important aspects of their own Gay culture, a culture they could not define or acknowledge, even though their lives represented a manifestation of it and even though the contribution they made to their society as a result of acting out their culture was enormous. They gave up much of their personal lives to accomplish this, because they had to suppress who they really were. One of the last survivors of the group, a literature teacher presently in her eighties, for a dozen years was very curious for news of a long-term relationship I had with one lover. Every year I would go to visit my parents and of course stop by to say hello to M., who always took me aside to ask a special question: Was my friend the same girl I had brought last time? Seeing how bright her eyes were when she asked about this, and how pleased she was when I told her we had bought a house together, I realized she was proud of our relationship and that she was vicariously living out her own desire to live so freely while still remaining a respected teacher. In that one facial expression I had a glimmer of all she had had to give up of warmth and affection and nighttime companionship to fulfill her Gay spinster calling. If only there had been a formal institution of female-to-female marriage for her, a way of uniting her with another woman under the spirit of her own kind of "Doublewoman."

We would have liked that ourselves, wouldn't we, Von? A little public ceremony, maybe a nice ribbon, "Spinster Dikes of the Year." Well, the Gay office is still an underground one, in our culture. Nor are there yet the ceremonial or religious aspects that would have helped us understand our place in the universe. There are hints of such ceremonial aspects, however, in the customs of people who still retain strong tribal memories.

Carrying the Sacred Trust

Same-sex bonding, such as is implicit in the Indian phrase two-saris-together or two-turbans-together, is one aspect of being Gay. A traveler to another land looking for Gay people would seek those who form relationships with members of the same sex and would see that young men cruise each other near the fountains of Rome, for instance, or meet in the baths of Turkey. One American Gay man was "picked up" by a man in Yugoslavia, not for sex but just to sit in the hotel room and freely talk about their lives and about being Gay, since that freedom was missing in the Yugoslavian's life under Communist rule.

One Black American who visited African countries said she had no problem finding lovers, though there was no identifiable Gay culture separate from the rest of the culture. A white woman visiting an African country governed by a harsh dictator in 1978 reported that women crowded around her at a party, turning the record player up as loud as possible while whispering questions about her knowledge of Lesbianism and feminism in America and other parts of the world. Given a combination of suppression and invisibility within our societies, it is no wonder that Gay people sometimes feel isolated, "the only one."

In addition to bonding lover to lover, a second pattern of Gay existence is present in societies, however diverse they may seem. This is a pattern of Gay office, a social, historical, and occupational function that may both reveal us and shelter us, hide us behind a list of descriptive characteristics that neglect to mention same-sex bonding. Gay offices include the major domains of spinsterhood, of spinster teachers and spinster weavers, and they represent the access of unmarried women to money and independence and a more self-defined life. Other contemporary Gay offices are revealed in the stereotypes of the Fairy in fashion design, the faggotry and Lesbianism of many movie stars, the Amazon in the armed services.

Tribal people make use of ceremonial homosexual behavior, so in such cultures an identification of a person as Gay, in the sense that industrial society means it, is actually irrelevant. Healing, shamanism, divination, or special access to the spirit worlds may be the qualities by which a person is known, and the sex rites she or he follows are simply connected to the office.

In *Witchcraft and the Gay Counterculture*, Arthur Evans lists some of the tribes in Africa known to have the institutions of Gay shamanism and transvestite Gay medicine people. He includes the Ovimbundu and Kimbundu people of northern Angola, the Lango of Uganda, the Konso of South Abyssinia, the Cilenge-Humbi Quillenges, the Barea-Kunama and the Korongo and the

118

Masakin, all of Northeast Africa. He mentions magical Gay people of Madagascar, where the Manghabei people called their sacred transvestites *tsecats*. The Ambo people of Southwest Africa called their Gay shamans *omasenge*. Among the Bantu and the Kwanyama, Evans says, all the medicine people were Gay transvestites.[16]

Historically, the office of shaman/priest often included the practice of homosexual relations. A homosexual love bond existed and exists very often between the sorcerer or priest and his or her apprentice or novice. Edward Carpenter pointed out this relationship in one (immense) section of the world: "Throughout China and Japan and much of Malaysia, the so-called Bonzes, or Buddhist priests, have youths or boys attached to the service of the temples. Each priest educates a novice to follow him in the ritual, and . . . the relations between the two are often physically intimate.[17]

In 1492 a North African writer, Leo Africanus, described "women-witches" or diviners of Morocco. He said they seduced younger women to join them as apprentices. The Moroccans called the sacred diviners *Sahacat*, translating as *fricatrices*, "tribadists," in Latin.[18]

In Chile the Mapuchi Indians, who have managed to survive colonization, call their shamans *Machi*. The Machi, mostly women, have Lesbian love relationships with their apprentices, according to one observer.[19] However, according to Carol Robertson, an ethnomusicologist who has lived and worked in the area for years, the Mapuchi women shamans usually apprentice a daughter or a niece and have been labeled Lesbian by white outsiders because they are willful, admired, feared, independent women. On the other hand, she says, male shamans *are* sometimes Gay, and the Mapuchi also have a special word describing homosexual relationships in the tribe as a whole. This may be a case of mislabeling that ignores genuine Gay elements in a culture while falsely describing others. How much of this kind of misrepresentation exists in the stories describing Gay apprenticeship in shamanism cannot be known, certainly not until more accurate, careful research is done.

For most tribal people, Gay cross-dressing has been virtually a prerequisite for a certain kind of male participation in shamanism, divination, and wizardry. Writing about Greece in 400 B.C., Herodotus described certain kinds of diviners, the "Enarees," and told a story about their origins as cross-dressers. The Scythian army was withdrawing from Ascalon, a town in Syria, he said, when "a small number of men got left behind and robbed the temple of Aphrodite Urania — the most ancient, I am told, of all the temples of this goddess . . . The Scythians who robbed the temple at Ascalon were punished by the goddess with the infliction of what is called the 'female disease,' cross-dressing, and their descendents still suffer from it. This is the reason the Scythians give for this mysterious complaint, and travelers to the country can see what it is like. The Scythians call those who suffer from it 'Enarees.' " [20] Thomas Falkner in 1775 said of the Patagonians, who lived at the tip of South America, "the wizards are of both sexes. The male wizards are obliged (as it were) to leave their sex, and to dress themselves in female apparel, and are not permitted to marry, though the female ones or witches may." He said boys were chosen to be wizards as children, preference given to those who showed an "effeminate disposition," and were dressed as girls and given the drum and rattles of the shaman, ordinarily a woman.[21]

Around 1800 a Russian traveler wrote about the Konyaga people living in the Alaska region. He said there were men with tattooed chins on the island of Kodiak who worked and lived as the women did and took husbands, even more than one. These men were respected, most of them being wizards; they were called *Achnutschik*. As with the Patagonians and many other tribes, the son was dedicated to his profession early in childhood either when his parents noticed his bearing or sometimes when they had wanted a daughter. The Achnutschik was considered a great acquisition by his husband, who was accorded status on account of his marriage.[22] Another writer, Westermarck, noted a similar institution among another northern tribe, the Kamchadale. He called the male cross-dressed magician a *Koe'kcuc*, a man transformed into a woman.[23]

Oh Yeah, Oya

As I searched for characteristic patterns in the mythic/spiritual/religious aspects of Gay culture, my attention was drawn, not surprisingly, to a particular goddess of the modern Macumba religion of Brazil. In this religion the gods are called the *Orisha*. One chant to the Orisha named Iansa ends with the lines "Here comes Iansa / queen of the wind and rain." [24]

Maria-Jose, whose Macumba title is "Mother of the Gods," describes the nature of the Orisha Iansa:

"Iansa, whom we associated with Saint Barbara or Joan of Arc,[25] is a woman warrior, an Amazon . . . Like Ogum [a warrior god] she lives alone in the sky, armed, helmeted and ready to combat injustice. Her children's necklace is made of red beads. She is storm, tempest and rain. She is the goddess of the River Niger. She likes to dance, her face hidden by the fringes of her crown, holding in her hand a scepter topped with a horsetail.

"Although she's a woman, she often wears men's clothing. She's not afraid to confront the most dangerous powers. She is cold and implacable and watches over her children like a jealous mother. She destroys everything that gets in her way. She is very beautiful, but she can seem very distant to those who do not know her. I'm very fond of Iansa because I know that I can count on her in times of need. She is stubborn and never gives up once she has undertaken a task.

"Sometimes she is death. She carries off the souls of the dead on her wings. She's the only [Orisha] who dares to confront the spirits of death — the *egums*.

"She moves from place to place with the speed of lightning. She is as pure and as luminous as ice. Like Ogum, she is difficult to corrupt. Her feast day is December 4th and is celebrated both inside and outside the terreiro [house of the gods]. We sacrifice a chicken to her. We greet her with the cry Epazzei!" [26]

At times thinly disguised as Catholicism for protection, Macumba actually draws most of its substance from the Yoruba religion of West Africa, brought by slaves in the seventeenth and eighteenth centuries and heavily mixed with the indigenous Indian spirit religions of South, Central, and North America. The gods, Orisha, are many and richly varied, including the trickster/coyote Eshu, a bawdy provocateur of the crossroads; his woman counterpart Pompagira; the feisty thundergod Shango; the virgin male warrior Ogum; the prominent Great Sea Mother Yemanja, who is often called Mary so the religion can escape detection. In this living religion, the gods visit their people through trained mediums, usually women, who are known as the gods' children and who are able to enter into a trance during ceremonies in order to "lend their bodies" to one of the gods. Special drummers call the gods from Africa or from the sacred ground of the American continent. Dressed as Iansa to help facilitate the transformation, an entranced medium carrying a sword and horse tail speaks to questioners with the words, feelings, and translated imagery of the goddess herself. Macumba is a religion used primarily by women and has been vital in keeping African culture from being crushed by slavery and Indian culture from being crushed by slavery and genocide. Macumba has been able to remain intact especially in Brazil, the Caribbean Islands, and the New Orleans area. Nonpractitioners know the religion as Voodoo. In the eighteenth century the powerful Macumba Queen Marie Leveau had tremendous popular support and so much influence inside the political networks of southern Louisiana that she might as well have been the mayor of New Orleans for half a century or more. Huge ritual dances held on a nearby island during her reign attracted much scandalous attention, and it is said that white people, especially women, as well as Black people, attended the rites. The origin of jazz, America's major contribution to world music, has been attributed to the ritual performances on the island. Special houses dedicated to the Macumba religion flourish today in the United States.

"I grew up in the house in New Orleans that had been Marie Leveau's," Luisah Teish told me. A tall, compelling Black woman with the kind of speaking voice that resonates in the hearer's chest for hours after hearing it, Luisah Teish was an initiate in Macumba, about to become a priestess at the time she talked to me about the nature of Iansa, the warrior goddess. I had seen her dance and had heard her read her own poetry and talk to women in the San Francisco Lesbian/feminist community about the goddesses of the Yoruba religion. I knew she often conducted rites involving a wide cross section of women. I told her that I had come upon Maria-Jose's description of the Orisha Iansa, which had a number of characteristics that I had identified from other stories around the world as having to do with Lesbian and homosexual rites and institutionalized Gay power. Did she know Iansa? I asked.

"Oh yes," she said, "that's Oyá, or so-called 'twice-born Athena.' In northern Brazil she is called Yansa, in some parts of Africa she is called Osa; in Yoruba her name is Orunsen; in Puerto Rico, Yequa; and in Cuba and Nigeria she is Oya. She is sometimes said to have nine heads, and the nine tributaries of the Niger River are hers, as is the Niger River itself. The city of Owo in Nigeria belongs to her. Her color is purple. She is Uranus, actually. She's Uranus because of her domain: storms, lightning, sudden tumultuous changes such as volcanoes and windstorms. She also is the only Orisha who is not afraid of the dead; in fact she comes down to collect the souls of the dead and carry them up to the sun on her wings. In my religion people are afraid of Oya."

I asked Teish about any openly acknowledged Gay aspects of Oya or the other Orisha. I referred to some information I had read in the book *Macumba*: "Maria-Jose is called the Mother of the Gods in Brazil," I said, "meaning she's head of the children of the Orisha in a Macumba house. She said there were beginning to be a few male mediums and even some Fathers of the Gods and that they were often homosexual. Is there any open acknowledgment of Gay people that you know of here in the United States?"

Teish answered, "If you say to the sisters in the religion, 'Well, isn't Oya a Lesbian?' they would back off from you and be very angry. Still, it's said that the daughters of Oya are secretive and ought not be asked about their business. There are Lesbians in the houses, and Gay priests, and they are gossiped about, but nothing is ever allowed to be said openly. They are excused as 'Obatallah's mistakes.' Obatallah created human beings. This took her a long time, so long that she got tired and so she drank a little wine, and then a little more wine and got so drunk toward the end that she made some mistakes. They are accepted as her children also. So a priestess will say of a Gay person, 'You know Obatallah made us all."

"Oya is a warrior, and she often dresses as a man. She's the female side of Shango, really. Now everyone divides people into either male or female, but at one time the gods were both, sometimes manifesting as a female and sometimes as a male, while still being the same god. So Eshu the trickster god has a female counterpart, Pompagira, which is an Indian word. She was probably an Indian deity when the Black people were brought as slaves, and they incorporated her into their religion. There has been a lot of mixing back and forth with the Indians. Anyway, Pompagira is known now as Eshu's 'wife,' when really she is the female side of the same god. So Shango is the male side of Oya.

"In Spanish, Oya is called *Macha* — 'masculine woman.' Oya has an aspect of herself called *Ochumare*, the rainbow after a storm. She wears a skirt of nine colors which she uses to raise the wind by squatting to the ground and then whipping the skirt to get the wind up. Nine is her number." With her tall dancer's body, Teish demonstrated the wind-raising motions and I felt a rush of the power and the beauty of Oya's dance as she uses her nine-colored skirt to whip up the wind.

Originally the lightning bolt belonged to Oya. She gave it to Shango, and that is his only source of this power. In fact, Teish said, everything Shango has, he got from the female gods, including his double-headed ax, his drum, everything.

The daughters of Oya are not permitted to eat mutton, because sheep once saved Oya's life when Shango was angry and had hurled a bolt of lightning at her. She hid among a flock of sheep who died in her stead, their bodies falling protectively on her. Oya is one of a trinity of goddesses, Teish explained. The oldest is Yemanja, the ocean. "The second sister goddess, the one in the middle, is Oya. She is made of three elements: the river Niger and its tributaries, plus wind, plus fire. No wonder she is so tempestuous! And then the youngest is my own, Oshun. I am her daughter. Her domain is fresh water, lakes, rivers, streams. She is the goddess of beauty and love, like Venus."

Teish described Oya's characteristics: She carries a little black horsehair whip or quirt. Her herb is the locust bean, a pod about eighteen inches long, with nine big seeds inside in a line. The herb is used to stop death. When she dances, Oya whirls this pod around her head and it makes the *tssst-tsssssst* sound of the locusts.

"Oya is not afraid of death," Teish said. "Her daughters wear bones, human bones." She widened her eyes in horror, but I felt curiously unmoved. I was remembering some necklaces I had once made, using mouse bones I found on the desert floor. I was realizing that if I were a daughter in Teish's religion, Oya would be my goddess as Oshun is hers. "Her priestesses wear necklaces of human spines," she said. I grinned. I could imagine wearing one myself. I was imagining that I could begin to understand Hekate, the Greek goddess of the underworld and the crossroads; I was wondering about the character of Hela, the Norse goddess of death and the otherworld. I was grateful to Teish and to Oya for what they were teaching me.

Audre Lorde kindly took time to tell me more about Oya and the other Orisha of the Yoruba/Macumba religion. Oya is love as well as tempest, she said, and she is the vanguard. When she is aroused to rage through injustice she punishes by robbing the transgressor of speech or inflicting him with a throat disease. As for the trickster god Eshu, Lorde says in Yoruba ceremonies he is always danced by a woman who straps on a straw phallus and chases the other women. He is also called Elegba. Originally he was a female, Afrikete, in the old thunder god religion that preceded Yoruba. Yoruba incorporated the older religions just as Catholicism has. Eshu/Afrikete is the rhyme god, the seventh and youngest in the old Mawulisa pantheon, Mawulisa being male/female, sun and moon. As the trickster, he/she makes connections, is communicator, linguist, and poet. Only Afrikete knows all the languages of all the gods. Afrikete always appears in guises, so it is wise to be nice to stones and bees, for instance, or anything at all that might be the mischievous Afrikete.

The Children of Gaia and Uranus

Only a Western mind, trained in fragmented ideas, could split one Orisha from the others and label her with "universal Lesbian characteristics," as I have done. The Orisha form a whole; they do not have an existence separate from one another. I expect that anyone who approached a practitioner of the Yoruba religion asking about a "Lesbian goddess" would rightfully be treated as a nincompoop.

Yet we can learn something about the history of Gay people from the story of Oya. Her rainbow self and her color purple remind me of the Greek Iris, the messenger goddess, and of the pervasiveness of purple as a Gay color. Oya is a transvestite, a crossdressing figure like Joan of Arc, like women warriors of the Plains Indians. She is a storm goddess like the Greek Dike, and her province is justice, as is Dike's and Maat's. Her symbols are the arrows used by shamans and medicine women and Gay men in other parts of the world; she is in charge of the spirits of the dead like Persephone and Hecate. She wears red beads as do the children of Kali; she carries a horse tail and is a warrior like the African and Mediterranean Amazons. Her element is fire like the sun goddesses and fire guardians with their Gay shamans and priests of Asia and Scandinavia and other parts of the world. Oya has more characteristics of worldwide institutionalized, ceremonial Lesbian shamanic power than any other single goddess I have come across; she is more Lesbian than Lesbos and very nearly more Sapphic than Sappho.

Oya is part of a living religion, a living Pantheon of Orisha. I like to imagine what a living Greek Pantheon must have been like, what it could have meant to be a daughter of Artemis, to be a medium through whom the goddess spoke; to be a son of

Hermes or Apollo; to be a child of Gaia or Uranus or Demeter, in the Macumba sense of taking years to become a proper medium through which the god acts and is made manifest, comprehensible, and physically real.

The Mahu in Tahitian Village Life

In another part of the world, in the South Sea Islands, the Gay cross-dressing figure of Tahiti, member of a special class of such persons, is called the *Mahu*. One of the Englishmen (Morrison) who first sailed to Tahiti on the notorious ship *Bounty* in 1790 described how the Tahitians "have a set of men called Mahoo [Mahu]. These men are in some respects like the Eunuchs of India but are not castrated. They never cohabit with women but live as they do. They pick their beards out and dress as women, dance and sing with them and are as effeminate in their voice. They are generally excellent hands at making and painting of cloth, making mats and every other woman's employment. They are esteemed valuable friends in that way." [27]

Captain Bligh himself wrote of seeing one of them when he visited island leaders: "On my visit this morning to Tynah and his wife, I found with her a person, who although I was certain was a man, had great marks of effeminacy about him ... On asking Iddeeah who he was, she without any hesitation told me he was a friend of hers, and of a class of people common in Otaheite called Mahoo, that the men had frequent connections with him and that he lived, observed the same ceremonies, and ate as the women did ... The women treat him as one of their sex, and he observed every restriction that they do, and is equally respected and esteemed." [28]

Fellatio, called *'ote moa*, is reported as the sexual method of choice by the Mahu, with modern Tahitian men claiming that the Mahu performs it on them and they do not return the favor. A member of the London Missionary Society in 1801 reported (with great disgust) that he walked in on the "chief of Hapy-ano" as he sucked another man's penis while lying on one of his attendant's floor cloths, indicating that in former times men commonly sucked, as the Mahu does, or that homosexuality had a connection with the office of chief. A belief of the modern young Tahitians is that being sucked is like feeding the *mahu* with the penis. "He 'ate' my penis," one man said. He said that the *mahu* believe that semen is "first class food for them. Because of that

126

mahu are strong and powerful. The seminal fluid goes throughout his body. It's like the doctors say about vitamins. I have seen many *mahu* and I've seen that they are very strong." [29]

"The Mahu" seems to be the title of an office. Robert Levy says, "People speak of 'the *mahu*' of a village or district, and say that most villages have a *mahu* (even if they do not know who it is)." The people report that there is only one Mahu per village and that when one of them dies another takes his place. " 'God arranges it like that,' one man said. 'It isn't allowed . . . two *mahu* in one place.' " [30]

Apparently, Levy says, either one is a Mahu or one is not, and "can discontinue being a *mahu* as one can discontinue being a chief," by deciding to cast off the role, dress, and mannerisms and become simply an ordinary man. [31] "The *mahu* appears to be a village role like the *tavanau* (village chief) of the Protestant pastor," Levy reported. [32] The Mahu apparently selects his own role, by often demanding very early in life to wear girl's clothing, and the Tahitians feel that the role is a "natural" one, even though many of them presently disapprove of it, following three centuries of exposure to Western culture. The early missionary who voyeured the chief in 1801 wrote of his horror at witnessing the homosexual act: "Satan has them in his arms . . . and the planting of the gospel on this island must evince the power of the grace of God in saving sinners very conspicuously." [33]

In the contemporary English-speaking Gay underground language, the word *mahu* is a modern Hawaiian slang term for the prancing effeminate homosexual. *Gay Talk*, a Gay slang dictionary, lists the term as Hawaiian, meaning "the shaman who played a woman." The expression *alano mahu*, "thou art a mahu," is a Gay Hawaiian version of "Come down to earth, you're just like the rest of us." [34] A generalized and recent term in Tahiti, referring to male homosexuals (but not cross-dressers) is *raerae*, believed to have come from the nickname for a particular Mahu. [35]

Forms of Dressing and Cross-Dressing

Cross-dressing is not a prerequisite for all the offices of Gay men in tribal life, as the following portrait shows. Evidently, at times a special Gay manner of dressing, imitative of neither men nor women, is what is most appropriate. George Catlin described trying once to paint a portrait of a homosexual shaman of the Mandan tribe. He was struck by the shaman's handsome presence and

127

elegant dress, though he was "not wearing the eagle's feathers of warriors." When he asked the man to pose, "the youth was over-joyed at the compliment, and smiled all over his face. He was clad from head to foot in the skin of the mountain goat, which for soft-ness and whiteness is almost like Chinese crape [*sic*], embroidered with ermine and porcupine quills; and with his pipe and his whip in his hand, and his long hair falling over neck and shoulders, made a striking and handsome figure, which showed, too, a cer-tain grace and gentleness." [36] This man was not dressed as a woman but nevertheless wore a special outfit befitting his unique Gay office, without the emblem of warriors yet still considered a man among men.

Cross-dressing and carrying on a traditional Gay office in a society that also at times attempts to prohibit the office has its own hazards as well as its own humor. In Barbados, according to Tonia G., whose family comes from that island, calypso has tra-ditionally been much more than a musical form. Calypso sing-ers use the lyrics to pass on news from village to village, for the gossip, scandal, political opinion, intrigue, and satire, along with some lively licentious joking. The office of calypso singer–news bringer belongs primarily to the women, Tonia said, and to special Gay men who dress as women. "The authorities clamped down on them when I was there," she said, "demanding that the men dis-play five pieces of male clothing whenever the police wanted to search them. So you know what they would do," Tonia said, giv-ing me a wink, "flaming faggots that they were. They would obligingly show the policemen their belt — a man's — and their men's socks and undershirt and shorts and maybe a necktie. And everything else they had on: high heels, bracelets and wigs, skirt and blouse or dress, and a brassiere — all that would be female clothing. So they couldn't be arrested, and they had a joke on the police besides."

What clothing may be special to ceremonial Lesbians or other cross-dressing women in tribal life I do not know, but male cross-dressing has been widely chronicled. It was practiced even among the ancient Hebrews. The Hebrew word for the female sex-rite priestess of the temple was *Kadosh*; the word for men who dressed in women's clothes and served a similar ritual sexual purpose was *Kadosha*.[37] Edward Carpenter lists them as *Kedeshim*, meaning "male-consecrated ones," and says, "it is probable they united some kind of sexual service with prophetic functions." [38]

Many of the Gay shamanic or priestly duties have a religious or sacred character. They have what Paula Gunn Allen would call "ceremonial" aspects. That is, the religious matrix or framework of the society ascribes specific sacred acts, offices, gods, and religious stories to the Gay side of universal human life.

When the Spanish conquistadores reached Central America and then the Yucatán, they found a prevalence of Gay priests and sacred statues and stone sculpture depicting the homosexual union as a sacred act. The Spanish soldiers destroyed the Gay elements of the culture first, before attacking other parts of the native religious and philosophical network. In the Yucatán the god Chin is said to have established sacred homosexuality and a Gay priesthood serving in the temples just as was true of the temples in ancient Babylon and Sumeria.[39]

Then the Ondele Seized Them

Arthur Evans reports that some African societies used (or perhaps still use) sexual rites in which people would be taken over by spirits who engaged in homosexual sex.[40] He quotes Baumann: " 'During these orgies it sometimes happens that a masculine *ondele* enters a woman, causing sexual desires that lead as an evil consequence to Lesbian acts.' " Being in condition to be taken over by a spirit force is a province of mediumship, requiring long training and discipline. During the rite, the medium "lends" her or his body so the spirit can freely enter it and speak and act in a comprehensible human form for the communication of advice or prophecy to the supplicants.

Many aspects of shamanism had homosexual content, and many of the gods, spirits, and divinities of the world have been associated with Gayness. In Tahiti there were special divinities for homosexual worship.[41] The ancient Shinto temples of Japan display scenes of sexual ritual orgies similar to those of the Bacchanalia of the Romans.[42] Evans, quoting Scott, says that the Great Mother Goddess of ancient China, Kwan-Yin, was worshiped with sexual rites that included homosexuality.

As I mentioned earlier, many of the Greek gods such as Apollo, Zeus, and Artemis participated in Gay love affairs, according to stories commonly told of their deeds; and Gay terminology has descended from Hermes, Aphrodite, Dike, Gaia, and Uranus. The threefold goddesses Demeter, Persephone, and Hekate had Lesbian elements in their stories and Lesbian rites at the center of their elaborate agricultural rituals.

B. Z. Goldberg in *The Sacred Fire* says that "at the service to Demeter at Pellene not only were men excluded but even male dogs so that there would be no disturbing element whatever for the rites to be performed." He says the goddesses Mise, Pudicitia, and Bona Dea were worshiped by women using sacred dildos and that the Phrygian deity Cotytto was worshiped by Gay men in some places and by Lesbians in others.[43] In Egypt the worship of the Great Goddess of Justice, Maat, is said to have included Lesbian ritual, and in India the same has been said of Kali and of the fire-stick goddess Arani.[44]

Areas of the world where the sun has been or is still worshiped as a female deity, including ancient Scandinavia, also have institutions of Gay shaman/sorcerers and remaining traces of Lesbian ritual.

Going Around the World Again

Gay culture has been largely invisible because of a combination of cultural bias on the part of all of us and because of its deliberate suppression. Yet because Gay people function in an analogous fashion all over the world, once we have delineated some of the patterns and the relationships Gay men and women have to their own societies, we can be named, seen, and found. That is, we can find ourselves, in spite of suppression and cultural bias. We can see both the forest and the trees, and even ourselves watching, if we have a place to stand and names to use for what our eyes tell us.

I wish, Von, that you were here now so I could say these things directly to you, how what we did in bed together was the least of it, in some ways. How your being a teacher was so definitely Sapphic, a Gay office you were carrying out, as I carry out mine of poet. And how can you get more Sapphic than "poet"? We could never imagine Gay people in other countries or in other groups within our own country. To us "We Go Around the World" was a slang sexual phrase meaning to kiss a person on every part of her body. Not a bad way to travel, but still . . . It's good to know there are other places to go, too. To be welcome.

My thoughts and research have only touched the tip of the vast world that lies under the lie, which says there are no homosexuals, no queers here, no history in the word *Gay*, no Lesbians on heaven or earth, nobody here by that name. Once we can hear the names and understand something of their history, their meanings, and origins, we can see that not only are the Gay people here, but they have always been here and they always will be here fulfilling offices and functions that may have altered drastically and may be hidden, distorted, or called something entirely other than what our own language calls them, but nevertheless are analogous to each other, are parallel in what effects they have on their societies, and are powerful, necessary, and vital parts of human social life.

CHAPTER SIX

Butches, Bulldags, and the Queen of Bulldikery*

I am the wall at the lip of the water
I am the rock that refused to be battered
I am the dyke in the matter, the other
I am the wall with the womanly swagger
I am the dragon, the dangerous dagger
I am the bulldyke, the bulldagger

and I have been many a wicked grandmother
and I shall be many a wicked daughter.

From "She Who," [1] Judy Grahn

---

* The words in the title of this chapter apply to women in Gay culture. *Bulldag* is short for *bulldagger*, a synonym for *bulldike*. While these three terms are used to describe a Lesbian and never to describe a Gay man, *butch*, especially as a complementary adjective, is in the vocabulary of Gay men and is discussed further in Chapter Eight.

133

WHEN I first went to live with you, Von, my first lover, we certainly didn't know a great deal about what Lesbians were supposed to be. Lesbians were warriors, that much we understood, and we affirmed the bravest, dikiest qualities in each other quite consciously. As you prepared to become a physical education teacher, everything about you made perfect sense to me — your muscles, your athletic ability, your physical courage all told me that you were acting out being a warrior. Somehow to me then in those early years, when you were in college and I was a renegade hiding out in your room, everything you did was a "dyke" thing. After all, I had no comparison, and you were utterly everything to me — husband, lover, friend, teacher.

I thought that your short hair, your square, muscled hands, your craft of leather tooling, even your habit of wearing electric-blue sweaters, were all "dyke" things. You had worked all through high school carving leather belts and purses to sell, so your hands were beautifully shaped: square, strong, precisely skilled. (And a Lesbian's hands are so important. We knew that, then, too.)

You were a warrior to me, and you knew it. You signed all your notes to me, "Your hero." You were completely cocky about this, and prideful. I loved those qualities about you; I hated it when you knuckled under to fear and to the Gay-baiting that was a constant factor in our lives, especially out on the street, where hostile boys would often follow us for blocks, taunting and threatening. I pressed you to be brave, and then I could be braver, too.

We both knew we were warriors, not that anyone else knew this. We were called "dikes," you said, raising your thick black brows and shrugging, for this word was a real mystery. And when we overheard boys calling us "bulldikes," it hurt our feelings. It made us afraid. The word "bull" sounded as though we were being compared to men, and we did not like that.

Being Called a Bulldike

After I entered the underground Gay bar culture, at the tender age of twenty-one, I could never forget the characters I met there, some of whom were me. The drag queens and faggots, the dikes and the bulldikes, the couples who called themselves butch and femme became a part of my definition of myself as a Gay person. I learned that a dyke was one way of being a Lesbian, and a bulldike was even more so.

Bulldike is the kind of word most women hope to avoid all

their lives, for few things are more horrifying to be called, especially if a woman is walking alone in an anti-Gay and masculine-dominated street, surrounded by hostile bulks. Few words are as guaranteed to set off an explosion of fear in her belly as the word *bulldike* when it is used on a woman like a whip. Usually, heterosexual men wield this particular verbal lash. I remember being so jeered once by an entire four-story building-full of construction workers, at seven o'clock in the morning in New York City, which I had never before visited. A woman so confronted will either slink into a defensive posture, deny everything, and flee — or she will get mad, she will raise her head and swing her arms in a sudden, hell-with-you, butchy swagger. And the minute she takes this last action, she may feel from the name-callers something more than their utmost derision, their contempt, and threat to her person. She may feel also a grudgingly granted hint of respect not present in the other anti-Lesbian or down-with-women words she may ever hear used against her.

For many years the mystery of this strange word *bulldike* has burbled and thickened in my mind, along with the milder *dike*. I called my first book of poetry *Edward the Dyke* in order to begin to defuse the terror people have of the word, for it is considered as bad a word as *cunt* and more taboo to say out loud than *lesbian* or *queer*. And I used it to tie it to me, so I could never deny it; everywhere I go as a writer and performer, the word *dyke* goes with me. It is a lower-class word, not written into literature or the dictionary. It did not appear even in slang dictionaries until the 1940s, although a wonderful reference is made to it in the song "B-D Women Blues," recorded by Bessie Jackson in 1935.[2] The *Oxford English Dictionary* lists *bulldike*,[3] having taken it from an American Gay writer, John Rechy, who used it in *City of Night* in 1963. Only truly, obstinately honest and tough dikes use the word *bulldike* about themselves. Really nice girls of any sexual persuasion have never heard of it, and your nicer sort of boy thinks it means "prostitute" or "shady lady."

Bulldike (also spelled *bulldyke*), *bulldiker*, and *bulldagger* are also used somewhat interchangeably, and all of them are loaded, taboo words. They are used, especially by lower-class, "straight" people, to describe a tough, brave, bold Lesbian who is considered "mannish" or "butchy" in her characteristics and mannerisms. The word does not apply as much to her Lesbianism, although this is always part of the definition, as it does to her toughness — her muscular physicality and aggressiveness, her free-striding manner. In the 1950s, underground bar dykes and fairies took the word and updated it from *bulldike* to *dieseldike*, applying it to women who seemed to them particularly butchy, the *most* butchy a woman could be and still not be passing as a man. This suggested to me that the word dates from a time when bulls were as everyday a part of the culture as trucks were to America in the fifties.

These particular Gay slang words sounded as though they stemmed from Old English, so I began searching English history for a historical people who once worshiped or otherwise valued bulls. I soon came across references to the Celtic people of ancient Europe and Britain, tribal people who had horned gods and goddesses and whose Druidic priesthood sacrificed bulls in sacred rituals. The Celts depicted cows and bulls more than any other animals in their art. I also noticed that in two Celtic dialects, *cow* was spelled *bo* (Irish) and *buwch* (Welsh).

At the same time I listened closely to my friend Sharon Isabell, to the special way she had of speaking. She has been a Lesbian all her life and has had plenty of experience in the Gay bar culture, where she was a bulldike with a leather jacket, motorcycle, everything.[4] She still retained a particular Euro-American dialect. When she said "boa constrictor," she pronounced it *"bull* constrictor." Then I noticed two other people who are descendants of settlers from the British Isles and who still speak in the older manner. They each said *"buadike"* instead of *"bulldike,"* making a soft "h" sound instead of an "l" sound. I asked them to repeat the word until they gave me funny looks; I was amazed and excited, realizing I was hearing remnants of older English dialects and being given an important clue in my search for the meaning of *bulldike.*

Freshly inspired, I went looking for a word that could have the *bull* part spelled *boa* or *bua* and that would be likely as the source of *bulldike.* What I found was a historical personage, a woman listed as Boadicea, Queen of the Iceni, a tribe of Celtic people living in what is now Norfolk, England. They called themselves Hicca, "people of the horse." Like tribal people everywhere, they had Gay customs. Their queen is remembered through twenty centuries as the leader of a major Celtic revolt in A.D. 61 against the Roman conquest of the tribal people of Britain. A statue of Boadicea and her two daughters stands under Big Ben in the city of London, which she burnt to the ground.

Some mention of this queen, however brief or caustic, for she produces a mixed reaction in people's minds, now appears in most books of Celtic history. She appears, as "Boadaceia," on a plate of Judy Chicago's *Dinner Party* art piece — in deep crimson with a shapely spear in the center of Stonehenge-shaped dolmens. Her real name, however, was never Boadaceia or Boadicea. I believe those are modern attempts to soften her character and hide her ferocious history. Her name was Boudica and came to be pronounced "Boo-uh-*dike*-ay." [5] Or, as we would say (those of us who say such things) in modern American English: *bulldike*, or *bulldiker*.

Gay Customs Among the Celts

The Celts were not the first people to occupy the land that became Great Britain; they were preceded by the Fairy folk, whose spirit-worshiping, woman-oriented ways they assimilated into their own, which were originally more nomadic and warlike. Beginning around 1500 B.C., Celtic tribes spread in waves from Turkey to the British Isles, emerging with a culture considered to be midway between the ancient matriarchal and newer patriarchal. Women still wielded tremendous authority, owned much of the property in common, dispensed most of the values, and had rights over their houses and their bodies.

> Many types of marriage existed, including marriage for a specific length of time; marriage between one wife and one husband; between one husband and many wives; and between one wife and many husbands. If a woman had greater wealth, she and not her husband was considered head of the family. [6]

Elaborate marriage laws recorded in the eighth century provided for the property that was due a woman if her husband left her for a young man. Older women taught younger men the arts of love, which undoubtedly included methods of birth control and tenderness toward women's bodies. Older women also taught the men to fight with arms, for novice Celtic warriors of ancient times went to school under experienced warrior women, who were at the same time sorcerers. [7] The martial arts teachers of the best-known legendary Celtic hero, Cu Chulain, were two powerful women, Buannan ("The Lasting One") and Scathach ("The Shadowy One"). [8] The men usually went to battle naked, having put all their wealth into the decorations for their horses; displaying proper courage was the purpose of the battle, not total conquest of

137

other people. Groups of women warriors (ceremonial Lesbians with institutional power) called *gwiddonot* are recorded in a medieval saga, *Kulwch and Olwen*; these women fought in battles, lived together, and uttered prophecies for the tribe.[9]

A prominent and typical goddess of Boudica's old Celtic people crouched in stone over the doorways of her temples, legs angled steeply apart, to welcome her people. A number of chiseled rays radiated out from her pudenda in a stone visualization of the *aura clitoridis*, the self-sustained, generative power of the female residing in and coming from her clitoris.[10] I like using the word *pudenda*. I like it so much better than *genitals* or *crotch*, certainly, or *pussy*; better than *mons veneris* (Mound of Venus), *labia majora* or *minora*, or any of the other Latin euphemisms; and most certainly I like it better than my mother's shamefaced "down there." Even though in Latin it means "something shameful," the word *pudenda* sounds so officiously welcoming and so religiously businesslike: a cross somewhere between *agenda* and *pagoda*. Boudica was a barbarian and a Celt and her pudenda would have been active, unashamed, and radiating with female power all her life.

As for the Celtic men, the main god with whom they identified was an amiable-looking bearded man with antlers. He was the Horned One: "The horned god was especially linked with male sexuality and often appears with an erect cock. Moreover, when erect, he is sometimes portrayed in the company of men, not women."[11] Horny was his name, giving us our slang word for sexual desire, *horniness*.[12]

Writing just eighty years before the A.D. 61 rebellion of Queen Boudica against Roman occupation of her tribal lands, the Greek historian Diodorus Siculus had this to say about the homosexuality of Celtic men:

> Although they have good-looking women, they pay very little attention to them, but are really crazy about having sex with men. They are accustomed to sleep on the ground on animal skins and roll around with male bedmates on both sides. Heedless of their own dignity, they abandon without a qualm the bloom of their bodies to others. And the most incredible thing is that they don't think this is shameful. But when they proposition someone, they consider it dishonorable if he doesn't accept the offer![13]

Considering this Celtic custom, it might have been dishonorable of Queen Boudica not to have been a Lesbian some time in her life. She was, after all, a queen and a military leader of her people. The Celtic tribesfolk would have certain expectations that her behavior would not differ markedly from their own. They would have expected too that a woman who roused and led them into battle against the Roman state would herself be a fighter. A Roman, writing three hundred years after Queen Boudica's time (and referring to the Celts as "Gauls"), described with Roman astonishment the reality of Celtic women:

> Nearly all the Gauls are of a lofty stature, fair, and of ruddy
> complexion; terrible from the sternness of their eyes, very
> quarrelsome, and of great pride and insolence. A whole troop
> of foreigners would not be able to withstand a single Gaul if he
> called his wife to his assistance, who is usually very strong,
> and with blue eyes; especially when, swelling her neck, gnash-
> ing her teeth, and brandishing her sallow arms of enormous
> size, she begins to strike blows mingled with kicks, as if they
> were so many missiles sent from the string of a catapult.[14]

Boudica's Electrifying Name(s)

Queen Boudica's name could very well have been a title rather than an individual queen's name: *bulldike* and *bulldagger* may mean bull-slayer-priestess. As high priestess of her people, perhaps the queen performed the ceremonial killing of the bull (who was also the god) on the sacred altar-embankment, or dyke. As bull-slayer she may also be related to another Lesbian/Gay word: *butch*, a word that comes originally from *goat* and may have re-ferred to the slayer as well as to the goat-as-god.[15] If Boudica is in fact a title, meaning sacred Bull- or Cow-slayer, or sacred Bull-slaying-altar, she would have been vested with the power of the people transferred through her from the dying bull. The bull, stag, goat, cow, and pig killing of pagan tribal religion was sacrificial, after the animal had been pacified in a dance or other hypnotic rite, for the purpose of transferring its life-blood power to the peo-ple and of divining their collective future from its internal organs.

In Boudica's territory, the sacrifice was carried out on the flat tops of large mounds of earth, special sacred embankments, "dykes," used by the Celtic priesthood and the wisewomen for bull sacrifices. Centuries later, "over the dyke with it" was an ex-pression reported to have been used by some English witches dur-ing coven ceremonies.[16]

The modern bullfight is a secular version of the old pagan

139

bull sacrifice practiced in ancient Crete, for instance, and carried on now in a less covertly religious fashion in Spain and Mexico. Instead of the innards used to divine the fate of the people, the ears and tails are cut off as prizes to the matador and the meat is given to the poor. Women sometimes still perform as the bull-fighter, although most matadors are men. In her pretty and very ceremonial black and silver and red pants and vest and white silk shirt, carrying a black and red cape, the female matador looks not unlike many dykes I have known who love to dress in similar fashion.[17]

If *dyke* meant sacred "altar," "sacrificial mound," then the title Bull-dyke just possibly meant "altar of the people's power," as the people's power was vested in the god-spirit of the bull. Altar originally was the lap of the goddess, the Great Mother of the people.

Whether it was a formal title or not, Boudica's name has a large number of puns and associations surrounding it. For instance, soldiers in A.D. 61 made defensive embankments consisting of a long ditch with the earth from the ditch piled into a wall on one side; the soldiers stood in the ditch while they waited for the enemy to advance. These embankments are called *dikes*, and they abounded in Boudica's war. Her association with dikes as a military structure is amply evident; she stood on them, made speeches on them, her enemies built them, and she stormed them. So many women warriors fought in this war that the women constituted the line of defense, just as the line of earthen dykes did. Large, ancient, ruined dikes around London were long credited to Boudica's war by historians. Her most famous statue is called "Boadicea on the Embankment." *Embankment* is a synonym for *dike*. Another version of her name is Bundaca;[18] *bund* was a word used in British colonial nineteenth-century military slang, and it meant "dike."

Bulldagger, which may be Boudica's name pronounced in a slightly different dialect, strongly suggests the sort of knife or short sword a priestess would use in sacrificing bulls for religious purposes, and in modern slang *bulldagger* strongly suggests "castrating woman," something Lesbians are often accused of being merely by our existence. The Gaelic word *biodag* means "short sword."

The fact that Queen Boudica was married to King Prasutagus and had two daughters doesn't interfere with her association with fierce Lesbianism, or suggest any imperative heterosexuality. Given one study's finding that over 70 percent of contemporary American Lesbians are mothers, probably a majority of Lesbians marry men at some time during their lives. Sappho herself, the mother of Lesbianism if anyone is, was probably married at some time, since she had a daughter. And several English kings were also both openly Gay and married. Customarily, royal marriages in earlier times were arranged for political reasons, not romantic ones. According to researcher Kathy Kendall, Queen Anne of England (1702–1714) was a Lesbian.* Married to King George, her primary royal duty was to produce a male heir to the throne, though tragically for both: the king had syphillis, causing Queen Anne to carry eighteen children to term only to have them each die soon after. Her Lesbian lover, Sarah Jennings, held the office of First Lady of the Bedchamber. Fortunately, they are close enough to us in time that their histories have survived.

Without the common folks' habit of retaining old words in slang, Boudica's name could never have survived so many centuries, especially during the aftermath of her rebellion, when the Romans heavily suppressed her tribe. Then it would have been suicidal to say "Boudica" in front of people of authority, "nice" people. But she has become a lady of many names, after all.[19]

Boudica's War

Rome colonized in a classic manner, flooding a territory with highly trained soldiers who had been promised pieces of colonial land for their retirement. The Roman-established provinces, guarded from their own populations by military posts, were headed by governors-general who levied taxes on all the resources of the provinces. From these they were expected to make personal fortunes and build major political and military careers.

After the military colonization of the British Isles came Roman money lenders and merchants, who promised economic "progress" to all who became indebted to them. They loaned back to the native peoples, at high interest, some of the riches that had already been stolen from them by the soldiers and governors. In this way the patrician Roman class acquired new labor and new fruits of the land. In addition, captured Celtic people were sent to Rome to become slaves. Some went to the houses of patricians as male and female prostitutes, artisans, musicians; some went to

---

* Private correspondence. (I have been unable to reach Kathy Kendall.)

rapid deaths laboring in heavy industry; some went to be used for sport in the arena, as gladiators.

The Celtic tribal people were angrily divided between those who cooperated with the Romans, crowding into the colonial centers such as London, and those who stayed in the countryside with their own people and did not cooperate. In their dealings with the Hicca people, Boudica's "people of the horse," the Romans negotiated an arrangement with the king, Prasutagus, rather than the queen. The arrangement turned half of all Celtic goods over to Nero, Emperor of Rome at the time. Then in A.D. 60 the Hicca king died, leaving the rulership clearly in the hands of redheaded Queen Boudica. Refusing to acknowledge a female head of state, Roman army veterans gleefully and roughly seized land and property from Hicca noblemen and relatives of the king. They increased their persecution and massacre of the Druid priesthood.

Outraged, Queen Boudica protested their behavior, whereupon the Romans had her hauled into a public place and flogged. Then they raped her two daughters, to discredit her queenship and her female powers.

There is no reason to believe Boudica had ever agreed to the original treaty with Nero, since it turned the Celtic people over to the Romans without a fight. Now, seeing the bitter results of the treaty and feeling them so personally, Queen Boudica rose up in a terrible rage. Secretly, and biding her time, she met with the other Celtic leaders, who were equally outraged by the Roman use of force. In a few months she united the greatest number of tribes and raised the largest army that had ever been seen in Britain — 120,000 people turned out for the war, according to Cassius Dio, who described how the Romans saw Boudica.

> In stature she was very tall, in appearance most terrifying, in
> the glance of her eye most fierce, and her voice was harsh; a
> great mass of the tawniest hair fell to her hips; around her neck
> was a large golden necklace; and she wore a tunic of divers
> colours over which a thick mantle was fastened with a brooch.
> This was her invariable attire. She . . . grasped a spear to aid
> her in terrifying all beholders.[20]

Waiting until the governor-general, the Roman Paulinus Suetonius, was occupied miles away (where he had trapped priests and priestesses of the Celtic religion along with other refugees and was slaughtering them), the Celts under the fierce leadership of Queen Boudica gathered and took the town of Colechester, then London and one other town; they dealt fiercely with the people they found there, Roman and Celt alike. "Beautifully timed and vigorously pressed, the sudden outbreak of the rebellion brought immediate success to the Britons," according to one account.[21]

Suetonius rushed to London in a panic when he heard that half of Britain had risen against him, and then he fled London, leaving it to the fury of the rebels. Boudica and company took London to the ground, undoubtedly dealing especially harshly with the Romanized Celts, for Dio reports that they bloodily sacrificed large numbers of prisoners in a sacred grove.[22]

One last, tremendous, grinding battle between the two forces decided the outcome of the rebellion, which hinged entirely on differences in the way the two peoples fought. On the Roman side, Suetonius came to the battlefield with a small, mobile, well-armed army of professional soldiers. He told his men not to be afraid of the Celts as they were mostly women anyhow, and badly armed. Boudica arrived with, it must have seemed, the whole countryside, for it was customary for the whole tribe to turn out for a Celtic battle, even the children hanging on the wagons shouting encouragement to their relatives. Dio claimed that 230,000 people participated in the battle.

Tacitus described Boudica on this day and paraphrased the speech she made to her army of united, furious peoples:

> Boudica drove round in a chariot, her daughters with her. As they reached each tribal contingent, she proclaimed that the Britons were well used to the leadership of women in battle. But she did not come among them now as a descendant of mighty ancestors, eager to avenge her lost wealth and kingdom. Rather was she an ordinary woman, fighting for her lost freedom, her bruised body, and the outraged virginity of her daughters. Roman greed no longer spared their bodies, old people were killed, virgins raped. But the gods would grant a just vengeance: the legion that had dared to fight had perished: the others were skulking in their camps and looking for a means of escape. They would never face the roar and din of the British thousands, much less their charges and their grappling hand-to-hand. Let them consider how many they had under arms, and why! Then they would know that on that day it was victory or death. That was her resolve, as a woman; the men could live, if they liked, and be slaves.[23]

It was altogether a remarkable speech for Boudica to make, the warrior queen who was leading women as well as men to war,

143

to protect the ancient female and tribal powers. The tight Roman lines, all modern iron and leather, moved in close at a slow trot, using their short swords like bayonets against the British mix of women warriors, naked men warriors, children, dogs, and oxen. Some of Boudica's vast number escaped that day; the rest were penned against their own overturned wagons, and 80,000, warrior and civilian alike, were slaughtered, as Tacitus boasts.

The tribal resistance against Roman rule did not stop, however, nor did the vengeance that Suetonius extracted throughout the countryside, especially concentrating his hatred on Boudica's own people. He submitted the Hicca villages to so much genocidal "fire and the sword" that the spareness of the archeological remains in those areas is attributed by historians to his extreme harshness against them.[24]

The Romans were told that Boudica took poison after the last battle, and they particularly hunted for her grave, "for they would not allow any memorial of Boudicca to survive." [25] Suetonius was so vicious that he finally had to be removed and a man with a less murderous colonial policy installed before Roman government could be reestablished in the area.

At this time Boudica's name would have gone underground, become a loaded, emotion-filled word meaning suicide if pronounced in front of the wrong people in the wrong tone of voice. *Bulldike* is the kind of name to come very early to America — perhaps directly from the slang of rebellious descendants of her tribal people. These were also exactly the people who would be most likely to remember, metaphorically and through common slang, that their ancestors practiced homosexualism as a matter of choice and as a matter of social rite and tradition. They would remember that their great, rebellious, loud-voiced queen — who came from a female warrior tradition, carried a spear and a sword, and took her people to war against the mightiest patriarchal military state ever seen to that time — that she and warriors like her were to be called bulldikes.

Perhaps Boudica and some of the other Hicca women in that war were ceremonial Lesbians; perhaps like other tribal folk they also had special homosexual gods of their own and special rites concerning their social functions. In any case, through their slang, her descendants and others like them gave to Lesbians — the most rebellious, armed, "masculine," warriorlike, dangerous, and deserving — and give them still the ancient, proud, frightening, street-talk title: *bulldiker, bulldagger, Boudica.*[26]

144

> And so we went to war.
> Our men went with us.
> And for centuries since, the foe has
> searched for us in all our havens,
> secret circles, rings and covens;
> almost always we elude him,
> we who remember who we are;
> we who are never not at war.[27]

Butches and Femmes

Butch is another Gay slang word that makes reference to a particular office or life-role — like *dike* — that a Lesbian-may take on
for herself early in her life. Unlike *bulldike*, which is usually
spoken by a straight person, *butch* and *femme* are words from inside Gay culture, part of the working vocabulary of most American Lesbians.

The "role-playing of butch/femme," as it came to be called
(rather negatively) during the Lesbian/Feminist movement of the
1970s, was in full swing in the Gay bar cultures of the fifties and
sixties and of course remained in many of them during the next
decade as well. It is easy enough to tell from old photographs of
Lesbian couples that the women early in the century used the designations too. You can often tell the butch from the femme in the
pictures of well-known Lesbian couples: Gertrude Stein is certainly butch while Alice B. Toklas is femme; Bryher is butch and
H.D. femme; Vita Sackville-West is butch and Virginia Woolf
femme; Rosa Bonheur is clearly butch in every regard; Radclyffe
"John" Hall was so butch she wore men's underwear, while her
lover Una Lady Troubridge was extremely femme. With other
couples it is not so easy to make the designation. The very butch
Amy Lowell, for instance, called her lover, Ada Russell, "Peter." [28]

*Perhaps Ada and Amy were more like you and I together,
Vonnie dear, for while you were always butch and I was always
femme, anyone had to look close to tell the difference.*

Butch and *femme* are French words. *Femme* derives from
femina, "woman," more literally "who gives suck" or "who nour-
ishes." [29] If the taking on of butch/femme roles were merely the
imitation of male/female roles, we could expect the partner of a
femme to be an "homme," which is French for "man." Gay characteristics, as we have seen with the drag queen and the bulldike,

145

are far more original to the Gay underground culture than they are imitative of the aboveground heterosexual culture. The word *butch* does not derive from *man*, but more likely (and even if it is also short for "butcher," the French *boucher*) it is from the French for goat, *bouc*.[30] This in turn is related to *bucca*, "buck," the male stag, hare, or goat; *buck* is also a slang word used in a derogatory manner in the United States to designate Negro or Indian males and to refer covertly to their recent tribal connections. The stag and the goat, like the bull, were sacred to European tribal people, especially on the continent. Tribes in what is now the nation of France valued the goat in particular. All these animals were part of special festivals and ceremonies, were impersonated as gods, and were sacrificed on certain holy days. The goat-god (a version of the Horned God) and his impersonators were sometimes titled "Puck." Puck, or *puca* (Irish for "elf"), appears in Shakespeare's play *A Midsummer Night's Dream* as a Fairy character who can be played by either a male or a female.

If the ancient ceremonial role of bulldike was fulfilled by the Warrior Queen, the ancient ceremonial role of butch for women was probably a priestess taking the part of Puck — the Fairy goat-god who was sometimes also sacrificed ("bouchered") to keep the people prosperous. This ceremonial office of impersonating the goat-god (in butch drag) was last acted out in the grand public manner by Joan of Arc.

Certainly Joan was the quintessential ceremonial dyke, the warrior maid who listened to Fairy spirit voices under a sacred beech tree, who cropped her hair at the age of sixteen and put on men's clothing and armor because her own spirit voices told her she must do so for the sake of her people and her dauphin, the as yet uncrowned King Charles VII. Joan the Maid ("La Pucelle"), or Maid of God as she would be titled after her death in 1431, perhaps had a beloved female companion, as she preferred to sleep with young girls,[31] but her reputation for innocence and chastity is pervasive and it is doubtful that physical desire troubled her; she had other things to do. Nevertheless Joan is every inch a Gay figure and a ceremonial butch.

After her successful military battles against the English who had invaded her French homeland, she was arrested, accused of paganism, of consorting with fairies, and of cross-dressing. Anthropologist Margaret Murray believed that no hand of her own people was raised to save her because she was a self-chosen sacrifice, a stand-in for the dauphin whose battles she had fought and won.[32]

146

Joan could have saved her own life during her trial by agreeing, as the court suggested, to put aside her men's clothing and to put on a woman's dress, *but she refused,* and this refusal was taken as a signal of tremendous significance by everyone concerned.[33]

Her cross-dressing was apparently a ceremonial decision, a signal to the populace with their still-potent pagan beliefs that she would not give up her special office of Warrior Maid and that she was truly a stand-in sacrifice for the dauphin. As such, she would of course have worn men's clothing. She was burned only after her refusal to give up her men's clothes.

Margaret Murray was convinced that Joan was part of the still-existent Old Religion of Europe and was standing in for the dauphin with the full backing of pagan elements in the army, the royal government, and the populace. Joan not only led and inspired the dauphin's army, she went on to be sacrificed in his place in order to pass on to the people the traditional sacred strength of the office of kingship. In pagan terms, the dauphin was the horned god of the people, the goat-god power, and Joan was the scape-goat, the substitute sacrifice. According to Murray, Joan volunteered, took it upon herself to go to the dauphin as a warrior and save his crown from the foreign invasion because, as she said, her spirit voices instructed her to do so.

Murray thought that Joan was a member of a secret coven whose members helped direct her actions and decisions. Certainly the common people understood her ceremonial nature, and they followed her, a sixteen-year-old girl, into battle and virtually worshiped her person before and after her death. People brought sick children to her for her blessing and asked her advice as though she were already a saint in her lifetime. They valued her butch characteristics of physical courage, short hair, men's clothing, disarming forthrightness, honesty, quiet but intense intelligence, and contact with the Fairy or spirit world. And of course, people valued her piety.

She cross-dressed with great significance, like many another shamanic Gay person fulfilling a particular office in her or his society. She had self-containment and the kind of integrity that takes its value from within or from natural or spiritual elements rather than from the worldly marketplace of ideas. She was a model dyke of high degree, a warrior-maid, the female Puck, a ceremonial butch, Maid of God, and a woman with whom many Lesbians have identified.

Baby Butch in the Modern World

I certainly identified with Joan of Arc. And I was a tomboy, of course. It is no exaggeration to say that in general women who become dykes were known as tomboys when they were children. Of course, many aggressive, athletic, rambunctious tomboys never become Lesbians, and many Lesbians were never tomboys. Nevertheless, having once been a tomboy is a major theme in the life stories of a great majority of Gay women, especially those designated in Gay culture as dikes, and especially those dikes who are particularly butch. In England, a slang word for Lesbian is *tom*.[34] *Tomboy* is also an old and perhaps spirit-based word, for one of the witches persecuted in England during the thirteenth century was accused by the authorities of having an imp, or spirit, in the form of a grey cat whose name was Tomboy.[35]

My mother tells me that at the age of three or four I invented or perceived an imaginary imp or playmate who went everywhere with me; no street could be crossed unless I first held his hand to make certain he was safe; no goodnight passed but that he must get a kiss too. And this little character, my innocent and unworldly mother has told me I told her, was named Butchie. I fought to wear pants at the age of five, and the snapshots my mother took of a curly-haired, pink-dressed person were all contrived, family lies. For at heart and at every opportunity I was a tomboy — out on a limb, up on a ledge, down a chimney, adrift on a raft, playing mumblety-peg barefoot with toes spread, daring some other child to throw the knife. I identified myself not only as Jo in *Little Women*, but as a pirate, cowboy, soldier, doctor, lumberjack, and, finally, adventurous writer in all my games and stories. Alone all day, I chose to play with my father's sparse property: knives, a handsaw, pistols, rifles, a machete, a bandana, bull's horns. Stomping around our tiny apartment in my brother's enormous engineering boots, sneaking a shotglass from the top kitchen shelf and repeatedly filling it with double shots of Pepsi Cola, I practiced becoming a tough-talking frontier drunkard while engaging in terse cowboy dialogues with the spirits who surround isolated eleven-year-old tomboys. That was the year I made myself a Roman breastplate out of beer-can tops. Later I would memorize Shakespeare's speeches by Marc Antony and Julius Caesar, having already become completely familiar with the metal and the leather, the postures and the play-acting of a man's world.

As a brazen twelve-year-old I sexually courted an unsuspecting married woman until her husband's astute suspicions interfered: "Are you sure she's supposed to lay her head on your breast like that?" he would ask worriedly. "But like *that*?" I loved her big firm breasts, and her big-boned body, and her thick blond hair. For the next two years I courted Pamela, a girl one year younger than I, going with her everywhere she would dare to go with me, pedaling madly on our bicycles, showing off to get attention, putting my arm around her shoulder in the movie house, overstaying my welcome at her large, well-kept house, writing her passionate philosophical poems. Her mother did not allow her to go to my house, for we were poor and in disgrace, I suppose. Their maid had as much social standing as my family did, perhaps more. They had a piano that Pamela played with much sneering and reluctance, while I hung over her, panting for a chance to get my hands on the keyboard. Pamela was outwardly a very boring person with little in the way of personality showing, self-control being her major attribute; consequently, I could imagine anything about her and it *might* be true. I imagined her as a brave, adventurous person who was completely crazy about me.

At night I would sneak out a window and go to her house and throw pebbles against her window, as I had read in romantic boys' stories, especially Mark Twain. She would crawl out her window and we would ride for miles in the moonlight on our bicycles. During these episodes I called her Tom Sawyer, and I called myself the more renegade and lower-class Huck Finn, my version of early butch/femme based on class difference. One night my mother caught me sneaking back in and was terribly angry. I explained, stuttering, that I had heard a noise and, thinking it was a prowler, had gone to investigate. She praised my courage. I felt very heroic.

Romeo and Juliet Replayed

Good-night, good-night! parting is such sweet sorrow
That I shall say good-night till it be morrow.
Sleep dwell upon thine eyes, peace in thy breast!
Would I were sleep and peace, so sweet to rest! [36]

In 1954 a peculiar, small, Levi-clad figure strode boldly along the silent streets of a small class-bound southwestern town, reciting Shakespeare in a loud voice and plainly ready for any mischief. At fourteen I was ready to move on to more exciting body contact than holding sweating hands, hoping Pamela felt more than some girlish crush. I wanted to kiss Pamela, who had by her actions, or rather her lack of negative actions, led me to believe she liked me a lot, and I thought I had found a foolproof method of bringing up the subject of kissing in a nonthreatening manner. Shakespeare! Literature! Shakespeare was going to help me kiss Pamela. Oh good for you, Shakespeare. It happened that both Pamela and I were invited to a timely sleepover party at the house of her best friend, Jo Ellen. Riding merrily to Jo Ellen's house on my trusty blue bicycle, with a hard-earned copy of *Romeo and Juliet* in my back pocket, I was very disappointed to arrive and learn that Pamela's mother had not allowed her to come. And no one else had been invited. Oh no. All my scheming and rehearsals would be for nothing unless — did I dare? Did I dare to try to kiss Jo Ellen? Did I even *want* to kiss Jo Ellen? She was so crazy. You could never tell what she would do. But so what? I would try it.

Jo Ellen was a strange person, extremely thin and anemic to the point of translucence. She did not exactly move, she flitted in a sideways direction and then abruptly came to rest. She had boyish bushy hair and was very nervous. Both she and Pamela were under increasing pressure to be respectable, to be on display at the country club, to prepare to take a highly regulated place among the elite of the town. What was a horsey crooked-toothed character like me doing at her house? I didn't know. She had invited me. Now she lay stiffly beside me in a sleeping bag stretched out on the floor of her parents' garage. I was reading *Romeo and Juliet* to her by flashlight and asking if she wanted to read a scene with me. She did, and I had it carefully prepared and marked, a scene in which Romeo kisses Juliet. First we just read the lines out loud, and that went fine. Then I suggested we do it again, only this time, I said, "We could act out the actions."

"OK," she said.

"And when we get to the part where Romeo kisses Juliet, Romeo will kiss Juliet," I said.

"OK," she said.

"OK," I said, "I'll be Romeo."

"OK," she said. She lay perfectly still on her back. This made me terribly uneasy because of its similarity to the joke in *Romeo and Juliet* about Juliet spending a lot of her time on her back once she was married, a joke I hated. Why did being married involve lying on the back, I wondered in horror. It sounded slavish to me.

Nevertheless, my fourteen-year-old heart thumped and whacked as we read the romantic lines of the play, and when I got to the kissing place I leaned over and kissed Jo Ellen's warm though will-less mouth like a passionate grown-up lover. Her green eyes widened and she seemed a little amazed, but she did not respond or twitch or say anything, and as the silence deepened and I said, "Well," and she said, "Well." I got nervous myself, feeling I had slid into water way over my head. What if Jo Ellen spread the news at school or among the adults that I had taken it into my head to kiss her and left out the part about Shakespeare? And about its only being a play? I decided nothing would help except to get her to be committed and as far in over her head as I was, and the way to do that was to induce her to make an aggressive sexual move.

"Well," I said as firmly as I could manage in the breathy atmosphere, "now it is your turn to be Romeo, and I'll be Juliet." I laid out flat and stiff on my back in imitation of her and waited. This time the pause was as deep as a well and as wide as a barn door.

Then her voice came. "OK," and she raised up on one elbow to read by the gleam of the flashlight on the floor by my ear. We got to the vital part, and then she stopped. "Well, come on," I said, impatient with sudden social terror. "Romeo kisses Juliet. It's in the play." And to my intense relief she leaned over to kiss me. Then just before her lips arrived a massive earth-rattling, thundering-end-of-the-world banging began in one side of my head that drove me into an instant frenzy and sent me hollering and pounding my poor skull on the cement floor. Had lightning struck, or psychosomatic illness? No. Drawn by the flashlight, a simple-minded moth had bumbled into my ear and was thrashing its great wings against my eardrum. The result was similar to being in a load of cement inside a cement mixer.

Humiliation followed, Jo Ellen's mother having to be called to warm some oil and pour it into my ear canal to drown the idiot, and when everything settled back into place with the moth blissfully dead and washed away, Jo Ellen had retreated into a deep, complete, nervous silence.

I saw both her and Pamela a few more times, and something volcanic must have built up in our tense relationships. Both of them were under increasing pressure from their parents to voluntarily drop me as a friend, particularly as they were beginning to attend Rainbow Star dinners and Cotillion dances where their formal gowns billowed awkwardly around their skinny, undeveloped bodies, and the fact that the children of cooks and clerks were excluded was what gave the event half its meaning. Jo Ellen and Pamela were cultivating the closed, artificially smiling faces and tight nasal voices of women expected to direct servants. I was of

151

the altogether wrong class to follow them along their narrow and difficult path. However winsome and appealing, my pirate Huck Finn ways could no longer be tolerated; soon I would be banished from Pamela's life. Never again would she say a word to me, even in the hallway at school, let alone be Tom Sawyer to my Huck Finn.

The last summer afternoon before my banishment from the kingdom of the Cotillion, we were all three together when something strange happened with the flitty Jo Ellen. Perhaps her thirteen-year-old mind just went berserk. That afternoon as I got to Jo Ellen's front door, Pamela met me. "Go upstairs," she ordered anxiously. "Jo Ellen is acting funny."

As I leaped up the stairs to the rescue, Jo Ellen charged out of her parents' bedroom holding a loaded derringer. Rushing down the first step and then steadying the blunt-nosed pistol with both hands, she aimed at the center of my astonished forehead just six inches away and pulled the trigger two or three times. Enraged when the derringer failed to fire, she continued down the steps aiming at Pamela, chasing her out of the house and across a field. The wispy and outwardly passive Jo Ellen had out-butched everyone and had gotten the plot all screwed up and was trying to murder Romeo, Juliet, everybody! We never mentioned the incident; it wasn't a terribly unusual occurrence, given the number of pistols, rifles, and unexploded bombs in any household in our little town. Well, goodnight, Jo Ellen; goodnight, Pamela and Huck and moonlit rides; goodnight! goodnight! Romeo and Juliet, goodnight!

Butch to Femme in One Easy Step

The only day in my life I voluntarily wore a dress was the day I went to my first lover. Unsophisticated and untraveled, unmoneyed and extremely optimistic, I put on a red quilt jumper and a white blouse from Penney's Dry Goods to ride the Greyhound bus seven hundred meandering southwestern miles for my "elopement" to a love so secret no one from my high school would guess for years what I was really doing.

Feeling certain that my dress would win her heart, I arrived in my lover's life like some bright-red, short-haired, self-created pagan bride. Yvonne came to meet me in her black cowboy hat and black boots, clean-pressed Levis and the Future Farmers of America jacket she had worn when she was rodeo queen of her diminutive town. With a dazzling open-hearted smile illuminating her handsome brown face and shiny eyes, with her expressive voice kept in the soft lower ranges, her well-kept muscles and strong square hands, she was the perfect dyke. Moreover, she was smart, proud, ambitious, and she had a strongly developed social conscience. Though I never again wore a dress except for the direct necessity of keeping a job, and not always then, we began our life together clearly organized as butch and femme. Our first two lovers' squabbles were about her needing to be more publicly daring and my not knowing how to cook well enough to cook for her. Yet in spite of our pretense I was as butch as she, and I hated having to play the femme, especially when she used it to get out of doing household chores.

We dykes of the fifties and sixties were not like the other women around us; our gestures, our manner of dressing, our expectations of life, our bodies and carriage, our philosophy were all different. We would be spinsters, we knew, and self-supporting, and sometimes painfully socially isolated. We would learn to defend ourselves and each other. We were also sexually active as our mothers and even our sisters were not, but we never said this openly. The fact that our kind were so completely misunderstood made us skeptical of authoritative ideas and the complacent acceptance of surface appearances. We would be quick to notice other forms of social injustice. We lived in two worlds at once, neither of them comfortable or safe. Unlike the women around us who schemed to capture husbands by putting out signals of helplessness, we kept our bodies physically active, and though we didn't dare show them to anyone except each other, we had a big bad butchy secret — we had muscles.

Yvonne was especially proud of her sturdy, athletic body, which was beautiful and solid and skilled. She concentrated on difficult acrobatic accomplishments. At nineteen she was one of only two athletes in the state who could do a triple back flip on the trampoline. Leaping and leaping until she was high on a column of thin air, suddenly her head would snap, her legs would pull up to her chest and over and over she would go, backward, like a rolling rock, to land balanced, graceful, and triumphant with her big grin, and then duck her head modestly and give out an "Aw-shucks-twarn't-nothin'" remark when she was praised.

"There's no such thing as a 'boy's way' of throwing a ball and a 'girl's way,' " she told me, greatly excited by this information. "There's just knowing the *way* to throw it, and then there's *not* knowing. Boys teach it to each other. Girls throw in that awful dishrag way because no one teaches them differently."

Years later I went to bed with a woman, a feminist, who had the muscleless blobby flesh most women at the time claimed was "natural," or at least "appealing to men." She was amazed at my flesh. "Oh — you have a *hard* body," she exclaimed. "Most women are crippled," she said. My Lesbian lovers and my own dyke identification had never allowed my muscles and sinews to atrophy as hers had, for I have always expected physical tenacity and butchness in my lovers and they have expected the same in me. Even Von, who also wanted me to be femme. But not *that* femme. Of course, there have always been aphysical Lesbians and plenty of heterosexual women on ball teams — especially now in the eighties when the country is under so much Gay influence and crisscrossing of traditional sex roles.

Once, in the old days when I was living in a situation where I was isolated from other Lesbians, I made a painting of a woman. In an era when few women wore pants, she wore pants that hung a little below her waist, just tight enough to show off the shape of her narrow hips and muscled thighs. Shirtless, she had medium-sized round breasts with erect nipples, broad shoulders, and muscled arms. She faced forward, fisted hands balanced on her hips, meeting your eyes directly when you looked at her face, which had a serious expression. She had very short hair and delicate features. My heterosexual roommate was very upset by the painting, spending two hours impatiently lecturing to me that women did not look like this and that what was wrong with me and my painting was that I had no idea what women look like. Because I was already in a great deal of trouble for being Gay, I could not explain to her that most of the women I had been to bed with looked precisely like my painting; in fact, if I myself gained ten pounds and stood up straight I would have looked precisely like my painting. I certainly couldn't tell her that the title of my painting was *The Butch*.

Establishing the Lesbian Bond

Within any era, the external appearances of the bond between two women vary according to what the society expects, tolerates and defines as a bond. When our society stressed the man-wife bond, many Lesbians formed the extreme butch-femme bond so evident in the 1950s. When the Lakota Indians stressed maternity as a prerogative for being truly a tribeswoman, *koskalaka* "Lesbians" bonded "in the spirit of Doublewoman" and ceremonially forged a "rope baby" between them to seal the bond and make it public. When class relations are most rigidly adhered to, the roles of lady/maidservant or mistress/handmaiden or author/secretary prevail as the models for two women together. When property rights are most at stake, the women formally marry each other and adopt each other's children, one of them taking on "father-owner" status.[37] When shamanism, sorcery, and access to the spirit world are a major part of social relations, two Lesbians or two Gay men together may be shaman/apprentice or priest/novice. Among movement Lesbians during the 1970s in America, butch/femme was criticized and suppressed in favor of partnerships (often business partnerships) that stressed an equality of dikeness distributed between both partners.

Probably no matter what society is examined, same-sex bonds will be found that formalize along social lines using roles recognizable to society, yet across cultural lines the *bond* is essentially the same and for the same purposes — to strengthen the position of women in the society, for instance, to model alternatives to existing forms, and to retain older traditional forms in danger of being lost.

Butch and femme, the two extreme social roles of modern underground Lesbians in industrialized societies, seem on the surface to be simple-minded imitations of man/wife roles developed by heterosexual culture. And some Lesbians do act them out to an extreme, with one woman in short hair and men's clothing, the other in a dress and high heels. This is especially true of the proud working-class Lesbians, both Black and white, among whom the butch and her lady will dress to the teeth for a weekend date and have a hell of a good time. However, unlike "man and wife," the participants in butch and femme are often interchangeable, or actually much more similar than their Saturday-night garb indicates. The following excerpt from "My Lady Ain't No Lady" by Pat Parker illustrates the point:

> my lady ain't no lady —
>
> she has been known
> to speak in a loud voice
> to pick her nose,
> stumble on a sidewalk,
> swear at her cats,

swear at me,
scream obscenities at men,
paint rooms,
repair houses,
tote garbage,
play basketball,
& numerous other
un lady like things.

my lady is definitely no lady
which is fine with me,

cause i ain't no gentleman.[38]

When I was a young dike trying to stay alive in the ghetto of the city of Washington, D.C., I found my place in a scroungy downtown low-life bar. There we young dikes tried out the different aspects of butch and femme as though our entire future depended on the outcome.

One small woman, Tonie, went to the wildest extremes. A dental assistant who had been evicted from the marines for being a Lesbian, she would arrive at ten o'clock, with much ado, as Tonie the Butch. Decked out in a man's black tuxedo with black, polished shoes, a man's handkerchief, cuff links, her short red hair plastered to her head with Vitalis, she would ask all the femmes to dance. The next night she would appear, with the same amount of drama, totally transformed and nearly unrecognizable as Tonie the Femme, with a flaming red dress, mascara and lipstick, high heels, hair fluffed out and piled on her head, a little brown beauty mark decorating one cheek. She was trying out the extremes of how to be "in the life," as we sometimes called being Gay.

Most of us tried out the roles in moderation, using a slight modification of hair style. (Is it behind her ears? She must be butch. Does it resemble bangs? She must be femme.) Or we used the difference between a "blouse" and a "shirt." We would lead with one dancing partner, follow with another. Since the butch was the one who requested the dance, it took much nerve to learn to be aggressive toward another woman and to risk being rejected out loud in front of your buddies. On the other hand, the femme role seemed boring and even more nerve-wracking since it involved waiting for another, perhaps equally shy woman to hurry up and get aggressive toward you. Few of us novices wanted to be femmes or knew much about the art of being femmes, so we tried hard to be accepted by each other as butches.

The heterosexual male model is by no means the only factor involved in the mannerisms of butch women. There is a tradition, for instance, of short-cropped hair for Western women that is not connected to the short haircuts of men. (The male military haircut, the crewcut, was developed for the purpose of detecting and preventing lice in the close quarters of barracks life.)

Ancient Greek vases show short-haired women together, including some who were clearly Lesbians. One of Sappho's poems describes how young women cut their hair in mourning when one of their number, Timas, died unexpectedly and, "unmarried, went to Persephone's dark bedroom." [39] Cutting the hair was evidently a purification rite, or a sacrifice to a special power. Both Persephone and her striking mother Demeter are often shown as short-haired, dikish-looking women, as are numerous other goddesses, especially the arrow-bearing Artemis and the three intriguing friends Leto, Themis, and Hera, shown lounging over each other's laps in warm attitudes of sexual friendship. In Rome, the vestal virgins whose task was to tend the eternal flame, which once represented the interior power of the female, were required by their office to be short-haired, as were Roman Catholic nuns until recently.

Though I had believed for years that American dikes wore short hair in direct imitation of men and as an aggressive rejection of the perception of "femaleness" as a form of slavery, I saw for myself how waves of extreme hair-cropping took place in the Lesbian feminist movement at a time when the styles for men's hair had been long for years. The women were cutting their hair to become dikes, not to imitate men.

But however well I imitated the butches in that particular competitive underground bar scene, I soon learned I was not going to make it as a butch, at least not all of the time, and not even after I had screwed up all my courage to buy a pair of men's loafers. The shoes were so well made, they had so much more leather in them than women's shoes, I still treasure the memory of the weight of them. And I had found some friendly male barbers who thought nothing of cutting a young dike's hair any way she wanted it, no small feat in those harshly role-bound times. All day at work I combed my hair one way, then at night I put on pants and a boy's jacket, combed my hair another ("opposite") way, and went to my other life at the bar. Still, I could not sustain a relationship with another woman unless I modified my clothes and undertook to be the femme.

157

Once, more recently, a friend of mine took an informal head count in a Lesbian bar in "liberated" San Francisco. She found that few women wanted to say they were femme; one table of eight responded with eight enthusiastic butches, though some were in couple relationships with each other. These women were all highly active feminists; they were also traditional American dikes.

The Butch Is a
Magical Figure

For the purpose of attempting an explanation, admittedly simplistic, let me say that for Lesbians involved in the underground Gay culture, the butch is, ceremonially speaking, Puck. Cross-dressing is a magical function, and the butch is the equivalent of the traditional cross-dresser who may also become a magical/shaman of the tribe. She is the one who cross-dresses, becomes a hunter or a sooth-sayer or a prophet or the first woman in a formerly all-male occupation. She keeps the idea of biological destiny untenable. She usually takes on butchness as a lifelong destiny, irrespective of whether she has a lover. As a single individual she may act out the role of spinster or of the hermit who prefers living alone in the mountains or consorting with animals to the company of humans.[40] Conversely, she may fit in perfectly with masculine company as "one of the boys."

As the butch of a European tribe, she would have taken on the garb and the persona of the Horned God, or "devil," during the witch coven meetings or other festive gatherings of pagan times. In her modern form she is still entitled to wear leather, to decorate her body with tattoos and heavy jewelry in the ancient tribal manner, to walk and carry her body in the old way of the cross-dressing female. She is a child of Oya, of Artemis, of Wila Numpa, of the Amazons, of the Valkeryes, and of Joan of Arc.

In the tribal societies, as the accounts have described the cross-dressing butch Lesbian, she often married women who were not necessarily ceremonial dykes themselves, who were not butch in the same sense she was. These women, let us suppose, were "femmes" of the tribe or village, were regular women, were ceremonial femmes, were women with full female powers, being "wisewomen," "the Mother" (in the sense of creator), or "the High Priestess." No stigma attached to the femme when she married the

158

butch, and apparently no special "Lesbian" status attached to her either. The femme's next lover was as likely as not to be a man.

In our society such public marriage between women is prohibited, and the status of womanhood is greatly reduced. There are no ceremonial femmes as there are no ceremonial butches, no daughters of Oshun or Aphrodite as there are no daughters of Oya or Diana, in any publicly acknowledged sense. The contemporary dike is almost always forbidden to openly court women and to marry. I could never have married Jo Ellen or Pamela, for instance.

There are examples in recent history of women "passing" as men and marrying women, simply by tricking everyone. And there are, of course, plenty of Lesbian couples who manage to slip by, with a "Boston marriage," as the secret Lesbian bond has been called in that city. There are many butch women who become lovers with femme women, even openly in their neighborhoods in some sectors. However, there is no social sanctioning for such unions, and there are no public ceremonies celebrating them in straight society. The tradition of the ceremonial butch, like that of her male tribal counterparts, the *Winkte* or *Mahu*, gave her a special place in the village or clan; she has been almost entirely displaced in modern society.

Modern Dykes Have Had to Marry Each Other

The dyke, or butch woman in our society, unlike many societies in the past, has been an outcast figure. Women who have sexual/love relations with a dyke are themselves placed in the special, outcast category of "Lesbian" and usually feel the need to vehemently deny Lesbianism in order to return to ordinary female status after having one or two relationships with butch Lesbians. As I know from my brief experience in the military service, even *knowing* or being seen in the company of an open Lesbian may be considered grounds for suspicion of being a Lesbian.

In the prohibitive society of the 1950s American women would not risk the losses such a stigma entailed. I have met dozens of women who wanted to have a sexual and emotional relationship with a woman during that period of time and did not dare. And so the ceremonial dykes of the day gathered in little enclaves both rural and urban and married each other; in the case of Von and myself, I had to give in and play the femme although I much preferred being seen as a butch. I am as much of a cere-

159

monial dike as she was, and I resented giving up any of my hard-won subterranean status. Those parts of our society which are closer to the tribal traditions (including what is called "lower class" and the old aristocracy of Europe and England) are more likely to maintain the classic butch, a cross-dressing, assertive woman whose lovers are femmes. The femme of this kind is indistinguishable in any way from the other women of her group and is usually very assertively "feminine," wearing makeup, vulnerable pretty clothing, high heels, and in general displaying the full powers of the female.

Among middle-class American Lesbians, extreme butch-femme polarities are tempered. The dykes simply disguise both members of their relationship in a modified drag known as "Lesbian," with perhaps one haircut a little shorter, one voice thrown a little lower, or some other distinguishing butch mark. The couple probably makes a few jokes about it now and then, meanwhile following feminist movement rhetoric by maintaining that "roles" are "patriarchal" and beneath our advanced consciousness.

The reality is that we, who would formerly have been considered ceremonial dikes, are now mass-culture Lesbians who have been excluded from our own villages and towns by homophobia and antitribalism and are having to re-form in urban or semiurban settings where the more overtly Gay people are partially ghetto-ized, while the rest are heavily closeted.

The new urban manner of being Gay has produced a "middle gender" (sometimes called in Gay jargon "the clone") that combines qualities considered masculine and feminine in the society at large. We cross-dress — a little. Maybe keys hang at the belt, or one earring is sported, something a little out of balance. In this mass-cultural Gay movement, there is less presence of the extreme butch woman, and of the drag queen as well. Everyone is a little butch, and a little femme at the same time. Because we can no longer easily live as the openly Gay members of our "village" — that is, our American hometown, neighborhood, ethnic group, or church — we are propelled into the world at large. We are forced to become Gay people, to act out our traditional functions in the national context of mass culture. In so doing we lead mass cultural movements, we press for more balance among human beings; we practice combining a greater number of diverse characteristics in one life. A more cosmopolitan person and a more cosmopolitan culture emerge from this combining of traits from different sexual sectors of the population.

This is a very interesting and good thing, this modern way of being Gay. We are forced to the cusp between psychological worlds, between the objective and subjective in an individual life. This gives us a particularly balanced position from which to view our society, to make social statements by our very way of being two women together, and two men together; and it enables us to make a balance between what is considered male and female. And if this is painful to accomplish, it's also ingenious in the insights it produces.

I think the word *butch* will remain with us in underground Gay culture, as a useful description of another way of being a female, and "butch-femme" relationships as another form of marriage besides male-female or man-wife. Butch, like bulldike, designates a Lesbian office, one with apparently quite a long history.

In the old times, Von, you scoundrel, you could have "married" one of the women you knew in northern New Mexico, or perhaps several of them, in succession. They would not have been Gay, particularly, just married to you for a while; you would have functioned like a man as well as a shaman — dike. But in our time you could not make such a marriage of course. Lesbianism was anathema to all the people you knew. So you secretly married me, another dike who was willing to take the social risks, since after all, being Gay is my life. To marry you I had to restrain some of my butch impulses and play the femme for you. Then the two of us together went out into the world (well it was more like lurching out into the world, but we got there). We acted out our Gay natures on a stage much larger than our hometowns could have provided. Like other Americans, we became national. We claimed several major cities as home; we thought of our people as all people. We sought out the company of other Gay people who had also been forced to seclude themselves away from the group of their birth.

161

CHAPTER SEVEN

Riding with the Amazons

Adolf Hitler allegedly dreamed of fighting a trio of naked Amazons riding through space. He broke his spear against one of them in a vain attempt to kill her, for he was sure the Amazons were really Jews. His doctor, Kurt Krueger, interpreted the dream in the light of Hitler's past as a symbolic effort to arrive at sexual normalcy.

Kurt Krueger, *I Was Hitler's Doctor*[1]

Von, you were so butch, and in the middle of an era when few women were wearing pants, let alone tuxedos and sideburns. You wore heavy silver jewelry, men's sweaters and Levis, boots, cuff links, and never any makeup. You had a direct gaze and a guileless manner. I believe you got away with it because of your ability to use genuine charm. Because of the — how shall I say it? — purity of your soul, my mother was able to come to terms, if not with my Lesbianism (the word had too many negative meanings for her), at least with my love for individual women.

After nearly losing your teaching credentials when the Air Force told your college that you were connected to me, an open Lesbian, you stayed away from me for two years. How I begged you, to get you to come back to me. I even sent you money to ensure that you would make the thousand-mile trip, so you would know how seriously in love with you I was and how much I needed you. I simply couldn't launch my life without you. And you came back to live with me even though it meant risking your credentials all over again, for I was angry and restless for a better life for Gay people. I persuaded you to march in a Mattachine picket line for Gay rights, two of fifteen marchers in front of the White House and with the real threat of permanent unemployment if we were seen by the wrong people. The risk for me was not so great, since "writer" was what I intended to become. You were a teacher; you could have lost everything.

When I brought you home to meet my parents during the second period when we lived together, after 1963, my mother took me aside in the kitchen for a whisper session. The horror of the letter my parents had gotten from the Air Force years before concerning my disgrace and "undesirable" status as a perverted person still shadowed her face. She feared social disapproval above all terrors. Her hands and eyes, however, were fluttering and sparkling with a newfound understanding.

"I can't help liking her," she said of you, using her lowest voice. "She's such a good person, so warm, and smart, and unassuming." My mother's eyes met mine. "Why, she's just like you," she said. "I can't hate her. It would be like hating you." I knew she was surprised at this. "Lesbian" in those days was something filthy and different that came along to wreck your innocent daughter's life. I grinned at her, knowing we were going to become friends again. I knew that once more, Von my hero, you had braved the vast army of social hatred and had won the field.

1981, Los Angeles

MY PRESENT LOVER Paula and I watch an unusual ceremony on television, a parade in honor of the African tribal King of Swaziland. Swaziland is one of the last areas on earth to have kept its preindustrial, precolonial traditions. The vivid parade that catches our attention is of the king's wives, who stride, a dozen abreast, swinging great arched swords in front of themselves, guarding the kingdom.

"Look at that," Paula and I exclaim, "they all look like dykes!" And what looks like "dykes" about them is not their Amazon-style dress that leaves one bare breast or the graceful sword flashing in front, warrior fashion. What catches our American dykish attention is their carriage, their center of balance. The kind of energy they display: their full faces forward, direct eyes, the amount of weight they carry, the work-formed muscle-bulge of their arms, the solid length of their stride. They do not look like men. They do not look like military women soldiers in formation. They do not look like "wives." They look like dykes. That is to say, there is something about the carriage and expression of American dykes we have seen — brown and white and red as well as black — that is similar to the sword-bearing women of still-tribal Swaziland. We look like them.

125th STREET AND ABOMEY

Head bent, walking through snow
I see you Seboulisa
printed inside the back of my head
like marks of the newly wrapped akai
that kept my sleep fruitful in Dahomey
and I poured on the red earth in your honor
those ancient parts of me
most precious and least needed
my well-guarded past
the energy-eating secrets
I surrender to you as libation
mother, illuminate my offering
of old victories
over men over women over my selves
who has never before dared
to whistle into the night
take my fear of being alone
like my warrior sisters
who rode in defense of your queendom

166

disguised and apart
give me the woman strength
of tongue in this cold season.

— Audre Lorde[2]

When I was twenty years old, in 1960, I was rudely arrested in the armed service, confined, searched, interrogated without a lawyer, phone call, or friend for days by raincoat-clad investigators who played "good cop and bad cop" and frightened me into signing a "confession" of "sexual acts" (and thoughts and feelings) done with other women. I was told there was no use trying to fight the charges. My mail was read. Women who expressed too much warmth toward me were investigated. Everyone who knew me in the service was threatened with the same fate unless they stayed completely away from me and out of touch with me. And they did.

Confined to the barracks for three months while the investigation and subsequent undesirable discharge were prepared, I was virtually in solitary confinement — although surrounded by people. Two thousand miles away, my lover Yvonne was also investigated and was nearly denied her teaching credentials, just as she was only weeks away from graduating. She stayed out of any contact with me for two years, for fear that association with me would ruin her career.

But late one night weeks into my isolation in the barracks as I stood ironing my military uniform, by myself as usual in the basement, a woman, another enlistee, appeared and dared to speak to me. She kept in the shadows so I wouldn't recognize her, though I still remember smooth black hair and a white scared face. She whispered, rapidly and with no indication that she was going to deliver an important message, so that I almost missed what she was saying. "We think you're very brave," she said, "to speak up. A bunch of us are with you. But we're afraid to show it. I just wanted you to know. Don't give up." She was shaking. She touched my arm and then vanished quickly up the dark stairs. I lowered my head over the ironing board and wept.

1960, The Captain and the Fricatrice

A tall, sandy-haired ex-schoolteacher, the captain would have been a handsome woman except she had no giving in her person, and her eyes were cold with what I was too young to recognize as cynicism.

"Watch out for Lesbians," she said to my uniformed, obedient self as I stood rigidly in front of her desk. "And let me warn you about just exactly how they operate. They are very underhanded and don't reveal themselves to you. They don't just walk up and say, 'Hello there, I'm a Lesbian.' You'll hardly know what is happening. Instead they'll do things like introduce you to classical music and good books. Then they'll engage you in interesting conversations that may be witty, entertaining, and filled with intellectual ideas. They may invite you to plays or to dinner and serve you some nice wine, have some flowers on the table. Then when your guard is down and you trust them and like them, they will seduce you to try to get you to bed with them."

The captain spoke a stern warning. Exactly as though she had once absorbed the warning of Leo Africanus, the Roman historian who in 1492 so bitterly described the Sahacat of North Africa as Fricatrices, despising the "venerie" of Lesbian sorcerers who "seduce" young women into their own company and away from their husbands.

The captain owned a tiny, ugly dog that had gotten loose and was under her immense desk. She ordered me to crawl under the desk to get the dog, which I had to do or face court-martial for disobedience. I knew she was testing me, and I had the metallic sensation I would remember again years later being strip-searched in a Berkeley jail: Military authority rules by the breaking of pride and dignity as much as by any threat of bodily harm. Nor can anyone humiliate you as deeply as your own.

During the purge of Lesbians that altered life for some of us who were caught up in it, we learned through the underground information network that the captain had been lovers with her handsome, gray-haired first sergeant for something like eighteen years, and every officer on the base knew it. When the uproar of our sacrifice (about ten women from our barracks were purged out of the service for Lesbianism during this time) had died down a little, after the two of them, the captain and the first sergeant, had participated in administering the purge, in arranging the interrogations, arrests, spies, secret information, evidence-gathering, and convictions of enlisted personnel who were accused of Lesbianism or in some cases something even more insidious, "guilt by association," the two blatant officer-lovers were discreetly transferred to a base in Germany so they could continue living together. This information was leaked to us by heterosexual officers who were apparently outraged by the hypocrisy at work. One of them, a male captain, was convinced that if only I went to bed with *him*, I wouldn't get into any more "trouble." But he was wrong. I got into a whole lot more.

1961, Making a Spear of My Own

My parents were sent a letter describing my "crime," and my father, who had been a close friend to me in adolescence, withdrew from me for many years. Although my mother remained warm to me, her devastation plagued her for a decade. She carried the burden of incomprehension and social ostracism alone, having no one with whom to discuss this unspeakable subject, whose very books of indictment were locked from us ordinary citizens.

Discharged into a poor area of Washington, D.C., with $80 and utter demoralization, I worked as a bar maid serving hard liquor to dying winos. I did not believe there was any farther to go on the bottom of society than where I was. But as I found the company of other Gay ex-service people who also had the state fall on their heads, living in an area mixed with people at the bottom of Washington's perpetual ghetto of Blacks and whites and a scattering of Asians, I found that despair has no bottom; it can multiply itself indefinitely, inside the mind and outside.

I took a night job as a sandwich maker and went to laboratory technician school during the days, even though I hated hospital work. But I had to put the pieces of my life back together somehow. The state had declared its hatred of me and my friends and family — with one or two exceptions — declared their fear, contempt, and disgust.

For more than two years, while other idealists of my generation joined the Peace Corps, I thrashed about at the bottom of the well of degradation among the more demoralized of America's people. Then I spent years emerging, fighting, studying, making notes on my own about Gay people I knew. I joined Mattachine Society to picket in a slender line for Gay rights at the White House in 1963, and by then Yvonne had come back to me and marched too. *Life* magazine printed pictures of Gay men and women who looked like me and quoted a cop saying we were germs.

Using a pseudonym (Carol Silver?), I wrote a pro-homosexual

article for *Sexology Magazine* in 1964, the first I had seen in print in any magazine except our own Lesbian *Ladder*. I met Barbara Gittings and she came from Philadelphia to talk to us. She was editor of the virtually underground Lesbian magazine. She spent an afternoon trying to persuade me to take over the editorship of the magazine. But I didn't have confidence in my abilities; I didn't know my knowledge was real, that *I* was an expert on the subject of Lesbianism, by virtue of experience, courage, writing skill, and brains. I did not know that organizing autonomously for their rights and history and cultural traditions and rightful place in society is *all* that people ever have, that this is the weapon, territory, nation, power. All the rest is despair, the whining of dogs who cannot speak, except to beg for bones.

The *Ladder* of Barbara Gittings passed into the hands of Barbara Grier, who changed its formal, legalistic format to a more popular Lesbian culture vessel. I became a poet and a leftist, going to San Francisco with Wendy Cadden. In 1969–1970 we formed a separatist Lesbian/feminist organization and then a woman's press, The Women's Press Collective, which published mostly Lesbian work for eight years until its merger with another Lesbian publisher, Diana Press. Beleaguered with difficulties and having taken some unpopular political stances, Diana Press crashed in a hail of attack, physical and psychological and economic; the group of us were not functional as publishers after 1978.

Meantime other independent Lesbian presses had grown up. In 1964 I had begun doing research on the nature of Gay people in society. I had taken notes on Lesbian couples I knew, then I had to destroy my notes when I heard through the underground grapevine that such material was illegal and was being confiscated by government agents in New York City.

In 1974 I took up the research task again, not stopping this time until I had finished a book, this book. This book is a spear from my good right arm, fiery arrow from my well-earned bow, and shield, and horse, and tent, and blanket, and comrade in this hard war. This book I have lived with longer than I have with some of my lovers and I have known it longer than some of my friends; this book is my flaming sister-in-arms. May she flame for centuries.

3000 B.C.

Historically, there were two distinct groups of Amazon peoples on the European and African continents. The oldest were Libyan, in

Northwest Africa; some stories connect them to the continent Atlantis, off the coast of Africa. They were known not only as warriors but as founders of cities. One well-known queen, Myrina, took her wandering army on a tremendous trek across North Africa, through Egypt, up through the islands of Greece and around the coast of Anatolia, establishing cities. Throughout the northern areas there were local monuments, called "Amazoneia," established by local people who hailed them as liberators and told legends about their adventures.

Most of the cities they founded were in the area of Ionia and were named for their own female generals: Myrine, Mytilene, Elaia, Anaia, Gryneia, Kyme, Pitane, Smyrna, Latoreia near Ephesus, and Ephesus itself, said to have been ruled by an Amazon queen, Smyrna. Dressed in red leather, carrying moon-shaped shields and bows, the Libyan Amazons were the targets of one of the giant-killing chores assigned to the patriarchal hero Heracles.

Etymologists have attempted to trace the word *Amazon* from *mazos*, "breast" plus *a*, "without," to get the word "without breasts," for stories have long circulated that the Amazons had to mutilate themselves by removing one breast in order to handle a bow and arrow. Others have tried to make the word "without bread," without grain; and of course the implication is always that they were "without men." The Amazons ruled in some places for four or five thousand years; it seems unlikely that they were without anything. The derivation of the word *Amazon* that I prefer is listed by Donald Sobol and is from a Phoenician word meaning "Motherlord." [3]

The Amazons characteristically ruled with a two-queen system; one queen was in charge of the army and battle campaigns, the other staying behind to administer the cities. And although they were ferocious and merciless in battle, once a people had given in, the Amazons were known for ruling with justice. Because of this they were often hailed in an area as a liberating army, and monuments were raised by the local people to praise and honor them. It is said that in their army life the warrior women had only two rules: no lying and no stealing.

Sometime after the Libyan Amazons had played out their part on the stage of history, a second group of women warriors arose, this time in the south of Europe, near the Caucasus region of the Black Sea, along the River Thermidon. Their home city was Themiscyra, and they pitted themselves against the young men of the rising Greek states, who were so impressed that they considered the defeat of the women their greatest victory. And, incidentally, although for a thousand years and more after the passing of the Amazons, their sculptors and artists depicted them in real-life battle scenes hundreds of times, not a single representation showed an Amazon with a breast missing, although typically they did have one breast *showing* because of the way they arranged their tunics. Stories of a breast missing did not happen until much later, as a kind of scare-story to imply that "men's weapons" (tools, cars, planes, horses, knives, guns, muscles, sports, animals) were too dangerous for women to attempt to use.

At the city of Ephesus the Amazons established a shrine and a magnificent statue to the Goddess Artemis. The skirt of Artemis is covered with breasts, which have been erroneously called "sacrificed Amazon breasts" by modern writers seeking an image to fit the rumors. Nothing about the statue could be further from the image of sacrifice, amputation, or blood. The breasts cover the front of her long formal skirt, and they are rich, ripe, full breasts in the prime of their lives, sensual, exuberant, and giving. On her crownlike hat and in her necklace are carved animal heads — cows, goats, and camels. All of these are herd animals, all of them give milk as an important contribution to the cultures that keep them. And their breasts, too, are included in some of the carvings. A few fruits and four-lobed flowers also form part of the motif of the great, stunning, sometimes black and sometimes white statue, but the overwhelming image is that of the giving of milk, of the breast in both its human and herd animal form. This beautifully wrought, warm, lush image is the opposite of the biased picture of brutally mutilated female warriors patriarchal mythology would like us to believe the Amazons were. Far from being "without breasts," their finest religious statues say the opposite: For them, the breast was essential, aesthetic, economic, and all-giving. The idea that women have to sacrifice something personal of themselves, to "unwoman" themselves, to practice war, hunting, athletics, or other arts that have for centuries been considered male-only domains simply doesn't hold up when we consider all the women around the world who have been hunters and warriors without any suggestion that they ever needed to remove any part of themselves to be successful.[4]

In honor and remembrance of her sister Mytilene, Libyan Amazon Queen Myrina established a city named Mytilene on the island of Lesbos. A few centuries later the city of Mytilene would be established for thousands of years in Western history as the home of the oldest surviving woman poet: Sappho. Described as "little and dark" and informally titled "The Black Swan," Sappho in her verse reveals herself as a teacher and a priestess of Aphrodite. She taught daughters sent to her from far-off lands, schooling them in the arts and graces and values suitable to the older matriarchal ways as well as her own tumultuous, clashing world of 600 B.C. Twice exiled for her political views, Sappho taught that pacifism is preferable to tyranny and militarism. Her work advocates protection for wives, appreciation for handwork and fine quality, and the equation of flowers, love, loveliness, and natural beauty with wealth. Extolling sexual love between women as well as giving advice to young brides and grooms, her poetry was sung and was characterized by its extreme popularity, the only thing that saved it from being lost even though it was burned by patriarchal zealots. In a poem of modern times, "Athens," Jacqueline Lapidus gives a succinct list of Sappho's apprentice-lovers. The travel folder for Lesbos, she says, does not say that Sappho slept with women:

> but we're not fooled
> we lock our door at the YWCA
> and fuse, faces flushed,
> palms damp, tongues
> tasting the names of Sappho's lovers:
> Anactoria
> Andromeda
> Atthis
> Damophyla
> Erinna
> Gyrinnô
> Gongyla
> Gorgô
> Herô
> Mnasidika
> Pleistodika
> and Timas of Anatolia who died young
>
> — Jacqueline Lapidus[5]

2000 B.C., Pantariste Avenges Her Lover

Seven individual masculine heroes dominate the mythology of the Greeks, who made the first historical steps from the old gynarchy civilizations of Gaia, Isis, Ma, and Anat with their multi-

173

farious pantheons into the age of the singular male God. Of the seven heroes, no less than three — Bellerophon, Theseus, and Heracles — were sent to pit themselves against the Amazons, true guardians of the older order.

The Greek hero Heracles fought the Amazons of Libya to win the sword of their great queen Hyppolyte. He took with him to do this the bravest heroes and masculine fighters in all of Greece, and they were nearly defeated by the Amazons in a battle that was won only because Heracles had a special weapon, his protective lion skin. The Amazons at first fought him one at a time, out of pride for this way of fighting, and they had lost a number of women before they dispensed with pride and utilized the strategy of encirclement to put him in danger. As they surrounded him, those in the rear attempted to snatch the tail or hanging hind legs of the lion skin and strip it from his body. He fended them off but soon grew hoarse with gasping and red in the face from the great effort, which he was losing. Three Greek captains saw his problem and leaped from their ships to help him. One of them, Tiamides, was singled out for attention by a young Amazon named Pantariste, because his sword had slain her comrade Thraso. I take "comrade" to mean lover, given how fiercely Pantariste avenged her fallen friend. Circling wide away from the other fighters, she approached Tiamides from the side.

According to Donald Sobol,

> Two muscular Greeks contested her path. The first she snared
> by the hair and wrenched off his feet. Holding him down on his
> shield, she stabbed him in the breast before the second Greek
> was upon her. Unable to free her spear, she jumped erect and
> took two steps in pretended flight, then whirled lightly around
> on the tips of her toes. She shot out her hands and clutched
> her surprised attacker by the throat, jerking him to a halt. His
> sword, arrested in mid-stroke, slid weakly from his grasp, and
> he howled like a tortured animal, writhing and tugging at
> Pantariste's wrists. His knees quivered and buckled. The arm
> that had raised the sword to kill her now lifted, palm turned,
> imploring mercy. Pantariste denied him, releasing his throat
> only after the pulse had gone and the light had left his eyes.[6]

Then Pantariste went into her final attack on Tiamides himself. He heard her war cry and knew it was for his ears only. Sobol describes the Amazon as wearing a starry tunic, hair tied in bands of blue, not bothering with shield or helmet, but holding her spear in the air like the athlete she was. Tiamides stopped her spear with his shield, although the impact knocked him off his feet. Then the woman warrior picked up a bloody war-ax, and took his head off with one great, angry swing. Having thus taken vengeance in behalf of her beloved Thraso, she returned to the main battle.

1960, Skeletons in Sergeant Kirk's Closet

Sergeant Kirk was a large, friendly, competent Caucasian woman, not sparkling, woody rather than brilliant or metallic, whose peppery black hair was only beginning to go to salt as she approached her middle years. She had made a career of being a noncommissioned officer in the Air Force, working her way up the chain of command from the bottom to the center. She had joined near the beginning of the establishment of the women's branch of the military, during World War II, when so many American women filled jobs that had traditionally been reserved for men. At least in our millennium, Sergeant Kirk (which is not her name) had many tasks in her responsibility as barracks supervisor for seventy women; she had many tasks and one obsession: Lesbians.

Sergeant Kirk had seen her share of official purges of Lesbians in the military, directed at eliminating the outspoken and daring, especially those who are dark-skinned but including plenty of white women too. She knew what could happen to the too honest and those unwilling to knuckle under to a man's definition of what women should act or look like. Though ostensibly aimed at removing "Lesbians," the purges are actually for the purpose of getting rid of "dikes," that is, the more independent women who have pride, intense loyalties, and strong, often romantic feelings about each other. One early veteran, Pat Bond, who was caught in the first wrenching, catastrophic mass arrest/interrogation program affecting thousands of American servicewomen on the eve of the victory of their army in World War II, fantasizes her own version of how the purges began. "After the American commanding general, General Douglas MacArthur, watched the women soldiers disembark in Japan, he said to his officers, 'I don't care how you do it, but get those dikes out of here.' "[7]

So the "dikes," the ones who had been the first to break with women's traditional roles, the more short-haired, muscular, intense, aggressive, passionate, and woman-identified of the servicewomen were suddenly arrested and charged with the crime of Les-

175

bianism. These women were humiliated, disgraced, isolated from society, turned against each other in vicious police tactics of extracting "confessions" and proof of guilt from their sister GIs, and bounced out of the army they had served with loyalty and trust. They were left without benefits, self-esteem, jobs, and all too often with shattered family ties, since letters were sent to their parents telling of the charges against them. Suicide, psychosis, fear of sex, great mistrust of other women, lifelong terror and bitterness were the fruits of the general's seemingly so casual words "get those dykes out of here."

Sergeant Kirk had safely gotten through *that* big nightmare, and then the others followed with terrifying persistence, sweeping over the intimate world of army bases every few months with stern, repressive edicts from the highest offices, accompanied by officers from the Office of Special Investigation (OSI), dressed in their FBI-type trench coats, opening women's mail to search for innuendos of too much affection, searching rooms for letters or photographs of friends inscribed "with love," training women to act as spies against each other, and conducting interrogations with no lawyers or hint of prisoner's rights in an ongoing war against women that no one talks about.

Sergeant Kirk did her job, gritted her teeth, survived these conditions, and learned to live with them by pretending that she herself was different from the others. They were the overt, the caught, the "criminal" types. She learned to warn the women in her command about the dangers of Lesbianism, how seductive Lesbians can be, what to watch for and be suspicious of in the women around them. "If you see two women kissing," she would say, "even if it's a harmless-looking peck on the cheek, let me know at once. Lesbians can be very sneaky. Or if you see them holding hands, or spending a lot of time together. If you think someone is spending too much time in another woman's room, you let me know at once, because she might be a Lesbian." Women who would not turn another woman in were themselves suspected of being Lesbians.

Sergeant Kirk survived the purges against Lesbians accused of having sexual relations with each other and those accused of *maybe* having sexual relations, or *trying* or *planning* or *wanting* to have sexual relations. And when the military tightened still further, introducing the concept of "guilt by association," meaning that anyone who associates with, is friendly to, spends time around, or even speaks to someone who is believed by the OSI to be a Lesbian is the same as a Lesbian, Sergeant Kirk spoke even louder and even more often about the nefarious evil and horrendous dangers of Lesbians in our midst.

On the other hand, Sergeant Kirk had the curious habit of breaking a cardinal rule prohibiting officers and enlisted drudges from seeing each other socially. This is called a rule against fraternization, brotherhood, though in this case, sororization, sisterhood, between the officer middle class and the enlisted working class is prohibited by the army as it is in the economic system. She liked to single out lowly and lonely enlistees who appealed to her, or perhaps showed symptoms of boldness and intellectual curiosity (as most of us did), and take them to her room after lights out for a game of chess or even in her car to Church's drive-in on the highway toward San Antonio, for a hamburger and a Coke. She did this to me, and I was sometimes naively tempted to want to press her into admitting that she was really a dike underneath all that spy stuff. She had so many familiar mannerisms, a direct gaze, honest, emphatic hands, beautiful New England plain folk's speech. There was something romantic, almost sexual, in her warm eyes. But her remarks about recruits who were being suspiciously friendly stopped me from showing my hand. Since any break from the ugly boredom of barracks life was appealing to any of us, perhaps she just used these little illicit trips as a ploy or bribe to get more anti-Lesbian information.

She made the same friendly overtures to another young woman, who years later and in a different part of the country became a friend of mine and told me parts of the sergeant's story I otherwise would not have known. Kathy Sparks, a tall nineteen-year-old enlistee with a very romantic nature, also went for hamburgers with Sergeant Kirk. She also told her nothing about Lesbians in the barracks since she was too inexperienced to know anything about sex or Lesbianism anyhow. But one weekend Sparks, like almost everyone who has recently entered the military, having no idea what was dangerous, fell into an even worse anti-Lesbian trap. The barracks were full of traps, for the OSI trench coat men had been busy and had developed a new weapon to ferret out the dykes in the army: decoy Lesbians. Earlier that year they had arrested another noncommissioned officer, a thirty-five-year-old sergeant who, like Sergeant Kirk, wanted a lifetime career. Sergeant Johnson had already been in for a decade and had worked her way up to recruiting officer, a pleasant job compared to some, when she was accused of Lesbianism. Confronted with the "proof" against her, she was given another choice. All charges would be dropped and she could stay in the service if she would serve as a spy and catch other Lesbians. She was to do this by using romantic entrapment as her method, and so she did. She invited the sergeant's new favorite, Kathy Sparks, to visit her on a ranch near the base, which was a training base in Texas. Sparks went, and the recruiting sergeant served her a nice dinner and wine, played soft music, and after a while began to make loving overtures to her. When Sparks reciprocated, she was arrested for Lesbianism, taken into custody, interrogated, and badgered into signing a "confession." Her parents were then informed, she was ostracized from the other women and finally discharged three months later with a criminal record, no friends, no skills, no self-esteem, and no idea why this had happened to her.

Then an unexpected thing happened. Sergeant Kirk had an apartment in town, and she very quietly moved the devastated Kathy Sparks into it. They began a strange, intense, highly romantic relationship in which neither was allowed to touch the other, even in the warm manner of friends. Sergeant Kirk brought her presents and flowers, using all the tenderest language of love and affection, up to the point of anything sexual. Sex was taboo. This continued for two years, until Sparks was feeling emotionally well enough to try again to venture into the shocking world by herself, and, leaving the sergeant's care, she got a job in another city.

This is where I met her and heard of her strange affair with Sergeant Kirk. There, although she became a top-notch typist on a newspaper and had the possibility of putting herself through college, for she was very quick, she suffered instead from feelings that she had done a great wrong and deserved punishment. She became a Tragic Figure, keeping company with demoralized minor criminals who wore dark clothes and had violent underpinnings. She often went to a Lesbian bar in the city, and she had two lovers that she kept in a state of rivalry, refusing to live with the one she had sex with, refusing to have sex with the one she lived with. And one night, in a deep fit of despair, she went into an alley and beat her head savagely against a brick wall until she fell bleeding and unconscious. When she was found in the morning, she told the police she had been assaulted by some men. And, of course, she had. She had been assaulted by the entire government and its army two years before.

The story of her "beating" appeared in the paper, and she showed the article to her friends. "Just look at the sort of thing that happens to me," she said. She painted her apartment entirely in black enamel, ceiling and floor too, and she wore black clothing whenever she was off work. She did not recover from this period of her life for many years, although she later finished school and became a college teacher.

As for Sergeant Kirk, she completed her twenty years in the service and retired. She was given a big send-off and a pension and congratulated. She went home to a small town in Minnesota and stayed with her parents. On her first Christmas evening out of the service, having filled herself with liquor, the forty-year-old ex-sergeant climbed heavily onto the steep roof of her parent's home in the middle of the little town and stood knee-deep in the bitter snow. Then she removed every stitch of her clothing. For several hours she stood there, oblivious to all threats or pleading, waving a shirt clutched in one hand, her face turned from the frozen earth as though signaling the fiery stars over her head, and bellowing at the top of her lungs, "I'm Gay! I'm Gay! I'm Gay!" And so she was.

1960, American Military Service

What I loved about my short stint in the military service was the challenge of basic training, the tremendous physical strain, and the demands put on my system to be disciplined — demands rarely made on the young women of that era. Being forced to exercise strenuously and then stand at attention in formation for hours at a time in Texas summer heat while sweat poured down our uniforms in streams that were white with starch dissolved from our uniforms — now that was hard. Not moving a muscle while salty water pours into your eyes is hard, but all of it gave me wonderful muscles and a sense of self-control. Leaping out of bed to the harsh voice of a bellowing loudspeaker at 5:00 A.M. and then having ten minutes to dress, hope for a place in the bathroom to piss and wash was excruciating, embarrassing, and nerve-wracking, but it made me very alert. And having to crawl around on a stinking floor scrubbing all the brown left by total strangers in the toilets and sponging other people's hairs out of sinks while someone in authority stood over me screaming about my deficiencies was terribly, hideously enraging. But it taught me a particular humility without which there can be no real pride of accomplishment. Having my personal letters (in which I had described all of us as looking "like Jane Eyre") confiscated from my bunk and then read aloud to the other recruits to make an example of me (by name) was acutely humiliating, but it taught me a genuine appreciation for the principle of freedom of speech.

And being on barracks guard duty at night helped teach me to be brave. And that bravery comes at a price. Barracks guard was a rotating duty — names were posted on a roster for the four-hour long shift, and we each had to do it about once a week. We could not make up the lost sleep during the day, so it took real discipline to stay awake, since our day's work was long, hot, and physically exhausting. All I ever wanted to do was sleep and eat anyhow. I had learned to sleep while standing up and to eat so fast that even though we had only ten minutes I could manage second helpings if no one caught me.

Staying awake while on guard duty at two o'clock in the morning was hard, and we had to do it alone. No radios, no one to talk to. The chore was made a little easier by the terrifying fact that an officer — a lieutenant or even a major — would randomly knock on the barracks door on some nights. If we listened to her tale of woe ("Airman, I have misplaced my ID, open up") and blindly opened the outside door for her, we were dead. We would be severely "chewed out" and punished. Instead, proper procedure called for an elaborate rite of code words and appropriate identification, the paper totem of the modern state. This was just in case she was an enemy soldier, a spy, a Russian, or someone trying to break in. This wartime practicing was part of the job of the barracks guard.

Another part of the job was hourly checks of all the locks in the building. For this we took a flashlight and a checklist that we would turn in at the end of our shift. The check was done by shining the light and perhaps tugging with our hand on every lock of every door and window and locker in the building, walking down every hall wing into every room where four women exactly like ourselves lay sleeping in their narrow bunks; walking between them to test the window locks and then turning back to check the closet locks where their uniforms and soap were stored (we owned little else — perhaps a Bible; even these were suspect); then swiveling the flashlight onto their beds to make certain they were in them. It was an eerie business. But it was necessary; every barracks did this as a practice for wartime conditions when our own country was in a war with foreign nations.

But in the women's barracks, the barracks guard also guarded against a second enemy, in a second war. Several times a month enlisted men from the surrounding barracks, where the men outnumbered us a hundred to one, would try to break into the barracks. To rape one of us. So when the light of the flashlight skimmed over the windows, the barracks guard holding it watched for a man's face on the other side. An enemy, not foreign, but American, one of our own brother soldiers. We did not talk about this. But we had a system for protection inside the barracks during the daytime too. Anytime a man set foot inside a woman's barracks for any purpose whatsoever, as a plumber or painter or carpenter, the call went out from the women, "Man in the barracks!" and every woman who heard the call repeated it, and then it was continued intermittently until he had finished his business and left.

We women did not need to be shipped overseas to a war zone to be on the alert to the dangers around us. Some of us on barracks guard had a method for keeping ourselves mentally active during the long, boring night hours. We read murder mysteries. We had a dare among us that no one could read all of a particular mystery story, *Psycho*, while on duty by herself. Never one to be outdone, even by no one, I took on the bet and read the whole terrifying book in one shift, bragging about it for a week afterward. The book centers on a particularly gory hatchet murder done on a young woman while she is taking a shower in a motel room, by a crazy man who is dressed up as a woman. And the last laugh was on me. For to this day, years later, I cannot bear to take a shower or a bath if I am alone in a house.

1000 B.C., The Amazons at the Battle of Troy

Penthesilea, Amazon queen, had accidently killed her own sister Hippolyta in a hunting expedition with a spear intended for a stag. She was downhearted about this, and her sister warriors of Thermidon were angry with her over it. So she decided to assuage her grief by taking on a battle campaign. According to Donald Sobol's version of the story, she arrived one day with twelve stalwart maiden warriors to the great siege of Troy, then in its tenth year, and offered the city her help. The Trojans were ecstatic that the fabulous warrior Penthesilea had come, all the more so because they had just lost their brightest star, King Priam's son Hector, in a hand-to-hand contest with the Greek Achilles, whose mother had dipped him in the River Styx to render him invincible.

Long angry with the Greeks for defeats her own army had suffered because of wars waged on them by the Greek heroes Bellerophon, Heracles, and Theseus, Penthesilea stood in the hall of the Trojans with no doubts about her own motives. She addressed the royal company, who included the king and queen, Priam and Hecuba, and also the gorgeous Helen, Queen of Sparta, whose illicit love of Prince Paris was said to be the cause of the arduous bloody war, of the 1,186 ships and 100,000 men led by her angry husband, Menelaus, surrounding the city.

Penthesilea, hand on hip and head thrown back, promised to turn the war around in favor of the Trojans with her twelve warriors and her own fierce right arm. She promised to rout the Greeks one by one and to leave even their invincible Achilles, terror of the plains, groveling in his own innards. She promised to send the men running to their ships, grateful to get away from Troy with their skins intact.

The Trojans of the royal house stood and cheered, for they lived on hope, and she and all her kind had such a fearsome reputation. The Greeks for a thousand years after would say that of all the old-world armies they went up against, of all the monsters, supernatural sorcerers, giants, horsemen — the Amazons of Thermidon, the women warriors, were the bravest and most difficult, the most memorable, the most beautiful, the most worthy to be called a foe.

Queen Helen and Queen Penthesilea toasted each other and exchanged looks that night, the one so curiously passive as her husband railed at the gate to regain her person by force, the other who had come, trained all her life to take up arms with him on his wife's behalf.

In the morning Penthesilea dressed meticulously in a rainbow-colored corselet. She wrapped her athlete's legs in light gold armor leggings and put on a gold helmet with long streamers. Her flashing sword, cased in a scabbard of ivory and silver, hung over one shoulder. Over her left arm she slid the crescent shield of the moon-maidens of Thermidon. In her left hand she gripped two javelins and in her right hand the double-edged ax of the old gynarchy she represented. Then with her similarly dressed twelve warriors around her she rallied the Trojan men and led them all onto the field that lay before the city. Thus she went up against the young, all-male Greek army.

The names of her warriors were Clonie, Polemusa, Thermodosa, Harmothoe, Derione, Evandre, Antandre, Bremusa, Hippothoe, Harmothoe, Alcibie, Derimacheia, and Antibrote, each seasoned in battle and fierce in reputation. It was their last campaign, the last of the Amazons who had their own territory.[8]

They went out against the Greek army who outnumbered them and all the citizens of Troy by ten to one, and yet the women were so fierce they left all the soil around Troy red with the blood they hewed out of the soldiers. As the afternoon bore on and other Amazons fell around her, nothing could withstand Penthesilea as she taunted and struck, struck and taunted. Achilles, had his mother not given him his magical protection, could never have withstood her. But he did have magical protection, and he not only withstood her, letting her tremendous spear throws crash off his armor, he slew her. And in the sculptured art through all the centuries of conquest, just as there would be "The Last Indian" and "The Dying Gaul," so there would be "The Wounded Amazon," the beautiful fallen warrior, Penthesilea.

And as she lay dying, Achilles decided that he "loved" her. Seeing the warrior stilled, seeing the blood run from wounds in her body, he became excited. Seeing her female might conquered by his own hand, he raped her. And when a fellow soldier protested this peculiar behavior toward a military enemy, Achilles chopped the soldier's head off. The sorrowing Trojans pulled Penthesilea's body from the river where the Greeks had thrown it. They gave Queen Penthesilea a hera's funeral and buried her in a special mound, her fallen warriors buried close around her. Troy went down soon after and was burnt, its women captured. Menelaus took his wife, Queen Helen, to her homeland as a slave; and she was soon murdered by her nephew. The gynarchic rule had crumbled, and a new wave of authority had arisen to establish patriarchal rule. In our age this rule has ripened and is beginning the decline that will give rise to a new cycle.

What matters about the Amazons is not that they fought and not that they lost — as thousands of armies have done before and since — but *what* they lost and how they lost. That they lost the Thermidon and their cities and their Libyan queendoms. That they lost their belt, the belt of female power, the blood-power girdle. And that they lost each other. And that Penthesilea was raped, her very soul stolen as she lay dying. And this was for her "beauty," he said, that is, he wanted her very life force, her sexual essence. So they lost, the women-warriors, the warriors for women:

183

their territory, their single-minded sisterhood, their magical power, the autonomy of their bodies.

Nor have we regained these since the Trojan War, losing them over and over, nor have we stopped trying to regain them, nor have we stopped understanding that it will be done.

A.D. *1600–1850, King Nzingha and the Rhani of Jhansi*

Women warriors have led armies against colonial occupation in modern historical times, too. Roman colonial rule in the south of Britain was nearly overthrown by Queen Boudica in the general uprising she led against the Romans in 61 A.D. During that same period of expansion by Rome, the Candace of Nubia in North Africa brought an army down the Nile just after Rome had defeated Cleopatra. The soldiers of Candace captured the city of Syene (Aswan) and tore down the statue of the Roman emperor. Rome retaliated by razing the capital cf Nubia, Napata, where the Candace (which is the title of the ruler, not a given name) had her royal seat. Roman historian Strabo described this particular Candace as "a masculine-appearing woman with one eye." What a warrior she must have been to warrant such a dykish description.[9]

In the domain of Ndongo, which later came to be called Angola, a brilliant head of state and military leader attempted to turn back both the Portuguese and the Dutch. This was Queen Nzingha, also known as Jinga or Ginga. Coming into her rulership at the age of forty-one and keeping back the massive expansion of the Portuguese slave trade until her death in 1663 at the age of eighty-one, Nzingha forbade her subjects to call her Queen, preferring the title King. When leading her army into battle, she wore men's clothing.

King Nzingha's diplomatic powers were even stronger than her courage and military might, and she was a visionary political leader who awakened a new sense of nationalism and resistance to the slave trade and colonial system. Following her death, African women and men alike mounted offenses and resistance against European domination all over Africa. They were inspired by forty years of the self-sacrificing example of a woman in total opposition to slavery: King Nzingha.[10]

During the nineteenth-century invasions of India by the British, an Indian woman leader, the Rhani, of the province of Jhansi, led an army of women as well as men against the colonizers. In

1979 my friend Linda Marie talked to people in Jhansi for stories about the Rhani. Old women who said the Rhani was their ancestor had come to pray at a particular temple she had once used. They wore their saris hitched up from front to back so they looked as though they wore pants, and they wore heavy silver bands tight around their upper arm muscles and snake-shaped bands looped around their ankles.

A taxi driver said, "Jalkari was a general in the women's army and never left her Rhani's side. She was so faithful." The all-women contingent of the army wrestled each morning, practicing and preparing to defend their territory. The Rhani herself rode along the wall of the British fort during a major battle on a white horse, holding the reins in her teeth and wielding two swords in her hands. She wore a pearl necklace, bloomers, and a turban.

Hard pressed by the British, she escaped death one night, after ensuring the escape of her people from the burning palace. First seeing that the men, the old people, and children found an underground tunnel and that her women warriors found horses near one of the walls, the Rhani herself then dressed in servant's clothing and rode hard away on horseback, her eight-year-old adopted son strapped to her back. In a later battle she and her woman companion, a general named Jalkari, were both killed in the same skirmish. Their bodies were burned under a tree to honor them and to prevent defilement and rape.[11]

Judith the Hebrew and Others

Certainly there have been traditions of women warriors other than the stories of the Amazon armies and bands or Queen Boudica and Queen Candace stories and other than the sorcerer/warrior traditions of Asian Uzume or Irish Scathach. Judith from the Old Testament represents yet another way of being a female warrior.

Having been married by arrangement to an old man, Judith was a widow still young and attractive when her people were besieged by General Holofernes' Assyrian army. Pitching his tents within their view, week after week the general kept the tribe of Jews imprisoned behind their own village walls, while he picked off their men one by one in small skirmishes. As they watched their supplies and water dwindle, the people grew panicked, yet no solution presented itself. But the widow Judith thought she knew God's plan, which one dark night she and a companion (an anonymous woman referred to in the story as her "handmaiden") carried out. The two women dressed Judith to the teeth in finery and packed a picnic basket of homemade goodies and a bottle of fine wine. Perhaps they laced the wine with a drug causing deep sleep: a Jewish Mickey Finn.

Then the two women crept across the no-man's-land of the war zone and found their way, with an Assyrian escort, to the general's tent. Judith said she would help him win against her people; but after three days of looking at her he determined to seduce the beautiful Judith. Instead he guzzled too much wine, which promptly put him into a sound coma. As the great painter Artemisia Gentileschi portrayed the story in her eighteenth-century studio, the companion kept watch while bold Judith took from her basket the weapon she had packed with the food — a short, sharp sword. With it she hacked off the sleeping General's head and packed the grisly thing into the basket under a pretty cloth. When the two women returned to their beleaguered town, Holofernes' head was put on display on a tall pike in full view of his troops, who fled in horror, and this ended the war.

Judith was hailed as a hero of her people; in fact the name Judith means "she who is praised" and perhaps was bestowed as a title. She was awarded two prizes: She was to be given food and her own lodging all her life, and, at a time when all Jewish women were required to marry in order to live, Judith was exempted from marriage and granted the privilege of remaining a single, independent woman all her days. I like to think that she and her "handmaid" companion settled down together.

As I think about my experience of the Lesbian/feminist movement from 1969 until the present, 1983, the number of Jewish Lesbians I can think of who have been catalysts, organizers, founders of institutions, writers, poets, artists, analysts, and general thinkers is virtually legion. Natalie, Wendy, Kate, Ginny, Judy, Evelyn, Beverly, Susan, Susan, Rita, Marian, Blanche, Janet, Suzanne, Evan, Alice, Nancy, Nancy, Martha, Susan, Susan, Adrienne, Irena, Ellie, Amy, Beth, Robin, Gloria, Lynda, Leigh, Laura, Melanie, Naomi, Ellen, Jan, Maxine, Deborah, Bella jump into my mind as a I scroll through the last twelve years of activity, and I know there are many more in my own life alone.

A generation of Jews in America lost people in the Holocaust of Nazi Germany as well as through the great displacement and annihilation of entire villages of people, especially throughout Eastern Europe during World War II. I believe this generation produced in its turn a generation of dedicated radical youths who came of age during the sixties with the injunction "Never again." Committed to opposing fascistic behavior every time they saw or believed they saw it happening, they joined every movement for social justice in America during the sixties and seventies; in many cases they led these movements, helped connect them to each other and helped develop their philosophies. They repeatedly brought up issues connected to human rights and racism; and when the mass liberation movement ideology and activity spread from Black, Chicano, and Indian people to women, feminists, Lesbians, and Gays, they "came out" in droves; those who had come out earlier through the underground bar culture now entered the political movement, often by founding some particular aspect of it as a new entity.

The Jewish dikes came out as Lesbians with a built-in sense of special purpose; they came out not as bar dikes and spinsters but as political Lesbians, and that is what they called themselves. They led a new movement, based on a combination of principles taken from the left, the Civil Rights and anti-Vietnam war movements, and feminism. They participated in the founding of independent, Lesbian-owned counterinstitutions that produced records, films, newspapers, magazines, presses, distribution services, bookstores, health centers and other health-oriented groups, production companies, and theater groups. They represent a very particular way of being dikish, and of being warriors, that descends from Jewish traditions in addition to Christian Anglo-Saxon traditions.

The Jewish dyke is not modeled after Celtic Boudica, the stolid, large-bodied, redheaded Celt who raised armies and in modern bar life is often quick to take a rival out in the alley for a fist fight or even to break a bottle over her head. The style of Jewish dykes, in my observation, is verbal, personable, argumentative, and sometimes extremely heady, while still courageous and completely determined. As post-World War II activists, fighting oppression and the Nazi legacy, Jewish women provided much political theory to the Lesbian and feminist communities. Primarily they have used organizing, argumentation, and emotional commitment as their tools and to further their ideologies; more than other Lesbians, they believe in words and ideas and the deliberate spread of images toward a particular end. More than non-Jewish Lesbians, they would use a word like *ideology*.

My lover Wendy Cadden, with whom I lived for fourteen

187

years, represents such a warrior and such a Jewish dike tradition, a descendant of Judith the Warrior and her companion. A child of radical parents, she used her organizing principles and analysis that she learned from her radical family in her work at the Women's Press Collective, always being quick to include white working-class women and women of color. Nor does this mean the Jewish dyke is a heady intellectual with a weak body. Like dikes everywhere, she pays attention to her physical being. Muscled and wiry, Wendy took on the hard labor of running printing presses and building darkrooms, tables, and shelves. One of my favorite stories is of the two of us picking plums in an orchard. I was high on the two-story, three-legged ladder with a bucket slung over one arm when I reached for one last ripe fruit, unfortunately using the same hand that held the heavy bucket. As the ladder began to fall to one side I yelled Wendy's name. She was fifteen yards away, picking on the ground. But by the time the ladder and I touched earth in a weltering tangle of legs and wood, she had taken a long flying leap and a baseball slide and landed under me, breaking what would otherwise have been a bone-busting fall.

Jewish Lesbians who came to full adulthood in the late sixties and seventies led the development of Lesbian-feminist politics and worked hard to produce Gay institutions that were not based in the bar culture, though they were usually formed in conjunction with dikes such as myself whose roots were drawn directly from the bar culture and earlier Gay civil rights organizations such as Mattachine and Daughters of Bilitis. (We became known as "Old World dykes"). Under the leadership of Jewish Lesbian feminists, working during those decades as assimilated people rather than being identified as "Jewish Lesbians" and in close personal conjunction with Lesbians from Christian and other backgrounds, alternative institutions flourished. Being a Lesbian became highly focused as a political choice, a voluntary method of becoming an independent female and of "overturning the patriarchy." The whole idea of Lesbianism as a "political choice" on the part of women who did not want to engage in an oppressive heterosexual marriage system, rather than as a personal accident or happenstance, grew out of this aspect of the feminist movement.

In an interview for *Lilith Magazine*, Evelyn Beck, editor of *Nice Jewish Girls*, was asked what she thought identified Jewish Lesbians as Jewish, aside from recognizing anti-Semitism. She replied that she sees Jewish involvement in Lesbian feminism as being "in a direct line with radical Jewish activity in this country.

Caring about others is a part of Jewish tradition as is an emphasis on this life and *this* world, and making it a better place." She continued, "The celebration of our holidays is something that Jewish lesbians see as particularly Jewish, particularly as the Jewish calendar is a moon calendar . . . Jewish lesbians hold seders all the way from Canada to Washington and Madison; they are writing their own *hagadas*, which are specifically both Jewish and lesbian and making connections with other oppressed groups. They are having Hannukah ceremonies. Many of these ceremonies are transformed, but are nonetheless very much both Jewish and lesbian." [12]

Reasons for lack of recognition of Jewish participation in the Lesbian/feminist movement are made clear by Beck: "I think there is a tremendous amount of Jewish energy in the Lesbian feminist movement. Many Jewish women have not wanted to recognize how much, partially for reasons of internalized anti-Semitism: namely, that when Jews have made ourselves visible as Jews, we have been seen as wanting to take over. That is part of the nature of anti-Semitism — that you don't have much space between being invisible as Jews or being too visible as Jews." [13]

In my own experience the Jewish participation in the Lesbian feminist movement greatly influenced and shaped its philosophy, especially of interconnectedness with other movements and oppressed groups, of the attempts to make an analysis of oppression, of antiracism, of attempting to improve current conditions, and of using organizing and the cultural media as tools. Frequently a Jewish Lesbian teamed up with a non-Jewish Lesbian to form a strong independent alternative institution that in turn sparked a ton of activity. (Sometimes whole neighborhoods of single women spring up around a bookstore, for example.) The founding mother-teams of the first all-women's press, bookstore, and music company each consisted of a Jewish Lesbian partner teamed with a WASP or Catholic Lesbian partner. These Jewish Lesbians were Wendy Cadden (who with Judy Grahn founded The Women's Press Collective in 1969 in San Francisco), Natalie Lando (who with her ex-lover Carol Wilson and Alice Molloy founded A Woman's Place Bookstore in Oakland) and Ginny Berson (who with her then-lover Meg Christian formed Olivia Records in Washington, D.C., in 1973). Natalie Lando (as well as Carol Wilson) had been an early member of San Francisco D.O.B.

Handsome Ginny Berson described her early life for me and the motives that led her to found Olivia Records. [14] Raised in a

189

suburb in Connecticut, with grandparents who were Eastern European, Ginny remembers "justice" as a main theme of her heritage. "I remember once in Sunday school they asked us for one word to describe God — *Just* was the answer I remembered. I always thought that God's main thing in life is justice. My father was always so fair; he started two different businesses but he was never enough of a capitalist to really succeed; he was too concerned with fairness." When civil rights issues began to gain national attention, teenage Berson knew where she stood on the issue without a second thought. A tomboy and a sportswoman, she knew where she stood on women's rights, too, and she told her rabbi that she intended to become the first woman rabbi. (Her other ambitions were to be on the New York Yankees' starting line-up and/or a senator and president of the United States.)

After a two-year stint in the Peace Corps, she moved to Washington, D.C., to work for radical government leaders. But she found they wanted her only as a secretary. Angered, she joined other women who organized and demonstrated "against imperialism" and "against racism"; in conjunction with other women who became strong Lesbian feminist leaders and image makers (such as author Rita Mae Brown and publisher Coletta Reid) she produced a furious and short-lived newspaper, "The Furies." But something else was nagging at her ambition. It seemed to Ginny that the movement excluded working-class people of all races, because it required so much leisure time. She wanted to start a women's institution that had a strong economic base so it could support, through jobs, the input of women she felt were not being heard inside the mostly white, mostly middle-class feminist circles. And she wanted her company to have something to do with images, images that could change the way people think. "I wanted national impact and something communicating ideas."

Berson exploded one day in a passionate letter to her lover Meg Christian, who had the unsatisfactory job of nightclub singing. "I described how her jobs depended on whether the male club manager liked her (meaning she was expected to simper) and how she had to play to the guys who would buy drinks. So when we Lesbians went to hear her we had to cower together and make ourselves small at a back table, because she was always being fired for 'attracting the wrong clientele.' And she was never really getting to write her own songs. In my letter I said she ought to start singing for women, and we ought to make a tape and send it out." Besides Meg's music, the other motive she had for founding a record company, Ginny told me, was that she wanted to record my poetry. "It was not only the first positive affirmation of Lesbianism that I ever read in my life, it was also the first poetry that really connected to me, even though I had studied it through high school and college." Singer/songwriter Cris Williamson suggested the company as a reality in a radio interview with Meg and Ginny, and in 1973 Olivia Records was founded. And to my eternal gratitude, a poetry album was the third album they produced, featuring my work and that of Pat Parker, a Black Lesbian/feminist.[15]

November 26, 1982, Olivia Records celebrated its tenth anniversary with a huge Carnegie Hall concert; both shows sold out most of their 5,600 seats months in advance, and every small-size tuxedo in New York City was rented out on that historic night. The concert featured Meg Christian and Cris Williamson with back-up singing by other Olivia recording artists, including Linda Tillery, who has her own album, and the exciting performer Vicki Randle. Program notes and a history of Olivia's star-studded success, founded entirely on the grass-roots participation of thousands of women all over America, was delivered by another early Olivia cofounder, Judy Dlugacz, a Jewish Lesbian.

Ginny's dream of an organization that uses business principles to promote political ideas and harmonious, artful Lesbian/feminist imagery came true and has involved artists and organizers across all kinds of race, class, and ethnic lines. She has gone on to become head of the Women's Department at a community-based radio station, KPFA in Berkeley. Ginny Berson has many tools in her picnic basket, more, perhaps, than the widow Judith had. I imagine her throughout her life, continuing to saw and hack away at Holofernes' heavy patriarchal head until it simply topples from the force of gravity.

1974, We Were Five Dykes

The year was 1974. We were five dykes, living in an all-women's household. We were highly visible and vocal Lesbian feminist organizers, a little grungy and eccentric in jackets and baggy pants, for we did not have a stake in what we looked like. We had started the first women's bookstore, the first women's collective press for publishing books, and a newspaper. Occupationally we were a carpenter-mechanic-accountant, a copy editor, a printer-poet, an electronics assembler, and a printer-artist. One day a woman came into the bookstore begging us for help. Her boy-

191

friend, she said, was trying to kill her because she did not want to see him anymore. She was afraid to tell her friends because he would tell them she was a whore. So he had beaten her up. He called her on the phone day and night to threaten and terrify her; he banged on her door in the middle of the night, and only that morning in broad daylight he had thrown a crowbar through her front door, which happened to be made of glass. And he had sworn he was coming in to get her. She spent hours cowering on the floor at the back of her apartment. The police had told her they couldn't — or wouldn't — do anything. They advised her to move.

"I don't want to move," she raged. "I love my apartment. Why should I move? He's the one who's in the wrong. Besides, he could just follow me home from work and start it all over again." We agreed. And we agreed to help. But, we told her, "You will have to help too."

That evening we went to her house, which had many windows and was as filled with lively plants as a hothouse garden. "We are starting a vigil here," we told her. "One or two of us will stay with you until the problem is solved."

She smiled gratefully. We did not smile in return.

"What are you doing to defend yourself?" we asked. She did not know.

"What do you want us to do to stop him?" we asked.

"Kill him," she said.

"No, no," we replied. "But you must protect yourself from direct physical attack and learn to feel safe in your house." We located hammers, umbrellas, heavy dictionaries, flowerpots, bricks, sticks, and the like and arranged them strategically around the house, showing her what to do with them. We talked a lot to each other about guns, knives, karate. We got her to agree to tell some of her friends about what was happening and to keep their numbers near her phone for emergencies.

Then we talked among ourselves about what plan of action to take, loud enough so she could hear there were a thousand alternatives to the drastic, essentially passive reaction "kill him." She went into the kitchen, returning with cookies and brownies. "I baked these for you," she said, smiling at us as though we were football heroes. We ignored her cookies.

"Why do you wear such helpless clothes?" we asked. "How can you run or kick in those shoes, that tight skirt?" She didn't know. "The police aren't going to help you," we said. "And for the most part neither are your friends. And you can't expect us to stay with you forever. We're not your personal bodyguards. You have to learn to defend yourself." She changed her clothes and began to pay attention to our plans. We asked questions about her boyfriend's habits. What does he value, we asked, his car, his motorcycle? Where does he work, where does his wife work, where do they live? Are his parents in town? Where do you think he is most vulnerable? We made a plan, one, two, three, four. First we would talk to him; if that didn't work then we would contact his wife, go see her if necessary, then his boss; if none of those tactics worked, we would go wreck his car.

She listened in amazement. She had believed the only way to stop him was to murder him. The two oldest among us — women in their forties — got on the telephone to him and took turns talking.

"Hello there," they said. They used his full name, they mentioned his address. "We're from the Women's Defense League of Oakland. We're a special protection group for women, and we've gotten a very serious complaint about you." They described his actions to him in detail. They mentioned his wife's name and where they both worked. "We've been checking up on you and we know quite a lot. If you don't agree — right now — to leave this woman completely alone, we're going to institute action." They left the nature of the action to his imagination. He began to stutter, then bluster, and finally to crack and beg them not to tell his wife.

He did not go near the woman again. Within two days she had changed her attitude toward her life, becoming much more assertive, especially with the several boyfriends she had. She came into the bookstore a month later to report to us and to thank us woman to woman. "This guy got drunk at my house last night and I ordered a cab, trundled him into it, and got rid of him," she crowed in triumph. She again owned her own space and peace of mind. And now that she was no longer using them to pay us for "protecting" her while she continued being Miss Helpless, we ate her cookies.

1981, One Amazin' Mornin'

One amazing morning in December just as Paula and I had begun to settle into living together in the strange town of L.A., to settle into the cramped smallness of our two rooms and the continual smog-dirty air that made us both sick, just when I had begun to overcome the grief and loss of self I felt with such devastation after leaving Wendy . . . just as we had gotten through some of the emotional terrors and our own shocking sense of being utter strangers to each other, women in our forties, she with grown children and so far from her family and from other Indians . . . Paula had finally felt at home enough with me to unpack some of her pictures and hang them up to cozy the place a little, and I had begun buying ordinary things we needed for the apartment . . .

And then one morning as we lay sleeping late to escape the smog-sickening rush-hour air, Paula opened her eyes to find a man standing over us with a knife raised as though to plunge down into her. With his other hand he touched his lips in a gesture of "shhh." But she did not freeze. Out loud she said, "Oh God, he's here." Still sleeping at her side I tried to open my eyes and murmured, "Huh?"

She said, "He's in here. He's standing here." Urgency in her voice opened my eyes. I saw a man's legs, a vague face obscured by the bedside lamp. The bed lay flat on the floor, so he seemed very far away. I thought he was our Gay landlord, Bob. What is Bob doing in here, I wondered. I blinked as Paula continued feeding me information. "He's got a knife," she said. Now my eyes saw him — a menacing stranger standing over us. The nightmare of all nightmares, the one I could never — quite — imagine getting through alive and intact. I had rehearsed what to do all my life, and I did not hesitate now. I became a whirlwind of activity. I flung back the quilt and in one motion sprang across the bed, took a huge step and swept a thin plywood sheet up into the air as vehemently as I could. Paula had been using it to stack her papers on; it was long enough to hold two stacks. Much had already gone through my mind by the time I wrapped my hands around it and wrenched upward. My heart had gone to my feet in fear and dread. My mind was registering my impression of the danger. Oh no, I thought with horror. This is really really bad. He's tall, young, aggressive, and he has a knife. What if there are more of them, one behind me, others in the hall or kitchen? Will they completely overpower us? What will Paula do? We would be completely at their mercy, for any purposes. None of our neighbors are likely to come. Or care. I am going to get hurt if I fight, especially if there is more than one; I will get hurt really bad. But I must fight, and now, instantly. I must throw something — Paula's heavy typewriter? No, better this plywood, something I can hold, wield. I must turn the situation around and fast.

194

I moved fast, whirling, racing, thrusting, making rapid aggressive motions. Papers and books flew nearly to the ceiling as I grabbed and swung my little weapon, which I thought of as a "heavy board." I flew straight at him, feeling only rage that he was threatening her, wanting only to get him away from her, to back him off away from the bed. And as I launched myself at him he took a step back. I locked eyes with his. And I began to chant, the most important poem of my life. "You get out of here," I said, "you get out. Get out of this house, you get out. You get out of here, you get out." To my left I could hear Paula, who was standing, yelling for Bob at the top of her lungs. The attacker's eyes widened. "Help, somebody help us! Bob! Bob!" Paula yelled and yelled, then changed her chant to match mine, "You get out of here, right now. You get out. You get out of this house."

He came into focus, a dark-brown-skinned man in his early twenties, medium-sized, athletic-looking, handsome, wearing a new royal blue running jacket with white stripes on the sleeve. The knife, which I kept myself from looking at directly, was a large-bladed pocketknife with a pearl handle. "Not too bad," I thought. "Try not to let him get your throat."

Then he began to recover himself, as I must have come into focus to him too, pale, fierce-eyed, a white woman in sloppy-looking pajamas, in her forties, carrying a little too much weight for easy motion on a slender frame. And waving, not an entire table top ripped off its moorings, but a little stick of plywood. He made a menacing face and gestured toward me with his knife, as though I might not at first have seen it.

To my great relief, rage poured through me. I swung my plywood like a great ax, hitting his arm in its arc, then coming around to slice into the lamp, gashing a great split in the lampshade as the lamp whirled up somersaulting into the air over my head. Keeping my eyes on his, a snarl on my lips, and my chant firm, I advanced on him again and backed him to the wall. His fierce expression crumbled as he saw that I would trade him hurt for hurt, and for the first time he looked away, looked for the way out. Looked at the door just a foot from him and decided not to turn his back on me. I did not press him now; I waited, relaxed back onto my heels, let him choose his point of exit. Did not drop my guard. I did not threaten to hit him, even when he reached over and grabbed some money Paula had on her desk. He ran toward the back where he had gotten in, stopping to grab my wallet, my little soapstone box of laundry change. I ran after him, lest he

195

go for my precious typewriter, the only other thing besides Paula and myself that I was willing to protect with violence.

Paula yelled for me to get the police on the phone as the guy ran out the back, and she ran out the front to get help. She found Bob and the rest of the story: There had been four of them; and a white guy and a black guy had surrounded him upstairs, boxing him in, while another one went into our apartment and tried to get to the front door to open it for the fourth to get in. Apparently, they planned to take us all, for whatever purposes our imaginations could design. Shaking with terror of what might have been, the three of us stood watching four policemen climb the steps. "And now," Bob, a Gay Black man, said, with his eyes on their burly forms, "who knows if things are going to get better or worse this morning."

"I know just what you mean," I replied.

THE WOMEN OF DAN DANCE WITH
SWORDS IN THEIR HANDS TO MARK THE
TIME WHEN THEY WERE WARRIORS

I did not fall from the sky
I
nor descend like a plague of locusts
to drink color and strength from the earth
and I do not come like rain
as a tribute or symbol for earth's becoming
I come as a woman
dark and open
some times I fall like night
softly
and terrible
only when I must die
in order to rise again.

I do not come like a secret warrior
with an unsheathed sword in my mouth
hidden behind my tongue
slicing my throat to ribbons
of service with a smile
while the blood runs
down and out
through holes in the two sacred mounds
on my chest.

I come like a woman
who I am

196

spreading out through nights
laughter and promise
and dark heat
warming whatever I touch
that is living
consuming
only
what is already dead.

— Audre Lorde[16]

1981, So You Will Know
You Are Heras

Los Angeles, December 26, 1981 — Journal Note:

Five women came over and gave us a protection ceremony so Paula and I can get through the destruction wrought inside ourselves and to our space and privacy by the knife attack two weeks ago. We have been unable to sleep; we sleep one at a time to watch out for the other one, and with all the lights on.

The five women were led by Nancy Angelo and Bia Lowe, the others were Eloise Healy, Terry Wolverton, and Geraldine Hanon. Eloise is a poet who sponsored a reading for Paula and me before we moved here. Nancy lived next door for a while and now lives in a downtown loft; she is a video filmmaker.

They brought various stuff to our house at 8 P.M. A bowl of salt, which we each held and vested with good thoughts and powers. Then we took the bowl outside, formed a seven-woman line, and took turns laying down a stream of white salt in a circle around the apartment. We made certain to include the back steps leading to Bob's apartment so he would be protected too. We made sure to circle the fig tree to save it from Bob who prunes it too heavily when he's feeling mad at the world.

Then we went inside. Each woman gave us a special present for our protection, while Bia lit six small white candles in beautiful heavy-bottomed glasses and burnt a little sage. Bia gave us each a large green laurel wreath, taken from two trees she had climbed and hidden in as a child, two laurel trees that had grown together as one. We put them on our heads. She said the wreaths were to tell us how heroic we had both been, and so we would know we were Heras. She said the wreaths were to remind us that we had the facility, the intuition, and intelligence to protect ourselves and each other, as we had already proved. We laughed and laughed at how handsome and also silly each other looked in the wreaths, with the sprigs of green twining into our short hair. Nancy had teary eyes from Bia's words, which were elegant and heartfelt. We applauded each gift.

Terry gave us a small oblong handsome mirror to put in the window facing outward. This is to turn threats away and direct bad feeling and evil intentions back to their sources. If we didn't want to use it in the window, she said, we could use it to look into, to see that we are who is here, and we are safe in this space.

Eloise gave us a tall glass candle with a color picture of Guadalupe standing with her foot on a serpent ("So you know everything is in place") and with light beams streaming from her hands. "Madonna of the Flashlights," Paula said she had always called her. Eloise and Paula were both raised Catholic. They talked about whether you could read by the light after your mother turned the lights out. Eloise said she had worn the medal as a child and it was special to her. The candle is titled "La Milagrosa," literally, "the Miraculous."

Geraldine gave us a tiny red plastic box. Inside is a tiny round mirror, the size of a pea, and on the mirror are two cat claws discarded by her cat. The bottom of the box says "Protection for Paula and Judy 9982." She lives in a 10,000-year-old world. Geraldine said, "The red is for fire and for love. Fire comes from women, it is our generative force. People used to believe it came from the tips of their fingers and this is what red nail polish means. The mirror is for contemplation and intuition, and the cat claws — you know what to do with them."

Nancy gave three big fat candles. (She had previously given us a purple one for higher spiritual power.) These were a gray one for setting limits, who could come in and who not; a blue one for protection and intelligence; a rosy one for creative intuition and for the love between us, to strengthen it if we got into trouble. We were to write what qualities we wanted on the candle before lighting it.

Then Paula got up from our circle. (They were sitting all around our couch bed and we were on it.) Paula got some pottery shards from a cup on the mantle and gave us each one. "These are from the mesa I climbed as a child and that is always home to me. This will help connect us." Then I read my mother-fire-source poem, "The Land That I Grew Up on Is a Rock"; meanwhile the cat Leonard Woolf rustled in the closet to get attention.

We talked about defenses. After Bia asked what measures we were taking, I said that we never fantasized the scene of him appearing again with his knife without following through to an end in which we were overcoming him — throwing him through a window, for instance, or knocking him senseless with heavy objects. Never did we leave the scene with him still in a threatening stance or ourselves frightened. In this way our own minds could not work against us. We talked about dogs — a Samoyed and a malamute Paula saw the day before. We talked about guns. I said that guns and dogs and husbands all seemed like the same amount of trouble to me.

Paula told how Bob had appreciated our part in stopping the attack. How he had rushed around putting new locks in and a peephole in the front door; how he had rented out his two empty apartments to the largest, straightest men he could find and their girlfriends. We rolled our eyes. "As though it was men who came to help him last time," we said. Paula told about the nailed-down windows, the bells she had hung on the door and windows, the plants she had lined on the ledges so they could easily knock over and make a sound, any sound. I said we did not want to move, although we had given it a lot of thought, and our friends seemed to expect we would.

Nancy said she "felt" we were safe here now, and I said the same. I said we'd been warned four times before the attack and had been psychically prepared. "The spirit people made certain we could get through this," Paula said. "What do you mean?" they asked.

I told about Leonard Woolf the cat acting strangely for three weeks, crying day and night and so restless that Paula was on the lookout for an earthquake or other disaster. I said another Indian woman, Joy Harjo, in a Tarot reading had predicted a burglary for Paula sometime this year. We described two dreams Paula had had in the past month, one of being robbed of her typewriter, the other a terrible nightmare. She woke me in the middle of the night screaming "No!" at the top of her lungs; then she leaped out of bed and went to the front window to look out. She'd seen a man, she said, standing by the bed. The spot she saw him was precisely where, a month later, our intruder would stand over her.

Then I told of the vivid spirit warning I had had thirty-six hours before the attack. As I lay in bed next to Paula, nearly asleep, a tall shadow figure appeared on my side of the bed, looming hugely over me, all the larger for the fact that the bed is just a foam mattress lying on the floor, part of a foam couch we make up during the day. The shadow was sinister and threatening, quite different from my usual spirit folk, and I was afraid of him. "You aren't friendly," I said.

Then as I began to doze I heard a grinding noise, as of teeth grinding — I looked at Paula and at the cat but they were still, sleeping. Then I saw the candle in the glass flickering crazily on the mantle that is more like an altar because we have so loaded it with loved objects. She had lit the candle because she felt uneasy after her dreams. There must be a breeze, I thought. I could feel the draft — there must be a window open. I went to the nearest window but it was closed tight. I went back to bed, scared stiff. I woke Paula and told her all my sights and sounds. And I suppose that when she woke me the following morning to tell me, "He's in here, he's standing here, he has a knife," I was prepared.

Bia talked a little about being raped in her bed at knife point five years ago — that she had opened her eyes at 4 A.M. and there he was with her kitchen knife, and she had frozen, unable to scream or fight back. "Some positive things have come out of it," she said, "for one thing, *I have gotten more in touch with my anger.*"

Suddenly I understood that phrase, that always seemed so strange to me. What it means to women who cannot make use of their own anger, cannot even feel it when they most need it. By not being allowed to physically express rage, by having to be so ladylike, she had been denied self-protection. She had been frozen in place long before the man arrived.

"But then," her lover Terry said, "you have responded every time since then to even a hint that another woman might be in danger by supporting her in every way possible, like in leading this ceremony and letting Paula and Judy sleep at your house for a couple of nights after what happened to them. And that has strengthened your self-defense." We talked about rape as the stealing of a person's soul. Paula, who worked at a rape crisis center, described the rapist as arriving with his own terrors, feelings of weakness and helpless rage. And when he leaves the victim, she has his fears and he has her confidence and goodwill toward the world. We talked about word processors that cause cancer and how secretaries were refusing to use them. We covered our ears and tried out Nancy's shrieker that she carries in her purse and discovered it was broken. We drank bottled spring water and ate apple slices and unbuttered popcorn. Then Nancy burned a dish of frankincense and, surrounding us with smoke, bade us to make three wishes. Good love, good work, and wisdom were what I wished — for myself, for Paula, and for the other women.

Then we hugged each other and they went home. I felt happy and so did Paula. The house was ours again and has remained so.

CHAPTER EIGHT

Flaming, Flaming Faggot Kings

———◆———

3

Madrone Tree that was my mother,
Cast me a cloak as red as your flower.
    My sisters don't know me,
    My father looks for me,
And I am by name the wind's brother.

Madrone Tree, from your thirsty root
feed my soul as if it were your fruit.
    Spread me a table and make it fair.
    Cast down splendor out of the air.
My story has only the wind's truth.

Madrone Tree, red as blood,
that once my mother was, be my rod.
    Death came when I was born.
    And from that earth now you are grown.
My father's a shadow, the wind is my god.

From "Four Songs
the Night Nurse Sang," Robert Duncan[1]

Faggot? A faggot is something that flames, a firestick. We used the word, Von, in those early months of our being together when every gesture was fraught with secret Gay meanings between us. We hung cigarettes from the sides of our mouths and talked tough. We called the cigarettes "fags" in a double pun, a joke both on our imagined dyke-toughness and on our Gay brothers. Like dike, faggot *is a Gay office; the Lesbian butch and the bulldike and the Amazon are related to female warriors and the Horned God. The faggot is related to Gay wizardry, to wands, and to the element of fire.*

THE OLDEST fire stories of Asia and North America say that an old woman-god, the Hag of fire, Spider Grandmother, brought fire and light for people to use. Grandmother kept the fire, some stories say, in the tips of her fingers. Perhaps the red nail polish traditional to women is a cultural reflection of this. Other stories say Grandmother had six fingers, the sixth being a firestick. Perhaps the wand of the Fairy Queen was at first a firestick.

Some stories say the Old Woman's grandson stole fire from her, and others that he misused it and even burned the world down. Asiatic and American Indian tribal stories name Spider Grandmother as the bringer of fire that she later gave to her grandson or that was borrowed or stolen by him.

The Greeks also have a story of the theft of fire, by a grandson of the female earth god, Gaia. Prometheus, with the help of the warrior Athena, took fire illicitly from the sun and was punished for his daring and his trespass by being chained to a rock in the Caucasus Mountains to remind him what he owed to the earth and that he is eternally bound to her. The gods who administered the punishment relented finally and agreed to his release, on condition that he wear a ring on his finger made of the earth's substance, in the form of a metal band with a chunk of rock, the earth's tissue, set into it. This was commanded so that he would never forget that he was bound to the earth, the Great Mother Gaia. And that, they say, is the origin of rings.[2]

Faggot, Faggot, Burning Bright

Prometheus carried his stolen coals in the stalks and roots of a particular plant, the ferula. According to Lawrence Durdin-Robertson, "There is a similarity between the Arani (the Lesbian firestick goddess) and the Ferula in which Prometheus, helped by Athena, carried away the fire."[3] The Ferula is the male firestick, as the Arani is the female. The ferula plant is familiar to us in America as the Italian salad vegetable called *fennel*. The Italian word for fennel is *finnochio*, which in Italy is derogatory slang for "effeminate man" and "faggot."[4] In San Francisco a nightclub extremely well known for its female impersonators and drag queens is called Finnochio's. My Gay slang dictionary refers to the club affectionately as "Finn's."[5]

Mythically speaking, what the story of Prometheus and his ferula plant suggests is that "faggots" (in all senses of the word) were the agency by which the magic of fire passed from the old female domain (with its sacred offices of ceremonial Lesbianism) into the newer, more male-oriented Greek tradition. In all likelihood this occurred through the offices of Gay male priest/sorcerer/shamans who cross-dressed and used wands of sacred trees as part of their magic-science. "Finnochio" and "faggot" are both very old terms referring to Gay men and to sacred fire as one and the same. They are references to the magical/creative powers specifically developed among the society of Gay males, both independently and with the "fire" taken, stolen, or received as a gift from the female side of tribal society, especially through such women's priesthoods as those of the Lesbian Arani. Or perhaps it happened at times through the functions of an intermediary who roughly corresponds to the modern "fag hag."[6]

Rods and wands belong to the Gay diviners. Herodotus writing of the Mediterranean region as it was in 400 B.C. described the use of rods in the divination technique of soothsayers in Scythia who worked with willow rods. "They bring great bundles of them, which they put down on the ground; then they untie them, lay out each rod separately and pronounce their prophecy. While they are speaking it, they collect the rods into a bundle again as before."[7] He then described a certain class of effeminate cross-dressed male priests, called "Enarees," who use a refinement of the rod method, "which they say was taught them (at the temple of Aphrodite Urania) by Aphrodite: these people take a piece of the inner bark of the lime tree and cut it into three pieces, which they keep twisting and untwisting round their fingers as they prophesy."[8]

Modern Gay fairies speak of themselves as having wands. In *Gay Talk*, a fairy wand is defined as "any phallic staff carried by a homosexual. Fairy wands include cigarettes stuck into rhinestone-studded cigarette holders, umbrellas carried when there is no possible chance of rain, pencils, long-stemmed American Beauty roses or even joss sticks. The hand holding a fairy wand usually performs wildly exaggerated gestures." [9] A penile braggart is called "Wanda Wandwaver."[10] Ordinary modern slang acknowledges the connection of the word *faggot* to *firestick*, when people refer to a cigarette as a "fag."

The sorcerer's wand with its burst of "fairy dust" (psychic energy? or semen?) at the tip, the diviner's stick, and the shape and sexual heat of the penis itself all contribute to the imagery. Participants in Greek all-women sacred ceremonies carried penis-shaped stalks called the "Thyrsus" in what were obviously uses of sexual magic. A tree whose wood was sacred to ancient (Gay male) sorcerers, magical kings, and wizards was the beech tree; the Latin word for the beech is *fagus*.[11] It was a huge and venerated fagus beech tree that Joan of Arc visited to get her voice messages and that she was accused of dancing around with the fairy people. "Faggot," as a sacred male sexual firestick, is a venerable term. The faggot as a wand for divination and sacred firemaking has apparently belonged to the province of Gay male wizards, sorcerers, and priests for thousands of years.

Medieval villages of Europe had the custom of calling upon the sacred male firestick and displaying its tribal roots in time of cold winter need. Two selected naked men made a public fire, called a "need-fyr," by rubbing two sticks together.[12] Medieval monks made a public fire while a large wooden lingum was posted nearby. The purpose was not warmth but rather the sparking of good hunting and farming and an early spring to ensure the survival of the village during extreme European winters.

Turning Tricks with Magic Sticks

Another fire association, at least in the sense of the sexual electric spark between Gay men, is the practice of tricking. Tricking, having sex with total strangers, is a province of some Gay men and of female prostitutes; that is, both groups call what they do "tricking." Some flaming queens brag of having sex with one thousand men in a one-year period. In *City of Night*,[13] John Rechy's novel about the urban Gay underground of the early 1960s, Rechy described exuberantly one special night of his life, a night spent standing with his back to a tree having sex with seven different men, all of it happening outdoors in a park. *That*

207

is what I mean by tricking. Even when two men have a long-term relationship with each other, tenderly living together as lovers, often they will trick outside the marriage. Michael Denneny's excellent account of a romance between two Gay men, *Lovers: The Story of Two Men*,[14] gives an honest discussion of the arrangement whereby one of the men might go out to have sex with someone he picked up at a bar or cruising on the street or met at a party, sex that lasts ten minutes or so. (The lover analyzes the motives for his behavior in terms of his having a fear of emotional intimacy with his partner, even though they love each other.)

Lesbians also sometimes have fears of emotional intimacy and go out with lots of other women, and still Lesbians do not trick in the way that faggots do, although some use the word *trick* (meaning sex for one night) and may even go through some motions similar to tricking. But entirely different archetypes are operating for Lesbians than for Gay men, perhaps because some of the oldest Lesbian archetypes have been more suppressed, as has so much of female culture. It isn't a matter simply of saying that men are different from women, although that is true enough. But some straight women do trick. Prostitutes, having an underground culture with a long history of its own, call their customers "tricks" and speak of their work as "tricking" or "turning tricks." And of course many prostitutes are Gay — an overlap of two undergrounds.

Gay men often go out tricking and call the men they pick up on the street or in bars "tricks." They also call them "trade," if the trick is someone who refuses to take an active homosexual part and is only acted upon.

All indications are that tricking began as a sacred and tribal act and was performed in village ceremonies and in the temples and sacred groves of the gods and goddesses, an act of worship (and much tribal worship is raucous, humorous, erotic) on the part of strangers who were erotically captivated and "tricked" into giving their sexual energy to the priestesses and cross-dressed male priests of the temple as an offering, the offering of orgasm. These people had special titles. For instance, two Hebrew titles for such temple offices are *Kadosh* and *Kadosha*. The priestesses, or sacred Gay men dressed as the priestesses, accepted the energy on behalf of the Divine Being. This exchange, or trade, or trick, often took place outdoors, in the wild woods or in a special grove of trees near a town or temple. In tribal societies all the people of the tribe gather for a ritual ceremony. The tricking that is the release of purely sexual energy is conducted not through a priesthood but through a trickster figure who impersonates the god-spirit and who is very erotic, bawdy, and at the same time comic.

Hermes of old Greece, Coyote of Indian America, Eshu/ Elegba of Africa and African America, and Wuotan of old pagan Europe are supreme trickster figures. Some of them carry huge phalluses, sometimes so large they are slung over one shoulder. The trickster gods provoke both men and women with their lewd behavior and ass-pinching. They joke and play tricks to induce strong emotional responses in their audience, to release certain kinds of energy, relieve some tensions and form new ones, stir up the fires of human expression. The female counterpart goddess (erroneously called "wife") of the cigar-smoking trickster god Eshu is not a Lesbian figure (although Eshu himself once was, being originally Afrikete/Elegba in his West African homeland). Eshu's current counterpart in the Americas is Pompagira, an Indian goddess absorbed into Macumba by the tribal Africans who were taken as slaves to Brazil. Pompagira wears heavy makeup and a red dress; she stands in doorways or on street corners in an aggressive female posture. In our society she is easily recognizable in her daily profane form as a prostitute, loud-mouthed, comic and witty, provocative, streetwise, supremely erotic and aggressive. She is a trickster figure and easily the match of the Gay street queens who imitate her. She speaks of herself as "turning tricks" (*turn*: to revolve, to rub, to bore a hole).

In bar slang humor, faggots speak of themselves and of each other as "whores." As a rule, Lesbians do not call each other "whores" and do not turn tricks. With rare exception, they do not pick strange women up on the street by displaying themselves sexually for the sole purpose of ten or fifteen minutes of genital sex; they do not perform cunnilingus or tribadism on total strangers in movie houses, restrooms, parks, alleys, tearooms, or baths, nor do they count these places as in any way having to do with themselves. Lesbians sometimes use the word *trick* when they really mean "one-night stand," that is, going to a bar or party, meeting someone, and going home with her to spend the night and have sex or at least hug and kiss and be in each other's arms. That isn't tricking. Lesbians have open and closed relationships, one-night stands, serial monogamy, affairs of long and short duration, several lovers at one time, group sex, and even grope sessions in the more flamboyant baths in openly Gay cities. But none of this is tricking. None of this is brief genital sex of a few minutes' duration performed with strangers, often with the details of the nature of the act worked out in advance through signals or direct discussion, and with or without a cash transaction.

I am not going through this definition as a means of making a moral judgment. I think there have been serious misunderstandings between Gay men and Gay women concerning tricking — with the men trying to assume that Lesbians operate exactly as they themselves do, and with the women trying to assume moral superiority because no, we don't. Our institutions and our precedents are different, I think only partly because women's sexuality in general underwent centuries of often very grotesque and heavy suppression. I think even more likely that whatever functions tricking serves for Gay men, Lesbians simply do not have that same driving purpose in their lives and are preoccupied with other equally pressing matters.

Frankly, I wish I could sometime stand against a tree in Washington Square Park or Golden Gate Park or across the street from the White House being sucked for the seventh time in one night by a seventh handsome dyke — if only to know what that experience could possibly feel like. Is it a feeling of erotic power only? Oneness with the universe or with the element of lightning? Total freedom from social restraint? Ownership of the air and space of the world? Of another's tongue and lips? Closeness to the tree? Extreme sense of erotic prowess? Frankly, I don't think I'll ever know. Not in this life. How could I possibly line up seven dykes willing to perform this public act and arrange for them to be in the area all night? How could I dress for the occasion? In a kilt? How could I display myself erotically to strangers with clothes that place emphasis on my genitals and hips and breasts without attracting men instead of women? No, it cannot be done in this society. Whores can trick and faggots can trick, but not dykes. It is not, anyway, a part of the archetype, the model for who we are, at least not since Baubo and Uzume pulled their G-strings down to titillate the female gods thousands of years ago. But for Gay men and for prostitutes there is a historical/mythic model for tricking.

They trick, Gay men and prostitutes. They elicit fire. That is, they release sexual/erotic/bawdy energy from strangers. The term "trick-or-treat," used on Halloween, the Great Gay Holiday, most certainly stems from the pagan trickster gods, as so must the term "tricks of the trade." Since the trickster is a gambler, card tricks are also in his or her bag. A trick is an energy exchange through masquerade, through being consciously fooled, or teased, or sexually aroused by a stranger in a semi-magical role such as the whore feathered and heavily made up who looks like one thing but is really something else or the elegant young queen who looks like one thing but who's really something else. And what they sell is as much the masquerade and the trick of the arousal as it is the sex itself. The Fool in the Tarot deck, the joker in the playing card deck, the court jester and the king's court fool are also Gay character figures stemming from the trickster gods. Divination was part of what they did, and this is recalled in the term "trick" used with regard to playing cards, whose original uses were divinatory.

Sex Magic

In all likelihood, the priestesses and sorcerers used different sex techniques depending on what they specifically wanted to conjure, what kind of social or natural power was being called on or solidified. Each has a different effect.

The dildo sex used by European witches in their Dianic Sabbats and other sexual ceremonies were for the purpose of uniting female initiates with the goat or stag-god, that is, with the masculine god or spirit of the animal world. This sacred act helped forge a vital close connection between human society and the herd animal societies on whom they depended for food and clothing, soap, fat, bone, and dozens of other products. The ceremonial dildo sex act was always described as very uncomfortable, and obviously inducing sexual pleasure was never its intention.

Likewise with male sorcerer/priest/shamans, different sex techniques produce markedly different psychic effects and are used in varied social and ritual contexts. For instance, Arthur Evans writes that in the old Buffalo Dance of the Sioux, the shaman would dress in a buffalo robe and be ritually fucked in the ass by the other male dancers.[15] This formed a sexual/magical connection to the animal world and to the all-important buffalo spirits. As an act it was the obverse of the all-female European witch circle in which the god/spirit, a Dianic priestess dressed in a goat or deer skin, "fucks" the initiate with a dildo.

Apparently the difference in effect between anal and oral sex is very significant among modern American Gay men, and

211

deep in the urban Gay underground culture participants have developed elaborate methods of signaling each other which (if not both) kind of sex they want. An earring worn on a particular ear, for instance, or a handkerchief of a certain color in the back pocket tell watchful, in-the-know strangers what type of sex the bearer desires. One man, a sailor who heard me speak on the radio, kindly wrote to tell me in what parts of the world Gay men prefer anal, and which oral, sex. I am certain that a different effect on the participants, and a different kind of psychic power or energy, is "raised" by anal sex than by oral, and by public sex rather than private, and that these are unconscious factors in the preferences Gay men have.

Bob Gluck, in *Elements of a Coffee Service*, describes some of those factors in the following love scene:

> That got old so I carried him to the kitchen table where he squatted like a frog and I fucked him. My own body knows what his experienced: each time my cock touched a certain point hot and icy shivers radiated outward. I burn and freeze. If you have a man's body that is what you would feel. A cock's pleasure is like a fist, concentrated; anal pleasure is diffused, an open palm, and the pleasure of an anal orgasm is founded on relaxation. It's hard to understand how a man can write well if he doesn't like to be fucked. There's no evidence to support this theory; still, you can't be so straight that you don't submit to pleasure. Ezra Pound claimed his poetry was a penis aimed at the passive vulva of London. Perhaps that's why his writing is so worried, brow-furrowed. We dallied with coming for a while but decided no. Brian loved to be carried and pleasure made me powerful, sent blood to my muscles and aligned them. I lifted him from the table and fucked him in the air.[16]

His description indicates a strongly felt distinction, the difference between sex that is assertion and sex that is acceptance, both states of being that are often combined in each person's sex life and that are available to both sexes. His description does not assign assertion to males and acceptance to females, as the classic (and heavily Romanized) heterosexual culture models have demanded.

"Madrone Tree That Was My Mother"

"Madrone Tree, from your thirsty root / feed my soul as if it were your fruit," Robert Duncan's poem sings.[17] "Fruit" is one of those derogatory words used in the street language of our society, like "pansy," to separate the straight men from the Gay men. It implies effeminacy, as "meat" implies masculinity. In terms of the Old Religion with its Gay priesthood, the term "fruit" opens into more significant meanings. The Mother Goddess of pagan belief was and continues to be represented in the form of a tree, the Tree of Life, whose "fruit" is her son. A "fruit" then is someone who is son to the mothergod. It seems significant to me that Gay men call the display of their genitals under tight clothing their "basket," since a basket is typically something used to contain flowers or fruit. According to *Gay Talk*, in Gay slang "fruit salad" is a Gay crowd, "fruit jars" are weights used for bodybuilding, a "fruit picker" is someone who blackmails or robs homosexuals, a "fruit fly" is a woman who enjoys the company of Gay men, and a "fruit bowl queen" is a Gay football player.

In a more sinister aspect of sacred trees, not only did Gay pagan priest/diviners take wands from trees, but special men among their number, or among the village at large, were often chosen for sacrifice and were "given back" to the mother tree by being hung from it, or buried inside it, or crucified from its limbs as a god/king sacrifice.

Though king sacrifice may seem like something that existed centuries ago in a far-off land, it is actually closer to us than we realize. You knew that, didn't you, Von? You once told me a story about one of your adolescent exploits in the wilds of northern New Mexico "Territory," as you called your homeland. Some of the people you went to school with were rumored to belong to a strange religion, known as the "Pentitentes." Brought to the people of the territory in the 1600s by the colonial Spaniards, the rites of Pentitentes, or "Penitents," as the name means in English, took the blood sacrifice of Christ very seriously. Not only did they flagellate themselves in a painful march at Easter, they also crowned as god-king a fourteen-year-old boy each year and crucified him. The boys, it is said, were selected early in their lives for this honor of renewing their people's collective lives by their total sacrifice each year.

As you told the story, Vonnie, the crucifixion ceremonies had been outlawed in the 1930s, and the Pentitentes had long been excommunicated by the Catholic Church, which of course wanted no part of such a pagan practice. But, you said, the Penitentes continued to have meetings back up in the hills and were the subject of much speculation in the town. One night you and a

213

friend went on horseback deep into the hills where you had spotted a strange wooden building that had no windows. You believed it was a secret meeting house.

Leaving your horses tied in the trees you two slithered through the grass on your bellies until you could peek into the cracks of the wooden slats of the church. Inside, you saw black-clothed people with candles moving around; the hairs raised on your arms and neck as you listened to the ceremonies (which were actually none of your business) and then suddenly you were spotted. Shouts, angry running men, shotguns, then shots fired over your heads sent the two of you running pell-mell for your lives, grabbing your horses' bridles with relief, and galloping off in the dark. What a cowboy you were, my friend. How I wish I had been with you then.

Medieval King Sacrifice
The Goat and His Butch

Since Gay power is so connected to the quality of transference, it is natural that pagan tribal-based people of ancient Europe would employ sacred Gay officials of the Druidic and other priesthoods to perform the various blood sacrifice ceremonies, because the old blood rites themselves represented a transference of power from one entity, or domain, to another, from the animal world to the human, from the human to the divine.

The animal blood sacrifice, like the European practice of king's blood sacrifice, was central to pagan religion during the centuries when women's oldest and most essential blood and birth powers were being transferred into men's hands. Women's oldest magical-science powers revolved around menstruation and birth, and the blood of both these states of being was considered sacred. In fact, I believe *sacred* itself meant the menstrual state. To ritually shed blood, meant the ability to take on women's ancient powers. The transfer of the rites and paraphernalia of blood power from secret all-female covens and temple ceremonies into male hands and into the hands of the people as a whole was pivotal in the transition from woman-based to man-based society. Gay culture effected and administered the changeover, as it continues to do today.

In *The Arrow and the Sword*, Hugh Ross Williamson relates a ceremonial myth of the slaying of the bull-god by the male god Mithra:

214

> Thereupon the Sun sent a messenger — a raven — to command
> Mithra to slay the Bull. Much against his will, Mithra carried
> out this sacrilegious mission. He overtook the Bull just as it
> was taking refuge in the cave it had left, and killed it with his
> hunting knife. Immediately a miracle happened. From the dead
> body of the Bull sprang all the useful herbs and plants. From
> its spinal cord sprang the wheat, from its blood, the vine. Its
> seed, gathered and purified by the Moon, produced all the
> species of useful animals; and its soul ascended into Heaven
> where, receiving the honours of divinity, it became Silvanus,
> the god of gardens, lover of the beautiful youth, Cyparissus.[18]

The sacrificed bull-god became a Gay god with a lover, to close
the cycle of this Gay creation myth, which perhaps once underlay
the sacrificial public bullfight.

The *slayer* of the sacred goat-bull-stag was a ceremonial person, and when the sacrifice was of the human king, as happened
all over Europe in its history, as well as parts of Africa, the king-
slayer was a sacred person too, and of course not subject to any
charge of ill-doing. Williamson believes that the relationship between the Gay Norman King William Rufus and his sacrificial
killer and longtime companion Tyrrel was a Gay connection. Although William the Conqueror had established a French Norman
court over the English people that fixed the class system of England, his son William Rufus, the pagan faggot king, was enor-
mously popular with the common people, who in the 1100s still
retained their own Old Religion in spite of centuries of influence of
the Church. They took Rufus to their hearts. King Rufus (the Red)
neither married nor took a girlfriend; no woman's name was ever
associated with his. His court was notorious for flagrant homosexuality and for "effeminati," men with long hair, extravagant manners, and luxurious dress, including shoes with upward-curling
points. The courtiers shaved in order "that their beards should not
chafe their friends when they kissed," according to Williamson.[19]

Tyrrel was described as the King's "intimate." Rufus worshiped the ancient god of light, Lucca, brother of Diana (who was
primarily worshiped by women). On the day of his death, a pre-
ordained and traditional sacrificial day, Rufus handed Tyrell a set
of arrows he himself had carefully sharpened and told him to use
them according to his obligation. Previously Rufus had dreamed
prophetically that he went alone into a chapel in the forest, whose
walls were hung with purple tapestries embroidered with ancient
legends. Then the tapestry vanished and he stood in a plain room

215

near a plain altar on which lay a naked man or, some stories say, a stag. The King tried to eat the body but the man/stag said, "Henceforth thou shalt eat of me no more" and vanished. After hunting all day at the site of a pre-Christian temple in New Forest, Tyrrel, waiting until the appropriate time of sunset, shot his king and longtime companion with the shiny new arrows, though he faltered at the last moment and was slow to shoot so that the king demanded it of him, in the name of the pagan god they both worshiped. Tyrrel then shot one arrow. The wounded king fell on it to ensure his own death.

All over the countryside the common people knew of the king's death before it happened, since it was a predicted sacrifice, and they took an enormous interest in the drops of blood that fell from his wound as Tyrrel carried his body home. The king's blood was considered sacred and extremely powerful, being a healing force giving good fortune and fertility to crops, animals and humans. As a king of the Old Religion, William Rufus was the Horned God personified, he was the goat — or, in this case, stag — whose powers passed on to the people by the special event of his death. And Tyrrel, his intimate companion, was his "butch," the sacred "goat-slayer," the king slayer. His was a task that had to be performed with perfect love.

The story of Rufus and Tyrrel is strongly reminiscent of that of Hyacinthus and Apollo and also of two women, the Amazon Queen Hippolyta, who was "accidently" killed by her sister Penthesilea, who "mistook" her for a stag. The fact that Penthesilea went to the battle of Troy with twelve warrior maidens, forming a coven number of thirteen, strongly implies the sacred nature of the slaying of one sister by the other.

Gay As a Goat

The goat-god appears in some references connecting him to Gay underground culture. In Gay slang the foreskin of the penis is called the "goatskin," as bitter semen is called "goat's milk." [20] *Gorky Park*, a novel about Russia by Martin Cruz Smith, describes two prison lovers, one of whom is called a "goat." His name is Swan, a man dressed in a leather jacket that emphasizes his narrow shoulders, long neck, and close-cropped hair. It seems that in prison a professional thief would select a less-experienced inmate, bugger him, and then throw him out. This gives the professional thief, the one who takes the top position, more points for masculinity. The "goat," the one on the bottom, is despised as the queer.

In Ireland there is a ceremony held in midsummer known as the Puck Fair. The Puck is a goat, representing the goat-king; he is crowned by a little girl "queen" and boys dressed in green and then carried in procession in a cart. Originally the Puck Fair was held on Lammas, the first of August, a formal Fairy holiday. The Puck in this ceremony is not sacrificed; it is not a blood ceremony. Margaret Murray derives his title Puck from Slavic *Bog*, for God.[21] Shakespeare, drawing on the folk culture of his time, formed the character of Puck in *A Midsummer Night's Dream* as a Fairy person, and he is usually played as a pretty person with a small, slender body, a mischievous innocent demeanor, and a graceful carriage — but without the exaggerated "effeminacy" of a Gay queen. Puck is a faggot, not a queen. I have seen him portrayed in such a way as to match the manner, look, and state of being of *both* a faggot and a dike — in that middle area where our styles overlap and duplicate each other and where we achieve a perfect balance of outward and inward (which we call butch/femme) in the same person. When I was fifteen I was lucky enough to see *A Midsummer Night's Dream* performed at a San Diego Shakespeare Festival. I identified completely with the character of Puck and within weeks of seeing him was able to understand that I was a Lesbian. I knew that summer that in some way Puck is what I am. He is also what I look for (and usually find) in my lovers and in Gay men.

The Whipping Stick

There is another kind of historical association, another strand of the story, between faggots and the vegetable finnochio of Prometheus, besides the fire-magical wand of wizards or the sacred branches of the fagus tree. Rome, excelling in conquest and colonization, used a bundle of sticks (the Fasces) to symbolize united male power. Although the Romans tolerated simple male homosexual sexual relations, they violently suppressed the older and more tribal and female-oriented Gay cultures wherever they found them. Using the classic colonial method of reversing a sacred tribal tradition, turning it on the people to terrorize them with their own most dearly held customs, Rome turned the sacred wand into a whipping stick. Among the cruelest and most physically punishing of any peoples, Roman patriarchs set up educational systems all over Europe that specialized in the whipping and torment of children, especially boys, who then grow up angry, stiff, frightened, and brutal. The stalks of Prometheus' sacred plant, the ferula, were used as a rod or whip for this purpose. In fact, the word *ferule* means such a rod or the punishment itself. In England, "fagging" is the word used to describe the system of hazing, sexually abusing, and punishing schoolboys, a system developed by the Roman occupation.

Though the Roman armies withdrew and Rome as a conquering supermasculine state declined around A.D. 500, the venerable history of the word *faggot* continued to take its negative twist during the Middle Ages. In a hideous turnabout of the old Paleolithic tribal customs, the Inquisition (another Roman legacy deliberately modeled on Roman methods) used women's essential and religiously recognized connection to fire as its most effective symbol of terror and pain by publicly burning alive convicted wisewomen in mass executions. Sometimes their daughters were required to stand and watch. Over a period of four centuries some nine million such hideous conflagrations occurred, driving Europe's women out of power and their tribal traditions completely underground. Sometimes to add to the horror and drive the lessons home further, the bodies of strangled Gay men were stacked in with the kindling at the witches' feet as "faggots" of a new and horrible kind and as a sacrificial symbol turned upon the people who had valued living faggots, sacred Gay men.

The Roman Way To Be a Man

The Roman army dressed and acted differently from the warriors of the vast territories it conquered. The barbarian tribes loved feathers and beads and gold decorations finely made and jingling bells to deck out their beloved horses. They favored natural talismans of all kinds, lion and leopard skins, eagle feathers and bear claws, wolves' teeth and snake skins to bring the powers of skill and courage of the natural world with them into the fray and to enhance their personal courage and connection to the other fanged folk.

In brittle contrast, the Roman legionnaires wore polished leather tunics, metal helmets, and metal breastplates. Marching in close formations of straight lines with their shields locked together, they were machinelike and industrialized, lacking in the individual duels and spontaneous bursts of personal courage and high feeling so dear to the hearts of the tribal warriors, who fought primarily to display their courage, for honor, and to be heroes in the eyes of their kinfolk.

In the tribal world conquered and forever altered by the Roman and other patriarchal war machines, women ruled with men, women governed and had economic control; women created large measures of the science, industry, and art. Celtic and Teutonic women went to battle alongside their uncles and sons and brothers, and many an armed queen led them. The purpose of tribal and barbarian battle was personal heroic display and the juggling back and forth of tribal boundaries, and though captured prisoners might be put to death, and horribly, as sacrifices, entire peoples were not annihilated or condemned to slavery or colonization. The purpose of Roman war was the acquisition of slaves, of property; of colonization and empire building.

Destructive to the tribal people as their enslavement was, probably even more destructive to their philosophical base were the gladiator games. Every city and province colonized by the Romans was required by law to hold gladiator games, and here the warriors of the old tribes were forced to relearn the principles of combat, which for them was its use as a voluntary display of masculine blood-courage. In the mass public arena of gladiator games they learned to think of warfare as conscription, as physical fear of death, as simple murder. As spectators or participants, they learned to strip it of tribal honor or personal courage, to strip it of choice and compassion, admiration or graceful display, to strip it of all ceremonial and shamanic aspects. The rules of the gladiatorial ring were simple; the combatants were threatened with immediate death unless they stood in the arena hacking at each other until one of them died. Women as well as men participated. The games used prisoners of war from the tribal territories, Britons captured under Claudius, or a host of Jewish prisoners taken after Titus sacked Jerusalem, for instance. It became customary for sons to stage games in honor of their fathers, with the contests reaching mammoth proportions. After the conquest of Dacia, ten thousand men fought continuously for four months, presumably until all were dead. All manner of animals were used also — elephants, bears, African deer and gazelle, lions, tall birds, goats, sheep, and cattle in a display of the "conquest of nature," somewhat on the order of the great buffalo shoots of the American West.

According to Otto Keifer in *Sexual Life in Ancient Rome*,[22] flogging, crucifixion, beheading, torture, the "living torch," slavery, sexual torment, and rape of both male and female were vital parts of the Roman conquest of the tribal European and North African worlds. They called their peculiar ambition *potentiae cupido*, "desire for potency." Control by force was the major Roman skill, and with it they subjected the creative skills and powers of the people on every side of them. The ideal Roman man loathed dancing, nudity, and sexual expression (unless its purpose was control, as is the case with rape). The father owned his household as his sole property, and this included his wife and children. If she committed adultery he could kill her.

Thrashing of children, especially boys, was an everyday part of Roman schooling as it was established throughout the conquered territories. The boy was held up in the air and even suspended from ropes while his nude buttocks were lashed with birch rods in front of the other children. Horace called a famous schoolmaster "The Thrasher."

> There was no such thing as a slave's evidence given without torture. Everyone not of free birth was always questioned under torture. The means used were all sorts of scourging, as well as the hideous torments which the middle ages took over from Rome and employed for centuries at every special investigation. Such were the *fidiculae* — cords for wrenching the joints apart, the *equuleus* — a trestle in which the slave sat while his limbs were dislocated either by a windlass and by weights attached to his feet; so also red hot metal plates were laid on the slaves' bare flesh, and so the dreadful leather scourges were intertwined with spikes and knuckle-bones to increase their atrocity.[23]

The Roman man, a marching soldier clothed in metal and leather, who watches others dance but never himself participates, who wields instruments of torture and makes certain through his beatings that his children, especially his male children, stay angry all their lives, and who makes war for the purpose of taking for himself the skills and services of others, is one model of masculinity, of "manhood" that has imprinted itself on all Western culture.

Mocking the Military Butch Man

The military butch qualities applied to men are clipped hair, clean-shaven face, polished leather trappings, boots and belts and jackets and straps; a young, muscled body. Then there is metal, like the shiny accoutrements such as buckles, buttons, clasps, keys, zippers, pins, medals, snaps. Leather and metal belong to the masculine idea of butch, along with bodybuilding and physical authoritativeness. The butch man is often admired by Gay men as he is by so many women, and he is sought after by many faggots as a love/sex object.

But military butch masculinity is also the object of deep scorn and social criticism on the parts of the core group of blatant and very nearly ceremonial dikes and queens at the heart of the Gay underground. Two Gay character figures make certain that society can never relax into the Roman-based definition of masculine role models. They are the Lesbian bulldagger and a particular kind of Gay queen, the male faggot leather queen.

Many leather queens presently live in large concentrations in a small area of the San Francisco Gay ghetto, an area known in Gay slang as the "Leather Belt." They parody the supermasculine role so often expected of men by publicly displaying themselves in tight leather jackets and tight leather pants, dark glasses, and slick-down hair. This all sounds "masculine" enough, but it is accompanied by high-pitched voices, limp wrists, a positively swishy walk, gossiping, and touching each other in a "feminine" manner, and a complete lack of visible body muscle. Sometimes the black leather pants are missing a round shape over the ass, displaying saggy gray long johns to complete the disturbing, clownish effect. But what else can you expect from people who refer to the draft as "Uncle Samantha's meat call"?

The second Gay cultural characterization and parody of "masculinity" is in the Lesbian butch as she appears in Gay bar society especially and in the Lesbian street ghettos and on Halloween, when she will add a mustache to the black leather jacket, boots, slicked-down hair, T-shirt, tattoo, and wad of keys hanging at the belt. Having muscles (or wishing to have them) and walking in big strides are part of the butch role for women, making it all the more of a shock when the observer sees or hears that what is so obviously "he" is really "she."

These two extremes of "role remodeling" are acted out in full by only a tiny number of Gay people, and usually only for that segment of their lives when they are passing through the Gay underground culture and are trying out different social attitudes learned from other members of Gay culture. Most of the time when Gay men use the word *butch* about themselves they are talking about much more minutely leatherish (or even tweedish) characteristics, such as an extra thick watchband. But when we observe the extreme butch and leather queen postures acted out, we can use them to separate characteristics from gender and begin to perceive the basis of this society's ideas of "masculinity" and "control, authority, strength."

And of course, social values influence how freely expressive the individual Gay person can be. One of my lovers had a long-legged, dykely stride to match her gestures, posture, low-pitched throaty voice, and general butch character until she was eleven or twelve. At that time her aunt and her mother cornered her and tied a rope between her ankles to teach her to "walk like a girl." After a week of this torment, her natural walk became a jolting, caught-up-short lurch that made her otherwise graceful body look as though she were about to fall over as she walked along. She hated this crippling, referring to it as "the time they hobbled me," but by the time she grew up it was permanent and she could not walk any other way.

Military Manhood

I walked more like a "man" when I got out of the service than before I went into it. What was different? Much of military training consists of learning to march in formation and to stand perfectly still without moving, no matter what calamities are happening around you. It is regimented passivity. A vivid memory remains of myself at age twenty standing in the blazing Texas July heat watching drops of sweat so mixed with starch they were eerie white drops, rolling monotonously down the backs and necks of the blue-clothed women standing identically in front of me in formation. Knowing my own back looked the same, soaked dark blue from shirt collar to mid-hip of the skirt as last night's effort of starching and ironing ran in sheets of white watercolor landscapes down our bodies.

Occasionally some soul collapsed, rolling to the ground unconscious; no one was allowed to move or flinch when this happened. I recall one such blistering afternoon standing at parade rest with a hundred other women for an hour or two, feet apart, back straight, hands clenched at mid-spine, numb everywhere, watching a pair of hornets climb up and down the bare arms and all around the fingers of the woman standing at parade rest in front of me. Not moving. Military butch means showing no emotion, taking no action on your own, holding the body utterly still, in a perpetual state of waiting to be told what to do next. The feeling is one of tense suspended animation, and the attitude is of passivity with regard to everyone who ranks above you and un-emotional, controlled aggression toward everyone who ranks be-low you.

To learn to march in formation, we were first retaught how to walk. Buttocks tucked under, never swaying the hips or twist-ing the shoulders, waist stiff, legs stiff, wrists stiff, face expression-less and tight, arms swinging in a line straight out in front and back, weight coming down hard heel first, eyes straight ahead, spine straight, everything *straight* and stiff, nothing crooked or kinked or round or gyrating or pelvic or supple or emotional. Or queer.

Remembering this experience, and taking notes and trying to really see what I was looking at, I watched various faggots walk down the street recently, and then some straight men, young and middle-aged. The faggot uses his hips and elbows and arms and toes in a sashay, side-to-side, light-footed, toe-using walk with arms used for side-to-side balance and grace. It is a floating, rhyth-mic, dancing sort of walk, and women often use a similar one. The center of balance is pelvic and such that the body rotates in a global fashion. Many straight white men (and also dykish women) walk stiff-armed, stiff-legged, heavy on the heels, and do not move their hips from side to side, although sometimes their shoulders do sway. It is a mechanical rhythmic marching motion, forward thrusting and progressive in a straight line, the heels be-ing the part of the foot emphasized, and the arms are used for forward motion and are otherwise stiff, the hands are utterly in-expressive, as are the neck and face and pelvis; the chin is thrust out, the buttocks are tucked under, and the center of gravity is in the torso and shoulders.

Reversing Tribal Powers

There is an oppressive or colonial technique of "reversing tribal, or indigenous, powers," that is, turning a people's most cherished rites, customs, and beliefs into weapons of humiliation, pain, and horror that can be used to frighten and control the nature of the culture itself. This tactic of reversing a positive cultural value into a negative one has long been utilized by "patriarchal" or state-oriented forces.

King-sacrifice of Europe and Africa, the cleansing and renew-ing ritual of tribal folk, was vested with the mainly Gay priesthood; over the centuries it has been reversed into a popular habit among certain groups of tormenting, torturing, beating, and even publicly assassinating Gay men. Lesbians come in for a certain amount of this harassment and murder, too, but in my experience it is far more often and more virulently directed at men. And usually the violence is performed by young men of the same race as the "scapegoat" faggot.

So one hears of Hispanic boys torturing and killing a Hispanic faggot during Christmas holidays, of Black youths in Oakland leaning out of a passing car to shotgun to death a Black drag queen standing in front of a Gay bar, of dynamite blowing apart Gay bars located near a white working-class area. The most dramatic of recent anti-Gay actions was the shooting in 1979 by Dan White of supervisor Harvey Milk (as well as liberal mayor George Moscone), and the fact that White was considered a hero for it in some sectors of his own straight community. Milk, the first openly Gay supervisor of San Francisco, was so certain he could be killed for his Gayness that he made out a will with that possibility in mind shortly before his election — hardly the usual precautions of a city supervisor.

The effect of being violently attacked within your own ethnic community is to effectively be in exile from it; this state of exile has characterized Gay people in the modern urban environment. Those of us who have remained overtly Gay for any length of time have also had to become ghettoized to a great extent, living primarily in those places that are safe for Gay people.

The violent reversal of a sacred institution is a form of terrorism that imprints itself into a population for centuries and is carried on by the bullies of a community, village, or tribe. Perhaps the irrational terror and disgust of Gay people expressed by large segments of the population had its origins in Inquisition-like formal attacks upon the ancient tribal and village institutions of Gay priesthoods and religious leadership.

By the Short Hairs

The Roman model for male behavior appears to be the basis for industrial militarism. If the model for "superbutch male" represents the cruel, metal-clad Roman conqueror marching through Europe and North Africa, the "ultrafemme" woman certainly represents the conquered tribe. Long-haired, walking light-footed, clad in bright colors, face paint, feathers, beads, earrings, sashes, flowers and fur — the trappings of the full-blown femme woman (and the faggot queen) of our society could easily translate into the garb of ancient tribal people of all continents. Except that the woman has added some deliberate symbolic effects of enslavement and total vulnerability such as silver or gold chains on ankles, wrist, and throat; high heels; sexual exposure of thighs and breasts; restrictive tight skirt in a hobbling effect; restrictive short-striding gait; and makeup that mimics a swollen, bruised, beaten look. Much heterosexual pornography centers on the dynamic between the man-soldier conqueror and the female-slave conquest.

The "military manhood" became the model for much Anglo-European "masculinity" and it has ever since been rejected by Gay "effeminate" men, queens, sissies, fops, and flaming faggots. Roman observers held the "effeminate" swishy walk of such people as Persian men in contempt. It is not so much that faggots march to a different drummer as that they refuse to march at all. They swish instead. And though it is true that faggots often look to the behavior and outward appearance of women to emulate and to aid their opposition to the military manhood model, this imitation does not account for all the mannerisms of Gay queens. Some of it they learn from each other. Secreted in their Gay underground culture, they retain, I believe, some of the characteristics of how men were, independent of how women were, *before* the military model for the masculine role was developed and spread by Roman and other patriarchal conquests of the older tribal traditions.

Affecting Somewhat of a Lisp

Gay men's "femme" faggotry appears on the surface to be an imitation of the mannerisms of straight women, and certainly some of it is such a conscious imitation. But only some of it. Some of it is an independent Gay cultural tradition. While much faggotry consists of the effects of cross-dressing (what is not butch is certain to be femme, what is not "like a boy" is considered "effeminate"), its most basic mannerisms are part of an independent cultural tradition handed along from faggot to faggot. These are remembrances and retainments of how men (and women) were in previous centuries, especially in the remembrance of tribal traditions, and how people were in "Fairyland."

It is commonly supposed that faggots lisp in imitation of women. Modern women, however, do not lisp, although unless they are utter dykes or have other reasons for plain speech, they do use inflections and intonations somewhat similar to faggot speech. But the sweet sibilant faggot speech is peculiar to Gay men, and completely distinctive. For the most part faggots learn their particular manner of speaking from each other. Lisping and other particulars of faggot speech can be heard most closely in Shakespearean actors, who are imitating sixteenth-century English and who are also themselves faggots or are imitating the speech retained in an acting community highly influenced by Gay culture.

Apparently, English-speaking people, both men and women, used the lisp as a form of speech in past centuries. Lisping is mentioned in Shakeseare's plays[24] as well as in this piece of the Prologue to Chaucer's *Canterbury Tales* describing a friar who was a beggar, wanton and merry:

> his robe was made of double worsted
> and was rounded like a bell right out of the mold.
> He affected somewhat of a lisp
> to make his English sweet upon his tongue;
> and when he harped at the end of a song,
> his eyes twinkled in his head just
> like the stars on a frosty night.

In Old English of the twelfth century lisping was called "awlispian," and Robert Gluck has found references in the Oxford English Dictionary dated 1375, 1386, and 1440. Perhaps lisping was once a form of court or special courting speech or at one time a ceremonial language, in English, as it was in Spain. Fourteenth-century Castilian, or court Spanish, is spoken with a distinctive lisp. Castile was a former kingdom (1313–1492) comprising most of Spain.

Since the definitions of romantic love were heavily influenced by the troubadors who emerged in areas that also produced the pro-Gay Cathar heresy, perhaps the historic formalities of courtly love, as well as the speech of the dramatic arts, were Gay provinces, vestiges of which have been handed down through word of mouth in Gay faggot culture totally independent of the "imitation of women."

Camping It Up

Gay participation and influence in every sphere of theater is well known — in ballet, television, the music industry, performance poetry, motion pictures (and much Gay male slang uses references to Hollywood: a "Hollywood uterus" being the anus, for example[25]) as well as stage theater. This participation is a natural inheritance, for theater began as the ceremonial dramas and rites whose purpose was the reenacting of spiritual events for the benefit of tribal and village people. And it was the Gay shamanic/priesthood who was in charge of these ritual dramas. The faggot sorcerer with his fagus wand and his costumes representing the god-forces and animal spirits of the universe in which his people lived took center stage and gave direction in the ceremonial theatrical functions and tribal origin stories.

The Gay word *camp* takes its origins from this theatrical Gay function. *Camp* as Gay people, especially men, use it, is like continual theater. The Gay slang dictionary *Gay Talk* defines *camp* as coming from a theatrical sixteenth-century term *camping*, meaning "young men wearing the costume of women in a play," from the French word *campagne*, the countryside "where strolling mime troops entertained" in medieval times. The dictionary gives a very full description of modern faggot camp:

> Camp is burlesque, fun, an ability to poke a jocular finger at one's own frustrations and guffaw at the struggles of other pathetics, homosexuals or famous, influential people . . . Camp personalities are sometimes loved because they are unpretentious, real . . . The funny thing about a camp is that the more seriously he or she takes himself, the campier he becomes. Batman became camp because his purpose in life — crime-fighting — became so serious it grew absurd. Items are also camp if they are so ostentatious they're considered good taste. So bad they're good. Some, such as pop posters, were once camp, but here comes the rub: as soon as an object is advertised as such, it no longer is camp.
>
> Camp is discovering the worthiness in something seemingly without value: finding the genius in something that flopped once upon a time; beauty in the grotesque . . . Camp is nostalgia . . . bringing back a lighter nonsense when things get dull. It is the means, the bridge, by which elaborate and necessary foolishness is briefly reclaimed. With personified Hollywood figures, it is also canonization. Women who are camp have donated, whether they know it or not, courage and bits of wisdom to the homosexual effeminate who often imitates them.[26]

The history of theater derives its origins from the rites and ceremonies of tribal times. When I think about the word *theater*, it is interesting to me that the word *Thea* was Greek for "goddess." The formal traditional theater retains much of its original purpose as rite, the reenactment of transformation. The curtain, or veil of vision or consciousness, opens to display a second world, a state of being different from the everyday one. It is a world which the audience agrees to enter by contracting both emotionally and intellectually to believe in the story being told. The players, using costume, makeup, and setting, take on or are taken over by the persona of characters who are not themselves, somewhat as the ancient shaman/medium in paint and mask was "taken over" by the god, spirit, or animal force being represented in the rite.

The faggot's "wand" of the theater is displayed as the baton of the orchestra director, the writers' pen, the "regie book" of the director (from *regie*, to direct, from *reg*, *rex*, *kingship*, meaning related to, *regale*, *regalia*),[27] the torch of liberty in certain motion picture logos, and the numerous canes, parasols, and other sticks and wands present in dance numbers, comic scenes, and the like.

Other theater-related words draw from the ancient rites of pagan times. *Comedy* comes from a Greek word, *komos*, meaning a festival procession and an ode sung at it. Tragedy means literally "goatsong," from the Greek *tragoidia* (*tragos*, "goat," and *oide*, "song"), relates directly to ancient rites of king-sacrifice and the practice of the singers in such dramas expressive of the sacrifice to clothe themselves in goatskins while they sang the drama. *Travesty*, "caricature," means literally "cross-dress" and is related to the term *transvestite*.[28]

It is in the sense of the ancient ceremonial festivals, processions, and rites that *Gay* means festive, and this explains where its tragic elements come from, too, for the ancient festivals celebrated life *and* death, in the acting out of stories related to forces and spirit-presences they called gods, such as Gaia and Uranus.

I believe that *Gay* and *Uranian* are the oldest English words pertaining to the Gay underground, having gotten their origin during times when Gay culture did not need to be closeted from the rest of society, at least not in an oppressive manner. It was integrated into the culture at large, which was mostly separatist; the men had their gods and so did the women. Before the invasions of light-skinned patriarchal people from the north, before "Greece" at all, there was a prevailing earth goddess, dark and grand and science-oriented and snakey/powerful, like Afrikete of Africa. Maybe she began her domain on earth in the millennia when science-based Egypt ruled the world, or perhaps prior to that, say seven to ten thousand years ago. The oracle at Gaia's shrine spoke in rhymed metrical riddles, and all manner of affairs of state were carried out through this poetic medium. In one form her name as *Ge* has been used to designate modern mathematical earth science ideas such as *geometry, geology, geography*. From another form of her name, *Gaia*, I believe derives the cultural/ poetic/oracular/contrary/priest/shamanic/cross-dressing/homo-sexual traditional cultural and group name *Gay*.

As a slang word, *Gay* was recorded in the sixteenth century using a socially acceptable definition, "loose man." In Castilian Spanish the word was pronounced the older way, *Gaya*.

The Gay Troubadors were very special poet/musician/singers who traveled in pairs in the eleventh and twelfth centuries in Europe singing songs that taught principles of romantic love taken from the philosophy of homosexual Plato and also from the philosophy of a Gay and woman-led heresy of the time called Catharism, concerning itself with the balance of power between good and evil. The first Troubador, according to Hugh Ross Williamson, was William, Count of Pouitou, the close friend and companion-in-arms of the Gay Norman King William Rufus, in a court notorious for "effeminate" homosexual customs. The count, who wrote the first Troubador poetry, was known as a brave, accomplished, irreverent, and immoral man.[29] The Troubadors were usually two men working together, traveling and singing, and the "ladies" to whom they addressed or dedicated their romantic songs were often other men.

Gay has long been associated with metrical, rhymed language. In India, right next door to the land of Gaia's shrine, the goddess of the Morning Prayer is named *Gayatri*. She is a companion to Kali, who has sometimes been worshiped with Lesbian rites. Gayatri's name is a Sanscrit word meaning a special meter, the Gayatri verse, from *gai*, meaning "to relate in a metrical language, especially to sing."[30] No wonder so much modern Gay philosophy and cultural, even political, understanding has been expressed through song and poetry, and no wonder Gay culture accounts for so many poets and poetic movements. Rhymed information is part of our inheritance from the rites of old Earth Goddess Gaia, whose shrine was the domain of an oracle who spoke in rhymes and whose festivities featured processions and dramas sung in verse. Greek Gaia appears to have lent her name to the gayness of festivities, or perhaps she got her name from the rites.

229

To sing in a metrical manner seems to be a major Gay cultural function. It is not surprising that the Gay Troubadors were often Gay men who could imagine calling the beloved object of song "she" with no problems. Other Gay phrases relate to the ancient rites as well: *Sapphic*, for instance, is directly from the name of the poet/priestess Sappho, who sang her work. As I noted in Chapter Five, in Spanish *marcha atras*, "marching backwards," refers to the trickster/Heyoka habits of Gay shamanism of mirroring and reversing human vision; another Spanish word for queer, *jota*, also means a Spanish courtly dance of old times in which the men made elaborate, pretty gestures. The term is used in the back country of northern New Mexico, where sixteenth-century Spanish is still spoken, and it is current in other Hispanic areas, such as Argentina. *Mariachi* is another term for Gay in the Spanish language, a reference to the festive garb and manners of the Mariachi singers and musicians who play at festivals. "Being in drag" is an expression stemming from riding in a drag, or dray, during a procession; the term *round*, meaning "Gay," may stem from the round or ring dance of the Fairy people; Fairy circles or Fairy rings were places where tribal ceremonies of the Fairy people took place; in Gay slang it is a coterie of male homosexuals who know each other. Fairy circles as deliberate enactments of celebrative and special ceremonies recalling a lost Gay heritage have recently become a part of American Gay culture. Gaia's co-ruler Uranus, or Ouranos as his name is sometimes called, was a thundergod, a god of weather and lightning and sudden stormy change. He is evidently very old and knowledge of him was widespread. In West Africa a thundergod is named Ouriganos. Brought to the Caribbean by Black people his name entered the English language as the word "hurricane."

In the occult sciences, Uranus is noted as a planet of certain change and of transformation. In later Greek times, the Muses were named and assigned the arts and sciences; the ninth Muse was Urania, Muse of astronomy. She was said to be the special Muse of Plato and of homosexuals; when she paid special attention to the needs of homosexual lovers, Aphrodite was sometimes called Aphrodite Urania. In the nineteenth century, progressive homosexuals of Berlin formed a society for the purpose of advocating homosexual rights. They called themselves Uranians and their society the Uranian Society, and they spoke of Gayness as "Uranian Love." [31]

What's in a Word

Metrical and poetic elements have come down from the tribal world of rite and ceremony, retained in Gay slang itself, which uses puns, vivid imagery, and rhyming slang, such as calling eyeballs "highballs," or referring to a heavy smoker as "Norma Jean Nicotine." Norma Jean is the Gay name for Marilyn Monroe, since it is her real, that is, her secret, name. An "erector set queen" is a Gay construction worker; "Queen Esther" is a Jewish homosexual; "Miss Scarlet" is a white racist homosexual (in Gay Black slang); "Miss Niagara" is someone who vomits profusely; "Miss Claudette Crowbar" is a clumsy queen; and "Miss Pick-up-sticks" is a Gay lumberjack. The speakers of Gay male slang may be the only group in America who really admire the female breast as a powerful characteristic: In Gay slang *tits* means courage, unmitigated gall, "the tits" means excellent. To "tangle tits" means to do battle, and "nit tits" are microscopic breasts.[32]

Using words as creative structures, Gay poets and writers continue the ancient functions of guiding, disturbing, re-creating human thought and cultural values. Using theatrical methods, faggot "kings" continue to act direct, edit, and display the images our society uses to help itself function as a cohesive whole. And using the ancient chaotic powers, Gay trickster queens of all descriptions keep the matrix of human thought in the disrupted, tumultuous state that prevents stagnation and keeps true creativity and flexibility possible. The poet-king Robert Duncan sings:

> Madrone Tree that was my mother,
> Cast me a cloak as red as your flower.
> My sisters don't know me,
> My father looks for me,
> And I am by name the wind's brother.

CHAPTER NINE

Friction Among Women

now you have left you can be
wherever the fire is when it blows itself out.
now you are a voice in any wind
     i am a single wind
now you are any source of a fire
     i am a single fire

From "Funeral poem: A plainsong
from a younger woman to an older woman,"
    Judy Grahn[1]

PERHAPS "tricking" is a vestige of the old pagan ceremonies, a small chip from ceremonies and rites that have been fractured, outlawed, driven underground, and in large measure forgotten. What purposes could they serve now, anyhow, in our modern industrial culture, so removed from the tribal world of King Rufus and Tyrell, of Amazons and Fairies, goat-kings, and women who worship Diana on mountaintops. Although I do hear rumors of Fairy Circles affirming their tradition of male connection to the earth and its powers; I know that Lesbians wear amethysts and opals in their Lesbian-made rings; I know that Lesbians call their institutions Diana Press, Persephone Press, *Sinister Wisdom* magazine.

The old ceremonies are fractured, they did not continue intact and purposeful through the centuries when Euro-American society suppressed its old tribal ways in favor of our more material and mechanical mass world. Yet just as it is possible to say that Gay offices of the butch, the bulldike, the faggot, and the drag queen have come down to us in an altered yet still vital form, it is possible to suggest that strands and chips of the tribal ceremonial rites remain with us too. They are suggested in the derivations of *faggot*, the sacred firestick of Gay men. And in Lesbian words fire also plays a major part.

This chapter is especially for you, my Von; we were lovers during a period of American history when women were almost inevitably assumed to be rivals with each other (for the attentions of men) and to be unable to be friends, let alone lovers. But we secret Lesbians were keenly aware of the real fire between us, the friction that warms. This chapter is for the fire between us, for fires that continue and for fires that go out.

Fires That Stay

Fire, in the oldest human memories, is a female province. The sun was once a female god for much of the world; and for people such as the Swedish Lapps, who may be related to the English Fairy people, she still is sovereign. The Japanese tribal Ainu do not personify their deities, preferring to pay respects to various spirits or essences, called *Kamui*. The greatest of these is the female force, the Kamui of fire. Heat is a female creative force whether actual material fire is involved or not; in Tibet when the esoteric hermits sit in stone huts keeping themselves warm in the midst of high

235

mountain snow, month after month, nude or clothed only in thin cotton nightgowns, they survive by concentrating their attention on and picturing a hot fire glowing in their own bellies or genitals, a fire that they understand as the essence of the female creative fire god-force.

The ancient belief was that fire resided in the wood, coming out when the wood was rubbed in a particular manner and that creative/sexual fire resided in the female pudenda, also coming out when it is rubbed a certain way. Wood itself was female and sacred, coming from the great representation of the female god-spirit, the Tree of Life. A number of Lesbian sex-words relate to the act of rubbing the clitoris or vagina. The Latin *fricatrice* means "she who rubs" in the sense of friction, firemaking. In English, the term for two women rubbing clitorises and mounds together with their thighs locked between each other's legs is *tribadism*, and the title of the woman who performs it is "Tribas." Sappho has been called "Tribas." [2] Tribadism, involving two female bodies rubbing together, could only multiply the amount of creative fire generated since it doubled the female potential for making creative fire. Cunnilingus means stroking the female genitals with the tongue. Frigging refers to rubbing with the fingers, either on the outside around the lips and clitoris or inside the vagina. Though often performed more secretly than other forms of sex, the Lesbian acts of cunnilingus, tribadism, and frigging have had many personal, social, and ritual purposes.

The oldest female-centered religions are reported to have had Lesbian rites at their center, designed to call forth the female sexual and creative fire for specific, tribal purposes. Although the stories exactly describing this Lesbian religious office have been largely suppressed, altered, or kept underground, sometimes it is hinted at in the stories that have survived, as in the following tale of the Sun goddess of Japan. [3]

She Pulled Down Her Skirt Band

In ancient Japan, the sun Goddess, Ama-terasu, was titled "Heaven Illuminating Great Sovereign Deity." The Sun Goddess was considered the most illustrious of all the family, and, according to Lawrence Durdin-Robertson, her parents sent her up to heaven by the ladder of heaven. This heavenly world was a place of mountains and rivers, a myth world, where she had three rice fields, which were called the Easy Rice Field of Heaven, the Level Rice

Field of Heaven, and the Village-join-in Rice Field of Heaven. They were all excellent rice fields and did not suffer even when there was continuous rain or drought.

One day, His-Impetuous-Male-Augustness, younger brother of Ama-terasu, decided to go live with his mother in the underworld. "But first," he said, "I will go say goodbye to my sister in the plain of Heaven."

The Durdin-Robertson account explains how Ama-terasu prepared for his visit by undoing her hair, wrapping it in hair-bunches on the left and right sides of her head. "On her back she bore a thousand-arrow quiver; on the side of her chest she attached a five-hundred-arrow quiver. Also, she put on an awesome high arm-guard; and, shaking the upper tip of the bow, stamping her legs up to her very thighs into the hard earth, and kicking the earth about as if it were light snow, she shouted with awesome fury, she shouted, stamping her feet."

When she greeted her brother, the Sun Goddess asked why he had ascended to heaven. Faced with this mighty warrior who was his sister, the Impetuous Male God replied that he had no malicious intentions. But then the younger brother did not want to accept the decision of the Sun Goddess that she should keep their eight children. And so he went on a rampage, breaking down the fences and boundaries of her rice fields, filling the water sluices of her canals with dirt, and tearing her beautiful gardens to shredded heaps of broken plants. Finally he set a wild horse loose in the great weaving hall of creativity, sending the weavers flying in all directions.

In response, the Sun Goddess shut the door of the cave in which the great weaving hall was located so that the whole Plain of Heaven and the Central Land of the Reed Plains, which is the Main Island of Japan, were darkened and night prevailed over everything. In great anxiety, eight hundred deities assembled in the bed of the tranquil river of heaven to propose plans for inducing the Sun Goddess to reappear.

But nothing worked until a lascivious madcap dance of enticement performed by the Mirth Goddess, Ame-no Uzume-no-Mikoto, called Uzume, "Terrible Female of Heaven," ritual dancer, priestess, shaman, ancestress of the Kimi women of the Sarume clan. To prepare for her seductive dance, Uzume the Mirth Goddess built a fire, bound up her sleeves with a cord of heavenly pi-kage vine, tied on a headband of the heavenly ma-saki vine, and bound together bundles of sara leaves to hold in her hands. Then

237

she overturned a bucket before the heavenly rock-cave door, stamped resoundingly upon it, and made a long, divinely inspired utterance, a poetic incantation. Finally she exposed her breasts, pulled on her nipples and pushed her skirt band down to reveal her genitals, which caused an uproarious response among the assembled goddesses and gods.

Now Ama-terasu heard this and said, "Since I have shut myself in the Rock-cave . . . How then can Ame-no Uzume-no-Mikoto be so jolly?" So with her august hand, she opened the Rock-door a narrow space and peeped out. When she saw what Uzume the Mirth Goddess was doing, she peeped out even further. The divine spirits then pushed a mirror they had made in front of the cave opening, and seeing her own reflection for the first time Ama-terasu was totally entranced and came all the way out, so that night and day again commenced. His-Impetuous-Male-Augustness was punished for his destructiveness and custody of the children went to Ama-terasu.

Uzume's dance is said to be the origin of the kagura or pantomimic dance now performed at Shinto festivals. The Sarume clan descended from Uzume, and they are described as an ancient family ruled by women Kimi claiming descent from the Mirth Goddess Ame-no-uzume-no-Mikoto, with the ideograph "monkeywoman." The members of this family served as participants in ritual dances performed at court.

The Column of Eternal Fire

Saint Brigid, or Bridget, of Ireland was Abbess of Kildare around A.D. 525. She was so influential and beloved that she equaled St. Patrick in importance and eventually her bones were interred in the same place as his. But she is a much older and more indigenous figure, with pagan antecedents, especially of the creation and fire and sun goddesses. After her death her nuns at Kildare kept a sacred fire burning in her name and memory until 1220 when it was forcibly extinguished by order of the archbishop during a period when many of the old female powers were being suppressed and the force and political clout of women in the abbeys were being overturned. Bridget's sacred fire burned at Kildare, watched day and night by her faithful sisters for seven hundred years, more than three times as long as the United States has been a nation.

One story about Bridget reveals her Godly capacity to control sunlight. According to the *Lives of the Saints*, "She is said, after a shower of rain, to have come hastily into a chamber, and cast her wet cloak over a sunbeam, mistaking it, in her hurry, for a beam of wood. And the cloak remained there, and the ray of sun did not move, till late at night one of her maidens ran to her, to tell her that the sunbeam waited its release, so she hastened, and removed her cloak, and the ray retired after the long departed sun." [4] In art she is portrayed with the symbol of her perpetual fire and sometimes with a column of fire, which was said to have arisen above her head as she took the veil.

In Rome an eternal fire sacred to the Hearth Goddess, Vesta, was tended for centuries by specially selected lifetime virgin priestesses (whose office, incidentally, required them to have short hair). Temple fires burn for millennia in honor of goddesses in all parts of the world, and torches are carried in processionals of many descriptions — for Isis, for Bridget, for Guadalupe (whose figure is surrounded with flames), for Diana, for Demeter hunting her lost daughter. Candles burn on altars in honor of the Virgin Mary, of the great Kali, of the Tree of Life, of Yemanya, of the people's heart, of the saints and gods and Kamui and elves and Orisha, of the life spark, of the spirit world, of magic and Kundalini and holiness. Candle burning is a major part of the ceremony of European witchcraft, as it is for Voodoo. Small wonder the English slang for Lesbian is "wick," as it is in English-influenced Barbados. The wick, that part of a candle or lamp from which fire can be called forth, is like a Kundalini column of fire, the very essence of the female sexual-creative soul-force.

Tribadic rites, to use one term for them, are credited to some of the rituals of Kwan Yin of China; Mise, Pudicitia, and Bona Dea of Rome; Demeter, Persephone, and Hecate of Greece; Kali and Arani of India; Diana and Holle in Europe; and Maat, the Goddess of Justice, in Egypt. Isis and Nepthys are said to have a Lesbian aspect to their relationship. Sister gods, Great Isis ruled above while her adviser Nepthys, "the basket," ruled the underworld of departed spirits. The Hebrew goddess Daath created the element Nephesh by means of tribadism.[5]

According to Paula Gunn Allen the major purpose of ritual as it developed in tribal life is the creation of shared images or, more exactly, creation *through* shared images. These images — whether dreams, stories, or rites such as two women creating a "rope baby" or two women reenacting how they worked together to get a deer's permission to take its life — connect tribal people not only to each other in a shared perception of reality but more important with all natural elements, who are perceived as alive and as producing images of their own. Without this understanding, people are left with only the patriarchal alternative: Alienation from an inert, uncaring universe needing human proprietorship and mastery.

According to tribal thought, images created during rituals become real things; in fact, the purpose of ritual is to transform material from one state or condition to another. It follows that the ritual sex of ancient goddess rites, the tribadism used by the Hebrew goddess Daath to create an element named Nephesh or the Lesbian sex rites reported as the secret and most sacred aspect of the Mysteries of Demeter were for the purpose of transforming some one or thing from one condition or state to another.

Journal Note, Los Angeles 1981

"There are times, when at the moment I touch my tongue to her clitoris, my whole mind 'sees' a blue light around the precious organ, and as my tongue folds around it, I seem to be licking a living yellow/red light, some essential stone-like flame with a blue light around it. I know I am entranced at those times, gone into another dimension, as she is, and our flesh is more than material, our lovemaking is more than love and more than sexual. The silver rays connecting between us fill me with strength, confidence, affirmation, joy, and some esthetic quality of beauty that is like another way of seeing, like being in another place."

In Hindu philosophical concepts this fire is called Kundalini when it is within us, Shakti when it is the female creative force of the universe, a force without which the creation god Shiva can do nothing. In the West, the idea is given only the narrowest and most exclusively sexual definition, as in "Come on baby, light my fire."

The blue light of the *aura clitoridís* is the essential female creative power, the emanating rays of life-giving force, the fire that lives in the wood of the female substance. In medieval Europe the Great Mother Goddess was sometimes represented with rays emanating from her vulva onto the earth with its greenery and its animals and onto the upturned faces of humankind, who looked to the aura for inspiration and life. In ancient Egypt the same and probably older idea was vested in Nut, the sky as a female God. Leaning her dark body over the earth, she allowed the precious rays to emanate from her vulva and her breasts onto the happy earth below. The earth in Egypt was a male God, Geb.

It was this sexual-creative force the ancient women used to contact, understand, and form social contracts with material fire, as well as with the energies of mineral and plant and animal life.

The Lesbian Firestick (Love Me Tinder)

As we have seen, *frig,* a slang verb meaning "to fuck or to rub a woman's genitals with the fingers," is connected to friction, fire-making by rubbing sticks, and to *fricatrice,* the Latin for she-who-frigs, the tribadic woman. Edward Carpenter notes that the Norse goddess Friga was sometimes thought of as a hermaphrodite, having the "members of both sexes, standing by a column with a sword in her right hand and in her left a bow." [6]

In India sacred wood itself is named for a Lesbian goddess. Her name is Arani, meaning "tinder-stick for producing fire by rubbing." In his encyclopedia of goddess lore from India and other countries, Lawrence Durdin-Robertson describes her: "The Arani, according to *The Secret Doctrine* [of Madame Blavatsky], consists of a piece of wood of the Shami tree. This is used for kindling holy fires: The word shami is the female name of a tree, the Minosa Suma, from the wood of which the Aranis or fire-sticks were made; perhaps from the root *sham,* work, owing to the frictions required in producing fire." Durdin-Robertson says that the Arani "corresponds to the wood used in kindling the holy fire of Vesta," the hearth goddess of Rome. Fire is born in the feminine wood, he says, for

> friction does not "make" fire, but merely calls it forth . . . the friction or tribadism, by producing the aura clitoridis, is a means both to expressing and evoking sexual love. Thus the epithet Tribas is applied to Sappho, the great and generous inspirer of love.
>
> In giving this aura or Shakti, woman is more than the Lover and the Beloved; she is also the Producer . . . she is engendering new life and new forms; she is the officiating priestess of Mother Nature. She is, in fact, exerting that power which belongs to the Female only, — the power to create. For this reason the cults of the Arani, the rites of Lesbian intercourse, are *the most occult and holy of all religious ceremonies.* (Emphasis mine) [7]

241

The aura, or energy field, of the clitoris, especially when produced by the sexual rubbing together of two women, was once held sacred. Significantly, Arani's titles are Matri, the Mother, and Mistress of the Race.

There is an uncanny (or a very canny) similarity between the Arani wood, *shami*, and the Sanscrit for friction-work, *sham*, and the Asiatic word for a tribal sorcerer, *shaman*. Moreover, the Fairy people's god of Halloween, celebrated by the Celtic tribes, was named *Samhain*. The sun deity (by that time male) of the Assyrians was *Shamash*, and the occult word for a sudden fiery change is *Shazzam*.

Beware the Venal Fricatrice

European women who were tried during medieval times for witchcraft described to the authorities that the "devil's" member was cold and uncomfortable and unaccountably stiff and unyielding. They clearly got no physical pleasure from the act. The ritual dildo sex described by the witches did not have as its primary purpose the sexual bonding of women. But probably bonding, as well as raising the Kundalini fire, was the purpose of the sex they described happening on special Wiccan days, particularly Thursdays, set aside for homosexuality, when after the candles were lit and the chants chanted they turned to the person next to them, the women with the women and the men with the men, and made love.

Other descriptions of ritual pagan Lesbianism make it clear intimate sexual relations and emotional closeness are part of the office. Edward Carpenter described the North African diviners called *Sahacat*: "With regard to the attribution of homosexuality also to female wizards, or witches, I believe that, rightly or wrongly, this was very common in Europe a few centuries ago. Leo Africanus (1492) in his description of Morocco . . . says, 'The third kind of diviners are women-witches, which are affirmed to have familiarity with divels. Changing their voices they fain the divell to speak within them: then they which come to enquire ought with greate feare and trembling [to] aske these vile and abominable witches such questions as they mean to profound, and lastly, offering some fee unto the divell, they depart. But the wiser and honester sort of people call these women *Sahacat*, which in Latin signifieth *Fricatrices*, because they have a damnable custom to commit unlawful venerie among themselves, which I cannot express in any modester terms.' " He goes on to say that these witches, carnally desiring some of the young women who come to " 'enquire,' " entrap and corrupt them so far as actually to cause them in some cases to " 'desire the companie of those witches' (and to that end, he explains, deceive their husbands)." [8]

The Sahacat sorcerers must have been irresistible women to arouse so much attention from local women and so much envious derision from Leo. Perhaps they apprenticed some of the women who found their loving so seductive, and these women not only deceived their husbands but left them altogether to become Sahacat diviner Fricatrice women-witches on their own account.

All Who Gather Around a Fire

In an article discussing women's collective spirit and the sororal commune that underlies society, Grace Shinell specifies the relationship between tribadism and the tribe:

> Without the politically motivated prohibitions against homo-
> sexuality enforced by patriarchal brotherhood, sisterhood must
> be firmly understood to include a sexual relationship, provid-
> ing the emotional-spiritual ties and life-supporting strength of
> the sex bond. From the root for tribe (Greek *tribe*: "the act of
> rubbing"; cf. tri-bao "tri-based") comes a cognate term, tribad-
> ism, exclusively defined as lesbianism. The hidden sexual
> preference throughout history, which can be logically ascribed
> to the sororal commune — the hidden social unit throughout
> history — is tribadism.[9]

Sisterhoods, tight, women-only groupings abound in ancient Western myth and history, and their names still ring down to us: Eumenides, Erinyes, Muses, Gorgons, Harpies, Lamiae, Sirens, Fates, Pleiades, and, in recorded history, Naditu, Danaides, Maenads, Bacchae, and Amazons, to use Shinell's list. Further north the names were Maedenheap, Gwyddonot, and Norns. In Africa women belong to women's market, medicine, and magic societies, some of which are secret and highly protective of women's rights. Sisterhoods have been a prominent feature of American Indian tribal life as well.

Separatist living was a feature of ancient society, as it is today a feature of Gay culture. In fact, the "togetherness" of men and women as couples is a recent feature of patriarchal marriage. Most human social interaction has been same-gender. Modern American Lesbians have their own bars, clubs, organizations, magazines and cliques separate from those of Gay men as a matter of history and tradition. That's part of what makes us "Gay." Most kinds of Lesbian separatism, whether or not it is consciously or "politically" undertaken, strengthen women (all women) considerably, especially in a heavily male-dominated environment where women are deliberately divided and weakened.

All who gather around a fire are the tribe, and fire, in its most basic sense, is the generating flame of the female. In the prototypical tribe, women and men live in separate communes, and lead entirely different lives. Male/female connection is as brother/sister through the female line; grandmother and aunts wield tremendous authority; sisters give their brothers power over and responsibility toward their children in an avuncular — unclebased — system. Fatherhood is irrelevant; men care for the children of their sisters in their tribe. Children's sexual feelings are acknowledged. People have sexual relations with members of both sexes. Ceremonies and sacred events may include sex magic or rite, the nature and gender of which depends on the intended effect and its place in the ceremony.

An all-encompassing net of tribal psychic mind, rather than "blood," unites a clan's people. The immediate maternal line is extended almost indefinitely by a clan system that unites huge numbers of people as "relatives," "cousins" — not by genetic inheritance but by clan identification and adoption. Some American Indian tribes used so much adoption to gain members that, for example, at one time the Cherokee were one-third white and Black and only two-thirds indigenous Indian, and the Iroquois of the early seventeenth century were largely made up of Algonquian adoptees.

These tribal people, related by and unified by tribal consciousness, participated in a psychic tribal mind rather than a genetic blood inheritance line or a patriarchal legal entity. They literally did not need to invent the telephone to communicate long distance. Their auras and other psychic structures were connected, and they were careful to keep competition and violent dissension organized in ritual ways so as to not to break the valuable supersensory perceptions among themselves. The medicine people, many times Gay as a matter of course, were especially skilled at psychic phenomena of all kinds, including the ability to use psychic power to effect as well as affect physical matter, shape-shift, make things appear, travel physically long distances by instantly transporting their bodies, bringing souls back from the dead, making brooms dance, and so on. But everyone, shaman or not, participates in the overall psychic mind of the tribe. And although psychic abilities have been very consciously suppressed in modern nontribal society, remnants peer through the surface, usually recognized as telepathy, telekinesis, intuition, "heightened awareness," or, barely acknowledged and as yet thinly developed, psychic power.

Since becoming lovers with Paula, I am astonished at the clarity of psychic message we can transmit to one another from distances of six hundred miles, three thousand miles, or through a wall. They are simple messages so far: "I love you," "I'm in trouble and afraid," "I'm lonely and sad," or "Come to the next room and sit with me." But they come through with a tremendous force, utterly compelling and unmistakable. My anxious need to talk to Paula on the phone from five hundred miles away in a crisis once sent her flying out of a café, dinner left unfinished, to rush home blocks away, arriving breathless to lift the ringing phone and find me, in a panic, on the other end. Likewise, when her need to hear from me is acute, no other thought can enter my mind but to call her. I once believed only mothers, and only a few of them, felt such things, and only toward their children. Not, surely, Lesbian lovers of totally different backgrounds who have known each other only a few weeks. "You're surrounded by spirits," Paula says. "The room fills with them wherever you go, spirits of all sizes and descriptions." She kisses me. "That's 'cause you're an elfkin," she says, referring to the old Celtic term for fairy people.

My own psychic abilities have caused me no end of trouble in this ultrarationalistic, linear-cause-and-effect society, and I have developed an elaborate protective system, as many people have, for covering up, denying, and lying about the tons of information that I just "know." When I was a teenager I remember hearing voices so acutely that I would stop on the street to look around, trying to see who was talking. I did not understand my voices until I was in my mid-thirties when a series of major events told me where they come from.

One summer I drove with my then lover Wendy to New Mexico to visit my first lover, Yvonne, for two weeks:

It was August, magnificently beautiful, with the huge sky filling with immense thunderheads and rainbows. I had left you

eight years before, Von, and our lives had diverged. I had become
a successful poet, a publisher and editor, and a Lesbian activist.
You had gotten a Ph.D. in education and developed an idealistic
program for teaching ideas and methods of independent thinking
to American schoolchildren, even in the deteriorating urban
schools. Although in my sharp-tongued manner I didn't let you
know, I admired you, my brainy Von, tremendously, and you
seemed on the verge of stepping into the world of influence and
leadership.

On the last day of our visit, you threw an I-Ching, something
I had never seen you do before. But we were all changing, leaving
the logical positivism and economic materialist theories in favor
of more subjective divinatory sciences. The predictions you read
were glowing for me and for Wendy, and for your current lover.
But for yourself, the coins spoke of sorrow, pain, loss, death. I
thought this meant your young lover would leave you, and I was
sorry.

In a torrent of New Mexico summer rain, Wendy and I drove
away from the North New Mexico town, and through the water
drops I waved good-bye to you, running through the rain in your
jacket, looking more like the beautiful dike I had once eloped
with in a funny red dress than the salt-and-pepper Ph.D. who was
about to embark on an illustrious administrative career in the
urban school systems.

> as the bond between women is beginning
> in the middle at the end
> my first beloved, present friend
> if i could die like the next rain
> i'd call you by your mountain name
> and rain on you
>
> — Funeral poem

That night Wendy and I parked our van near Ship Rock,
where hours later the howling wind woke me and I sobbed with a
grief I could not understand.

Back in my room in Oakland that October I wrote the
beginning of a novel, a novel that unaccountably centered around
a dead woman. I often worked until dawn and increasingly heard
voices in my ear, especially just after I lay down to sleep. I was
worried, too, for your lover called to tell me you were in the
hospital in Albuquerque with a mysterious problem in your leg —
a minor clot, your voice later reassured me on the telephone. All

that month I wrote at night, and when I stopped to rest, voices
rang in my ear, calling my name so that I turned my head to
answer "What?" out loud.

Once I heard a man's voice amplified as though by a
loudspeaker. Another time I was suddenly hearing a playground
filled with children's voices playing and yelling. I listened to it
for perhaps five minutes, and I could not understand where it was
coming from; I even leaned out my Oakland window into the
silent night in case someone's radio was playing schoolyard
sounds. I seemed to have become a receiver for bizarre and urgent
messages, and as fall deepened toward Thanksgiving of 1974,
they blathered on in my ear nearly every night.

All that month you stayed in the hospital, insisting when
I called that it was all nothing. "I'm going to come to California,
to see you guys," you said one day. "I can't wait to see you," I
said. The next day your lover called. "You had better come," she
said, "a clot has gone to Von's brain, leaving her unconscious."
Dazed, I stared out of the window of the airplane departing for
Albuquerque at a brilliant blood-red and storm-black sunset.
"She's dead," I thought, and it was true.

I could still feel your spirit near you as I bent over your
wasted, bony frame, with wired connections to green-lit machines.
An hour later I felt the spirit had said good-bye. We, your three
lovers and your parents, sat up all night in a hopeless, necessary
vigil.

When I went back to Oakland I found the night voices had
completely stopped. "I wonder if they came from Von," I thought.
But I had no way to prove it. I wrote a funeral poem to help myself
comprehend your death.

> life, as it stands so still along your fingers
> beats in my hands, the hands i will, believing
> that you have become she, who is not, any longer
> somewhere in particular
>
> we are together in your stillness
> you have wished us a bonded life
>
> love of my love, i am your breast
> arm of my arm, i am your strength
> breath of my breath, i am your foot
> thigh of my thigh, back of my back
> eye of my eye, beat of my beat
> kind of my kind, i am your best

— Funeral Poem[10]

247

My life did not go well for many years following Yvonne's death. But at least I was beginning to make sense out of the voices in my head. One night at 4 A.M. I heard my name said very distinctly, and this time I recognized the voice as that of a friend who is a performer with a very distinctive manner of speaking. There was no mistaking who it was: Pat Parker. I thought of calling her to ask if she needed something, then suddenly the door to my room opened and she stumbled in. She was drunk, and lonely, wanting company; she had driven across town in a needy stupor to see me. As she pulled back my covers and lurched into bed beside me, I grinned in elation and years' worth of relief. My voices were real! They had sources! I wasn't crazy or troubled with ear problems, I just sometimes heard what certain other people in my life were thinking when they directed their thoughts toward me. I had a piece of tribal mind.

> now you have left, you can wander
> will you tell whoever could listen
> tell all the voices who speak to younger women
> tell all the voices who speak to us when we need it
> that the love between women is a circle
> and is not finished
>
> wherever i go to, you will arrive
> whatever you have been, i will come back to
> wherever i leave off, you will inherit
> whatever we resurrect, we shall have it
> we shall have it, we have right
>
> and you have left, what is left
>
> — *Funeral Poem*

Modern Lesbian Sex Domains: Flaming Without Burning

For the purpose of describing modern Lesbian sex as a socially vital function, I have imagined that there are four domains, or levels or spheres, of power involved in the sexual dynamic between and among women. The four domains are the physical, the mental, the psychic, and the transformational. Each domain represents another level of the emergence of historical Lesbian sexual connection from its suppression over the centuries.

From Deep Within

Nature tests those she would call hers;
Slips us, naked and blank down dark paths.
Skeletons of the sea, this we would become
to suck a ray of sight from the fire.

A woman's body must be taught to speak —
Bearing a lifetime of keys, a patient soul
moves through a maze of fear and bolts
clothed in soft hues and many candles.

The seasons' tongues must be heard & taken,
And many paths built for the travelers.
A woman's flesh learns slow by fire and pestle,
Like succulent meats, it must be sucked and eaten.

— Pat Parker, *Movement in Black*[11]

The First Domain: *Vulva to Vulva*

The first domain is the physical, the basic flesh-to-flesh contact of sexual relationship. It is based in touch, sensation, smell, intense feelings, intimacy, sharing. In the first domain a Lesbian learns to receive sexual love from another woman, to trust her vulva to a stranger's hands and lips and tongue, to be able to let go and come in her presence, in her very face. And in the first domain a Lesbian learns to give love to another woman, to develop a sensitive and sustaining tongue and knowledgeable fingers, the physical confidence and competence necessary to be the lover, the ability to read another woman's responses and be able to respond to her body on its own terms.

(THE FLOATING POEM, UNNUMBERED)

Whatever happens with us, your body
will haunt mine — tender, delicate
your lovemaking, like the half-curled frond
of the fiddlehead fern in forests
just washed by sun. Your traveled, generous thighs
between which my whole face has come and come —
the innocence and wisdom of the place my tongue has found
    there —
the live, insatiate dance of your nipples in my mouth —
your touch on me, firm, protective, searching

me out, your strong tongue and slender fingers
reaching where I had been waiting years for you
in my rose-wet cave — whatever happens, this is.

— Adrienne Rich, *Twenty-One Love Poems*[12]

Sometimes a Lesbian couple will spend time learning how to come simultaneously, an exercise in controlling physical impulses that is also particularly valued in heterosexual lovemaking. Or a couple may be so close that they feel each other's sensations.

For women from families in which women's sexual expression has been denied or forcibly suppressed by church, state, and/or patriarchal ideas of ownership, the first sexual steps of Lesbianism may be very difficult to take and fraught with terror and excitement. As a teenager, I had rather cleverly learned to masturbate from reading the Kinsey Report while babysitting for a progressive family. However, I could not relax enough to come in front of my lovers until I was twenty years old. I literally ordered myself to relax with someone so I could do it. The lover I chose for the occasion was a woman I barely knew, older than myself. We were fully dressed and sitting in daylight in a parked car. She had her hand in my pants. She was patient and persistent and gentle and knew what she was doing. In that instant, she was a witch. After I came in her arms, with my face pressed against her cheek, I was released from my prohibition and could come with other women. I did not have any further sex with my teacher, though I suffered guilt pangs at having used her for such a thoroughly physical purpose. But it was the lack of emotional entanglement that gave me the freedom to let go and not worry so much about my partner's reactions so I could have complete feelings of my own.

At that time, 1960, for most of the women I knew, who were mostly white and lower middle class, sex was a source of embarrassment and various degrees of dissatisfaction if not outright pain and rape by boyfriends and husbands. Some of my high school friends seemed to be enjoying sex, but since straight women were told to fake orgasm it was difficult to know for certain what women were really experiencing. Sex with your clothes on and in the dark was still a prevalent mode.

We Lesbians, despised and negated though we were, had the advantage of not being watched, and we were sexually daring. Some of us had orgasms and taught others about it. Some made love in the daylight, were "promiscuous," and did other lascivious things. But I don't think we looked at each other's vulvas openly

— or our own. It would remain for the sexual revolution of the sixties and the development of independent women's groups taking gynecological childbirth and abortion functions into their own hands and developing self-help groups and clinics before Lesbian poet Olga Broumas could begin a poem, in 1976, with these lines:

> With the clear
> plastics speculum, transparent
> and when inserted, pink like the convex
> carapace of a prawn, flashlight in hand, I
> guide you
> inside the small
> cathedral of my cunt . . .
>
> — Olga Broumas[13]

But if in the late 1950s my experience among lower-middle-class, white Lesbians in a small western town was about how to crawl out of the pit of frigidity (into the Well of Loneliness — infinitely preferable), less sexually suppressed, more sophisticated, urban and urbane Lesbians had quite another story to tell as this fruity and passionate passage, set in New York City, from Black poet, writer, and professor Audre Lorde's *Zami* shows.

> There were green plantains which we half peeled and then planted, fruit-deep, in each other's bodies until the petals of skin lay like tendrils of broad green fire upon the curly darkness between our upspread thighs. There were ripe red finger bananas, stubby and sweet, with which I parted your lips gently to insert the peeled fruit into your grape-purple flower.
> After I held you, I lay between your brown legs slowly playing my tongue through your familiar forests, slowly licking and swallowing as the deep undulations and tidal motions of your strong body slowly mashed the ripe banana into a beige cream that mixed with the juices of your electric flesh. Then our bodies met again, each surface touched with each other's flame from the tips of our curled toes to our tongues, and locked into our own wild rhythms we rode each other across the thundering space.[14]

Lovers who explore the infinite sensual possibilities in the first domain may experiment by using acrobatic positions, making love in all kinds of beds and places, in the outdoors, in public, on a bus or plane or car, in water, sand, dark, light, hot, cold, in a rainstorm — trying for every variety and complexity of sensation. Some Lesbians add additional numbers of people to the lovemaking or add other elements such as sensual oils and fruits. A small number mix eroticism with other but highly charged body functions such as pissing and menstruating; a few Lesbians mix sexual sensation together with deliberate forcefulness and stylized "pain," vaginal stretching, pinching, slapping, vigorous frigging, and the like.

Sex in the first domain has become lightly industrialized and mechanized with the marketing of how-to-do-it sex manuals and electric vibrators. The purpose of sex in the physical domain is sensual contact and sensation, usually mutual, and bonding with other women in a network of lovers, ex-lovers, and potential lovers. Additionally it releases sexual sparks of a particular nature into the universe, and it helps to magnetize and direct the attention of women toward each other.

The Mental Domain: Fantasy and Control

I have on occasion been awakened by an orgasm in my sleep, accompanied by an erotic dream. And when I reached down to my vulva to continue the pleasant sensations and possibly encourage a second helping, I have found that my clitoris is quietly tucked into her vulval bed, not hot, not swollen, not sensitive, not even awake. The orgasm had not happened in my clitoris, or anywhere in my body. It had taken place in my "mind," or rather in the feeling-state of the dream imagery. I have known other women to whom this has happened.

Only some sexual experiences are physical and use the medium of the body's erotic organs and erogenous zones. Other sexual experiences take place in other domains, for instance from seeing pictures or reading descriptions of sexual scenes. This is mental sex, sexual feeling created by mental images. Most of the sex we have operates in more than one domain at once, and they enhance each other. Fantasy amplifies our physical erotic sensations and gives our sexual being much more scope and a second dimension, breadth.

The purpose of fantasy, the manipulation of images to construct possibilities other than what is actually happening, appears to be control. So someone who is having sex in the city may fantasize that she and her lover are in a woodsy setting far away with rain softly falling on their cabin or tent or blanket, and that the siren that blares as she is coming is the howl of a wild, wild she-wolf. This seems like simple wish fulfillment.

Fantasies let us "experience" what we have chosen not to experience, so someone who is having heterosexual sex may fantasize that her male lover is a woman and that his penis is a tongue. Conversely, a Lesbian may fantasize a man, or three or four, fucking her while she is experiencing cunnilingus. Some fantasies center on bondage, punishment, being onstage, illicit relationships, strange combinations of people and animals, or even rape.

By analyzing fantasies as though they are dreams, we can learn about ourselves and what we desire to control in ourselves. Forbidden levels of assertion surface in me as a particular kidnap-rape fantasy. A captive small woman is being slowly, rather patiently, fucked by a man with a penis "too large" for her. He is a sincere, determined, sometimes angry, huge man; other kidnappers who are medium-sized men and Lesbians perform other and multiple sex actions on her while the large one is telling her she can take him all the way in if she'll just concentrate on stretching. A little ashamed of this fantasy even to my private self, I decided to try analyzing it as though it were a dream. Since the fantasy occurs in my mind, not in real life, aspects of myself are each of the characters, including some that I do not like, some I respect or find amusing, some I fear or pity. All are "me" in dialogue and confrontation with myself, with something happening to me in my own life. I decided the fantasy says that I am trying to take on things that I believe are "too big" or too much for me. My little "female" energy pot is being abused by my enormous "masculine" ambition; or perhaps my svelte, slender ambition and success is being assaulted by my great hulking masculine work force. It happens the situation in my life is that I have taken on projects requiring decades of effort, and I am trying to do them all in a short time. My fantasy precisely describes my anxiety over pressure I have put on myself and helps me understand it. Moreover, the kidnap victim's little tight vagina has stretched considerably since the first of these episodes, and she is beginning to have massive orgasms along with the kidnappers.

My fantasy sex usually uses modern settings, a pizza parlor (?), a motorboat crowded with revelers, a fertility rite of old women frigging an essential central figure (myself), one woman fucking three or four men, people both straight and Gay having sex in public or in a great hurry. The fantasy is a pressure chamber for intensifying sexual feelings and for directing orgasm. If I am particularly tense and frustrated with my life, I notice that more of the fantasies include bondage or forced circumstances; for instance, my favorite under duress in my life is the fantasy of a line of nude, horny men tied to an overhead pole who are anxious to have sex and are not allowed and cannot touch each other, while a naked woman dances a sex dance directly in front of them, sometimes with a chosen male partner. It is a fantasy of thwarted desire and pretend revenge on forces I perceive as ranged against me. But all the characters in my fantasy *are* me.

My lover, Paula, who spent years being afraid to come out as a Lesbian, tells me she sometimes fantasizes being forced to have sex with women. The deliberate illusion of "no choice" and therefore "no fault" releases her from internal social controls and allows her sexual feeling to build intensely.

While control is the main feature of fantasy sex, arousal and coming are its goals. The control helps us be specific and focused, directed and assertive, and trusting. We need rely less on the vagaries of the body and its emotions, and can demand of ourselves and our partners more specific feelings, roles, activities as we become more open about our fantasies. Some people take their fantasies into the realm of theater, acting them out with each other in carefully proscribed, even costumed, ways. This is the exertion of the will in trying to gain control in the external world, by gaining control of the internal world. Blind acting out seems to me a dead-end street, however. I don't want to make a cult of my inner workings. By acknowledging all the parts of my fantasy as pieces of myself, I do have a tool for understanding my own limitations, ambitions, and fears, as well as my will to control myself or the parts of myself I see in others.

The Psychic Domain: Stroking the Rose

Journal entry, August 1981, Los Angeles: "There was a rose garden," I said, "and I became one of them, the flower, the stem and thorn and even the roots." I was speaking into Paula's mouth as her fingers relaxed trying to leave my vagina as I held her.

"The rose was pink," I said. "I didn't expect that, I have never cared for pink."

"Oh," she said, "I know that rose. When you made love to me, there was a pink rose. And Guadalupe was there. She was holding it," she said. "She was showing me how to stroke the rose. She was using her first two fingers inside the petals and holding the flower in her other hand, her left hand, saying, 'This is how to stroke the rose." She laughed,

"You learned very well," I said.

In the third domain the form of lovemaking between women is one that goes into a world beyond physical sensation, intimacy, fantasy, shared orgasm, mental control, and feelings of love. Beyond all these riches lies another domain, the psychic levels of consciousness, creativity and insight. If the physical domain represents length and the mental domain breadth, then the psychic domain represents the depth of field of the cube, the third dimension in space.

To produce the psychic state, the beloved does not attempt to control what the lover is doing. She gives her body to the lover. Nor does the lover try to force something to happen. She lets herself know what to do. If the heightened state is working, they do not need to control it. If they can control it, it is not happening. The lover lets her own spontaneous sensibilities, as she tunes herself to the beloved, tell her what to do, her fingers and tongue, eyes and ears, and all her body and mind, and she will find she can "see" what to do with her fingers and tongue and become so sensitive as to experience a kind of orgasm — just from stroking the beloved's neck or head or breasts or cervix — through her fingers, the firesticks. And by entering the beloved and paying attention to the feelings, she can guide or allow her to "leave herself" and go to a different world or state of being. And she, the lover, will also leave although she may not go so far as the beloved goes.

No fantasy is involved in this journey to the source of power. Within the altered state there is an absence of fantasy as there is an absence of pain or anxiety, violence, fear, distance, hiding from or acting out on each other in any way. There is no acting. There is rubbing. There is extreme feeling. There is receiving. There is sucking and tonguing. There is not much moving. There is staying real. There is frigging. There are highly dilated pupils. There is an altered state. There is a spinning out. There is a journey, and a return. There are visions and an understanding of the word *aesthetic*. There is no attempt or necessity by either lover to deliberately control and construct mental images in the psychic domain, for control only interrupts what is happening — as do pain, anxiety, force, struggle, or anger between the two lovers. The journey goes where it goes and the imagery constructs itself. This is what creative power *is*. As happens also to artists of all kinds when they are in a creative state, or trance, images — like feelings, dreams, thoughts, melodies, understandings, and patterns — appear of themselves. In the sexual creative trance, metaphors, scenes, personages speaking and moving, one's ancestors, mentors, spirit-guides of every description from earth and sky and parts unknown arrive with messages and meanings, as the lovers pass through level upon level of sexual and psychic feeling in a state that may go on for hours, at or near the level of intensity immediately preceding orgasm.

The experience is that of taking a journey to sources of power and creativity, of "making" something, and of being made. Of going somewhere and coming back different. Intimacy and pleasure and intense feelings, though present, are not the goals; orgasm is present but is not the goal. In fact, the construction of goals destroys the state of feeling, turns it aside, lowers it into the realm of fantasy and the necessity for control. When the creative sexual state proceeds on its own, the feeling or experience is prolonged, ecstatic, emotional, journeylike and with intensity barely short of orgasm over a long period of time; and though the orgasm when it finally and brilliantly happens may culminate an image or a sequence of images, its purpose seems more to be to bring the dreamer back, to return the beloved to the material plane. She is not only coming, *she is coming back into herself*. And she has been away, in the sexual/psychic domain. The orgasm is the way back from the trance.

One Lesbian who has also experienced what I am calling "psychic sex" is Nancy, a Los Angeles video filmmaker. She told me that she and her lover Julie would take turns being lover and beloved and would go "out," that is, enter an entranced state. Nancy said they had a term for what the lover was doing as the guide. They described it as "spotting." So, for instance, when Julie was being the lover and Nancy, as the beloved, had gone into a psychic state, Nancy said that Julie would "spot" for her to make certain she could come back to the present world. "The 'spotter' keeps you from getting lost or dying," Nancy said. They had taken the term from the "spotter" on a trampoline, the one who stands on the bouncing canvas with the athlete, holding the strap of the safety belt and guiding her through the somersaults and other balancing maneuvers high in the air.

During their lovemaking Nancy would sometimes stay out a

long time, until Julie would get tired and even worried. Julie would yell at her, "Come back! Come back!"

"Because I wouldn't always want to," Nancy says, grinning wistfully. "The other world is so harmonious and beautiful. I love it over there."

Harmony and beauty. I know just what she means. When I am at one with myself and with Paula, and we enter the psychic domain, I prefer it over anything I've ever felt — it's so rich and full and deep like *being* a painting or film or story, like *being* a wolf or storm cloud or fire. The feelings are varied, unpredictable, and not goal-oriented. Many natural elements are present and may predominate. The aesthetics are exquisite, to the point that I am willing to believe aesthetics and psychic sex and the creative trance are all the same feeling: truly the Golden Mean.

Often after psychic sex I remain in an altered state, the room and everything in it being very vibratory. The walls are three-dimensional and in motion, not still flat surfaces. I can see into them to some extent; could possibly reach into them. I can feel into her body and see her aura. I see "spirit lights" as they are called, flickering whitely in the air, and I sometimes come to understandings during that time that seem profound and help me in my work and Paula in hers. And she does the same.

The poet Hilda Doolittle (H.D.) apparently practiced psychic sex, describing it as having access to the "love mind," or the "womb mind," the mind of vision. In men, she said, the "womb mind" corresponded to their sexual center. She advocated that like-minded people try to gain access to the love mind, and her examples indicate she also meant "like-gender." [15]

It is not Lesbians or Gay people alone who have access to the sexual psychic domains, of course. Heterosexual culture has a well-developed tradition of sexual yoga (Tantra yoga) for the purpose of psychic vision. The *Kama Sutra* is an erotic text for this practice, which requires intense physical discipline. Perhaps this helps prolong the male's orgasm, for if the orgasm comes too quickly he cannot stay "out" long enough to enter the psychic world.

The psychic sexual experiences I have described between modern Lesbians do not require any physical discipline; they do require emotional discipline. This includes openness, trust, honesty, and a willingness to display both vulnerability and strength with each other. This means each person needs to have a well-developed femme side and a well-developed butch side. Needless

257

to say, alcohol and drugs interfere, while the study of therapeutic methods helps by clearing emotional tangles.

Entering the Fourth Domain

In the first three sexual domains Lesbians have the potential to attain sensation and female bonding through emotion and through the sexual organs of the body; to gain control and the specific ordering of forceful images and personal authority through the will of the mind and its fantasies; and to gain creative vision through the aesthetics and harmonies of the psychic world. From these uses of sexual power there is only one more step into the fourth domain, the plane of transformation. The powers released in this dimension can influence not only the participants but also the world around them and its future.

The fourth domain involves more than one person, for it is an exchange between at least two mind/bodies, who share an image between or among them, greatly intensified by their close sexual and emotional connection. If they choose to pour their mutual energies into a mutual image, they greatly strengthen it and bring it closer to becoming a real thing, a material being. A "tribe" (in Shinell's sense) of hundreds of thousands of women concentrating on images of women's returning powers by using all three of the Lesbian sex domains will be using the fourth domain; they will alter consciousness, establish psychic, physical, and mental communications of all kinds, and will literally be able to bring back the power of any "goddess" force they desire, to strengthen any elements of nature and human society they wish to, and to unite with, bring forward in themselves or bring to the attention of others outside their modern psychic "tribe" any ideas or altered understandings they want to see happen. They will be, once again, ceremonial Lesbians and ceremonial Dykes.

Transferring an Image During Sex

Transferring images during sex is a first step toward this domain, requiring a lot of effort and with a lot of reward. With us, it happened with a Diamond Light.

Journal entry, August 10, 1981, Los Angeles: I went out to the very tip of her clitoris with my tongue, staying soft and slow without pushing her into coming, and stayed there with a very soft and sensitive part of my tongue for about 5–7 minutes, a long time for that much intensity. This was about midway in her total journey, which was about 30 minutes or less. Cunnilingus alone seems to create a slightly shorter trip than frigging; and the longest is some combination of the two.

While I was out on that tip, which felt very special to me, her flesh became so smooth, and the organ feeling so shapely and full; I was moaning with excitement and "seeing" an exceptional fleshy rose around my tongue. Meantime she experienced being *very* far away out of herself, deep in the night sky, and she saw a goddess whose entire being was a deep intense shiny bluish black, who spread her legs, and then spread her vulvular lips, and from her cunt came a stunning, brilliant diamond light — which Paula entered, so she was sitting in it, a pure light more like a laser than other more reflective lights. It was piercing, not diffuse. Exact. She said she had read descriptions of the Diamond Light but had not previously known what was meant until that moment. She said the goddess sent blessings and love to me. (We since began calling her the Midnight Lady.) Then a voice said she could send a message to me. She concentrated on sending a yellow light to me, and I received it as a golden glow spreading in a warm ball over my eyes and face while I was tonguing the outmost tip of her clitoris. She says she entered the Diamond Light after concentrating on pulling the sexual energy up to her third eye and above, rather than leaving it down around her cunt. She said this was very difficult and she had to keep both places in her concentration to do it; and that the goddess with the Diamond Light between her legs appeared very suddenly and intensely. Since then we have transferred dozens of images during sex and intensified our ability to transfer images at other times, too.

Entering the Spirit World

I, too, entered the Diamond Light one night, to my surprise, and met an old friend.

Journal entry, October 29, 1981, Los Angeles: Last night we made love (after trip to New Mexico and recovery from road exhaustion).

A completely hooded, very skinny, and tall woman dressed in shiny black from head to foot insisted that I look into her crystal, which was like an eye — a white eye. She held it in both hands near the crotch of her blue-black dress. I didn't want to, but the

Midnight Lady demanded it, several times. I looked closer and closer, then saw rainbow lights emanating and flowing over me from the crystal in a flashing manner, waves of rainbows sweeping out and over me, directly into my eyes.

Then I entered the crystal and was immediately standing on a riverbank. A ship with white sails — a little barque — came and turned out to be smaller — a boat with sails — maybe thirty feet long or less. It took me across to a place I knew to be the land of the dead — very pleasant, light shore, sandy like any other shore. And there I had an ordinary-seeming conversation with Vonnie — the first since her death, the first contact. Though I have often felt her presence. And its absence. She said she is often with me and looks out for me. She told me funny stories and talked in the joking way she always had. I laughed out loud as I listened to her. I could hear the cadence of her voice clearly, though I couldn't always make out the exact words. She was very reassuring. She said, "You have made a wonderful choice," I assume meaning my renewed life — and she said not to worry about X. That I also would do fine in the future, that she was happy for me and would stay in touch with me. Then the boat reappeared and brought me back exactly the way I had come, across the river and through the crystal, past the lady in black, and back to the bed with Paula making love. I then proceeded to fantasize a sex scene in order to "come" back and Paula helped by talking, saying how much she loves to touch me, how sweet it feels to her, how swollen I was, and this helped. The orgasm was mild, but my mood and good feelings were ecstatic. A great rift in me felt filled in, and I was reunited with Yvonne in some way.

"To Suck a Ray of Sight from the Fire" (Pat Parker)

We speak of "carrying the torch" for someone and also of the "torch of knowledge," the "flame of hope," the "light of intelligence," of "civilization" and "at the end of the tunnel," of the "spark of life," the "fire of passion," "burning desire," the "cauldron of feeling," the "candles of the soul."

Perhaps these expressions are descriptions of the rainbow envelope of energies that move our material fleshy beings, the spirit that "goes" when our bodies, like the flowers they are, die back when their season is done. Or perhaps this electrifying force field can also be perceived as an entire matrix, one that connects to others, a psychic network overlying everything we know, a psychic net. It is a form of thought-being. And as the thought goes, so goes the being, for we are active participants in our own lives. A psychic net can be thought of as a shared mind, a third state of consciousness shared by two or more people who exchange thoughts on a nonphysical plane and who mutually create images. Close sexual and emotional bonds amplify the amount of energy poured into these images, giving them tremendous power to alter our consciousness and to influence the course of our lives. If enough energy is poured into an image, it will become actual in the material world. Perhaps "tribadic mind" is an apt term for this net as it applies to Lesbians.

Whoever enters this net in a directed and directing manner, singly and in groups, will alter future time, will "make" patterns for structures that will then proceed to manifest themselves as we act them out in accordance with our beliefs. The ideological battles of the cold war and all the hot wars in between are battles for the minds and attention of human beings on a mass scale. Psychic battles too, or at least competitions, are going on and will be increasingly waged. However, this does not mean that I feel that Lesbians and Gay men should rush defensively into the psychic domains in order to remake the future into a safer place for ourselves and our particular ideology. The shaman/priest/artist/teacher/leader does not operate for the sole benefit of herself and her kind but for the benefit of the people at large and of the universe and its patterns, as becomes what she perceives as fitting into place, into her sense of natural justice.

Perhaps the ancient priestesses and fire guardians stroked each other's roses, and entered the Diamond Light together; perhaps they became the raincloud and called in rain when it was needed; perhaps they called in peace when it was needed. Perhaps we modern Lesbians will learn once again to gather around our fires and locate our god-powers. Whatever the equivalent of these acts of ceremonial Lesbianism is for modern times, I feel we shall ultimately learn to do them and to direct them consciously toward purposeful and just ends.

> my first beloved
> present friend
> if I could die like the next rain
> I'd call you by your mountain name
>
> and rain on you . . .

want of my want, i am your lust
wave of my wave, i am your crest
earth of my earth, i am your crust
may of my may, i am your must
kind of my kind, i am your best

tallest mountain least mouse
least mountain tallest mouse

you have put your very breath upon mine
i shall wrap my entire fist around you
i can touch any woman's lip to remember

we are together in my motion
you have wished us a bonded life

— *Funeral poem: For Yvonne Mary Robinson*
(Oct. 20, 1939 — Nov. 22, 1974)

CHAPTER TEN

Gay Is Good

Who hears whom once once to snow they might
if they trained fruit-trees they might if they leaned
over there they might look like it which when it
could if it as if when it left to them to their use of
pansies and daisies use of them use of them of use
of pansies and daisies use of pansies and daisies
use of them use of them of use use of pansies and
use of pansies and use of pansies and use use of
them use of pansies and daisies use of use of them
which is what they which is what they they do
they which is what they do there out and out and
leave it to the meaning of their by their with their
allowance making allowed what is it.

Gertrude Stein, from *Patriarchal Poetry*[1]

Well, Von, first lover, what a journey this has turned out to be for me! My little sashay down the lavender trail led me through so many stories of the color purple and then into the tribal worlds underlying our modern one, not really buried either but often very close to the surface. I was ecstatic to learn some of the Gay names and Gay offices used by American Indian tribes: Das and Murfidai, Huame and Winkte and Koskalaka, Nadle and Choupan. I know you would have loved that part especially, my Von, you who were born in the backlands of the territory of New Mexico, delivered at home by a Spanish-speaking midwife, and steeped in so much original American southwestern lore. You who always drew pictures all over your hands and your Levis. You who painted katchinas on the wall in full color when we were so home-sick in Washington, D.C. But my investigation didn't stop in tribal America, although I learned such valuable tools there; it spread out over the world, to pagan religious stories from former centuries, to spinsters in China as well as New England, to North African Sahacat "fricatrice" sorcerers. I continued into the lives of the Fairy people who left us such rich stores and our big Gay holiday of Halloween; I remembered the Celtic wisewomen and men who were burned a few centuries ago for following the ways of the Old Religion of Europe and for practicing homosexual love "officially," so to speak. They worshiped a Horned God,[2] or the sun and moon together, or they followed the huntress Diana with her multitude of European names on moonlit journeys to wild dark places where they held tumultuous sensual dances in communion with wilderness spirits. And all the time that these ancient histories, these stories of Lesbian warriors and Gay kings and priests, were unfolding in my notebooks I continued to draw references and comparisons with our own personal history, my Vonnie, of the way it felt to be coming out as a Gay person in the second half of the twentieth century in America, of emerging from such obscurity and lost connections that you and I, like so many Gay people, believed we were the "only ones" (plus Sappho).

And all the time that I was busy researching and writing in notebooks, drawing together the strands of those two histories, the long general one and the short private one, a third history was taking place all around me, becoming an increasingly important part of my life, as the Gay civil rights and countercultural movement grew up during the 1970s.

Dennis Altman describes the urban Gay culture that has developed:

> A whole new range of images has been added to the traditional stereotype of the lisping hairdresser and the cigar-chomping diesel dyke; nowadays gay business, professional, and religious groups meet with mayors, members of Congress, and even (under Jimmy Carter) presidential aides; gay spokespersons appear regularly on television, speak at colleges and schools, and demand equal time in the press; and gay marches have become major events in a number of cities each summer. The very diversity of gays revealed in this new openness — the fact that the gay community cuts across divisions of sex, race, class, and geography — has helped make homosexuality an increasingly important political issue in contemporary American life.[3]

This diversity includes the rise of an independent Gay press, the production of a number of films, the organizing of political groups such as National Gay Task Force and the Lesbian Mother's Union; the Gay Academic Union and Gay libraries; the election of Gay people to national and local political office; the advent of yearly mass marches, street festivals, and public celebrations of Gay Pride Day drawing crowds of hundreds of thousands (almost completely ignored by the mainstream press), and an increasing number of openly Gay and nevertheless widely accepted writers, poets, and playwrights of all races and ethnic backgrounds.

Altman writes, "Just as in earlier times homosexuals were identified by tennis shoes, scarves and jewelry for men, shoulder bags, and floral shirts, so a new set of styles came to be identified as gay during the seventies: restaurants with plants and plate-glass windows; an art deco revival; greeting card shops; wicker furniture; high tech style; leather fashions; earrings for men and army fatigues for women; Perrier water. No doubt as the decade progresses these will be replaced by others. The crucial point is that as gays become more open, so too does their impact on fashions as a whole."[4]

Far more than fashion trends, buying styles, and the like constitute the Gay and Lesbian influence in America. Under the influence of Gay men, American men in the past decade have come to value their own beauty, to take care of themselves, and to take pride in appearing attractive to others. As Altman put it, the question is not so much why straight men are now imitating Gay men in beautifying themselves as it is why straight men neglected themselves for so long. And the new emphasis on male beauty is accompanied, at times, by tenderness, warmth, and an ease of touch between men that was not noticeably present prior to the phenomenon of mass Gay influence. Feminism, of course, also affected this process, but I really believe we learn most of our behavior from our own genders.

Speaking for the Lesbian/feminist side of the family at least, I know that the influencing of society was completely intentional; we set out to create a context in which our voices, experiences, and philosophical positions could be heard. The founders of Olivia Records, for instance, and of the women's presses and bookstores perceived themselves as creating something far different from businesses; they thought of themselves, we all thought of ourselves, as needing to create a social/political/cultural matrix in which people could comprehend and absorb our basic philosophical understandings. We developed bookstores, newspapers, magazines, presses, networks, meetings, groups, books, records, staged events, and many other things for the precise purpose of creating a community that would impact publicly and directly on American society. We were completely conscious of doing this, though we had no way of knowing how audaciously successful we would be. Through the cultural media in particular, we interjected into mainstream America the ideas that gender roles are never fixed, that women can be creative, articulate, and public and can engage in skills formerly designated as "men's work."

In its very way of operating, Olivia Records, a prime example of what has become known as "women's culture," has promoted a particular, 1970s Lesbian/feminist politic. It is collectively owned and run, embodying the difficult principle of sharing control on a horizontal rather than a vertical plane. The group has been strongly interracial at times and interclass. Grass-roots financial support sustains it, chiefly in the form of small, low-interest loans from individual women who invest in it because they want the company to exist. Grass-roots networking has created the matrix of distributors necessary to sell hundreds of thousands of records outside the mainstream record industry and to produce hugely attended concerts. And herein is a vital point about the semiunderground state of Lesbians (as Karla Jay has also pointed out): Because we are almost always ostracized and censored, because our records and books are so rarely produced by mainstream media, we have had no choice but to organize separate networks.

267

These wield tremendous influence and put pressure on mainstream organs to promote at least some of the ideas developing at the woman-centered ground level. It has been and remains a hard row to hoe, filled with the horrors of trying to establish a business organization within the context of a social movement, but it has had strong successes.

The mass all-women music festivals (attended by many, perhaps hundreds of thousands of women) grew out of Olivia's groundwork of organizing and presenting high-quality music with high pro-woman content.

What Did Sappho Teach Her Girls?

During the period since 1969, when I first entered the women's movement, I have seen how Lesbians worked with other feminists and undertook to organize around and often independently catapulted issue after issue of feminism into the public eye: doing "nontraditional" (male-controlled) work; demanding the right to abortion; treating rape as hostile aggression rather than as sex; advocating self-defense, athletic competition, and muscle building; establishing shelters for battered women; starting women-owned businesses; collectivity and other equitable work structures; women and money; women and alcohol; women-controlled space; women-owned land used for "women's" purposes; women-produced art, music, and writing; international feminism; being "woman-identified"; redefining power and control; creating woman-defined religion, philosophy, and language; women and racism; motherhood as a real job. And, of course, we have raised the issue of Lesbianism itself and what it might mean for women to "love each other" and ourselves.

"What did Sappho teach her girls, except how to love?" the Roman Ovid asked, and it is just possible that she not only taught her companions how to love women but that she taught her whole society as well.[5] Popular songs today are full of very specific advice about how men and women alike desire to be approached and courted, women's songs having gotten particularly graphic on the subject as the sexual revolution has unwound in the United States. Sappho was a popular song writer as much as a lyric poet, so popular and influential that coins were afterward minted with her picture on them.

The men of Sappho's day may have needed some instruction

about how to approach a woman, especially at marriage, especially since they were oriented toward the male body for their sexual and aesthetic attention. One marriage custom of the time required the woman to lie in wait for her new husband with her ass prominently displayed, so he would be certain of arousal. This is hardly flattering to women.

Sappho wrote bridal songs as well as woman-to-woman lyrics, and her works have helped men as well as women better understand how to approach loving the person and the body of a woman. That is certainly a function (one of many) that modern Lesbians have had, at least in the last fifteen years in America. As sexual inhibitions have dropped, many women have had affairs with Lesbians, learned about the possible responses of their own bodies, and gone on to teach the men of their choice how to be effective lovers. I was delighted to see this acknowledged on the cover of a standard slick women's magazine whose headline read: "A woman taught me to love — and my husband thinks it's wonderful!"

The position that Gay people take in society, the function we so often choose, is that of mediator between worlds. We transfer power, information, and understandings from one "world" or sphere of being to another. In a tribal environment, this means shape-shifting into wolves, birds, stones, the wind, and translating their wisdoms for the benefit of the people of the tribe. In a modern urban environment it may mean living in a port city, helping to absorb and translate new arrivals of all kinds; in the long patriarchal history that has gradually enveloped the world's people, the Gay function has been to make crossover journeys between gender-worlds, translating, identifying and bringing back the information that each sex has developed independently of the other. Gay men began crossing over centuries ago to effect the transfer of the religions, science, and agricultural development accomplished by women during the prepatriarchal period. Lesbians have in recent decades crossed over and increasingly do so to acquire for women male social habits that lead to, or at least appear to lead to, genuine social control in the working and management worlds (smoking, drinking, gambling, pool playing, wearing pants, driving cars and planes, handling machinery, developing muscles, and entering athletic sports). We have also broken into thousands of occupations, making it possible for women in general to enter; in the future I believe Lesbians will cross increasingly into religion, science, and technology, taking other women as well as pro-woman and pro-nature (unalienated) perspectives with them, and this will greatly alter the nature of our society.

Although we are "The Changer and the Changed," to quote singer Cris Williamson's album title, we also help society retain some of its oldest values and customs by keeping them and using them in our own subculture.

Subculture is what Gay culture as a whole has been called by sociologists, and though that is preferable to sickness, sin, or crime as designations, *supraculture* is actually what we have, an umbrella *metaculture* that reaches all around the world and through all time periods. *Transculture* is what we have, crossing every imaginable border with our functions, qualities and philosophical stances intact, with, of course, intercultural and interera variations. The qualities of Gayness are metacultural, they transcend eras of historical time, they transcend national borders, and they transcend social systems such as "tribal," "village," "feudal," and "industrial."

Life on the Cusp of Being

Homosexuals, and others who perform similar social functions, such as circus people, artists and musicians, prostitutes and clowns, are not living on the "fringe." This is an inaccurate image. The universe, let us say instead, consists of interlocking worlds. Gay culture is always on the cusp of each intersecting world or way of life, on the path between one world and another. This is why Hecate and Afrikete were worshiped at the crossroads. This is why Gay city ghettos are so often on the border between one ethnic or racial group or class of people and another and located in cities that are ports of entry between a multiplicity of "worlds." This is why the name of the Greek goddess Dike means "the way," "the path." This is why sailors are considered Gay in popular jargon, whether as a group they actually participate in Gay sex more than soldiers or not; sailors ply on ships between the land and the sea, between one country and another.

In large cities, especially port cities, where so many Gay neighborhoods have grown up since the 1940s, social interactions and even entire movements are heavily influenced by Gay culture. For example, the well-publicized hippie movement of "flower children" that flourished during the mid-sixties drew many of its values and underlying precepts from Gay culture. (In the countryside they drew from Indian people.) The hippie movement began its main course of life and remained centered, in the public view at least, in the area of the Haight-Ashbury District of San Francisco, an area that has been a Gay ghetto for decades before the arrival of acid, rock, and hundreds of thousands of young Americans looking for a new set of ideals and something to do for a few years. Before her untimely overdose of heroin and Southern Comfort, white rock singer Janis Joplin was a frequent customer, along with her girlfriend, at a long-standing Lesbian bar in the Haight. Gay poets Allen Ginsberg and Jack Spicer set a post-beatnik tone for the dropout culture. Gay slang phrases entered hippie language with such terms as "straight," meaning not us, others; "blow your mind," meaning to produce an altered state of consciousness through hallucinatory drugs; and "what a drag," meaning bad time or bad happening.

During the hippie heyday of the sixties and early seventies, the indigenous Gayness of the neighborhood all but disappeared under the rush of spectacularly costumed and bearded hippies, and then the tourists who came by the hundred thousand to gape at them, and finally the drug dealers and entrepreneurs of addiction and despair who came by the thousands to exploit them. The neighborhood deteriorated under these pressures, especially following the heavy influx of the dope industry and its attendant violence. Then around 1978 the Haight Ashbury began to revert to its Gay ghetto origins, this time with a new coat of paint, as it was "gentrified" by single white men with money to invest in the beautiful old victorian houses and to open small, attractive businesses. These investors were continually pointed out as Gay. Many poor people, especially Black, who had moved to the Haight to take advantage of the lower rents or who had been there all along, were pushed out and forced to move, accelerating the anti-Gay feeling in Black areas.

In its beginnings at least, the hippie movement advocated a loving outlook, flower power, peaceful behavior, free love, lots of every variety of sex, bright colors (especially on the men), love of nature, doing things yourself, and using altered states of consciousness induced by psychedelic drugs, using the tarot, and being relatively accepting of all kinds of people, including interracial mixtures. The movement advocated and manifested underground alternative communal cultures with their own territory, media, economic base, language, and shared value in sharp distinction with those of the major culture. All of these qualities are also Gay ghetto characteristics, though of course not on such a large scale. It is completely appropriate that the hippies called the above-ground people who were not part of their lifestyle "straight people," a term they learned, among other things, from the queers they found living in the Haight Ashbury District. (Unfortunately, they never did catch on to the really fine cooking and the aesthetic sensibility that can make neighborhoods of Gay men such a joy. And now that I think of it, we dykes are not always up to par in these regards either.)

In 1984 the Haight-Ashbury is no more staid and proper than it was when I first saw it in 1968. Bizarrely dressed young punk people walk around in flaming red or blue Mohawk haircuts, mixed in with musicians, artists, and writers and just ordinary denizens of every race, age, and description. It is a very appropriate Gay neighborhood, a mixing pot for what is going to emerge next to create culture in America.

Uses of Pansies and Daisies

Pansy and violet are not the only flowers connected to Gayness in language and culture. Actually *flower* itself is, in the Spanish language at least. One Hispanic Lesbian told me that her grandmother, who lives in the western United States, used *flores*, flowers, as the traditional name for Lesbians passed down to her, and she did not use it in a derogatory way. The masculine *flor*, is a Hispanic term for a Gay man, as is *margarita*, meaning daisy, according to a Gay Chicano who reported overhearing the words in bars and other places.

". . . use of pansies and daisies, use of them, of use," Stein wrote in her emphatic style in a paragraph from her long poem, *Patriarchal Poetry*, and I believe her. But what are some uses of Gay and Lesbian flowers in modern society?

In the mid-1980s an editor for *The New York Times* took me to a central location in Manhattan, to a very special Gay bar. What distinguished this large yet rather homey and extremely crowded bar from others was the community of newly arrived immigrants — from a Central American country — that made up its clientele. And while the bar, called "The Little Schoolhouse," was clearly Gay, with many same-gender couples of both sexes dancing together, a large number of straight people were also in evidence. These latter folks were not the typical tourists, heterosexual couples out looking for nighttime exotica to mingle with, nor were they friends spending time with their Gay buddies. These straight people were relatives, family members related to the Gay people, related to each other, and related to their common community.

The result was a bar filled with adults of all ages, gabbing away in a social gathering that resembled a big family picnic, birthday or two-day wedding. Nor did I doubt that the same people gathered for those events, too. This was an extended family worth wanting, worth working to realize, a family within a community in which everyone gets to be who they are, and to which each person contributes his or her own special intracultural traditions.

Noticeably missing among the dancing Gay couples was any kind of posturing or sexual costume; I saw no glitzy bids for attention or erotic displays for public consumption. These people did not have to show off to gain attention from strangers. They weren't strangers.

The dancing, like the country western dancing popular among Gay people in San Francisco, San Diego, and Albuquerque, was warm, affectionate, measured and engaged. Their clothing, neat and working-class, wasn't different for Gay and straight relatives, though a lot of women were in pants. Except for the multitude of closely dancing and openly affectionate Gay couples I would have thought it was any community event, one that made me homesick for such a heterogeneous community.

Near midnight on Saturday night, every Saturday night according to my guide, people gathered to sit near a small stage area. A drag queen emerged from behind the curtain, dressed as one or another prominent American female movie star, dancing with plenty of posturing and scanty, glittery costume. As s/he danced; people, men and women alike, rose from their places to tuck bills into her/his G-string, then sat back down to watch the Gay Queen recreate for everyone the great American goddess.

I thought about the bar's name, "Little Schoolhouse," and how, as a community, these people were perhaps using their own Gay culture to teach themselves about life and expectations in the new country, while at the same time using it to maintain cohesiveness with the culture they had brought from the old country.

My companion told me that small Gay bars were located block by block in sections of a New York borough settled by these people, "and it goes almost village by village," she said, "each neighborhood with its own central, community-style Gay bar."

Rainbows, Storms and Changes

Perhaps nothing was more particular to the inner heart of the Gay domain during the 1950s and 1960s than a theater full of fairies of all descriptions listening to a tragicomic actress or queen in drag, a person of either sex singing, after the manner of Judy Garland,

273

"Somewhere Over the Rainbow." Somewhere over the rainbow is another world, just follow the yellow brick road in your "red shoes,"[6] and soon your own inner nature will be revealed. The Judy Garland imitator at that moment is a ceremonial dyke or fairy queen, illuminating an otherworld dominion that has been part of subterranean Gay culture for millennia. The rainbow was perhaps sacred to the god Uranus as it was to the other Gay thundergods. Brazilian/African Oya wears a rainbow dress as she sweeps up the wind with her quirt; Queen Boudica's dress was described as multicolored. The goddess of the Greek rainbow, Iris, was "handmaid" to the goddess Hera. Let's hear it for the handmaids; we know that more than one lady and servant were lover/companions.

The power of the rainbow to transform is recorded by John Gunn in a story from the Keres (Pueblo) people of the Southwest.[7] Once in the village of Acoma lived a beautiful young woman, who had a handsome young man for a lover. Nearby lived a Ko-qi-ma, or hermaphrodite (referred to in the story as a "she"), who also wanted the handsome young man for a lover. Since the Ko-qi-ma was a Gay magician with magical powers "she" tricked the beautiful young woman into walking under a rainbow while chanting "I am a coyote." This turned the unfortunate woman into a coyote, who was too ashamed then to return to her village. After a while the handsome young man found her and brought a wise old medicine man who restored her to her original body and in addition gave her a magic object. With this she tricked the Ko-qi-ma in turn, turning "her" into a rattlesnake.

In another association between Gay transformation and the rainbow, the uncle of a family with both American Indian and Scots tribal affiliations told an adolescent tomboy daughter that she could become a boy if she only walked under a rainbow. Stalwartly, one summer day after a rainstorm, she set out toward a glorious multicolored bridge in the sky, but you know how rainbows are. Rainbows and storms are transitional forms, as the stories reflect. In every sense the people who act out the heart of Gay culture are storms themselves, agents of change.

"The common woman is as common as a thunderstorm," I wrote as a specifically Lesbian verbal portrait in 1969, using sheer intuition for the image of storm that I would find repeatedly ten years later in my research about Gay people. This subconscious knowledge of the shamanic archetype may also underlie the simpleminded actions of the first Christian Roman Emperor, Justinian, who condemned many Gay people to death. He believed we were responsible for causing earthquakes, which in my mind suggests that some Gay ceremonial figures were pretty good at predicting them. I'm glad he was not the dictator of California in 1989, when the October earthquake knocked out freeways and moved the Bay Bridge five inches to the east. Although, on second thought, his views are not that different from the blaming of AIDS and the high divorce rate on Gay people, a contemporary view promoted by some Christian fundamentalists, who might have felt completely at home under Justinian's rule.

Through an Ever-Revolving Door

In the absence, in most or all of America, of a holistic community spirit such as existed at the "Little Schoolhouse" bar, Gay-owned bars in the 1960s attempted to establish alternative communities for a clientele who had largely been excluded from the communities of their births.

A particularly central bar named "Maude's Study" was opened in 1966 by Ricki Streicher, a hospital technician who decided to strike out on her own as a businesswoman, and who helped form a massive social movement. Well-located in the Haight-Ashbury district of San Francisco, and started just as the area began burgeoning with the hippie flower-child phenomena, Maude's quickly became much more than a bar, more than the place rumored to be frequented by the rock singer Janis Joplin. It became a primitive social center, an entry point into the Lesbian lifestyle and point of view, a doorway to a different world entered by women from all over the country, and ultimately, the world.

By 1968, when I arrived in San Francisco, Maude's already had mystique, a welcoming atmosphere and warmth in the hearts of its clientele. As a woman-centered, woman-owned bar Maude's differed markedly from the alienating bars owned by the Mafia, and from the male-owned bars, where women were barely or not at all tolerated and, as in most of the culture, by and large invisible as individuals and as a public force.

Maude's was not a furtive place but a vibrant public space for women-only activities. The decor was warm, lots of wood and red wall paper. Ricki sponsored ball teams, monthly dinners, and birthday parties based in one's zodiac sign — completely democratic celebrations. For a Lesbian population starved for women-defined spaces, nurturing, encouragement and attention, Maude's was a launching pad for other activities. Like other Gay bar owners in

California, Ricki hired Gay people, so it was possible for a few women, at least, to come to work in Gay clothes, and to speak a Gay language, to have "style." She fought political and legal battles for our rights to touch each other in public and set limits to keep some amount of order in the fights that inevitably break out after hours (or earlier) in bar culture. Maude's Study was more sensitive, I have heard, to race and class issues than many other bars, listening to criticism from continually outspoken Lesbians, such as Pat Parker, trying to be fair about who was eighty-sixed in fights, who was carded most at the door, what kinds of music were on the jukebox, and so on. Ricki or her partner went personally to the police station to bail out Lesbians who left the bar too drunk and got into subsequent trouble.

Lesbian bar culture, even with our feminist opposition to its limitations, formed a strong underbase of the incredibly vital social movement that would by 1969 or 1970 be known as Lesbian feminism. We women needed to talk to each other, long and urgently, to locate our commonalities and differences, to raise consciousness of our political positions, to read, write and discuss our own literature, cooperate in projects and plan effective actions. Finding the noisy, alcohol-deadened atmosphere unsuitable for the kinds of gathering we needed, we set ourselves to form "alternatives to the bars." Yet even as we formed our Lesbian feminist meetings, dances and projects, the bars remained, along with "the Movement," one of our two primary mother-places. Those who first gained Lesbian public identity within bar culture were called "bar dikes" (not always a compliment), to distinguish us from the later "political Lesbians" — women who came out in the context of the new alternative, Movement-based institutions we founded and fostered and which by 1971 were spreading across the country from, most publicly, the urban centers of New York City and the San Francisco Bay Area, though already Lesbian feminism was being established in other places such as Iowa City and the Washington, D.C.–Baltimore area.

Wild in the Streets and in the World

Feminism in the form of grass-roots consciousness-raising groups was born, one woman told me, on the West Coast in Berkeley in 1967, when four or five graduate students from the University of California at Berkeley gathered around a suicidal friend and began to talk truly about the despair of being female in a male-dominated America. Consciousness-raising groups spread quickly into the disaffected white left where women were angry at being the overworked and overlooked auxiliaries of men who were imitating the paramilitary public posturing of the Black Panthers, and not, for instance, the Panthers' social programs such as breakfasts for children — programs run primarily by women.

In May of 1969 my then-lover Wendy Cadden and I were heavily involved in demonstrations, street riots and collective tree planting at the birth of the grassroots environmental movement, People's Park, in Berkeley. The day that a man named James Rector was fatally shot pointblank and another man was blinded by the police I too was fired on, one street over, running a little too far down the block for the shotgun pellets to do more than sting through the back of my jacket.

A month later, in June, we heard that some dikes and queens had rioted at a bar in New York City. These were the Stonewall riots that triggered the national Gay Rights Movement and though we were cheered up by news of the event we were not immediately affected, being already embarked on our own course, a course that eventually would pour us right back out into the Gay Movement.

In July Wendy and I joined women's consciousness-raising groups in San Francisco, tired of what we would learn to call the misogyny of the Left, and the nonexistence of a Lesbian base in the organizations of Gay men such as Mattachine, One and various literary groups. I was electrified by the ideas discussed in the consciousness-raising group, and then horrified when some of the straight women in the group reacted with such fear and objectified sexual charge toward me that I didn't feel my life story could be heard in common with the stories told by other women. I dropped out of the group.

In October I stayed home to write *The Common Woman Poems*, my own fantasy consciousness-raising group, a set of seven sonnetlike portraits of women related by their "commonality," in which one — "Carol, in the park, chewing on straws" — was an overt Lesbian. Carol did get to tell her story. By reading these portrait poems in public I would create feminism as I wanted to see it — completely inclusive of working-class and (at that time) ghettoized Black and Lesbian women, women of all shapes, ages, occupations, habits and connections to other humans and to nature.

In November Wendy and I tried again to find a place in a Gay men's gathering, this time a large political conference with many speakers. I read a paper and gave a talk urging Gay people to take a moral stand against the Vietnam War, and to work together, men

277

and women. Once again I felt that I was unheard, that my very emotional delivery was a source of embarrassment; as Lesbians we felt invisible and inarticulate, completely overshadowed by the concerns of the men. And what, anyhow, were the concerns of women? We weren't sure.

We had come with two friends, also organizers. One of them, a Black Lesbian named Amá, astonished us by disrupting the whole conference single-handedly to bring up the issue of the lack of women's participation. But to no avail, for there was no base of female power toward which to take the attention that continued unabatedly fixed on the very white, very articulate men. But instead of giving up, Wendy and I gathered up five other disgruntled Lesbians and arranged a separatist meeting.

Within two weeks sixty women were attending, and we had the first formal Lesbian-feminist organization that I know of. We called ourselves Gay Women's Liberation and we were consciously separatist, from men, from Gay men, and from straight feminists, though we always saw ourselves as part of "the Movement," the mass drives for civil rights and ecological balance, that impelled our generation from the moment Martin Luther King and Malcolm X took the public stage.

Meanwhile, on the East Coast, writer Rita Mae Brown had been a volatile Lesbian voice in the National Organization of Women of New York City since 1968, and when in 1970 feminists seized *Rat*, a left newspaper, Brown and another longtime Lesbian, Martha Shelley, published pro-Lesbian articles in it. I reprinted these tracts to distribute as organizational tools, along with my own *Common Woman Poems*, my satire *The Psychoanalysis of Edward the Dyke* and, later, Valerie Solanas's *SCUM Manifesto*.

Brown and Shelley, we heard years later, disrupted a women's liberation conference to talk about Lesbianism in 1970, the same year that seventeen of us on the West Coast interrupted a feminist conference to display our views and our public presence.

From the beginning our efforts on the West Coast were characterized by our attempt to include all classes and races, with strong leadership from both Black and white women.

Irish American Alice Molloy had been part of the Beat movement, carrying her anarchism out to the West Coast in 1960. Amá was from Harlem, active in the Black student movement and influenced by the Black Power movement, as was Pat Parker, a poet and activist whom Amá brought to my room one day in late 1969. Parker quickly began participating in our organization. Natalie Lando and Carol Wilson were white working-class women who had earlier, in the 1950s, helped organize Daughters of Bilitis and who now joined Lesbian feminism, founding public institutions and keeping them going for decades.

In our diversity and anarchism we consciously suppressed hierarchical leadership, opting instead for encouraging small group action and initiating projects that quickly became public institutions. Every woman, we said, was a leader in her own way. We retained a strong commitment to race, class and environmental issues as part and parcel of Lesbian feminism.

Pat Norman, a Black woman, founded the Lesbian Mothers' Union and went on to run for public office as a Lesbian in the 1980s. Pat Parker joined me in overtly Lesbian feminist poetry readings that established us as spokespeople for ideas from a community base, extended out to include liberation for everyone. For a period of time most of our audiences were entirely female, by our design; huge, vocal and enthusiastically screaming and standing on chairs to urge our voices on.

Parker, who died of cancer in 1989, was a giant voice of early Lesbian feminism, a succinct describer of racism and sexism, and a fierce promoter of equality for all people. When Pat in turn became disillusioned with the incipient racism in our large Gay women's group she dropped out to found a separate group of Lesbians of color, called Gente. It is a measure of the usefulness of separatism as a tool that she was able to do this without losing her ability to speak to and from the larger white-dominated base as well.

Meanwhile, on the East Coast, Rita Mae Brown had moved to Washington, D.C. in 1971, connecting up with Coletta Reid, who was an early founder of the feminist newspaper *Off Our Backs*, and with other women who were coming out as Lesbian feminists. This group, which included Ginny Berson and Charlotte Bunch, met for a while, published a newspaper and then exploded out in several directions, with individuals forming Olivia Records, Diana Press, a women's distribution service, and an important analytical journal, *Quest*.

In Iowa City, too, a women's press began publishing Lesbian feminist material, led by Joan Pinkvoss, who went on to merge her press, Aunt Lute, with Spinster's Ink in San Francisco, in the mid-1980s.

This exploding of the public Lesbian voice into national bases of institutional power coincided with the appearance of Gay organizations and the increasing public presence of Gay men and of old time Lesbian businesswomen like Ricki Streicher and other organizers who moved the Gay civil rights movement out into the public media view in massive annual parades celebrating Gay power, and into the political world to effect real change in the legal and social status of Gay people. Some of the largest gatherings in U.S. history have been of Gay people concerned with Gay issues.

Thousands of local Gay organizations in every part of the country, dozens of Gay national magazines, cable TV and radio programs, full length movies, and thriving communities of Gay writers and artists have continued to grow and give each other encouragement through the 1980s. The Gay movement has provided enough support, enough sense of community in enough areas, to enable many openly Gay people to bear, adopt and raise children.

The attention of Lesbians was brought sharply onto Gay men with the crisis of AIDS and the obvious and immediate need for women to be involved in the old female role of providing healing and caretaking services. However, as consciousness spreads of the accelerating rates of cancer and environmental disease among women, Lesbian attention is again turning toward the needs of women.

Separatism Is for Everyone

In the years of Lesbian separatism we deliberately gave the word *Gay* to the male movement since the popular media almost invariably centers on men when it hears *Gay* anyway, and we always need words to differentiate female from male concerns, as they overlap only to some extent. Like *fairy, Gay* is a word about both men and women, although the media ignores this, so that just as *people* often means men, *Gay* often means men, in the public view. This is a form of separatism, male separatism, though it is not called that.

Male separatism in the form of men being overwhelmingly preoccupied with their own concerns dominated the Gay male movement of the 1970s, though like other men across the country, they imagined they were somehow speaking for "everyone."

In the 1980s, as Lesbian feminism swelled out into the world, women established separatist grounds in the form of national music festivals, bookstores, media including feature length films on Lesbian subjects, and hundreds of businesses. From this power base women have again approached working with men, pulled along in part by the AIDS crisis, by the twelve-step addiction recovery movement, and by the clear need and possibilities for exchanges of information and caring between the Gay genders.

The nationwide recovery movement of twelve-step programs, originating with alcoholism in the 1930s and fifty years later extending to all obsessive behavior, provided a forum for exchange among different kinds of people. These programs, while appealing to many heterosexuals, have had an impact on a majority of the Gay population, at least on the West Coast. An estimated four out of five Gay people in California were believed by some social scientists to be alcohol abusers in the 1970s. One reason for this is that bars served for decades as the only public meetingplaces for Gay people of both sexes. Secondly, alcohol deadens pain among the socially dispossessed. As the openly Gay and Lesbian movements have taken charge of our public lives, the need to deaden pain has been replaced by activist activities improving the quality of life.

Early indications are that the decade of the 1990s will be characterized by more activism, more public presence, and more stability, rising from concern for Gay children and for developing alternative, varied family systems that work for people who have become conscious of abuse patterns handed down for centuries and who are determined to break these patterns.

Examples of genuine cooperation and successfully shared resources between men and women are already happening. This sharing is made possible by the success of separatism, used as a tool to give groups of women a power base from which to overlap with men. The impact of feminism is evident, along with slightly increased wage-earning, and hence greater independence among women. Men still make some 40 percent more money for the same work, while at the same time more openly craving and needing women's knowledge, so perhaps an equitable exchange can be bargained for.

Within Gay culture the same excellent use of separatism is happening with people of color, and people of differing ethnicities. We can thank separately founded institutions such as Kitchen Table Women of Color Press, and various Black journals, Hispanic anthologies, Jewish magazines, and most notably the anthology *This Bridge Called My Back* for the increasingly strong multicultural voices now gathering and being heard.[8]

Women comprised about half the panelists of the 1990 Outwrite Conference sponsored by the first Gay and Lesbian magazine, *Out/Look*, and the conference's honorees and keynote speakers were gender-balanced and also (to some extent) of varying race and ethnicity. This is a completely different approach to life and community than the one reflected by the 1969 conference in the same area of the country, in which Wendy and I gathered five other separatist Lesbians in frustration, and where Amá and I were the only female speakers to volunteer our voices, and where probably only about 3 percent of the attendees were female, and where I noticed no black or brown skinned men at all.

In New York City The Center, a complex Gay multicultural enterprise of services and the arts, is staffed by both genders. Bookstores that formerly carried few or no books for the opposite gender are now merging or moving in that direction. A Different Light, with stores in several cities, features literature for both sexes though it is male-owned. Even firmly Lesbian feminist stores now often have substantial stocks of books by Gay men.

When a man says to me, "I'm glad you're not separatist anymore," I wonder if he knows he could also say, "I'm so glad you were separatist for a while, and found your own base."

The Gay Crossroad

I said earlier that the German phrase referring to Gay people *Vom Anderen Uffer*, means literally "from the other side." In Spanish, especially in Mexican, Chicano and Pachuco dialects, there are several similar phrases, including *es de agua*, "is of water," in the sense of being from across the water; *de la banqueta*, "from the other sidewalk"; *del otro lado*, "from the other side"; and *de los otros*, "of the others" — all referring to Gayness.[9]

Some people perceive themselves and all of existence as having only one side, and I suppose that's sometimes a useful way to maintain a stable society; just as long as those on that one side don't insist that their monochrome perception is the only true one.

I believe that Gay culture at its heart is continually, however unconsciously, trying to reveal the other side, sometimes just to reveal the *fact* that there are sides. I believe we do this with regard to the sexes, to work roles, to the world of judgment and value, of aesthetics, of philosophies, of other realms of consciousness. We act out irony, essential humor, and paradox.

Old Gaya's children stand at the intersections of the universe pointing out the various directions. And the intersection may be a Dianic crossroad where offerings were left, an Indian four-direction cross painted on the ground, a Voodoo or an African cross marked in wood, or an Asian crossroad related in a story. Or the crossroad may be pointed out as a dream of another world, the possibility of going "over the rainbow."

In tribal culture we often formed a pool of potential initiates some of whom became the shamans and medicine people who can enter the spirit world, the wind, the mountains and rivers and the bottom of the sea; the worlds of the dead, or spirits, of other people's minds, of the gods and their forces; we it is who bring back the strange and old messages, interpreting them for the benefit of our tribe. Anciently we were sometimes rewarded and esteemed for this, though I don't doubt we were more than once stoned out of town or tarred and feathered. We can be very aggravating, moody people, even to ourselves. And of course we don't always bring good or easy news. What we perhaps have at the core is an uncanny ability to identify with what we are not, to die as one form and return as another, to go from shy cocoon to rampant butterfly, to enter the wolves' den to learn the wolves' wisdom and return uneaten, though not unmarked. We have been the oracles and inspired diviners, the mediums who interpret the stars, the cards, the king's idle remarks, the weather and innards of fowls, the gossip, the history and poetry and saga of a people. And we remain remarkably tuned to a particular inner vision that is compelling to us, leading us into sometimes painful, grueling, lonely lives. All the more so when we cannot say our names.

We are the essential center of the entertainers, actors, musicians, poets, and playwrights who interpret and portray the social types, stereotypes, archetypes, videotypes of our society. And sometimes, like the Jews whose medieval history is so often linked with that of Gay people, we have long been selected as the sacrificial victim and blame-all whether we will it or not. And sometimes we get caught in our own paranoia and forget that we have power, and we deny it.

Gay is good, yes, Gay is vital, Gay is much more powerful than even its own people realize, and I believe that Gay is always present in any society, whether covertly or in a recognized form. Gay is Good, and as with any other group or category, Gay is sometimes Bad, too. But to say "Gay is better" — now that is just wrong. Inaccurate, among other things. In the early days of the Lesbian/ feminist groundswell there was a song going around, and I remember singing it: "Any woman can be a lesbian."[10] I suppose the Gay men have had similar doctrines of enthusiasm for a reborn cause. But I have come not to believe it, and, not only that, I don't think it would be a valuable thing for "everyone" to try to be Gay all their lives even if it were possible. I like diversity, I like cross-cultural connections and for that you have to have some cross cultures to connect with. And if each one is respected for what it is, is autonomous and confident of its own history, roots, cultural traits, and general functions, that seems to me a most fruitful situation, far safer and more exciting than the attempts at total homogeneity could ever be. Straight and Gay culture are mutually interdependent and complementary in their social functions. They have a tremendous overlap of personnel. To define each one honestly and fully we are going to have to learn how to think in two different directions at one time, to understand that "bad" has a place in the universe, and to do this without becoming passive and losing the will to rebel against injustice and dogmatic thinking when we see it before us.

CHAPTER ELEVEN

And Gay Is Also Baed

What is called good is
perfect, and what is
called sin is just as
perfect.

"To Think of Time," Walt Whitman[1]

Von, when my mother said, on meeting you, that she couldn't hate you because you were such a good person, she was talking about the difference between a stereotype and a flesh and blood reality. And you tried so hard to be a good and useful person. You tried to integrate your strict Catholic upbringing, your teacher's credo, your intense caring for your students, especially the poorest of them, and your own internal integrity and desire to be honest about your love for women, your good Gay life. You were the most moral person I have ever met, and yet your strands of goodness did not braid together in the world as you found it. The physical reason for your death was blood clots from your heart that lodged in your brain, your fine brain. Being a poet who understands the power of metaphor I will always believe you died of a broken heart, because no matter how you tried to improve the schools, how generous you were with your time, how hard you tried to be good, it simply wasn't good enough to give you anything back, nor to let you be yourself in the world.

In the Oldest Literature Gay
Is Good — Sort of

The fragments of Sappho's poetry that remain for us don't mention goodness. She said that whatsoever you love is what you will find beautiful, and she also said the world would not forget her.

Sappho was not kidding when she said she would be remembered; as a literary figure she has had sexual and bonding behavior, forms of romantic love, various sins, and (with Lesbian feminism) political movements named after her. I expect a bottled scent to appear on the market one of these days: "*Sappho*, the perfume that irresistibly attracts women to women."

Ancient as the poetry of Sappho, writing in 600 B.C., may seem to us today, it is not by any means the oldest Lesbian work available to us.

The earliest poetry signed by an individual in any literature is the poetry of a woman of ancient Sumer in the Tigris-Euphrates region of what is modern day Iraq. Her name was Enheduanna, and she lived in 2300 B.C., nearly as many centuries before Sappho as we are after Sappho. As the Moon temple high priestess of the first city, Uruk, Enheduanna occupied the highest civil office in the land. Her long poems exalted the goddess Inanna as the most powerful of the pantheon of Sumerian gods, restoring the waning great goddess

287

religion at a time when her own culture was in great transition from farming villages to a centralized urban center.

Enheduanna's lushly sensual descriptions of Inanna's physical beauty, her unbridled love of her fierceness, the complete absence of heterosexual references, and her accounts of Inanna's undertaking of ceremonial Gay rituals — all make it highly probable that Enheduanna was a Lesbian. That she describes herself as "spouse" of the goddess makes it nearly certain that she was a Lesbian, and expressing a Lesbian office.

The Gay rituals described in detail in this ancient Middle Eastern poetry are cross-gender changes, called "head-overturning" ceremonies. Inanna takes under her godly care a young woman who sees herself as a man, and who has been scorned in the streets of the city, particularly by women sitting in their windows. Inanna bestows men's weapons, dress and tools on her outcast protégé, in a special ceremony in which the initiate is obviously consecrated to the goddess as a ceremonial dike. Then Inanna does the obverse, taking on a young man, not an outcast, but rather one who had previously scorned her. He too, is cross-dressed, with women's clothing. These two "head-overturning" ceremonies were accompanied by a title given the Gay recipients: *pili-pili* in Ancient Sumerian. After their consecration they have a special office and powers of ecstasy and trance.

Anonymous poets earlier than Enheduanna chronicled the brilliant mythology of Inanna, describing her open love of her own vulva ("boat of heaven"), her sexual love for and sacred marriage to the shepherd king, and her descent to the underworld of death and transformation. The underworld was ruled by another female goddess, Ereshkigal, and the archetypal dance of beauty, judgment, birth and death between the two powerful female forces is a drama of elemental butch/fem interaction as gripping as anything in mythology.

In areas bordering the cities of Sumer, Inanna was called Ishtar. In *Gilgamesh*, a later Babylonian poem, two male figures encounter the goddess, who kills one and sends him to the underworld. This is Enkidu, the wild god, while the other is an early patriarchal hero, Gilgamesh, who scorns the advances of Ishtar (though not, in general, sex with women). The relationship between the male human hero and the male wild god is described in terms of great loyalty and endearment: bonded male friendship with sexual implications. Gilgamesh is told to embrace his friend "like a wife," and to love him as he loves himself. He watches over the dead Enkidu in despairing grief and later when he speaks with his spirit, Enkidu describes "my body that gave your heart joy to touch."

Thus the most ancient literature, revolving around the great goddess Inanna, openly involves both Gay customs and the relation men and women had to the goddess who preceded the patriarchal great gods of our era.

So Von, this is an involved way of wishing you were here so I could tell you that even in 2300 B.C. dikes were wandering the streets feeling alienated — only to be swept up by the goddess (or by history or by the media or the Movement or the winds of change), taken up suddenly into the heart of society, given special office, special pressures, special responsibility. How many times in our lifetimes have we had "head overturnings"? I certainly have had many . . . perhaps you in your isolation needed one.

Gay is always good *and* bad.

Black American artists, caught in a similar exclusion/inclusion, leadership/pariah rubber-band dance, sometimes use the idea of bad to describe their special oppression, their misuse as a stereotype by white Americans, and their pride of difference. *We a Baaad People* the poet Sonia Sanchez called her book in the 1970's — in pride — and Rap poets today say they identify with a football team (the Raiders) with a tough reputation because "the team is bad and Rap is bad, and bad is Black."[2]

Gay is also bad. While looking up the word *bad* in a dictionary, I discovered (to my delight) that its origin is an Anglo-Saxon word, *baedell*, meaning "hermaphrodite." So Gay was "baed" before it became "bad." The very word used to judge whether something is to be acceptable or not acceptable is a word that once meant "Gay."

Today as we near the end of the twenty-fourth century since Sappho, *Gay* is a word schoolchildren use to describe behavior they disapprove of. For instance, two Black eight year old boys are playing baseball, and one says, "You swing like you're Gay." Or in a white high school a girl will say of a test she didn't like taking, "that was very Gay."

At the same time I see in my neighborhood brave young Black faggots of twelve or thirteen, already decked out in special clothing, leading or running from some pack or other, in the company of girls, steadily swimming upstream, preparing for the enormous forces that will reach out later to select them for their offices. Singer Blackberri and writers Joseph Beam and Essex Hemphill have already done this.

Thus the wheel continues to turn, churning out courageous Gay people who become rebellious as a matter of perilous survival. In their fighting for their rights to survive they see differently from others and influence and alter the culture for everyone.

Out of bad comes good and out of good, bad in the sense of a dance of equals.

Nor is *bad* the only word once associated with the older pagan rites and now in later times used to condemn or alter people's behavior. For instance, Sin is the name of a female god in some areas of the ancient world, a male moon god in others. Worshipers used sex-magic in their rites to Sin, or Sinh, or Sidna; in the ancient Middle East the people's sacred kings were Sinbad, Bur-sin, and the like. Sheol, Hell, the place of the condemning fire was orignally the womb-fire, the clitoral "fire" of energy and creation, female sex and enchantment, so suppressed during the more patriarchal centuries that women of all classes have at times been subject to clitoridectomies and other sexual atrocities designed to curtail our powers. Sexual energies, utilized in tribal and temple traditions alike for social and magical purposes, came to be identified as the "fires of hell" and suppressed forcefully, especially during decades of the tumultuous passage of women's ancient arts and skills from female hands into the masculine world of priests, doctors, judges, and military officers.

The relation between the word *evil* and the word *Eve*, and between the goddess of India, Devi, and the word "devil," and between *daimon* and *demon*, are unmistakable, at least to a poet's ear. The idea of "evil" as it is manifested in English and in our modern culture did not arise from nowhere but grew out of the history that preceded it. Patriarchal morality required one single male god and was naturally in deadly opposition to the histories and pantheons of gods and spirits that were everywhere around it as it developed. The "devil" as Church authorities perceived him in Europe was sometimes the Horned God, the Goat-king and his Gay priesthood, his Lesbian Maids and his Mother-god and High Priestess. Sometimes when the word *devil* was used it meant Diana of the wild woods and her brother Lucca, Lucifer, who "fell," that is, whose reign has been overthrown.

"Sinful," "of the devil," and "evil" are all expressions that have been used very effectively against Gay culture, as has "queer," which derives from *cwer*, crooked, not straight, kinked. Perhaps the difference between queer and straight originated very simply with the difference between the straight-line dance of male/female couples and the Fairy round dance. *Wicked* is another pejorative word with a rich history, coming from the wonderful group of words surrounding the Fairy arts of weaving, basketry, herbology, and magic and including, as I mentioned earlier, *wick* (which also means "Lesbian" in British slang), *wicket, wicker, withy, weak* (meaning "pliant"), *wiccan* ("wise"), *wicca* ("coven of the wise"), *wise* ("knowing the craft"), *witch* ("wise woman"), *wizard,* and finally the judgment word used by those who condemned those practices and people, *wicked.*

In medieval Europe during the Inquisition the words for heresy and homosexual were identical in a number of languages. According to Arthur Evans, words meaning both Gay and heretic were used in Germany (*Ketzer*), in Italy (*Gazarro*), and in France (*Herite*). A particularly popular heretical movement, the Bogomils, arose in Bulgaria and spread across Europe. They were heavily Gay-influenced and advocated female leadership, so that in several languages the word for Bulgaria also meant homosexual; for instance, the word was *Bulgaro* in Italian, *Bougre* in French, and *Bugger* in English.[3] *Bugger* has remained in the underground language as a description of an act of male homosexual sex.

What *heresy* means literally is choice, from the root word *hairein*, "to choose."[4] In the context of its connection to the ancient Gay traditions it means not only the ability to choose one's beliefs but also to choose the characteristics of gender identification and sex-related social roles one will live by. No interplay between the two worlds of masculine and feminine is allowed in a society that allows no "heresy," no choice, no leadership on the part of its women and its Gay people and their chosen priesthood.

So "bad," or, rather, "baed," meant to those long-ago Anglo-Saxon tribal people "hermaphrodite," two-sexes-in-one. Gay. That's all. Not bad as we use it today, not evil, not sick, not undesirable, not "to be destroyed," to be avoided, to be considered the worst enemy, to be crushed and driven out of existence. Just Gay. *Murfidai, Nadle, Huame, Das, Links, Finnochio, Baedell.*

And so, understanding that the gods of older times were sometimes sacred deities who could be both sexes at once, I could begin to understand what is actually being said when someone says, "You Gays, you faggots and queers and bulldikes are bad; you're evil and wicked and full of sin, and we good, righteous, upstanding people are going to destroy you." What is really being said, in the light of

291

the "real," that is, the historical, meanings of the words, is this: "You children of Gaia, you sacred male firesticks, round-dancers and Daughters of the Warrior Goddess of Justice and Balance, you who are part-man-part-woman like a combination of Hermes and Aphrodite, you who are fruits from Eve the Mother and who have a habit of gathering in covens and desiring to know, you who are full of the spirit of the Moon; we don't like you, and we who are children of One-God, and of the right side, we straight-up-and-down-in-a-line people are going to make your living and your expression of your being as difficult as we can." Well, so be it.

The Horns of Our Dilemma are not that certain groups and individuals in modern society hate, fear, and oppress us (though this does cause us many problems), but, more important, our dilemma is that Gay is Good and Gay is also Baed. For if Gay is Good, yes, and should therefore be accorded equal status, socially, morally, and legally in the modern nation-state — a status that is very appealing — then how do we also fulfill our ancient position as classic outsider, as cultural leader/antileader, as goat, as shaman/priest, as mirror reflection of the social fabric, as critic, as mover and shaker? That is the apparent contradiction between our increasingly successful and inevitable attainment of civil rights and acknowledgment and protection of us as citizens of the nation — and our understanding that, as Tede Mathews said, "Gay people are not nice — that is, we're nice, but we're not *nice.*"[5] Given that one definition of nice is "to be ignorant," from *nicere*, to know not, perhaps it is that we have, as a group, knowledge of the difference and, as well, the similarities between good and evil. As the court jesters traditionally had. We are, very often, astutely aware of the forces *other than those that appear on the surface of a situation.* And by and by, no matter how smoothly things are going (in fact, perhaps because of the very smoothness) we are bound to point out diversity, to upset the applecart, throw the machine off balance, step out of line, wear "inappropriate" clothing, give away the secret, take a different course.

To understand Gay people and the nature of "perfection" and "sin" the entire society will need to literally transcend, rise above, envelop the system of perceiving everything as "either/or." Double vision, what researcher Lee Francis has described as the "diachromatic" thinking characteristic of tribal people and Gay people,[6] is the ability to simultaneously see "both/and," inner *and* outer, male *and* female, black *and* white, the individual *and* the community, strong *and* tender. "Double vision" suggests the style of perception inherent in a full understanding of the wholistic stance toward which I believe we modern people are moving.

This is by no means an easy stance to take. In this book I have implied that "evil" colonial Romans crushed Gay culture and established anti-Gay customs. And that is part of the story. Romans hated "effeminacy" of all descriptions and were solidly patriarchal in their laws and customs. But the other part of the story is that the Romans had more overt homosexuality in their art, their government, and their military than any nation since their time, at least among the men.[7] Roman women had little part in public life. But homosexual poetry abounded in Roman writing; so many emperors were homosexual that it is noteworthy when one of them was *not*. Taking the passive role, however, was reserved for women, slaves, and boys and, according to historian John Boswell, this was often done so "under duress, economic or physical."[8] This indicates strongly that the purpose of the sex (a form of rape, as is much sex in our own society) was to strengthen adult free male prerogatives of all kinds over the rest of society. This is a far cry from the Gay cultural attributes I have been describing throughout the world. Julius Caesar, famous conqueror of Celtic male lovers and wondrous tribal women warriors, was known as a sissy because, rumor had it, he allowed his lover Nicomedes, king of Bithynia, to fuck him in the ass. One of his nicknames was "queen of Bithynia," and his own soldiers chanted, "Caesar conquered Gaul; Nicomedes, Caesar."[9] Rome used male homosexuality and masculine military bonding to establish a colonial doctrine and political structure of male domination over European societies, such as the Celts, who formerly had large measures of female freedom and leadership in the tribes.

The Inquisition deliberately copied Roman methods of physical torture in order to suppress remnants of female power, Gay power, and other tribal elements, such as the Jews, that throve during the eleventh and twelfth centuries. These artful folk, who would be branded as "heretics," flourished especially in Spain and the south of France, producing (in combination with Moorish culture) the troubadors, the Cathar heresy, the Knights Templar, and the Kaballa, the major book of Jewish mysticism.

In modern times Hitler, following the footsteps of Kaiser (Caesar) Wilhelm and imitating Roman torture methods, would suppress the same tribal and folk elements: The Jews, the Gypsies, the Gays, prostitutes, Eastern Europeans, and leftists advocating feminism and socialism were especially targeted for genocide. (Stalin was not kind to these people either, nor are modern totalitarian

dictators.) At the start of his military campaign in Germany against German citizens, Hitler made use of a few Gay men Brownshirts, a terrorist group; when he had succeeded to absolute dictatorship, he destroyed these troops. Tens of thousands of Gay men formed a separate category of concentration camp victims. They were forced to wear pink triangles, as the Jews wore yellow, and were mistreated and murdered in a similar manner, especially in the work camps.[10]
Heinz Heger makes the point succinctly:

There is a vicious slander, originally put about, unfortunately, by the opponents of Nazism in the 1930's, but still echoing today, that in some sense or other the Nazis actually condoned or even promoted male homosexuality. In fact, from its very origins through to its demise, the Nazi party consistently viewed homosexuality as an integral part of the "degeneracy" they were set on stamping out. Naturally, in the para-military organisation of the SA, Hitler Youth, etc., even the elite SS, the forms of homosexuality that are characteristic of such all-male bodies were as common as they always are; and before the Nazis seized power in 1933, they found it difficult to completely suppress this spread of "degeneracy" even among their own ranks. But it was quite fundamental to Nazi ideology that men were to be properly "masculine" and women properly "feminine," and that homosexuality went diametrically against this "Nordic" tradition. If there is any grain of truth mixed in with the slander, it is that when male homosexuality disguises itself as a cult of "manliness" and virility, it is less obnoxious from the fascist standpoint than is the softening of the gender division that homosexuality invariably involves when it is allowed to express itself freely.[11]

Because Gay people often go first, taking the risks, breaking through the veils and walls that lie in the frontier zone of ideas and ways of being, we fulfill a particular social role, and sometimes it is a dangerous and despised one. Easily enough, Gay people often feel (and are) evicted, punished, cruelly treated when we are displaced from our positions as originators, founders, and tradition breakers. It is easy at those times to feel like a "loser," to believe that the stereotypes of our Gay culture are shameful or aberrant rather than necessary functions that help the institutions of societies to change, to view themselves from another perspective, and to remain flexible. I believe we need to learn to honor ourselves and each other for our Gay traditions and to give real credit to the risk-takers and guides who lead social forces through the maze of human experience.

Even in the extreme negative areas, such as the current epidemic of AIDS affecting the Gay male communities, we need to be articulate and protective about our position in society. The sister of one Gay man who died of AIDS, an honor medical student, told me of his agony and shame, for the family did not know he was Gay until he came down with the disease. They were appalled and baffled, and he died bitterly. AIDS is a viral discase affecting the immune system. Panicking over the outbreak of AIDS and blaming it on the "Gay lifestyle," as both the rabid right and the television media are curently doing, is like calling for the abolishment of highways as a response to auto accidents.

If our modern society understood its Gay people as "who goes first" rather than as "who does bad things," research would be instituted on a wide scale to determine how we are all contributing to the breakdown of our own immune systems, as we are, and how the locus of disease is shifting from bacterial or even systemic disorders to immune system disorders, such as severe allergies, lupus, and now AIDS and other immune system breakdown cancers. Our society might understand that what research is being done on AIDS will contribute to medical knowledge about immune system diseases that will affect the lives of all people in industrialized countries in the future.[12] The response has too often been superstitious and anti-Gay: Thank God this is happening to *them* not *me* and if I can just stay straight, female, away from them, etc., I'll be safe. Some Lesbians, too, participate in this self-hating exercise.

However, AIDS also brings out deep compassion, and while it has made coming out sometimes more dangerous, it has at the same time made it more compelling and more necessary. The growing strength, both cultural and political, of the Gay community has made coming out more rewarding. The fact that AIDS is spread through semen and blood has turned Gay men from the heavily stressed, pure sex-oriented life in the fast lane to explorations of the many other exciting aspects of their culture and their bonding as men. These aspects have included the development of a literature, independent presses, self-help groups, alternative spiritualities, social activism, slightly more conscious inclusion of people of color on the part of whites, challenges to the medical establishment — all activities that dominated the movement of Lesbians in the 1970s and into the 1980s. Interestingly, the new cultural bonding of men is accompanied by a move toward more explicit sexual habits and vocabulary among Lesbians, a move led by Pat Califia and others of the highly controversial Lesbian S/M leather dikes and fem ladies, producing a commonality with Gay men that helps in bonding the two gender-based communities.

We need to understand that the Gay cultural history of the modern state during the last few centuries has been to some extent that of a defeated army, of wounded Amazon warriors and dying Celtic and other warriors, and of colonized tribes of every color and description, who have been absorbed (as much as they have allowed themselves to be) into the industrial state, bringing with them cultural "goods," values and understandings that the industrial state (in which we all participate) uses for its own survival. The fact that Americans have been looking to their Gay people increasingly for leadership is symptomatic of our society's readiness for a "new world," readiness to once again, and in a vastly expanded form, incorporate some of the ancient values that had to be left behind when mass, national culture developed.

Moving Toward Ceremonialism

Gay culture is far from "marginal," being rather "intersectional," the conduits between unlike beings. It is also central, not only to its own strong Gay cultural elements, but also within society as a whole. For instance, in her novel *Say Jesus and Come to Me*, Ann Shockley reveals the centrality of Gay people to Black American culture. Shockley's book carefully uncloaks the leadership roles played by Lesbians and Gay men closeted within the two major social institutions that Black Americans have used to maintain their distinct cultural identity on this continent. These are the Black church and its artistic mother, Black music, which has in the last fifty years become an industry exerting tremendous influence in American society.

It is in the sense of having been instrumental in bringing forth stories of Gay history with Gay religious myth included that I can now say that I am approaching the ceremonial state as a dike and can consider myself on the way to becoming something of a modern ceremonial Lesbian in spite of our fractured modern society. I cannot hope to attain the same levels of entire spiritual being that Sappho had with her prayers to a living Aphrodite, or that the sacred Gay men had with their statues to Hermes, or as Lakota women publicly united in the spirit of Wila Numpa had in their time. As the Gay men who participated in reenacting the myths of Mithra and the bull sacrifice were, as Apollo mourning Hyacinthus was, as Boudica and other Celtic warrior-sorcerer-queens practicing the bulldagger sacrifice and calling on their great she-gods were, and as King Rufus going into the sacred grove to be a holy stag with his beloved butch lover Tyrell was, with Rufus calling the name of his god Lucca as he fell on the arrow to spill his magical blood.

Still we can see from the novels and poetry of modern, openly Gay writers a combining of spiritual and political strands, of personal and public, internal and external. And I feel a groundswell of hope for a renewed ceremonialism, an intact culture, from the increasing visibility of groups of Gay people from every racial and ethnic background, and the pouring of tremendous new (ancient) energy into tired contemporary forms. We cannot live in the past, nor can we re-create it. Yet as we unravel the past, the future also unfolds before us, as though they are mirrors without which neither can be seen or happen.

A New Night in an Old Land

Well, Von, I have one more story to tell, and you know it already, for you were there; I felt your presence, and your peace at last. The occasion was a night in November 1982, in New York City. You had been dead for eight years, and I had taken some drastic and necessary steps to become a whole, an integrated person. I had become reconciled with my family, for instance, after twenty years of estrangement over the issue of my being Gay. I had heard my brother apologize to me for his anti-faggot attitudes of twenty years before; I had heard my sister say my lover's name; and I had decided to accept them for who they are, as well, and to accept family love. Big steps for someone as alienated as I had been.

And now in an auditorium at Columbia University I am about to hear what, personally speaking, amounts to a formal funeral for you, dear Von; a Gay funeral, a memorial to heal our sorrows. Friends from the Bay Area in Northern California, where I make my home, sent me. Friends from New York City sit on either side, Clare Coss on the left and Blanche Wiesen Cook on the right. The event is a concert, "Live Or Die," in commemoration of Gay and Lesbian victims of the Nazi Holocaust and other Gay martyrs. The composer, Calvin Hampton, has taken for his text selections from six Gay poets, three men — Tommi Avicolli,

Harold Norse, and Walt Whitman — and three women — Pat Parker, Irena Klepfisz, and me.

Hampton has structured the beginning and the end of his composition with a chorale incantation of Klepfisz's electrifying chant "These words are for those who died," from Bashert, which means "inevitable, (pre)-destined" in Yiddish. The men's chorus is to the right of us on the stage, as my friends and I take our seats; the women's chorus is to the left. It seems appropriately Gay to me that the women stand together in one place and the men stand together in another, while they take turns saying things that form a whole, and that whole is a poem. A small orchestra of violins, cellos, oboes, flutes is seated in the center of the stage. I know that we are sitting before some of the best musicians in the city. Safely sandwiched between my friends, I am already crying as the artists tune up. Hampton is dapper and handsome as he directs them in the playing of his diverse, dramatic, and at times inexpressibly lyrical music.

Following the opening chorus, in which the men and the women alternate saying each line, a formal poetic reader presents Avicolli's poem, the subject of which is the brutal rape of faggots by bully boys in jails and other places. The tenor steps forward to sing a lyric piece from Walt Whitman's Leaves of Grass, about lovers who roll and tumble in the ocean waves. And I am holding Blanche's hand, trying to aim my cassette tape recorder at the stage at the same time. Blanche, who is Jewish, has already told me that it is a very special occasion for her, too, that it is the anniversary of her father's death. Then another reader gives us a fine reading of Harold Norse's biting description of Gay poet Federico Garcia Lorca's murder, as told through the mouth of his fascist killer.

Women around me whisper restlessly. "Why are the men always so concerned with blood and violence," they wonder. But I think I know. If Gertrude Stein had been taken to a lonely road and shot, that would be a subject of our women's poems. You bet it would. It is a matter of history, and of experience; it is a matter of tradition.

And then it is the moment I came three thousand miles for. The contralto Sarah Young has stepped forward and stands beside the musicians. The room is riveted on her dramatic presence; she is tall and full bodied, a large, attractive concert singer dressed in shining black leather tunic and skirt, her lips blazing with vivid red lipstick to set off her white face and stark black *hair. Now she is singing my piece, a section of the "Funeral Plainsong" I wrote one brownly empty day to formalize your death, Von, to bring it home to myself so I could understand. Could stop shattering. Could claim you, Von, for us, your lovers. Hampton has selected pieces of the poem that are applicable to either sex and has matched it with the natural imagery of the Whitman piece. Nervous about handling women's material, he has done the music for it perfectly — lyrical, respectful, soaring. Sarah Young's articulation is perfect, superb, sensitive, acute. From the stage she delivers the last passage looking across the audience to my face; looking me right in the eyes as they are dissolved in tears, she sings the funeral oration "plainsong from a younger woman to an older woman," that I wrote for you my lover: "we are together in your stillness / you have wished us a bonded life"; and inside I am screaming, I am dying, I am able to feel at last the impact of your death, Von, and below that in a frozen pit the terror and the anger and the guilt we felt over the punishment and isolation meted out to us in our American lives, in the infernal shadow of the Nazi camps and the sense of having done something terrible to warrant those little pink triangles of horror, and behind that shadow another one, of the Inquisition, of the stoning in so many neighborhoods, of the bully boys and vicious women, of our families' rejection . . . I am able to absorb it and to feel it and to begin to heal it up again. I am sobbing and collapsing as Blanche holds me and our snuffles and breathing take up all the sound in the tape recorder. "Oh Baby," she says over and over, crying herself and wiping at my teary cheeks and whispering, "She did you proud." And she did. They all did.*

I watch through a blur of water and feeling as poet Cheryl Clarke, tall, Black, and handsome in her beautiful dike clothing, steps forward to read her rendition of my old friend Pat Parker's poem "Where will you be when they come?" Then the chorus is finishing with Irena's chant "These words are for those who survived," and the cycle is completed. You were there, Von, for I felt you; and so were many, many others, millions; and something grand was happening, something ceremonial . . . with something like the Gay sound of a piccolo following you down your spirit trail, like a little golden butterfly, singing rainbow songs . . . (i will be your mouth now, to do your singing).[13] You are always near me. I will always, always love you.

Notes

Bibliography

Index

Notes

1. Sashay Down the Lavender Trail

1. Lord Alfred Douglas (1870–1945), "Two Loves," in *The Penguin Book of Homosexual Verse*, ed. Stephen Coote (New York: Penguin Books, 1983), pp. 262–264.

2. The turquoise stone she bought me was light green. The stones Yvonne chose for herself were always dark blue. A Navajo or Zuni ringmaker had told her that blue was the masculine color of turquoise and green the color worn by women. By her choice of ring colors, Vonnie was designating us "butch and femme," something she always did with great attention to detail.

3. These of course were not the first formal Lesbian or Gay organizations in modern America. Daughters of Bilitis (DOB) was started in 1955 by Del Martin and Phyllis Lyon. Mattachine Society, which was composed mostly of men, had formed after Henry Hay (who spent several years on an Indian reservation in the Southwest) worked out its cultural ideals in 1948, then later it changed into a white-collar organization working for legal rights of (primarily male) homosexuals. DOB consisted of women only, fought for legal rights, established cultural identity, and founded a magazine, *The Ladder*, which sometimes featured legal struggles and sometimes literary, depending on the editor at the time. It was the only Lesbian vehicle during the fifties and sixties, a real "underground" magazine in a world of censorship.

4. *A Midsummer Night's Dream*, act 2, sc. 1, lines 165–172. Shakespeare calls the flower "Love-in-Idleness," which was one of several folk names for the pansy, according to Mrs. M. Grieve, *A Modern Herbal*, 2 vol. (New York: Dover, 1971), p. 386.

5. Thomas Bulfinch, *Bulfinch's Mythology: The Age of Fable, The Age of Chivalry, Legends of Charlemagne* (1898; reprint New York: Crowell 1970), p. 86. Bulfinch suggests that the purple flower that sprang from the blood of Hyacinthus might have been a pansy, iris, or larkspur.

6. Grieve, *A Modern Herbal*, 1, p. 30.

7. Bulfinch, *Age of Fable*, p. 25.

8. Grieve, 2, p. 573.

9. Apostolos N. Athanassakis, "To Demeter," in *The Homeric Hymns* (Baltimore: Johns Hopkins University Press, 1976), p. 1.

10. Bulfinch, *Age of Fable*, p. 85.

11. Bulfinch, *Age of Fable*, p. 85. The story of Hyacinthus and his lover Apollo includes another Gay male god, Zephyrus, the West Wind (domain of the spirit), who was also in love with Hyacinthus. Zephyrus has been blamed for deliberately blowing the discus off course out of avenging jealousy, having been rejected by Hyacinthus, who favored Apollo.

12. Grieve, *A Modern Herbal*, 1, p. 424. About "Ah! Ah!" Mrs. Grieve notes, "As our English variety of Hyacinth has no trace of these mystic letters, our older botanists called it *hyacinthus nonscriptus,* or 'not written on.' A later generic name, *agraphis,* is of similar meaning, being a compound of two Greek words, meaning 'not to mark.'"

13. Sappho, *Greek Lyric,* trans. D. A. Campbell (Cambridge: Harvard University Press, 1982), p. 99. "They say that Sappho was the first to use the word . . . 'mantle,' when she said of Eros: . . . who had come from heaven clad in a purple mantle." The count of references to purple and so on is taken from this very literal translation of Sappho's work.

14. *Sappho: A New Translation,* trans. Mary Barnard (Berkeley: University of California Press, 1958), p. 34.

15. Thanks to Joanna Griffin for locating the poem by Anacreon and for calling it to my attention. The poem in the text is from a tape of her reading. According to Greek scholar John J. Winkler (unpublished manuscript), the "purple ball" is also sometimes translated as a red ball, like an apple.

16. From an interview with Luisah Teish, a priestess in the Macumba religion.

17. Arthur Evans, *Witchcraft and the Gay Counterculture* (Boston: Fag Rag Books, 1978), p. 104. Evans quoted from George Dorsey, *Traditions of the Caddo.*

18. Paul Mariah, "The Spoon Ring," in *This Light Will Spread: Selected Poems, 1960–1978* (South San Francisco: Manroot, 1978).

19. It is of considerable interest that among Lesbians the first finger is also a favorite place for a ring. One Black longtime dike told me that she and her friends had worn their rings on the index finger until the Gay movement touched them in the early seventies. At that time they shifted the ring to the little finger. My experience is the opposite: Having worn a ring on my little finger in the Gay underground for years, I suddenly added an index-finger ring when I became a public Gay speaker, activist, and Lesbian poet. Lesbian writer Lee Lynch describes changing ring fingers similarly in her novel *Toothpick House* (Tallahassee, Fla.: Naiad Press, 1983). The index finger indicates an aggressive stance "out in the world." It is the public finger. When the two fingers are held out with the others tucked under, the result is an old magic sign of the horned god as a sexual, trickster figure; this is still considered a filthy hand gesture in some Euro-American subcultures. It refers to the "cuckold," that is, it indicates that a woman has been sexually free without her husband's permission.

20. *Random House Dictionary of the English Language,* unabridged (New York: Random House, 1966), s.v. "Hermes" and "Hermes Trismegistus."

21. Three Initiates, *The Kybalion: A Study of the Hermetic Philosophy of Ancient Egypt and Greece* (Chicago: Yogi Publication Society, Masonic Temple, 1912), pp. 17–18. See also the writings of Madame Blavatsky and Aleister Crowley.

22. Sayed Idries Shah, *The Secret Lore of Magic* (New York: Citadel, 1970) p. 283. Shah lists the god for each day of the week along with the god's characteristics, symbols, and colors. *The Practice of Palmistry* (Van Nuys, Calif.: Newcastle, 1973), p. 31, rendered the names and characters of the fingers.

23. Jeffrey Burton Russell, *Witchcraft in the Middle Ages* (Ithaca, N.Y.: Cornell University Press, 1972). See especially "Witchcraft and Rebellion in Medieval Society, 1300–1360," pp. 166ff.

24. Shepherd Edwin Peter, *Metaphysical Candle Burning and Color* (Albuquerque: Universal Church of the Holy Spirit, 1975), p. 6.

25. Dorothee L. Mella, *Stone Power: Legendary and Practical Uses of Gems and Stones* (Albuquerque: Domel).

26. John Allegro, *The Sacred Mushroom and the Cross* (Garden City, N.Y.: Doubleday, 1970), pp. 126ff.

27. Arlene J. Fitzgerald, *Everything You Always Wanted to Know About Sorcery* (New York: Manor Books, 1973), p. 176. Thanks also to Coletta Reid for her discussion of the properties of the amethyst.

2. The Original Underground

1. "Shamans and Spirits, Myths and Medical Symbolism in Eskimo Art," Eskimo shaman song, from the catalog of an exhibition jointly sponsored by Canadian Arctic Producers and the National Museum of Man (National Museums of Canada).

2. Originally the word *closet* referred to a private, enclosed place inside a house that was used for prayer, meditation, and special decisions. Another usage of the word referred to the special apartments or rooms reserved for the exclusive use of women, known as the *queen's closet.*

3. *The Oakland Tribune,* probably 1981. I regret not having the exact date. The group, the Santa Clara Moral Majority, advocated the execution of Gay people; they pledged to spend $3 million to turn non-Gay members of San Francisco's population against Gay citizens.

4. Adrienne Rich, "Compulsory Heterosexuality and Lesbian Existence," *Signs* (Summer 1980): 631ff.

5. Gertrude Stein, *Geography and Plays* (1922; rpt. New York: Something Else Press, 1968), p. 17. Thank you, Paul Mariah, for "loaning" your copy to me for more than a decade.

6. Hannah Arendt has written of this, for instance. I have heard testimony by a Gay male survivor of the camps about the openly Gay culture thriving in liberal pre-Nazi German cities.

7. The underground bar culture of Gay people uses nicknames and made-up first names for protection. Interestingly, so does the Lesbian-feminist movement, although women's rationale for their new names seems not to have anything to do with a consciously acknowledged need for protection and camouflage.

8. The *Winktes* of the Lakota tribe also called each other "sister," according to Lame Deer's account. John Lame Deer and Richard Erdoes, *Lame Deer, Seeker of Visions: The Life of a Sioux Medicine Man* (New York: Simon and Schuster, 1972). As mentioned earlier, the *Winkte* were buried together in a specially designated place, unlike their contemporary counterparts in white culture.

9. Bruce Rodgers, *Gay Talk: A (Sometimes Outrageous) Dictionary of Gay Slang* (New York: Putnam, 1972).

10. Apostolos N. Athanassakis, trans., "To Demeter," in *The Homeric Hymns* (Baltimore: Johns Hopkins University Press, 1976), p. 1.

11. R. Gordon Wasson, Albert Hoffman, and Carl Ruck, *The Road to Eleusis: Unveiling the Secret of the Mysteries* (Italy: Helen and Kurt Wolff, 1978). The authors discuss *ergot.* Lawrence Durdin-Robertson, *The Goddesses*

of India, Tibet, China and Japan (Eire: Cesara Publications, 1976), mentions the *aura clitoridis* under "Arani," pp. 192–193.

12. Lawrence Durdin-Robertson, *The Goddesses of Chaldea, Syria and Egypt* (Eire: Cesara Publications, 1975), p. 318. He connects Baubo to frogs and to Hecate, or Heqit. In *The Goddesses of India, Tibet, China and Japan* (Eire: Cesara Publications, 1976), p. 393, he lists Baubo as "sappic mistress" and compares his erotic dance before Demeter to a similar dance by the Japanese shamanic goddess, Uzume, who danced erotically before the cave of the Sun goddess to entice her out.

13. The word in the story that describes Hekate's relationship to Persephone as her companion means, literally, "she who goes before and she who follows after," according to Bella Zweig, a classicist.

14. *Rubyfruit Jungle*, a popular Lesbian novel by Rita Mae Brown, is named for the pomegranate. For more about women's menstrual powers, see my article on menstruation in *The Politics of Women's Spirituality*, ed. Charlene Spretnak (New York: Doubleday, 1981), and my book *Blood and Bread and Roses* (Boston: Beacon Press, forthcoming).

15. Quoted in Edward Carpenter, *Intermediate Types Among Primitive Folk* (London: George Allen & Company, 1914), pp. 18–20.

16. The *New York Times*, May 2, 1982.

17. George Thomson, *Studies in Ancient Greek Society* (New York: Citadel Press, 1965). Thomson discusses Dike as "the way," pp. 134–135. See also Jane Ellen Harrison, *Epilegomena to the Study of Greek Religion, and Themis* (New York: University Books, 1962), pp. 518ff. "The Ways of Day and Night are closed by mighty doors, and of these Dike Avenging keeps the keys that fit them," p. 518. Harrison speaks of Dike as an address for the moon, as residing in Hades, as associated with the Kore, the Maid, and with the Wheel of Life, that is, natural fate.

3. Gay Is Very American

1. Paula Gunn Allen (Laguna/Sioux), from "Some Like Indians Endure," in *"Skins and Bones,"* unpublished manuscript.

2. Edwin T. Denig, "Biography of Woman Chief," in *Gay American History*, ed. Jonathon Katz (New York: Crowell, 1976), p. 308. The story is of a Crow woman of great powers who became a hunting chief and married four wives. She did not cross-dress.

3. Sue-Ellen Jacobs, "Berdache: A Brief Review of the Literature," *Colorado Anthropologist* 1 (1968): 25–40. Jacobs lists all eighty-eight tribes. Thanks to Mary Redick for bringing the article to my attention. See also Carolyn Neithammer, "Lesbianism," in *Daughters of the Earth* (New York: Collier, 1977). Evelyn Blackwood, "Sexuality and Gender in Certain Native American Tribes: The Case of Cross-Gender Females," unpublished paper, has described cross-gender lives and the full acceptance of Lesbian marriage among five American Indian small-game hunting tribes along the Colorado River: the Mojave, Klamath, Maricopa, Yuma, and Cocopa. Among people who lived in small kinship bands and had egalitarian social structures, girls who rejected women's work as children would be accepted as men (among the Mojave this

included an initiation ceremony), and they married women who were not cross-gendered. They had Lesbian sexual relations; the woman might take a man for her next husband, or the two females might live together a long time, raising the woman's children. In Western Gay terminology, they are butch and femme. According to Blackwood, these free Lesbian practices have become suppressed since the mid-1800s as tribes have needed approval from the white world and as men's economic status in the world has been accorded more importance, leading them to see cross-gendered Lesbians as competition for the labor of women.

4. Jacobs, "Berdache," p. 35.

5. Jacobs, "Berdache"; I also drew names from "Native Americans/Gay Americans: 1528–1976," in Katz, *Gay American History*, pp. 281–332.

6. Katz, *Gay American History*, p. 289. See also Arthur Evans, *Witchcraft and the Gay Counterculture* (Boston: Fag Rag Books, 1978), for other accounts of the suppression of Gay Indians.

7. *Random House Dictionary of the English Language*, unabridged (New York: Random House, 1966). *Berdache:* from French *bardache*, Spanish *bardajo*, Arabic *bardaj*, "slave." The sense is of "kept boy prostitute." Many people, especially earlier white writers, have used the term *berdache* (usually pronounced *ber-dachie*) when discussing Gay Indian customs. As far as I know, the Gay customs of traditional American Indian people had nothing to do with keeping boy prostitutes, and I have preferred to avoid the European term *berdache* when possible, using instead more original tribal words and names even when I cannot determine the exact meanings. When I do not have the original Indian name, I have used *Gay* or *dyke* or *fairy* because these European words have ceremonial, tribal, and shamanic derivations and origins. They stem from underlying European Gay tribal cultural functions, rather than implying their suppression, as I believe "Arab slave boy" does.

Currently, an intertribal network of modern Indian Lesbians are calling themselves "berdache" or "berdache women." I assume this is to distinguish themselves from white Lesbianism and to make certain they are known and identified as Indian women with a separate American history of their own, while using a term that does not spring from one tribe in particular, as each tribe is quite different from another.

8. Katz, *Gay American History*, p. 293.

9. Katz, *Gay American History*, p. 314.

10. Katz, *Gay American History*, pp. 315–317.

11. Paula Gunn Allen, "Beloved Women: Lesbians in American Indian Cultures," *Conditions* 7 (1981): p. 70.

12. Jacobs, "Berdache," p. 29.

13. Jacobs, "Berdache," p. 28.

14. Edward Carpenter, *Intermediate Types Among Primitive Folk: A Study in Social Evolution* (London: George Allen & Company, 1914), p. 18.

15. Carpenter, *Intermediate Types*, p. 19, quoting Elie Reclus.

16. Carpenter, *Intermediate Types*, p. 18.

17. Mike Wilken, "Transformations: Shamanism and Homosexuality," unpublished paper.

18. Katz, *Gay American History*, p. 305.

19. Evans, *Witchcraft*, p. 102.

20. Allen, "Beloved Women," p. 67.

21. Allen, "Beloved Women," p. 67.
22. The poem, by Paula Gunn Allen, was first published in *Conditions* 7 (1981); reprinted in *Lesbian Poetry*, ed. Elly Bulkin and Joan Larkin (Boston: Persephone Press, 1981).
23. Allen, "Beloved Women," p. 81.
24. Allen "Beloved Women," p. 81.
25. Katz, *Gay American History*, pp. 293–298.
26. Katz, *Gay American History*, p. 298, quoting Francis Simon.
27. Allen, "Beloved Women," p. 82.
28. Neithammer, "Lesbianism," pp. 230–231.
29. Alvaro Estrada, *Maria Sabina: Her Life and Chants*, trans. Henry Munn (Santa Barbara: Ross-Erikson, 1981), p. 65.
30. Estrada, *Maria Sabina*, p. 44.
31. Estrada, *Maria Sabina*, p. 67.
32. John Lame Deer and Richard Erdoes, *Lame Deer, Seeker of Visions: The Life of a Sioux Medicine Man* (New York: Simon and Schuster, 1972), p. 149.
33. Lame Deer and Erdoes, *Lame Deer*, pp. 149–150.
34. From "WINKTE," by Maurice Kenny, in *Only As Far As Brooklyn* (Boston: Good Gay Poets, 1979).
35. Katz, *Gay American History*, pp. 301–302.
36. Hamilton A. Tyler, *Pueblo Gods and Myths* (Norman, Okla.: University of Oklahoma Press, 1964), pp. 194ff.
37. Jeffrey Burton Russell, *Witchcraft in the Middle Ages* (Ithaca, N.Y.: Cornell University Press, 1972), pp. 50–53. Tyler in *Pueblo Gods and Myths* compares the Koshari with European Fool's Kings.
38. Katz, *Gay American History*, p. 324.
39. John M. Gunn, *Schat-Chen* (Albuquerque: Albright and Anderson, 1917), p. 173.
40. Jacobs, "Berdache," p. 28.
41. From a conversation with Paula Gunn Allen.
42. Cited in Jacobs, "Berdache," p. 209.
43. Evans, *Witchcraft*, chapters 7, 8, 9.
44. Jacobs, "Berdache," p. 30, quoting Dorsey.
45. Jacobs, "Berdache," p. 30.
46. Katz, *Gay American History*, p. 311.
47. Katz, *Gay American History*, p. 311.
48. Wilken, "Transformations," suggests these parallels.
49. Katz, *Gay American History*, p. 313.
50. Following a discussion with Lee Francis, a San Francisco educator who specializes in studies of empathy and multicultural concerns.

4. Fairies and Fairy Queens

1. Carl Morse, from "The Curse of the Future Fairy," *Fag Rag* 40, Boston, 1983.
2. Margaret Murray, *The God of the Witches* (London: Oxford University Press, 1952), chap. 2.
3. Murray, *God of the Witches*, p. 56.

4. K. M. Briggs, *The Fairies in Tradition and Literature* (London: Routledge and Kegan Paul, 1967), p. 18.

5. Murray, *God of the Witches*, p. 59.

6. Murray, *God of the Witches*, pp. 108–110.

7. The connections to Fairy people were concrete and directly physical, as they intermarried. The Fairy Tree round which Joan danced was owned by a man, Sieur de Bourlemont, who was married to a Fairy woman. Murray, *God of the Witches*, p. 50.

8. Margaret Murray, *The Witch-Cult in Western Europe* (London: Oxford University Press, 1921), app. B, "Names of Witches," pp. 255–270. Of a list of 732 witches from covens in the British Isles, 118 are men's names and 614 are women's.

9. Jeffrey Burton Russell, *Witchcraft in the Middle Ages* (Ithaca, N.Y.: Cornell University Press, 1972), p. 58: "The festivals most important for the development of the witch idea were the fertility rites associated with Diana or Hecate, the festivals on Thursday, which later became a favorite day for witch meetings, and the hunting celebrations on the first of January... The synods and Caesarius also bear witness to the custom of transvestitism at the same New Year's festival, where men dressed as women, a masquerade probably originating in a fertility rite of some kind." ("Fertility rite" is one of those generalized terms used to vaguely describe what is imprecisely understood. Imagine it if applied to a modern Halloween drag ball.)

10. Russell, *Witchcraft*, p. 218.

11. Russell, *Witchcraft*, p. 48.

12. Barbara Falconer Newhall, "Halloween: Ancient New Year's Celebration," *Oakland Tribune*, October 31, 1980.

13. E. M. Broner, *A Weave of Women* (New York: Bantam, 1982), p. 115.

14. Broner, *Weave of Women*, p. 117.

15. Aaron Shurin, from "Woman on Fire," in *The Night Sun* (San Francisco: Gay Sunshine Press, 1976).

16. Tede Matthews appeared in *Word Is Out*, a film on contemporary Gay life by Peter Adair et al.

17. He means that the actress Tuesday Weld displays no dikish, or what he calls "gutsy," qualities.

18. Eloise Klein Healy, "I Spent the Day with You," in *A Packet Beating Like a Heart* (Los Angeles: Birds of a Feather, 1981). I have not used the second stanza here.

19. Murray, *God of the Witches*, p. 100.

20. Murray, *God of the Witches*, p. 100.

21. Murray, *God of the Witches*, p. 100. One woman, Jeanne D'Abadie, said that "when the Devil marked her on her right shoulder he hurt her so much that she cried out, and felt at the same time a great heat as if a fire had burned her."

22. Sharon Isabell, "The Tattoo Parlor," unpublished manuscript, 1979.

23. Eric Partridge, *The Macmillan Dictionary of Historical Slang* (New York: Macmillan, 1973).

24. Russell, *Witchcraft*, p. 67.

25. Arthur Evans, *Witchcraft and the Gay Counterculture* (Boston: Fag Rag Books, 1978), p. 69. Harlequin: Harla the quin (king). Harla is another form of *Herne*, "horn."

26. Russell, *Witchcraft,* p. 49.
27. This is not true of Lesbians involved in sadomasochism, who advocate use of the dildo.
28. Murray, *Witch-Cult,* p. 178.
29. Murray, *Witch-Cult,* p. 180.
30. Murray, *God of the Witches,* p. 181.
31. All from Murray, *Witch-Cult,* "The God."
32. Murray, *Witch-Cult,* p. 31: "The evidence of the witches makes it abundantly clear that the so-called Devil was a human being, generally a man, occasionally a woman." In Scotland the Devil was often reported as a woman and named the Queen of Elphin, or Elphame (p. 44).

5. We Go Around the World

1. Audre Lorde, from "Timepiece," in *The Black Unicorn* (New York: Norton, 1978).
2. I first heard *mariposa* from Pat Parker, who heard it in Spain. I would like to know if butterflies represented the spirits of the dead in ancient tribal Spain, as they do among many American Indian tribes. The other terms in this paragraph are contributed by Dr. Carol Robertson, an ethnomusicologist who grew up in Argentina.
3. My thanks for these observations to two Dutch Lesbians who talked to me at San Francisco State University.
4. Thanks to Aleida Rodriguez.
5. Robert I. Levy, *Tahitians: Mind and Experience in the Society Islands* (Chicago: University of Chicago Press, 1973), pp. 140–141.
6. Thanks to Nellie Wong.
7. Thanks to Tonia. Barbados was colonized by the English so I assume an English origin for both expressions.
8. Thanks to Rena, from Italy.
9. Thanks to Ursula Heinegger for much of this German terminology; see Therese Iknoian, "Out of the Closet in Germany," *San Francisco Sunday Examiner and Chronicle,* April 17, 1983. Iknoian mentions that an accepted estimate of the number of Gay people currently active in Germany is 2.4 million, of a total population of 64 million.
10. Linda Marie, "Antonia," unpublished manuscript, 1980.
11. See the magazine *Connections: An International Women's Quarterly,* especially Winter 1982 and Summer 1982.
12. Carol Lee Sanchez, from a private conversation. She is an artist who does fabric paintings, a poet, and a teacher. She grew up on a Spanish land grant west of Albuquerque, New Mexico.
13. Two spinsters of the Northeast who managed also to become poets were Amy Lowell and Emily Dickinson. Lowell was an even-featured, classical blond beauty from a wealthy mill-owning family, in an obviously highly marriageable state of being. At puberty she developed a mysterious glandular disease that caused obesity. Her "ugliness" and lack of "desirability" allowed her to maintain an independent life of spinsterhood and to become a full-fledged writer and prime mover in a new poetry movement. She wore men's clothing, smoked cigars, came and went as she pleased (she worked nights and

slept all day, for instance), and had a woman as her lover. Without her "disease" she would have been pressured all her life to marry, and her life story raises interesting possibilities about the nature of the "ugliness" required of the "Old Maid" during periods when marriage is her expected occupation. From indications in her letters and many of her poems, Dickinson was also a Lesbian.

14. See Agnes Smedley, *Portraits of Chinese Women in Revolution* (Old Westbury, N.Y.: Feminist Press, 1976), pp. 103–110. What follows is a heavy paraphrase of her account. I am grateful to the Feminist Press for making this material available by publishing it.

15. Smedley, *Portraits of Chinese Women*, pp. 103–110.

16. Arthur Evans, *Witchcraft and the Gay Counterculture* (Boston: Fag Rag Press, 1978), p. 106.

17. Edward Carpenter, *Intermediate Types Among Primitive Folk* (London: George Allen & Company, 1914), p. 33.

18. Carpenter, *Intermediate Types*, pp. 38–39.

19. L. C. Faron, *Hawks of the Sun*.

20. Herodotus, *The Histories*, trans. Aubrey de Selincourt (Baltimore: Penguin Books, 1954), p. 263.

21. Quoted in Carpenter, *Intermediate Types*, pp. 36, 37.

22. Carpenter, *Intermediate Types*, p. 37. The Russian traveler's name was Dawydow.

23. Carpenter, *Intermediate Types*, pp. 16, 17.

24. Serge Bramly, *Macumba: The Teachings of Maria-Jose, Mother of the Gods* (New York: Avon, 1975), p. 114.

25. The reason for the association with the two European saints is that the practice of Macumba is covered with a veneer of Catholicism to escape detection by the antipagan authorities. The warrior saints of Europe are code words for a female god with similar attributes. They, in their turn, are coded also, for they represent more vestiges of European paganism than they are generally given credit for.

26. Bramley, *Macumba*, p. 115.

27. Levy, *Tahitians*, pp. 130–141.

28. Levy, *Tahitians*, pp. 130–141.

29. Levy, *Tahitians*, pp. 134–135.

30. Levy, *Tahitians*, pp. 130–141.

31. Levy, *Tahitians*, pp. 130–141.

32. Levy, *Tahitians*, p. 472.

33. Levy, *Tahitians*, quoting from London Missionary Archives, p. 472.

34. Bruce Rodgers, *Gay Talk* (New York: Putnam, 1972), p. 130.

35. Levy, *Tahitians*, p. 140.

36. Quoted in Carpenter, *Intermediate Types*, pp. 21–22.

37. B. Z. Goldberg, *The Sacred Fire* (Secaucus, N.J.: Citadel, 1958, 1974), p. 79.

38. Carpenter, *Intermediate Types*, p. 29.

39. Goldberg, *Sacred Fire*, p. 79.

40. Evans, *Witchcraft*, p. 106.

41. Goldberg, *Sacred Fire*, p. 79.

42. Goldberg, *Sacred Fire*, p. 79.

43. Goldberg, *Sacred Fire*, p. 79.

44. Lawrence Durdin-Robertson, *The Goddesses of India, Japan, China*

and Tibet (Eire: Cesara Publications, 1975). See entries under individual names of deities.

6. Butches, Bulldags, and the Queen of Bulldikery

1. Judy Grahn, "I Am the Wall," from "She Who," in *The Work of a Common Woman* (New York: St. Martin's, 1978), p. 98.

2. Allan Berube, *Lesbian Masquerade*, presentation notes from a public slide program. "B-D Women Blues," sung by Bessie Jackson, 1935, reissued on *AC/DC Blues: Gay Jazz Re-Issues, Vol. I*, collected by Chris Albertson, Stash Records, ST-106, 1977.

3. *The Compact Edition of the Oxford English Dictionary*, 2 vols. (Oxford: Oxford University Press, 1971).

4. Sharon Isabell, *Yesterday's Lessons: An Autobiography* (Oakland: Women's Press Collective, 1974).

5. Donald R. Dudley and Graham Webster, *The Rebellion of Boudicca* (London: Routledge and Kegan Paul, 1962), p. 143. The philologist K. H. Jackson says it was spelled *Boudica*. The Romans recorded the queen's name as Boudicca and Boudouica.

6. Jean Markale, *Women of the Celts* (London: Gordon Cremonesi, 1975), pp. 36–37.

7. Arthur Evans, *Witchcraft and the Gay Counterculture* (Boston: Fag Rag Books, 1978), p. 18, quoting Markale.

8. Anne Ross, *Pagan Celtic Britain* (New York: Columbia University Press, 1967), p. 228.

9. Evans, *Witchcraft*, pp. 18–19, quoting Markale.

10. Lawrence Durdin-Robertson, *The Goddesses of India, Tibet, China and Japan* (Eire: Cesara Publications, 1976), under "Aura clitoridis."

11. Evans, *Witchcraft*, p. 21.

12. Eric Partridge, *The Macmillan Dictionary of Historical Slang*, abridged (New York: Macmillan, 1973), pp. 457–458. Also *hornification* (a priapism), *old horny* (the male member), *horns-to-sell* (a loose wife, also a cuckold), *horny, horney, hornie* (Scottish colloquial for the devil—*auld Hornie*), *horny* (disposed for a carnal woman), *at the sign of the horn* (in cuckoldom).

13. Evans, *Witchcraft*, p. 19, quoting Diodorus Siculus.

14. C. D. Yonge, trans., *The Roman History of Ammianus Marcellinus*, XV, xii (London: Henry G. Bohn, 1862), p. 80.

15. *The Random House Dictionary of the English Language* (New York: Random House, 1966). The entry for *butch* as the partner in a Lesbian relationship who "takes the part of the man" suggests, with a question mark, "short-haired one" as the possible derivation. I believe there is far more reason to look to the Horned goat-god and the Gay tribal sacraments surrounding him.

16. Margaret Murray, *The God of the Witches* (London: Oxford University Press, 1952), p. 109, and *The Witch-Cult in Western Europe* (London: Oxford University Press, 1921), p. 133. An English witch, Isobel Gowdie, testified that the Maid of her Coven, Jean Marein, was nicknamed "Over the dyke with it" because the Coven god-figure always takes the maiden's hand when the dance was Gillatrypes, and they leap while both chanting "Over the dyke with it."

17. Among some Mexican villagers and Southwest Indians, the bull-killing rite is accompanied by Mattachino dancers who form lines to make a corridor

that leads to the bull. They are dressed in special conical hats, ribbons, glass decorations, and flowered scarves. They each hold a tree of life in one hand and rattles in the other. The American Gay rights group Mattachine Society (whose founder, Harry Hay, spent years living among southwestern Indians) is named for French Mattachines, who were jesters or wisemen in the medieval court.

18. Minna M. Schmidt, *400 Outstanding Women of the World and Their Costumology* (Chicago: Minna Moscherosch Schmidt, 1933), p. 129. Dudley and Webster, *Rebellion of Boudicca*, also list "Bunduica." Interestingly, American frontiersman reporting on "Berdache women," that is, cross-dressing Indian "bulldikes," wrote the French word *berdache* variously as *bowdash* and even *bundash*, as though combining the French term with one they recognized from an Irish, Welsh, or English tradition: Bundaca/Boudica. Jonathon Katz, *Gay American History* (New York: Crowell, 1976).

19. Perhaps it is because Boudica's name is so close to the slang word *bulldike*, which derived from her story, that it apparently unnerves people who want to deny a "strong" female name or any suggested connection to Gay terms. In recent centuries, writers have tried to soften and romanticize the original name. Of the Roman historians who reported the queen's rebellion, Cassius Dio (writing in Greek) spelled the Celtic queen's name *Boudouika*, and Cornelius Tacitus (writing close to her time and in Latin) spelled it *Boudicca*, both of which clearly indicate a hard "c" sound. For ten centuries following the decline of the Roman Empire, these records were lost from discussion. When Roman writings were resurrected about four centuries ago, prominent English writers discarded Boudica's classical name and other remembered versions, such as Bunduca, in favor of Boadicea, Boadaceia, and the like, I suspect because they thought these sounded less threatening and more ladylike. And even though a few scholars have insisted that Boudica and Boudicca must be closer to her original name, many modern writers have been strangely reluctant to use it. T. C. Lethbridge, for instance, in *Witches* (New York: Citadel, 1968), said he used Boadicea because he "dislike[s] the correct name, Boudicca," p. 78. Another author, with credentials from the British Museum, explained his persistent misuse of the name and his personal preference for Boadicea: "The name is, I admit, indefensible, except on the grounds of euphony and popularity. But though I am prepared to champion most forlorn causes, I confess it seems hopeless now to substitute the appalling, yet more correct, Boudicca or Buddug," T. D. Kendrick, *The Druids: A Study in Keltic Prehistory* (London: Methuen and Company, 1927), p. 5. Even well-known writers have problems with the name and what it represents. Writing of the queen more than 1600 years following her infamous battles, John Milton flew into an unseemly rage over Boudica's story in his *History of Britain*, published in 1670. Interrupting a paraphrase of Boudica's rousing battle speech as it was interpreted by Cassius Dio, Milton raged, "a deal of other fondness they put into her mouth not worth recital: how she was lashed, how her daughters were handled, things worthier of silence, retirement, and a vail, than for a woman to repeat, as done to her own person, or to hear repeated before a host of men ... And this they [the Classical historians] do out of vanity, hoping to embellish their history with the strangeness of our manners, not caring in the meanwhile to brand us with the rankest note of barbarism, as if in Britain *women were men, and men women*" (emphasis mine). The quote is from

Dudley and Webster, *Rebellion of Boudicca*, p. 123. A present-day Celtic philologist, Prof. K. H. Jackson, has a different perspective. Interpreting the name through Welsh sources, he says: "The name is derivative of *bouda*, 'victory,' and is of course the Mod. Welsh *buddug*, 'Victoria.' But *buddug* is a secondary development, with vowel-harmony from (older) *buddug*, and this is from British 'Boudica,' which is the correct form of the lady's name," Dudley and Webster, *Rebellion of Boudicca*, p. 143.

20. Cassius Dio, *Dio's Roman History*, VIII, bk. LXI–LXX, trans. E. Cary (Cambridge: Harvard University Press, 1925), p. 85.

21. Dudley and Webster, *Rebellion of Boudicca*, p. 61.

22. Dio, *Roman History*, pp. 85ff. Boudica must have been especially angry with women collaborators, for "their breasts were cut off and stuffed in their mouths, so that they seemed to be eating them, then their bodies were skewered lengthwise on sharp stakes," in a sacrifice to the ferocious goddess Andrasta.

23. Dudley and Webster, *Rebellion of Boudicca*, pp. 138ff.

24. *The Encyclopaedia Brittanica*, 13th ed., s.v. "Boadicea."

25. Dudley and Webster, *Rebellion of Boudicca*, pp. 76–77.

26. Boudica's story has passed in a folk version through the Irish folk tradition, with her name pronounced BOO-duhca. I believe it was the British who put the long "i" sound into her name, as they have for so many other words: pronouncing "mike" and "tike" for *make* and *take*, the drink daiquiri as "dikery." Some American dialects reflect a similar phenomenon, changing "decked out" to "diked out."

27. Judy Grahn, "Queen Boudica," based on the research I did for this chapter. The poem was first published in *Extended Outlooks*, ed. Jane Cooper, Gwen Head, Adalaide Morris, and Marcia Southwick (New York: Macmillan, 1982). "Queen Boudica" is part of my book *The Queen of Swords* (Boston: Beacon Press, 1987).

28. Jean Gould, *Amy: The World of Amy Lowell and the Imagist Movement* (New York: Dodd, Mead, 1975). Stein and Toklas have been seriously disclaimed for the public "man-wife" aspect of their relationship, although it served to camouflage them. Feminists both straight and Gay have been critical of the two women's "role-playing," in spite of their obvious working partnership, in spite of the completely female-defined writing it produced, and in spite of the tremendous credit Toklas received from Stein, appearing in most of the photographs and in the title of her autobiography (as a little joke they must both have had on the world). This is in contrast to the lack of credit or attention given to the wives of the famous male artists and writers of their day.

The very dykish Bryher took care of the poet H.D. (Hilda Doolittle), their partnership lasting several decades.

I believe Woolf modeled her brilliant half-male, half-female character Orlando after Sackville-West.

Bonheur's paintings of heavy horse flesh and early morning hunting gatherings of men and dogs could only have been accomplished by a woman if she dressed as a man, as Bonheur did.

29. *An Etymological Dictionary of the English Language* (Oxford: Oxford University Press, 1978), p. 753.

30. *The Random House Dictionary of the English Language*, unabridged (New York: Random House, 1966), s.v. "goat."

31. Regine Pernoud, *Joan of Arc* (New York: Stein and Day, 1966), p. 63.

32. Murray, *Witch-Cult*, pp. 270–276.

33. Evans, *Witchcraft*, chap. 1, and Murray, *Witch-Cult*, both discuss the transvestite aspects of Joan's trial.

34. H. Montgomery Hyde, *The Love That Dared Not Speak Its Name: A Candid History of Homosexuality in Britain* (Boston: Little, Brown, 1970), p. 22.

35. Murray, *Witch-Cult*, p. 216. Deep into the 1600s English witches were still calling imps, spirits, familiars and "the Devil" by the name Tom, making it even more interesting that modern-day English Lesbians are called by that term (pp. 211, 213, 214, 225).

36. *Romeo and Juliet*, act 2, sc. 11, lines 184–187.

37. Denise O'Brien, "Female Husbands in Southern Bantu Societies," in *Sexual Stratification*, ed. Alice Schlegel (New York: Columbia University Press, 1977), pp. 109–126.

38. Pat Parker, "My Lady Ain't No Lady," in *Movement in Black* (Trumansberg: Crossing Press, 1983), p. 113.

39. Willis Barnstone, trans., *Sappho* (Garden City, N.Y.: Doubleday, 1965), p. 101.

40. See, for example, Gina Covina, *The City of Hermits* (Berkeley: Barn Owl Books, 1983). The novel includes a well-drawn portrait of a Lesbian hermit, a lover of horses and desert life whose butch qualities are so extremely defined as to make her a ceremonial figure, an archetype of Lesbian literature.

7. Riding with the Amazons

1. Kurt Krueger, "I Was Hitler's Doctor," *The Amazons of Greek Mythology*, ed. Donald Sobol (London: Barnes, 1972), p. 155.

2. Audre Lorde, from "125th and Abomey," in *The Black Unicorn* (New York: Norton, 1978).

3. Donald Sobol, *The Amazons in Greek Society* (London: Barnes, 1972), p. 161.

4. Florence Mary Bennett, *Religious Cults Associated with the Amazons* (New York: AMS Press, 1967), p. 13. Sobol and others confirm.

5. Jacqueline Lapidus, from "Athens," in *Conditions: Seven* (N.Y.: Conditions, 1981), p. 91.

6. Sobol, *Amazons*, pp. 45–46, on Pantariste's and Heracles' story.

7. From a radio panel on Lesbianism in the armed services with Pat Bond, me and others. Produced by Karla Tonella for KPFA, Berkeley.

8. Sobol, *Amazons*, pp. 61–77.

9. Strabo, *The Geography of Strabo* (London: Covent Garden, 1958), vol. 3, p. 268. The Candace is described in Cheikh Anta Diop's *The Cultural Unity of Black Africa* (Chicago: Third World Press, 1963), p. 163.

10. Roy A. Glasgow, quoted in the introduction of Diop, *Cultural Unity of Black Africa*. The last major war in Africa against the white colonialists led by a woman was in Ghana in 1900 when Queen Mother Yaa Asantewa said, "If you the men of Ashanti will not go forward, then we will. We the women will. I shall call upon my fellow women. We will fight the white men. We will fight until the last of us falls in the battlefields" (introduction to Diop, *Cultural Unity of Black Africa*, p. xv).

11. The story of the Rhani of Jhansi is from an unpublished manuscript by Linda Marie and lengthy discussions with her. She traveled to India and England to research the story.

12. Evelyn Beck, interviewed by Aviva Cantor in *Lilith: The Jewish Women's Magazine* (Winter 1983); 11.

13. Beck, interview.

14. Interview with Ginny Berson, 1983. Thank you very much.

15. Pat Parker and Judy Grahn, *Where Would I Be Without You: The Poetry of Pat Parker and Judy Grahn* (Oakland: Olivia Records, 1976).

16. Audre Lorde, "The Women of Dan Dance with Swords in Their Hands to Mark the Time When They Were Warriors," in *The Black Unicorn* (New York: Norton, 1978). Dan is Dahomey.

8. Flaming, Flaming Faggot Kings

1. Robert Duncan, from "Four Songs the Night Nurse Sang," in *Roots and Branches: Poems by Robert Duncan* (New York: Scribner's, 1964), pp. 59–63.

2. Dorothee L. Mella, *Stone Power: Legendary and Practical Uses of Gems and Stones* (Albuquerque, N.M.: Domel).

3. Lawrence Durdin-Robertson, *The Goddesses of India, Tibet, China and Japan* (Eire: Cesara Publications, 1976), p. 192.

4. Thank you, Rena of Italy.

5. Bruce Rodgers, *Gay Talk* (New York: Putnam, 1972).

6. Often an articulate, ambitious, perhaps artistic woman, the fag hag keeps company almost exclusively with Gay men, feels at home with them, exchanges information with them. And because Gay men are so often highly skilled at "women's arts," such as articulate personal conversation, cooking, acting, decorating, creating an image, gardening, and so on, the fag hag is getting a mirror reflection of some of the more highly valued skills of her own gender, with a bit of inadvertent Gay philosophy as well.

The Tahitian woman leader visited by Captain Bligh of the *Bounty* in 1775 was "best friends" with her village Mahu, and for good reason; he could only increase her already highly esteemed womanly powers. The Mahu, in turn, acquired the high status accorded to all the women of that society, in addition to his own status as holder of a special Gay office.

The modern American fag hag may be best friends with her male hairdresser or decorator or the director of her summer theater group, or she may have an affair with or even marry a faggot and bear his children. She may live for a time in or near a Gay urban ghetto absorbing the culture, the aesthetics, attitudes, and values from the shops, art galleries, schools, theaters, run by Gay people, as well as from intellectual friendships she may engage in with Gay men.

Occasionally she may proceed to come out as a Lesbian. (See Marilyn Hacker, "The Dyke in the Matter," a review of *The Work of a Common Woman* by Judy Grahn, *Christopher Street* [July/August 1980].) But for the most part I think the fag hag is adamant in her straight sexual orientation, sometimes so vehemently protective of her heterosexual status as to be vocally contemptuous of dykes. She may be relaxed and confident within the Gay culture she has chosen for company or she may be highly critical of it, as though needing to maintain her own identity even while taking advantage of the Gay culture surrounding her. The term "fag hag" is almost always spoken with a certain amount of derision by both faggots and dykes, a measure, I believe, of both sexism being expressed toward her as a woman and suspicious fear of the powers of straight women that she represents. In former times, and in other terms, the fag hag would have been a queen or a powerful medicine woman, establishing a political friendship bond with the Mahu or Fairy or Winkte and sharing her high status with him.

7. Herodotus, *The Histories* (Baltimore: Penguin, 1954), p. 263.

8. Herodotus, *Histories*, p. 263.

9. Bruce Rodgers, *Gay Talk* (New York: Putnam, 1972), p. 78.

10. Rodgers, *Gay Talk*, p. 116.

11. *The Random House Dictionary of the English Language*, unabridged (New York: Random House, 1966). A Yiddish term for faggot, *feigle*, variant spelling *fagola*, is translated as "birdie." From Rodgers, *Gay Talk*.

12. B. Z. Goldberg, *The Sacred Fire* (New Jersey: Citadel, 1974), p. 98. Margaret Murray also discusses it.

13. John Rechy, *City of Night* (New York: Grove Press, 1963).

14. Michael Denneny, *Lovers: The Story of Two Men* (New York: Avon, 1979).

15. Arthur Evans, *Witchcraft and the Gay Counterculture* (Boston: Fag Rag Books, 1978), p. 102.

16. Robert Gluck, *Elements of a Coffee Service* (San Francisco: Four Seasons Foundation, 1982), pp. 33–34.

17. Duncan, from "Four Songs."

18. Hugh Ross Williamson, *The Arrow and the Sword* (London: Faber and Faber, 1947), p. 21.

19. Williamson, *Arrow and Sword*, p. 116.

20. Rodgers, *Gay Talk*, p. 123.

21. Margaret Murray, *The God of the Witches* (London: Oxford University Press, 1952), p. 43. This book also has pictures of the crowning of the goat Puck. Perhaps *Bog, bouc, bouch, Bogey, buck,* and *Puck* are all related words.

22. Otto Keifer, *Sexual Life in Ancient Rome* (London: Abbey Library, 1976).

23. Keifer, *Sexual Life in Ancient Rome*, p. 93.

24. Thanks to Bob Gluck for pointing out the references to lisps in Shakespeare: "You jig and amble and / you lisp" — *Hamlet*, act 3, sc. 1, line 144; "look you lisp and wear strange suits" — *As You Like It*, act 4, sc. 1, line 34; "The pox of such antic, lisping, affecting" — *Romeo and Juliet*, act 2, sc. 4, line 28.

25. Rodgers, *Gay Talk*.

26. Rodgers, *Gay Talk*, pp. 40–42.

27. *Random House Dictionary*.

28. *Random House Dictionary*. See also Murray, *God of the Witches*.

29. Williamson, *Arrow and Sword*, p. 115.

30. Ralph Blum, *The Book of Runes* (New York: St. Martin's, 1982), p. 116, includes a prayer to the sun that is called the *Gayatri*. Durdin-Robertson, in *Goddesses*, cites her as a goddess of morning prayer in India; *Random House Dictionary* lists "song, hymn" as the basic meaning.

31. John Lauritsen and David Thorstad, *The Early Homosexual Rights Movement (1864–1935)* (New York: Times Change Press, 1974).

32. Rodgers, *Gay Talk.*

9. Friction Among Women

1. Judy Grahn, excerpt from "A Funeral: Plainsong from a Younger Woman to an Older Woman," part of the series "She Who," in *The Work of a Common Woman* (New York: St. Martin's, 1980). The poem has been used many times in memorial services.

2. Lawrence Durdin-Robertson, *The Goddesses of India, Tibet, China and Japan* (Eire: Cesara Publications, 1976), s.v. "Arani."

3. Durdin-Robertson, *Goddesses of India, Tibet, China, and Japan,* s.v. "Ama-Terasu, Sun Goddess of Japan." Also Mircea Eliade, *From Primitives to Zen,* part 1 (New York: Harper & Row, 1974), has another good version of the story.

4. James Frances Webb, *Lives of the Saints* (Baltimore: Penguin, 1965).

5. Durdin-Robertson, *The Goddesses of Chaldea, Syria and Egypt* (Eire: Cesara Publications, 1975), p. 242: "DAATH. Heb. daath, n. fem. knowledge, insight, wisdom of magicians ... In her Tribas aspect she creates Nephesh and other elements ... The function of Daath seems to be the making of a variety of forms for different sorts of beings; and in this process she works in conjunction with Malkuth ... It is said that Daath has legions of angels and other beings of the denser Lower Realms as her followers ... Daath is sometimes associated with the Scarlet Lady of Babylon and, in a Kabalistic tradition, with the Egyptian goddess Sothis."

6. Edward Carpenter, *Intermediate Types Among Primitive Folk* (London: George Allen & Company, 1914), p. 77.

7. Durdin-Robertson, *Goddesses of India, Tibet, China and Japan,* s.v. "Arani," pp. 192–193.

8. Carpenter, *Intermediate Types,* quoting Leo Africanus, p. 38.

9. Grace Shinell, "Women's Collective Spirit: Exemplified and Envisioned," in *The Politics of Women's Spirituality,* ed. Charlene Spretnak (New York: Doubleday, 1981).

10. Judy Grahn, "A Funeral."

11. Pat Parker, "From Deep Within," in *Movement in Black* (Trumansberg: Crossing Press, 1983).

12. Adrienne Rich, "(The Floating Poem, Unnumbered)," from "Twenty-One Love Poems," in *The Dream of a Common Language* (New York: Norton, 1978).

13. Olga Broumas, from "with the clear/plastic speculum," in *Lesbian Poetry,* ed. Elly Bulkin and Joan Larkin (Watertown, Mass.: Persephone Press, 1981).

14. Audre Lorde, *Zami: A New Spelling of My Name* (Watertown, Mass.: Persephone Press, 1982), p. 249. Zami is a carriacou name for women who work together as friends and lovers, p. 255.

15. H. D., *Notes on Thought and Vision* (San Francisco: City Lights Books, 1982).

10. *Gay Is Good*

1. In *The Yale Gertrude Stein* (New Haven: Yale Univ. Press, 1980).

2. Perhaps Lesbians continue the Horned God tradition by having a great fascination with the magical one-horned horse, the unicorn. Lesbian feminists flocked to singer/songwriter Margie Adam concerts expressly to hear her sing about unicorns. My eleven-year-old stepson, an expert on the subject, tells me unicorns in the past were associated with other horned animals, including the goat.

3. Dennis Altman, *The Homosexualization of America and the Americanization of the Homosexual* (Boston: Beacon Press, 1982), p. viii.

4. Altman, *Homosexualization of America*, p. 34.

5. John J. Winkler, classics scholar, has had this thought too, developing in a lecture titled "Psappo and Eros" the idea that "Psappo was the first, or one of the first, 'teachers of Eros,' that she scripted for later generations the cultural role of being a lover." Unpublished manuscript, delivered as a lecture at New College of California, fall 1982.

6. Bruce Rodgers, *Gay Talk* (New York: Putnam, 1972); "red shoes" are fancy dancing shoes, as were Dorothy's red shoes in *The Wizard of Oz*.

7. John M. Gunn, *Schat-chen: History, Traditions and Narratives of the Queres Indians of Laguna and Acoma* (Albuquerque, N. Mex.: Albright and Anderson, 1917), pp. 205–208. (Reprinted New York: AMS, 1977.)

8. See *This Bridge Called My Back: Writings by Radical Women of Color*, edited by Cherrie Moraga and Gloria Anzaldua (Latham, NY: Kitchen Table Press, 1984).

9. Spanish phrases thanks to John Ponciano, a Chicano English teacher with a special interest in Pachuco slang.

10. Alix Dobkin, "Lavender Jane Loves Women."

11. *And Gay Is Also Baed*

1. *Leaves of Grass*, Malcolm Cowley, ed. (New York: Penguin, 1976).

2. From an article on Rap poetry in *Keyboard Magazine*.

3. Arthur Evans, *Witchcraft and the Gay Counterculture* (Boston: Fag Rag Books, 1978), pp. 55–56.

4. *The Random House Dictionary of the English Language*, unabridged (New York: Random House, 1966).

5. Interview with Tede Matthews.

6. Lee Francis, unpublished research paper on responses of people of color, women, and white people to colors.

7. John Boswell, *Christianity, Social Tolerance and Homosexuality* (Chicago: University of Chicago Press, 1980), p. 87: "But Roman society was strikingly different from the nations which eventually grew out of it in that none of its laws, strictures, or taboos regulating love or sexuality was intended to penalize gay people or their sexuality; and intolerance on this issue was rare to the point of insignificance in its great urban centers. Gay people were in a strict sense a minority, but neither they nor their contemporaries regarded their inclinations as harmful, bizarre, immoral, or threatening, and they were fully integrated into Roman life and culture at every level."

8. Boswell, *Christianity*, p. 74.

9. Boswell, *Christianity*, p. 75.

10. Heinz Heger, *The Men with the Pink Triangle* (Boston: Alyson Publications, 1980).

11. Heger, *Men with the Pink Triangle*, pp. 10–11.

12. "The Medical Mystery, Special Report on AIDS," by David Perlman, Science Editor, in *This World*, January 15, 1984, p. 11: "The tragic human toll of AIDS and the mysteries surrounding it offer at least one ironically hopeful aspect: As research intensifies, there is a real possibility that major new insights will emerge to clarify the molecular nature of the defensive mechanisms the human body has developed to fight disease over millennia of evolution ... Understanding the immune system fully would enable science at last to work a host of wonders: possibly to cure or even avert cancer ... or to expand the still-limited numbers of patients who can successfully retain organs transplanted from the dead to the living. The spread of the AIDS diseases, and the public's fearful reactions, will themselves add to the understanding of medical epidemiologists and behavioral scientists."

13. Judy Grahn, "A Funeral: Plainsong from a Younger Woman to an Older Woman," part of the series "She Who," in *The Work of a Common Woman* (Freedom, CA: Crossing Press, 1984).

Glossary

AFRIKETE: Early West African trickster/warrior goddess whose characteristics later passed over to Eshu/Elegba.

APHRODITE: Greek goddess of love, Sappho's god. Aphrodite Urania was said to be the goddess special to homosexuals.

BAD: Word used to judge behavior; from *baed, baedell,* Anglo-Saxon meaning "hermaphrodite."

BUGGERY: Gay male anal sex act; from "Bulgaria," source of a Gay and female-led religious philosophy arising in that country and spreading over Europe in the eleventh century.

BULLDIKE, or BULLDYKE: In slang, a strong, warriorlike Lesbian, assertive-looking Gay woman; from the name of a warrior Queen of the Celtic Hicca people (Boudica, "boo-dike-a") who rose up against Roman colonization in A.D. 61. Variations of the slang word are *bulldagger, bulldag,* and, in the Gay bar slang of the fifties, *Dieseldike.*

BUTCH: Cross-gender mannerisms in a woman. Usually considered very attractive, especially by one's lover. Among Gay men the term loosely refers to assertive, "masculine" characteristics but also may be a term of endearing fun; for instance, giving someone a teddy bear with the word "Butch" lettered across the chest means he doesn't have to relinquish his Gay characteristics to be attractive. In straight culture *Butch* has military masculine characteristics. For Gay people it probably derived from the French for goat, *bouch,* reference to the ceremonial cross-dressing of Gay pagan "priest/shamans" taking the part of the horned god or goat-god (done by both women and men).

CAMP, CAMPY: Indigenous Gay theatrical/satirical qualities of dress, speech, and attitude. From English *camping,* young men wearing women's clothing in a play, from French *campagne,* outdoor area where medieval minstrels and players performed. Camp operates by allowing a characteristic to continue so far in a single direction that it becomes its own opposite; "so bad it's good" (Bruce Rodgers, *Gay Talk*). And of course, so good it's bad.

CUNNILINGUS: Lesbian act of oral sex; from Latin *cunne*, "female pudenda," and *lingus*, "tongue"; punned as "cunning linguist."

DRAG: Cross-dress, especially "being in drag," "going in drag"; formerly "on the drag"; from *drag, dray*, meaning "cart." Gay men and women cross-dressed to imitate the gods and rode in carts or "drags" in processions honoring pagan gods during the festivals of New Year's, Halloween, and other holidays.

DYKE, or DIKE: A regular Lesbian, who participates in her Gay culture in her dress, mannerisms, attitudes, and so forth. Short for *bulldike*. In addition, Dike ("natural justice") was a goddess of Greece whose female companion was Truth, Aletheia.

FAGGOT: A regular Gay man, who participates in his Gay culture in his dress, mannerisms, attitudes, and so forth. From the sacred firestick of ancient Gay wizards, branch of the *fagus* (beech) tree. Related both to the Fairy wand divining rod and to the Roman *fasces*, a bundle of sticks signifying collective masculine force.

FAG HAG: A straight woman who keeps company with Gay men.

FAIRY: In general slang, an "effeminate" or nonmilitary Gay man; some regions use the term generically to include Lesbians. Originally the Fairies were brown-skinned tribal people of ancient Europe and the British Isles. In children's lore, tiny people who live in a different world or plane than our earthly one, perform magical acts, and leave "fairy circles" in the woods where they do their dancing.

FELLATIO: From Latin, "to suck"; male oral sex act.

FEMME: French for "woman"; "who gives suck." A person who participates in, or imitates the style of, female culture. A Lesbian who takes on a femme style or who modifies her butch characteristics as a way of participating in Lesbian culture.

FINNOCHIO: Italian slang for fairy or faggot; from *finnochio*, "fennel," a plant whose roots were used as coals when Prometheus stole fire from the (originally female) sun, giving it to humankind.

FRIG: Lesbian manual sex act; related to "friction," making fire by rubbing; possibly related to Frig, Norse female god of the sun who is sometimes portrayed as a hermaphrodite.

GAIA: Earth goddess of ancient Greece; her consort was Uranus.

GAY: Pertaining to homosexual culture and to homosexual people, and also to simple male homosexual sexual behavior, as in "Gay sex." Culturally the word applies to both women and men; anciently it referred to ceremonies and festivals.

HERMAPHRODITE: Two sexes in one, often used to indicate a cross-dressed Gay person; from the Greek trickster-messenger god Hermes and the female god of love and beauty, Aphrodite.

HWAME: Pima Indian name for Lesbian medicine woman.

JOYA: Spanish for "jewel," title once given to Gay magical men by American Indians of a coastal tribe near Santa Barbara, California.

KOSKALAKA: Lakota (Sioux) Indian name for Lesbian medicine women whose formal initiation as a pair included "making a rope baby" in a public ceremony.

LESBIAN: A woman who has sexual relationships with other women, and who may or may not participate in her Gay culture. From the island of Lesbos in Greece, home of the poet Sappho, who wrote love poems to women, among other subjects.

MAHU: Polynesian name for Gay shaman or fairy, from a title of special office preceding Western contact.

MARIPOSA: Spanish name for male homosexual, "butterfly."

OYA: Warrior goddess of the Macumba and Yoruba religions, sister of Yemanja and Oshun.

SAHACAT: North African Lesbian sorcerer/wisewoman (fifteenth century). Name possibly related to Hecate?

SAPPHIC, SAPPHISTRY: Lesbian, art of Lesbianism; from Sappho.

SODOMY: Gay male anal sex act; from Sodom, a city renowned for Gay practices, apparently destroyed by patriarchal antihomosexual forces during biblical times.

TRIBADISM, TRIBADIC: Lesbian sex act; rubbing a woman's pudenda with the thigh; from Greek word *tribe,* meaning "the act of rubbing"; probably related to tribe, as in all who gather around a fire.

TRIBAS: Title for a tribadic woman; for instance, Sappho has been called Tribas.

TRICKSTER: Special god with many Gay characteristics. Some tricksters include Hermes (Greek), Coyote (American Indian), Loki (Nordic), Eshu (West African), and Elegba (West African), all males; and Uzume (Japanese), Baubo (Greek, North African), and Afrikete (West African), females.

TSECAT: Gay "medicine man" of Madagascar, off the coast of Africa.

URANUS: Consort of Gaia, thundergod and sign of transformation.

VOM ANDEREN UFER: German expression, "from the other side," to be homosexual.

WARM BRUDER: German expression for male homosexual, meaning to love a man in a tender way; literally, "warm brother." WARME SCHWESTER, "warm sister," means Lesbian.

WINKTE: Lakota (Sioux) Indian name for Gay medicine man. The "sisterhood" of Winktes are or in the past were given a special burial ground.

Bibliography

Allegro, John. *The Sacred Mushroom and the Cross: A Study of the Nature and Origins of Christianity Within the Fertility Cults of the Ancient Near East.* Garden City, N.Y.: Doubleday, 1970.

Allen, Paula Gunn (Laguna-Sioux). "Answering the Deer: Genocide and Continuance in American Indian Women's Poetry." *American Indian Culture and Research Journal* 6, no. 1 (1982).

———. *The Sacred Hoop: Recovering the Feminine in American Indian Traditions.* Boston: Beacon Press, 1987.

———. "Beloved Women: Lesbians in American Indian Cultures." In *Conditions: Seven.* New York: Conditions, 1981.

———. *The Woman Who Owned the Shadows.* San Francisco: Spinsters, 1983.

———. "Red Roots of White Feminism." In *Sinister Wisdom.* Rockland, Me.: Sinister Wisdom, 1984.

———. "Some Like Indians Endure," from unpublished manuscript, "Skins and Bones." First published in *Common Lives/Lesbian Lives, Number Three.* Spring 1983.

Athanassakis, Apostolos N. *The Homeric Hymns.* Baltimore: Johns Hopkins University Press, 1976.

Avicolli, Tommi. *Magic Doesn't Live Here Anymore.* Philadelphia: Androgyny Collective, 1976.

Barnard, Mary, trans. *Sappho: A New Translation.* Berkeley: University of California Press, 1958.

Barnstone, Willis, trans. *Sappho.* Garden City, N.Y.: Doubleday, 1965.

Barr, James. *Quatrefoil.* Boston: Alyson Publications, 1982.

Beck, Evelyn. *Nice Jewish Girls.* Boston: Beacon Press, 1989.

———. Interview by Aviva Cantor in *Lilith: The Jewish Women's Magazine* (Winter 1983).

Bennett, Florence Mary. *Religious Cults Associated with the Amazons.* New York: AMS Press, 1967.

Berube, Allan. *Lesbian Masquerade,* a slide-lecture.

Bethel, Lorraine, and Barbara Smith, eds. *Conditions: Five, The Black Woman's Issue.* New York: Conditions, 1979.

Blackwood, Evelyn. "Sexuality and Gender in Certain Native American Tribes: The Case of Cross-Gender Females," unpublished manuscript.

Borror, Donald J. *Dictionary of Word Roots and Combining Forms.* Palo Alto, Calif.: Mayfield Publishing Company, 1960.

Boswell, John. *Christianity, Social Tolerance, and Homosexuality.* Chicago: University of Chicago Press, 1980.

Bowman, Walter Parker, and Robert Hamilton Ball. *Theatre Language: A Dictionary of Terms in English of the Drama and Stage from Medieval to Modern Times.* New York: Theatre Arts Books, 1961.

Bramly, Serge. *Macumba: The Teachings of Maria-Jose, Mother of the Gods.* New York: Avon, 1975.

Brewer, E. Cobham. *Brewer's Dictionary of Phrase and Fable* (revised by Ivor H. Evans). New York: Harper & Row, 1959.

Briggs, K. M. *The Fairies in Tradition and Literature.* London: Routlege and Kegan Paul, 1967.

Broner, E. M. *A Weave of Women.* New York: Bantam, 1982.

Brown, R. Allen. *The Normans and the Norman Conquest.* London: Constable, 1969.

Brown, Rita Mae. *Rubyfruit Jungle.* New York: Bantam, 1975. (Orig. pub. by Daughters Publishing Company, 1973.)

Bulfinch, Thomas. *Bulfinch's Age of Fable, or Beauties of Mythology.* Philadelphia: Sherman & Company, 1898.

Bulkin, Elly. Introduction to *Lesbian Fiction.* Watertown, Mass.: Persephone Press, 1981.

————, Joan Larkin, eds. *Lesbian Poetry.* Watertown, Mass.: Persephone Press, 1981.

Bullough, Vern L. *Homosexuality: A History, from Ancient Greece to Gay Liberation.* New York: New American Library, 1979.

Caesar, Julius. *The Gallic War and Other Writings by Julius Caesar,* translated by Moses Hadas. New York: Modern Library, 1957.

Califia, Pat. *Sapphistry: The Book of Lesbian Sexuality.* Tallahassee, Fla.: Naiad Press, 1980.

Campbell, D. A. *Greek Lyric,* vol. 1, *Sappho and Alcaeus.* Cambridge: Harvard University Press, 1983.

Campbell, Joseph. *The Masks of God: Primitive Mythology.* New York: Viking Press, 1959.

Carpenter, Edward. *Intermediate Types Among Primitive Folk: A Study in Social Evolution.* London: George Allen & Company, 1914.

Chambers Etymological English Dictionary. Edited by A. M. MacDonald. New York: Pyramid Books, 1966.

Clark, R. T. Rundle. *Myth and Symbol in Ancient Egypt.* London: Thames and Hudson, 1978.

Clarke, Cheryl. *Narratives: Poems in the Tradition of Black Women.* New York: Kitchen Table, Women of Color Press (distributors), 1983.

Compact Edition of the Oxford English Dictionary. 2 vols. Oxford: Oxford University Press, 1971.

Covina, Gina. *The City of Hermits.* Berkeley: Barn Owl Books, 1983.

Daly, Mary. *Gyn/Ecology: The Metaethics of Radical Feminism.* Boston: Beacon Press, 1978.

David-Neel, Alexandra. *Magic and Mystery in Tibet.* Baltimore: Penguin, 1929, 1971.

Debrida, Bella. "Drawing from Mythology in Women's Quest for Selfhood." In *The Politics of Women's Spirituality,* edited by Charlene Spretnak, p. 138. New York: Doubleday, 1982.

Deren, Maya. *Divine Horsemen: The Voodoo Gods of Haiti.* New York: Delta Books, 1970.

Dillon, Myles, and Nora K. Chadwick. *The Celtic Realms.* New York: New American Library, 1967. (Ammianus Marcellinus from Book XV, xii.)

Dio, Cassius. *Dio's Roman History*, vol. 8, books 61–70. Translated by E. Cary. Cambridge: Harvard University Press, 1925.

Diop, Cheikh Anta. *The Cultural Unity of Black Africa*. Chicago: Third World Press, 1963.

Douglas, Lord Alfred. "Two Loves." In *The Penguin Book of Homosexual Verse*. Edited by Stephen Coote, pp. 262–264. New York: Penguin, 1983.

Dover, K. J. *Greek Homosexuality*. New York: Random House, 1980.

Dudley, Donald R., and Graham Webster. *The Rebellion of Boudicca*. London: Routledge and Kegan Paul, 1962.

Duncan, Robert. *Roots and Branches*. New York: Scribner's, 1964.

Durdin-Robertson, Lawrence. *The Goddesses of Chaldea, Syria and Egypt*. Eire: Cesara Publications, 1975.

———. *The Goddesses of India, Tibet, China and Japan*. Eire: Cesara Publications, 1976.

1811 Dictionary of the Vulgar Tongue. Foreword by Robert Cromie. Northfield, Ill.: Digest Books, 1971.

Eliade, Mircea. *Gods, Goddesses and Myths of Creation*, part 1, *From Primitives to Zen*. New York: Harper & Row, 1974.

Estrada, Alvaro. *Maria Sabina: Her Life and Chants*. Translated by Henry Munn. Santa Barbara, Calif.: Ross-Erikson, 1981.

Evans, Arthur. *Witchcraft and the Gay Counterculture*. Boston: Fag Rag Books, 1978.

Evans, Bergen. *Dictionary of Mythology*. New York: Dell, 1970.

Fitzgerald, Arlene J. *Everything You Always Wanted to Know About Sorcery*. New York: Manor Books, 1973.

Fletcher, John. *Bonduca*. 1647. Reprint. Oxford: Oxford University Press (Malone Society), 1951.

Foster, Jeannette. *Sex Variant Women in Literature*. Baltimore: Diana Press, 1975.

Friday, Nancy. *My Secret Garden: Women's Sexual Fantasies*. New York: Pocket Books, 1973.

Gluck, Robert. *Elements of a Coffee Service*. San Francisco: Four Seasons Foundation, 1982.

Goldberg, B. Z. *The Sacred Fire: The Story of Sex in Religion*. 1958. Reprint. Secaucus, N.J.: Citadel Press, 1974.

Goodrich, Michael. *The Unmentionable Vice: Homosexuality in the Later Medieval Period*. Santa Barbara, Calif.: Ross-Erikson, 1979.

Gould, Jean. *Amy: The World of Amy Lowell and the Imagist Movement*. New York: Dodd, Mead, 1975.

Grahn, Judy. "Menstruation: From Sacred to the Curse and Beyond." In *The Politics of Women's Spirituality*. Edited by Charlene Spretnak. New York: Doubleday, 1982.

———. *The Queen of Swords*. Boston: Beacon Press, 1987.

———. *The Queen of Wands*. Trumansberg, N.Y.: Crossing Press, 1982.

———. *The Work of a Common Woman*. New York: St. Martin's, 1978.

Grieve, Mrs. M. *A Modern Herbal*. 2 vols. New York: Dover, 1971.

Groden, Suzy Q., trans. *The Poems of Sappho*. New York: Bobbs-Merrill, 1966.

Gunn, John M. *Schat-Chen: History, Traditions and Narratives of the Queres Indians of Laguna and Acoma*. Albuquerque, N. Mex.: Albright and Anderson, 1917.

Hacker, Marilyn. "The Dyke in the Matter." *Christopher Street* (July/August 1980).

Harrison, Jane Ellen. *Epilegomena to the Study of Greek Religion, and Themis.* New York: University Books, 1962.

H.D. *Notes on Thought and Vision.* San Francisco: City Lights Books, 1982.

Healy, Eloise Klein. *A Packet Beating Like A Heart.* Los Angeles: Books of a Feather, 1981.

Heger, Heinz. *The Men with the Pink Triangle.* Boston: Alyson Publications, 1980.

Herodotus. *The Histories.* Translated by Aubrey de Selincourt. Baltimore: Penguin, 1954.

Hyde, H. Montgomery. *The Love That Dared Not Speak Its Name: A Candid History of Homosexuality in Britain.* Boston: Little, Brown, 1970.

Iknoian, Therese. "Out of the Closet in Germany." *San Francisco Sunday Examiner and Chronicle,* April 17, 1983.

Isabell, Sharon. *Yesterday's Lessons.* Oakland, Calif.: Diana Press, 1974.

Israel, Lee. *Miss Tallulah Bankhead.* New York: Dell, 1972.

Jacobs, Sue Ellen. "Berdache: A Brief Review of the Literature." *Colorado Anthropologist* 1:25–40.

Kanter, Emanuel. *The Amazons: A Marxian Study.* Chicago: Charles H. Kerr, 1926.

Katz, Jonathon. *Gay American History: Lesbians and Gay Men in the U.S.A.* New York: Crowell, 1976.

————. *Gay/Lesbian Almanac.* New York: Harper & Row, 1983.

Kendrick, T. D. *The Druids: A Study in Keltic Prehistory.* London: Methuen, 1927.

Kenny, Maurice. *Only As Far As Brooklyn.* Boston: Good Gay Poets, 1979.

Kerenyi, C. *Eleusis.* New York: Schocken, 1977.

Kiefer, Otto. *Sexual Life in Ancient Rome.* Translated from the German. 1934. Reprint. London: Abbey Library, 1976.

Klepfisz, Irena. *Keeper of Accounts.* Watertown, Mass.: Persephone Press, 1982.

Kramer, Heinrich, and James Sprenger. *Malleus Maleficarum.* 1486. Reprint. London: Arrow Books, 1971.

Kunz, George Frederick. *Rings for the Finger.* New York: Dover, 1973.

Lame Deer, John (Fire), and Richard Erdoes. *Lame Deer Seeker of Visions: The Life of a Sioux Medicine Man.* New York: Simon and Schuster, 1972.

Lapidus, Jacqueline. "Athens," in "Voyage to Lesbos." In *Conditions: Seven.* New York: Conditions Publishing, 1981, pp. 91–96.

Lauritsen, John, and David Thorstad. *The Early Homosexual Rights Movement (1864–1935).* New York: Times Change Press, 1974.

Leach, Maria, ed. *The Standard Dictionary of Folklore, Mythology and Legend.* New York: Funk & Wagnalls.

Lesko, Barbara S. *The Remarkable Women of Ancient Egypt.* Albany, Calif.: B. C. Scribe, 1977.

Lethbridge, T. C. *Witches.* New York: Citadel Press, 1968.

Levy, Robert I. *Tahitians: Mind and Experience in the Society Islands.* Chicago: University of Chicago Press, 1973.

Leyland, Winston, ed. *Orgasms of Light.* San Francisco: Gay Sunshine Press, 1977.

Linda Marie. *I Must Not Rock.* New York: Daughters, Inc., 1977.
————. "Antonia," unpublished manuscript.
————. "The Rhani of Jhansi," unpublished manuscript.
Lorde, Audre. *The Black Unicorn.* New York: Norton, 1978.
————. *Uses of the Erotic: The Erotic as Power.* New York: Out & Out Books, 1978.
————. *Zami: A New Spelling of My Name.* Watertown, Mass.: Persephone Press, 1982.
Lynch, Lee. *Toothpick House.* Tallahassee, Fla.: Naiad Press, 1983.
MacCana, Proinsias. *Celtic Mythology.* London: Hamlyn, 1970.
MacDonald, A. M., ed. *Chambers Etymological English Dictionary.* New York: Pyramid, 1968.
Maquet, Jacques. *Civilizations of Black Africa.* London: Oxford University Press, 1972.
Marcellinus, Ammianus. *The Roman History of Ammianus Marcellinus,* XV, xiii. Translated by C. D. Yonge. London: Bohn's Classical Library, 1862.
Mariah, Paul. "The Spoon Ring." In *This Light Will Spread: Selected Poems, 1960–1978.* South San Francisco: Manroot, 1978.
Markale, Jean. *Women of the Celts.* London: Gordon Cremonesi, 1975.
Mbiti, John S. *African Religions and Philosophy.* New York: Doubleday-Anchor, 1970.
Meatis, Georges. *The Mysteries of Eleusis.* Translated from the French by J. van Isselmuden. Madras, India: Theosophical Publishing House, 1932.
Mella, Dorothee L. *Stone Power: Legendary and Practical Uses of Gems and Stones.* Albuquerque, N. Mex.: Domel.
Moraga, Cherrie, and Gloria Anzaldua. *This Bridge Called My Back: Writings by Radical Women of Color.* Watertown, Mass.: Persephone Press, 1981.
Morse, Carl. "The Curse of the Future Fairy." *FAG RAG* (Boston), No. 40 (1983).
Murray, Margaret. *The Divine King in England.* London: Faber & Faber, 1954.
————. *The God of the Witches.* London: Oxford University Press, 1952.
————. *The Witch-Cult in Western Europe.* London: Oxford University Press, 1921.
Mylonas, George Emmanuel. *The Hymn to Demeter and Her Sanctuary at Eleusis.* Washington University, 1942.
Myron, Nancy, and Charlotte Bunch. *Lesbianism and the Women's Movement.* Baltimore: Diana Press, 1975.
————. *Women Remembered.* Baltimore: Diana Press, 1974.
Neithammer, Carolyn. "Lesbianism." In *Daughters of the Earth.* New York. Collier Books, 1977.
Nestle, Joan. "Butch-Fem Relationships." In *Sex Issue, Heresies* #12, p. 21. Brooklyn: Heresies Collective, 1981.
Neumann, Erich. *The Great Mother.* Princeton: Princeton University Press, 1955.
Newhall, Barbara Falconer. "Halloween: Ancient New York's Celebration." *Oakland Tribune,* October 31, 1980, p. B-6.
Norse, Harold. *Hotel Nirvana.* San Francisco: City Lights Books, 1974.
Nowak, Margaret, and Stephen Durrant. *The Tale of the Nisan Shamaness: A Manchu Folk Epic.* Seattle: University of Washington Press, 1977.
O'Brien, Denise. "Female Husbands in Southern Bantu Societies." In *Sexual Stratification.* Edited by Alice Schlegel. New York: Columbia University Press, 1977.

Parker, Pat. *Movement in Black: Collected Poetry*. Oakland, Calif.: Diana Press, 1978. Reprint. Trumansberg: The Crossing Press, 1983.

Partridge, Eric. *The Macmillan Dictionary of Historical Slang*. 1937 Reprint. New York: Macmillan, 1973.

Patterson, Rebecca. *The Riddle of Emily Dickinson*. New York: Cooper Square Publishers, 1973.

Perlman, David. "The Medical Mystery, Special Report on AIDS." *This World*, January 15, 1984.

Pernoud, Regine. *Joan of Arc*. New York: Stein and Day, 1966.

Peter, Shepherd Edwin. *Metaphysical Candle Burning and Color*. Albuquerque, N. Mex.: Universal Church of the Holy Spirit, 1975.

Philippi, Donald L. *Songs of Gods, Songs of Humans: The Epic Tradition of the Ainu*. Princeton: Princeton University and University of Tokyo, 1979.

Picano, Felice. *A True Likeness: Lesbian and Gay Writing Today*. New York: Sea Horse Press, 1980.

Raynolds, Robert. *Boadicea: A Tragedy of War*. New York: Poets Press, 1938.

Rechy, John. *City of Night*. New York: Grove Press, 1963.

Reed, Evelyn. *Women's Evolution*. New York: Pathfinder Press, 1975.

Rees, Alwyn, and Brinley Rees. *Celtic Heritage*. London: Thames and Hudson, 1961.

Reymond, Lizelle. *Shakti*. New York: Knopf, 1974.

Rich, Adrienne. *The Dream of a Common Language: Poems 1974–1977*. New York: Norton, 1978.

Robbins, Rossell Hope. *The Encyclopedia of Witchcraft and Demonology*. New York: Crown, 1959.

Robinson, David M. *Sappho and Her Influence*. New York: Cooper Square, 1963.

Rodgers, Bruce. *Gay Talk: A Dictionary of Gay Slang*. Originally published as *The Queen's Vernacular*. New York: Putnam, 1972.

Rolleston, T. W. *Myths and Legends of the Celtic Race*. London: George G. Harrap, 1911.

Ross, Anne. *Pagan Celtic Britain*. New York: Columbia University Press, 1967.

Rothery, Guy Cadogan. *The Amazons in Antiquity and Modern Times*. London: Francis Griffiths, 1910.

Russell, Jeffrey Burton. *Witchcraft in the Middle Ages*. Ithaca, N.Y.: Cornell University Press, 1972.

Sappho. *Lyrics in the Original Greek*. Translations by Willis Barnstone. New York: Anchor Books, 1965.

———. *Sappho: A New Translation*. Translated by Mary Barnard. Berkeley: University of California Press, 1958.

Schafer, Edward H. *The Divine Woman: Dragon Ladies and Rain Maidens*. San Francisco: North Point Press, 1980.

Schmidt, Minna M. *400 Outstanding Women of the World and Their Costumology*. Chicago: Minna Moscherosch Schmidt, 1933.

Schneebaum, Tobias. *Keep the River on Your Right*. New York: Grove Press, 1969.

Shah, Sayed Indries. *The Secret Lore of Magic*. New York: Citadel Press, 1970.

Shakespeare, William. *A Midsummer Night's Dream*. Modern Library Edition.

Shinell, Grace. "Women's Collective Spirit: Exemplified and Envisioned." In *The Politics of Women's Spirituality*. Edited by Charlene Spretnak. New York: Doubleday, 1982.

Shipley, Joseph T. *Dictionary of Word Origins.* Ames, Iowa: Littlefield, Adams, 1959.

Shockley, Ann. *Say Jesus and Come to Me.* New York: Avon, 1982.

Shurin, Aaron, *The Night Sun.* San Francisco: Gay Sunshine Press, 1976.

Sisley, Emily L., and Bertha Harris. *The Joy of Lesbian Sex.* New York: Simon and Schuster, 1977.

Skeat, Walter W. *An Etymological Dictionary of the English Language.* Oxford: Clarendon Press, 1978.

Smedley, Agnes. *Portraits of Chinese Women in Revolution.* Old Westbury, N.Y.: The Feminist Press, 1976.

Sobol, Donald J. *The Amazons of Greek Mythology.* London: A.S. Barnes, 1972.

Sojourner, Sabrina. "From the House of Yemanja: The Goddess Heritage of Black Women." In *The Politics of Women's Spirituality.* Edited by Charlene Spretnak. New York: Doubleday, 1982.

Spretnak, Charlene, Ed. *The Politics of Women's Spirituality.* New York: Doubleday, 1982.

Stein, Gertrude. "Miss Furr and Miss Skeene." In *Geography and Plays.* 1922. Reprint. New York: Something Else Press, 1968.

Stone, Merlin. *Ancient Mirrors of Womanhood: Our Goddess and Heroine Heritage.* Boston: Beacon Press, 1984.

Strabo. *The Geography of Strabo.* London: Covent Garden, 1958.

Summers, Montague. *The History of Witchcraft.* New York: Citadel Press, 1970.

Thomson, George. *Studies in Ancient Greek Society: The Prehistoric Aegean.* New York: Citadel Press, 1965.

Turville-Petre, E. O. G. *Myth and Religion of the North: The Religion of Ancient Scandinavia.* New York: Holt, Rinehart and Winston, 1964.

Tyler, Hamilton A. *Pueblo Gods and Myths.* Norman, Okla.: University of Oklahoma Press, 1964.

Wasson, R. Gordon, Albert Hoffman, and Carl Ruck. *The Road to Eleusis: Unveiling the Secret of the Mysteries.* Italy: Helen and Kurt Wolff, 1978.

Wedeck, Harry E. *Treasury of Witchcraft.* New York: Philosophical Library, 1961.

Weekley, Ernest. *An Etymological Dictionary of Modern English.* New York: Dover, 1967.

Wilken, Mike. "Transformations: Shamanism and Homosexuality," unpublished paper.

Williamson, Hugh Ross. *The Arrow and the Sword.* London: Faber and Faber, 1947.

Woodul, Jennifer. "Emily Dickinson." In *Women Remembered.* Baltimore: Diana Press, 1974.

Yonge, C. D., trans. *The Roman History of Ammianus Marcellinus,* book XV, xii. London: Henry G. Bohn, Bohn's Classical Library, 1862.

Young, Ian, ed. *The Male Muse: A Gay Anthology.* Trumansberg, N.Y.: Crossing Press, 1973.

Zografou, Mina. *Amazons in Homer and Hesiod: A Historical Reconstruction.* Athens, Greece, 1972.

Index